Conventional Arms Control Perspectives on Verification

Conventional Arms Control

Perspectives on Verification

Sergey Koulik and Richard Kokoski

sipri

OXFORD UNIVERSITY PRESS
1994

Oxford University Press, Walton Street, Oxford OX2 6DP
Oxford New York
Athens Auckland Bangkok Bombay
Calcutta Cape Town Dar es Salaam Delhi
Florence Hong Kong Istanbul Karachi
Kuala Lumpur Madras Madrid Melbourne
Mexico City Nairobi Paris Singapore
Taipei Tokyo Toronto
and associated companies in
Berlin Ibadan

Oxford is a trade mark of Oxford University Press

Published in the United States
by Oxford University Press Inc., New York

British Library Cataloguing in Publication Data
Data available

Library of Congress Cataloging in Publication Data
Koulik, Sergey.
Conventional arms control: perspectives on verification /
Sergey Koulik and Richard Kokoski
p. cm.
"Sipri, Stockholm International Peace Research Institute"
Includes index.
1. Arms control 2. Arms control—Verification. 3. Europe–Defences.
I. Kokoski, Richard, 1952– II. Stockholm International Peace Research Institute
III. Conventional Arms Control: Perspectives on Verification
JX1974.K68 1992 327.1'74'028—dc20 92–37898
ISBN 0–19–829149–3

Typeset and originated by Stockholm International Peace Research Institute
Printed and bound in Great Britain by
Biddles Ltd., Guildford and King's Lynn

Contents

List of tables and figures

Preface

The signing within a relatively short period of time of both the 1990 CFE Treaty—emerging from the arduous negotiations of the 1970s and 1980s on conventional armed forces in Europe—and the 1992 Open Skies Treaty (first suggested in 1955 by US President Dwight D. Eisenhower in his talks with Nikita Khrushchev of the Soviet Union) bears witness to the new possibilities which radical changes in the political climate of Europe are now making possible.

The CFE Treaty, signed in a rapidly evolving Europe, has demonstrated remarkable flexibility in adapting to the new political landscape—including the unilateral restructuring of military forces. This is due in no small measure to the strict verification measures which allow a degree of transparency with implications far beyond those of the quantitative limits which the Treaty must uphold. The transparency will be greatly enhanced by the Open Skies Treaty which places all parties on an equal footing with respect to the fruits of aerial monitoring, regardless of their technological capabilities.

None the less the new political landscape necessitates a radical reassessment of traditional approaches to enhanced security through furthering transparency, predictability and openness. First steps have been taken which have the potential to usher in a new era of international co-operation and, while a very positive occurrence in principle, the sheer scope of the emerging regional security concerns will doubtless require new approaches and solutions. The time is ripe to set common European standards, a kind of code of conduct in the field of security. In this context the concept of an Arms Control Agency in Europe should also be considered. It might be instrumental in monitoring the implementation of and verifying compliance with concluded multilateral agreements.

Newer verification and transparency mechanisms will of necessity, however, rest in large measure on the foundations of those already incorporated in the CFE and Open Skies treaties. Written as it was in a time of rapid flux in events and evolving security concerns, this book delves into the structure and functioning of the associated verification measures of these two important agreements. It then goes on to explore the manner in which they may be built upon, augmented or complemented in future arms control agreements or confidence- and security-building measures to address more directly the new and more complex situation in Europe.

Adam Daniel Rotfeld
Director of SIPRI
September 1994

Acknowledgements

As was the case for the first volume in this study, the work could not have been accomplished without the tireless efforts of our editor Billie Bielckus. Her comments and questions on the text have been invaluable and her constant good cheer made working together a pleasure indeed.

The SIPRI library worked its usual miracles and our thanks go out to Christer Berggren, Nenne Bodell, Gunnie Boman, Olga Hardardóttir, Olle Persson and Sten Wiksten.

Thanks as well to the former Director of SIPRI, Dr Walther Stützle, for initiating the project and for his valuable advice at the outset, and to SIPRI's current Director, Dr Adam Daniel Rotfeld, for much appreciated interest and encouragement through the final stages.

Sergey Koulik   Richard Kokoski
Moscow   SIPRI

Acronyms

ACV	Armoured combat vehicle
AEW	Airborne Early Warning system
AIAM	Annual Implementation Assessment Meeting
AIFV	Armoured infantry fighting vehicle
APC	Armoured personnel carrier
ATTU	Atlantic-to-the-Urals (zone)
AVLB	Armoured vehicle launched bridge
AWACS	Airborne Warning and Control System
CBM	Confidence-building measure
CC&D	Camouflage, concealment and deception
CDE	Conference on Disarmament in Europe
CFE	Conventional Armed Forces in Europe
CIS	Commonwealth of Independent States
CSBM	Confidence- and security-building measure
CSCE	Conference on Security and Co-operation in Europe
CWC	Chemical Weapons Convention
DCD	Divisions of coastal defence
DCI	Director of Central Intelligence
DIA	Defense Intelligence Agency
DPSS	Designated permanent storage site
EDC	European Disarmament Conference
EMIS	Electromagnetic isotope separation
FAA	Federal Aviation Administration
FRG	Federal Republic of Germany
GDR	German Democratic Republic
HACV	Heavy armoured combat vehicle
HLTF	High Level Task Force
HLWG	High Level Working Group
IAEA	International Atomic Energy Agency
ICAO	International Civil Aviation Organization
INF	Intermediate-range nuclear force
JACIG	Joint Arms Control Implementation Group
JCG	Joint Consultative Group
JOIC	Joint Operational Intelligence Centre
JSTARS	Joint Surveillance and Target Attack and Radar System
KTO	Kuwaiti Theater of Operations
MBFR	Mutual and Balanced Force Reduction talks
MD	Military district
MLM	Military Liaison Mission

MLRS	Multiple-launch rocket system
MTI	Moving target indicator
MTM	Multinational technical means
MURFAAMCE	Mutual Reduction of Forces and Armaments and Associated Measures in Central Europe
NAEW	NATO Airborne Early Warning
NATO	North Atlantic Treaty Organization
NNA	Neutral and non-aligned
NSC	National Security Council
NTM	National technical means
OOV	Object(s) of verification
OSCC	Open Skies Consultative Commission
OSI	On-site inspection(s)
OSIA	On-Site Inspection Agency
PEEP	Permanent entry and exit point
PFP	Partnership for Peace
POMCUS	Prepositioned Material Configured to Unit Sets
PSM	Plano Spaziale Militaire
R&D	Research and development
SAR	Synthetic aperture radar
SIGINT	Signals intelligence
SPOT	Système Probatoire d'Observation de la Terre
START	Strategic Arms Reduction Talks/Treaty
TLE	Treaty-limited equipment
UNSCOM	UN Special Commission on Iraq
VCC	Verification Coordinating Committee
VSS	Verification Support Staff
WEU	Western European Union
WTO	Warsaw Treaty Organization

1. Introduction

I. Overview

The period 1990–92 was marked by a series of achievements in conventional arms control. In the changing political climate in Europe at the end of the cold war the emphasis was on enhancing stability and security and a number of arms control negotiations were brought to a successful conclusion. Capping a period which included the drawn-out Mutual and Balanced Force Reduction (MBFR) Talks (1973–89) and the important signing of the Stockholm Document in 1986, the signing of the Treaty on Conventional Armed Forces in Europe (the CFE Treaty) in November 1990, together with that of the 1992 Concluding Act of the Negotiation on Personnel Strength of Conventional Armed Forces in Europe (the CFE-1A Agreement), soon thereafter ushered in a new era in European arms control.

Inextricably linked to these agreements, verification measures of unprecedented breadth and scope were negotiated which serve not only to ensure successful treaty implementation but will doubtless also provide a basis for future agreements and greater transparency. In addition, although much broader in scope, the Treaty on Open Skies signed in 1992 will provide for unprecedented access to monitoring capability throughout its wide area of application from Vancouver to Vladivostok.

From a more overarching perspective, although not directly linked with verification activities, the Partnership for Peace (PFP) programme launched by the 10–11 January 1994 North Atlantic Treaty Alliance (NATO) summit meeting, by inviting the former Soviet republics and East European countries to strengthen their ties to NATO, has the potential to further enhance political and military co-operation in Europe.

II. Conventional arms control and reductions

The January 1989 Mandate for the Negotiation on Conventional Armed Forces in Europe stated that

the objectives of the negotiations shall be to strengthen stability and security in Europe through the establishment of a stable and secure balance of conventional armed forces, which include conventional armaments and equipment, at lower levels; the elimination of disparities prejudicial to stability and security; and the elimination, as a matter of priority, of the capability for launching surprise attack and for initiating large-scale offensive action . . . These objectives shall be achieved by the application of militarily significant measures such as reductions, limitations, redeployment provisions, equal ceilings, and related measures, among others.[1]

The Treaty on Conventional Armed Forces in Europe signed on 19 November 1990 reaffirmed the commitment to these objectives in the agreed provisions and emphasized that the states parties signed it 'Striving to replace military confrontation with a new pattern of security relations among all the State Parties based on peaceful cooperation and thereby to contribute to overcoming the division of Europe'.[2] Thus, the CFE Negotiation in Vienna and its results set out measures which deal strictly with the military aspects of security but which are aimed at broader political objectives.

In a Joint Declaration signed on the same day the heads of state or government of the 22 original signatories of the CFE Treaty stated that they were 'confident that the signature of the Treaty on Conventional Armed Forces in Europe represents a major contribution to the common objective of increased security and stability in Europe' and 'convinced that these developments must form part of a continuing process of co-operation in building the structures of a more united continent'.[3]

The Vienna Document 1990 of the Negotiations on Confidence- and Security-Building Measures (CSBMs) convened in accordance with the relevant provisions of the Concluding Document of the Vienna Meeting of the Conference on Security and Co-operation in Europe (CSCE), also signed in November 1990, recalls the aim of the Conference on Confidence- and Security-Building Measures and Disarmament in Europe, 'to undertake, in stages, new, effective and concrete actions designed to make progress in strengthening confidence and security and in achieving disarmament, so as to give effect and expression to the duty of States to refrain from the threat or use of force in their mutual relations as well as in their international relations in general'.[4]

The Vienna Document 1992 of the Negotiations on Confidence- and Security-Building Measures convened in accordance with the relevant provisions of the Concluding Document of the Vienna Meeting of the CSCE was signed in March 1992. It repeats these aims and includes the lion's share of the provisions of the Vienna Document 1990,[5] thereby representing continuity in

---

[1] The Mandate for the CFE Negotiation is reprinted in SIPRI, *SIPRI Yearbook 1989: World Armaments and Disarmament* (Oxford University Press: Oxford, 1989), appendix 11B, pp. 420–22.

[2] See the Treaty on Conventional Armed Forces in Europe, Paris, 1990, reprinted in this volume as appendix A.

[3] The Joint Declaration of Twenty-Two States is reprinted in SIPRI, *SIPRI Yearbook 1991: World Armaments and Disarmament* (Oxford University Press: Oxford, 1991), appendix 17A, pp. 601–602. Article XVIII, paragraph 1 of the CFE Treaty reaffirms that 'the States Parties, after signature of this Treaty, shall continue the negotiations on conventional armed forces, with the same Mandate, and with the goal of building on this Treaty' (see appendix A).

[4] The Vienna Document 1990 of the Negotiations on Confidence- and Security-Building Measures convened in accordance with the relevant provisions of the Concluding Document of the Vienna Meeting of the Conference on Security and Co-operation in Europe, 17 Nov. 1990, is reprinted in SIPRI (note 3), appendix 13B, pp. 475–88.

[5] The Vienna Document 1992 of the Negotiations on Confidence- and Security-Building Measures convened in accordance with the relevant provisions of the Concluding Document of the Vienna Meeting of

seeking to reduce the risk of military confrontation and in providing measures to deal with military aspects of strengthening security. While by no means confined to monitoring conventional forces, nor even to Europe, the Treaty on Open Skies signed in March 1992 ushered in a new era of openness and transparency. It will serve to facilitate the implementation of the various conventional and other arms control agreements, but with the added dimension of aiding in conflict prevention and crisis management as well.

Finally, the Concluding Act of the Negotiation on Personnel Strength of Conventional Armed Forces in Europe, signed on 10 July 1992 by 29 countries as the main result of the CFE follow-on negotiations (the CFE-1A Agreement), set a ceiling on the military personnel of each participating state.[6] As a politically binding document, it represents a further successful effort in enhancing security in Europe and widens the range of military potentials under limitation.

The CFE Treaty

The stated objectives of the Mandate for the Negotiation on Conventional Armed Forces in Europe determined which weapon categories should be included as treaty-limited equipment (TLE) in the CFE Negotiation agenda. The capability of certain categories of weapon system for waging war and launching a surprise attack was a key factor. Capabilities were assessed on the basis of several criteria, including fire-power, mobility, protection, radius of target engagement and accuracy. It was decided that the negotiations should cover limitations on and reductions of battle tanks, armoured combat vehicles, artillery, combat aircraft and attack helicopters. Although naval forces meet these criteria, they were excluded from the CFE Negotiation.[7]

The selection of TLE categories was also based on assessments of probable threats and on concerns about the main elements of military doctrines of the various parties to the Negotiation. In addition, the selection of TLE categories depended on the negotiability of limitations on, or reductions in, these systems. This was demonstrated by the resistance on the part of several NATO countries to dealing with naval and air forces in Vienna on political and military grounds, citing the immense difficulties connected with the 'global character' and high mobility of these components. Other considerations included difficulty in verifying restrictions by national technical means (NTM) and on-site inspections (OSI) as well as the prospects for a sudden and substantial violation of an

---

the Conference on Security and Co-operation in Europe, 4 Mar. 1992, is reprinted in this volume as appendix B.

[6] The Concluding Act of the Negotiation on Personnel Strength of Conventional Armed Forces in Europe, Helsinki, 10 July 1992, is reprinted in SIPRI, *SIPRI Yearbook 1993: World Armaments and Disarmament* (Oxford University Press: Oxford, 1993), appendix 12A, pp. 683–89.

[7] See note 1. In fact the Mandate stated that naval forces would not be addressed and that the subject of the negotiations should be the conventional armed forces based on land within the territory of the participants in Europe from the Atlantic to the Urals.

agreement.[8] All these interconnected considerations were the subject of intensive discussions in Vienna.

The approach adopted by the CFE process has been labelled by several experts as the 'structural approach', that is, the scaling down of military structures—manpower, units and equipment. The second approach to conventional arms control in Europe, which has been implemented to some extent in the CSBM negotiations and documents, has been characterized as the 'operational approach'. It focuses on regulating the activities of military forces. It allows for advance forecast or notification of manœuvres or concentrations of troops above certain thresholds and for the invitation of observers to these activities, and it also demands verification arrangements such as the conduct of on-site inspections of questionable activities.[9]

The new military–political landscape in Europe after the dissolution of the Soviet Union at the end of 1991 and the collapse of the Warsaw Treaty Organization (WTO) in the same year has to some extent invalidated the basic criteria of these approaches. The 'structural approach', for example, focused on maintaining 'balance'—understood by the negotiators in Vienna in the context of the CFE agenda as quantitative equality in the main categories of offensive systems in the reduction area for the two groups of states, NATO and the former WTO.

The changing military–political situation has also quickly invalidated many concepts and approaches, involving mainly military considerations, to the creation of common denominators of balance and criteria for further negotiating efforts. Moreover, the real challenges for security have shifted to political, national, economic and ecological areas. Arms control is in the process of finding its proper place in the security agenda, of moving into new areas of military problems, including, for example, ballistic missile and weapon technology proliferation.

Some basic goals of the CFE Mandate have already become redundant, particularly the elimination of the threat of large-scale offensive actions between two blocs. Nevertheless, many problems remain on the European arms control agenda. Despite the dramatic and rapid evolution of the political and military situation in Europe the stated goals of the CFE and CSBM negotiations—the removal of the threat or use of force, the reduction of the dangers of misunderstanding or miscalculation of military activities and the elimination of disparities prejudicial to stability and security—are still relevant for strengthening military security within Europe. The creation of new states on the former Soviet territory and their inclusion in the CSCE process have complicated the task of implementing these goals. The instability in some regions of the former Soviet Union, the armed conflicts underway in some of the newly independent states

---

[8] *Past Experiences of Verifying Restrictions on Conventional Forces and Armaments,* Western European Union, Paper prepared by the staff of WEU in Paris for the Fifth Annual Symposium on Arms Control and Verification, Carleton University, Ottawa, 23–26 Mar. 1988.

[9] Darilek, R., 'The future of conventional arms control in Europe, A tale of two cities: Stockholm, Vienna', SIPRI, *SIPRI Yearbook 1987: World Armaments and Disarmament* (Oxford University Press: Oxford, 1987), p. 339.

and the war in the former Yugoslavia have set new priorities for the security agenda.

Nevertheless the November 1990 documents, especially the CFE Treaty, represent solid ground for creating complementary or perhaps alternative arms control arrangements. Such arrangements are particularly needed for the stable transformation of Europe, especially of Eastern Europe and the former Soviet Union. The documents contribute to the elimination of many uncertainties and much speculation in constructing different arms control scenarios and, more importantly, will serve as a testing ground for future attempts to cope with the changing reality. They made a very positive contribution to the successful process of the CFE follow-on negotiations (CFE-1A) and the signing of the CFE-1A Agreement.

In the military sphere, withdrawals and reductions of substantial quantities of offensive weapons and negotiated zoning of the reduced limits within the European continent have a far-reaching positive impact on reducing force concentrations. The reduction of offensive systems undermines demands for maintaining large offensive contingents for mobile defence and large-scale counter-offensive operations on a tactical and operational level. It also stimulates the stationing of reserve forces in distant rear areas.

It should be emphasized that all the above-mentioned documents are of increasing importance in the transitional period in Eastern Europe and the former USSR. The agreements serve to neutralize the potentially uncontrolled restructuring of forces, the disputed division of Soviet military potential among the former republics and other changes in the former Soviet armed forces. The CFE and CSBM agreements serve to test the willingness of the new states to implement internationally accepted arrangements and to follow the documents signed by the Soviet Union. That the major plans of the restructuring process coincide with the timetable of the CFE Treaty's implementation increases the value of the terms of the Treaty.

The CFE Treaty provides a basis for making and implementing unilateral decisions in former WTO and NATO countries on reducing and restructuring their military potentials in a more radical mode than is prescribed by the signed agreements themselves. In tandem with the new military–political realities and the opportunities for reductions beyond the limits of the Treaty, the Treaty itself serves as a guideline for decision makers both in the East and the West.

The conventional arms control agenda faces challenges regarding the coordination of defence and arms control planning. As the agreements already in place directly influence substantial changes in defence planning for conventional forces, the task of increasing their positive influence on further formulation of adequate defence needs would seem to be one of the most important for the implementation of both these agreements and the future arms control process in Europe. The Partnership for Peace programme represents a new dimension in facilitating transparency in national defence planning and budgeting processes as well as interoperability. Nevertheless, the existing arms control arrangements remain the basis for future decisions on military postures and possible arms control endeavours.

The challenges facing monitoring and verification measures are particularly acute. Failure by the states parties to implement a robust and effective verification regime could negatively affect the debates on the future of arms control; success could open up new possibilities for more comprehensive measures.

The road to transparency

The implementation of conventional arms control agreements depends on the approaches which a participating state or group of participating states is willing to accept. What are the basic hopes for a verification regime—that it will provide item-by-item compliance or verify basic obligations according to the stated objectives of agreements and focus on early-warning functions? What are its most important tasks in the new military and political situation in Europe— to detect and deter violations or to enhance confidence-building for creating new security structures? Naturally, the approaches cannot be so clear-cut and they comprise overlapping priorities. Finally, is it necessary to change previous approaches, criteria and tasks for verification because of recent trends in Europe?

One of the basic needs for military–political stability in Europe is predictability of military developments as a means to eliminate short- and long-term security concerns. Such predictability continues to be the principal requirement for the further strengthening of security in Europe. The past record has shown the vicious circle of action–reaction in military preparations. Predictions or perceptions by one state of 'bad intentions' on the part of another state or groups within a state could prompt reactions which might also be implemented without the ability to predict counter-reactions.

The predictability resulting from far-reaching arms control accords and other arrangements can help to alleviate the domestic and international impetus for such destabilizing activities in the military arena. The more complete the knowledge of the other side, along with the co-operation that the process of accumulating this knowledge engenders, the better the chances for eliminating concerns. The problem is to find the threshold at which security could be damaged—a threshold that could be higher as co-operation improves.

The arms control agreements signed in 1990 and 1992, including the verification regimes, are the binding nucleus of the process of co-operative security and of enhancing predictability. In examining the role of verification, Harald Müller wrote that aside from its direct role, the acceptance of far-reaching verification obligations reflects the following:

The parties create a unique opportunity to demonstrate to each other their political preference for security cooperation over self-help cooperation:
    – they give priority to transparency over secrecy . . .

– Moreover, they prove their readiness to incur even serious changes in their domestic structures in order to eliminate elements that hamper cooperation.

. . . more liberally formulated verification schemes will inevitably lead to a growth in collateral information conveyed to the verifying party. . . . More important is political and social information which will be learned by inspectors and, through them, by the political systems on both sides.

. . . there is the gain in human contacts among those parts of either society which need mutual recognition and appreciation most: the military. Verification schemes bring together people who are supposed to fight and to kill each other if it comes to it.[10]

He concluded that in the world of security co-operation, 'verification measures designed to provide information about capabilities will also convey information about intentions. . . . And through this enhancement of mutual trust verification will greatly contribute to the transformation of the East-West conflict'.[11]

Despite the dramatic changes in the military and political situation in Europe it will be some time before the accumulated military potentials are reduced to levels appropriate to this new or emerging co-operative environment. The task remains of dismantling the mechanisms of the former confrontation which, although drastically reshaped, has yet to completely fade into oblivion. A new security mechanism has to be based not on the presence of the military threat, but rather on the reliable absence of this threat. Mechanisms and regimes are needed to provide the maximum predictability of the actions and intentions of the CSCE participating states. Especially in the light of the January 1994 Partnership for Peace initiative, the time is ripe at least to talk about the military co-ordination of CSCE states. This must go in parallel with the elimination of the 'cold war' heritage, including the accumulated military potentials. In this case, verification is becoming an integral and important part of the process of achieving greater transparency.

The process includes two interrelated tasks. The first, more limited in scale and goals, deals with a given concrete regime to provide and check data and information about military activities and relies primarily on technological and detailed practical arrangements. The second task, which underlies the first, is to build up overall co-operation among states to provide predictability of actions and intentions, to eliminate images of opponents or rivals, and to form real partnership relations. Among other things this requires mechanisms of military co-ordination and joint bodies to counter outside threats.

One of the key requirements for transparency is a successful verification regime. The demands for costly and comprehensive means of verification could be reduced, while at the same time optimizing insight into new military potentials, by methods such as monitoring of military activities outside the scope of a given arms control agreement or *ad hoc* checking of the data exchange.

[10] Müller, H., 'Transforming the East–West conflict: the crucial role of verification', eds J. Altmann and J. Rotblat, *Verification of Arms Reductions: Nuclear, Conventional and Chemical* (PRIF, Springer-Verlag: Berlin, Heidelberg, 1989), pp. 7–8.

[11] Müller (note 10), p. 9.

Verification and monitoring regimes are important practical tools with which to achieve transparency, and they fulfil several requirements. First, they can provide an opportunity for equal participation by states parties and permit them to gain equal experience. This opportunity may then stimulate further transparency, for example, by promoting reduction of military production, conversion and limitations on military research and development (R&D) and the transfer of armaments and technology. Second, they provide a guarantee in the initial stages of the process against potential negative trends during the transitional period. This guarantee mechanism is based on strict legal obligations and arrangements for implementing certain agreements and activities.

Analysis of the verification aspects of the documents, and of the CFE Treaty in particular, should take into account how they might best contribute to the successful pursuit of transparency and the strengthening of security and co-operation in Europe. In the initial stage of the process, however, one should start by analysing verification problems in the context of present-day realities, taking into account the following:

1. The agreements are still in the process of implementation.

2. States parties are still accumulating proper experience in these very comprehensive conventional arms control enterprises.

3. The process of substantial reductions must be dealt with in the face of potentially sensitive and many unforeseen problems.

4. There is widespread concern as to how to cope with residual forces so as to ensure stability and predictability of further military developments.

A verification regime can be supplemented by a monitoring regime covering some activities which go beyond the agreements mentioned above. The Open Skies concept has been acknowledged by politicians and experts as a promising means of easing the burden and increasing the effectiveness of the verification regime in Europe as well as expanding transparency to include areas outside Europe and to contribute to stability at lower levels of armed forces. The verification regime as a system can be affected by outside factors. Unregulated military activities within and beyond the area of application of the agreements may require still further co-operative measures. Whether or not this is the case depends on assessments of the adequacy of the verification regime and political decisions with regard to the necessity for further transparency. The signing of the Open Skies Treaty in March 1992 indicated that the participating states acknowledged the benefits of expanding transparency.

Whether Europe pursues further arms control agreements or has to rely upon the present regime for some years to come, the existing verification arrangements will deal with the problems of co-operative security and provide valuable new experience, including that which may affect new forms of co-operation. Co-operative monitoring beyond the CFE framework may bring different approaches in improving transparency for stability and elimination of the threat of war.

III. Verification

While the precise definition and main tasks of verification are st/ cussed, political and academic communities have worked out a extensive framework of arrangements, some of which have already been tested and some of which remain as possible theoretical foundations for future arms control agreements. Despite differences in arms control agreements, changing environments and the range of details and priorities in verification arrangements, several basic concepts of verification remain valid. They dictate the specifics and functioning of a verification regime. Those which are relevant to further analysis are described here.[12]

Definition

According to an important UN study,

Verification is a process which establishes whether the States parties are complying with their obligations under an agreement. The process includes: collection of information relevant to obligations under arms limitation and disarmament agreements; analysis of the information; and reaching a judgement as to whether the specific terms of an agreement are being met. The context in which verification takes place is that of the sovereign right of States to conclude and their obligation to implement arms limitation and disarmament agreements. Verification is conducted by the parties to an agreement, or by an organization at their request.

. . . Compliance refers to the actual behaviour of a party with respect to the provisions of a binding agreement. It denotes behaviour that is in accordance with the forms and requirements of the agreement.[13]

In this report experts from different countries emphasized the agreement-specific approach to defining verification. At the same time they acknowledged that a package of methods and activities specifically assigned to verification implies rather broader tasks.

Verification of compliance is a process with several unilateral and/or co-operative steps. It starts with monitoring, examining and analysing information relating to compliance. The analysis includes problems associated not only with specific categories limited by an agreement, but also with the agreement-relevant activities of the other side.

Monitoring/data collection: monitoring is the process of watching, observing or checking objects, activities or events, for a specific purpose. It is one generic form of information collection, which can include other activities such as exchange of information. Monitoring, and data collection in general, constitute the first step in the verification

---

[12] The authors leave aside some broader aspects of verification covered in Kokoski, R. and Koulik, S. (eds), SIPRI, *Verification of Conventional Arms Control in Europe: Technological Constraints and Opportunities* (Westview Press: Boulder, Colo., 1990), pp. 3–13.

[13] UN Department for Disarmament Affairs, *Study on the Role of the United Nations in the Field of Verification* (United Nations: New York, 1991), p. 4.

process. In verification, this information is collected for the purpose of assessing compliance with a binding agreement.

Monitoring/data collection and analysis can be undertaken for a much wider range of purposes than verification including, *inter alia*, crisis prevention, peace-keeping and general intelligence gathering. Verification procedures must be carefully designed to prevent, as far as possible, collection of data unrelated to the purpose of verifying the treaty concerned.[14]

The last requirement was a stumbling-block in negotiations on verification arrangements for many arms control agreements. It has continued to be a particularly sensitive problem because of security, legal and economic concerns, and the fear of military or industrial espionage.

Verification (the process of determining compliance with a treaty's obligations) includes monitoring (the process of collecting, analysing, and reporting data on the activities of the parties to an arms control agreement). On the other hand, monitoring is usually mainly a technical activity, collecting objective facts, while verification includes an interpretative activity which deals not only with evidence, but also with the meaning of the terms of the agreement itself. The verification process as a whole is the responsibility of the national political authority and not of the intelligence agencies; the role of intelligence is supportive.[15] Verification policy is a result of conflicting interests at the national and international levels, and the analysis and interpretation of compliance may have a political and ideological character.[16] The functional requirements of verification have been described as follows:

The basic function of any verification regime is information collection. A steady stream of data, ideally provided by each participant to the agreement, is necessary as evidence of good behavior and future good intent. A second function of verification is the ability to provide timely warning should war preparations occur. Warning requirements are the bedrock of compliance monitoring. Relative certainty about one's own ability to mobilize against an attacker serves as an important way of gauging the level of verification needed. A third function is transparency. Information about the disposition and location of forces, along with the right to observe exercises, is vitally important to maintaining stability.[17]

Finally, verification of compliance may allow a different response to ambiguities or violations: monitoring the 'unusual' activities of one side may provide an argument for the other side to start or speed up certain military programmes or activities. The compliance mechanism gives an opportunity to clarify the

---

[14] UN Department for Disarmament Affairs (note 13), p. 4.

[15] *Security and Arms Control: The Search for a More Stable Peace* (US Government Printing Office: Washington, DC, Sep. 1984), pp. 75–76; Feer, F., *The Intelligence Process and the Verification Problem*, RAND Report P-7112, RAND Corporation, Santa Monica, Calif., July 1985, pp. 11–12.

[16] von Riekhoff, H. (ed.), *Compliance and Confirmation: Political and Technical Problems in the Verification of Arms Control of Chemical Weapons and Outer Space* (Carleton University: Ottawa, 1986), p. 1.

[17] Altmann, J., Deak, P., Kelleher, C. M. and Makarevsky, V. I., 'Verification and conventional arms reductions', eds F. Calogero, M. L. Goldberger and S. P. Kapitza, *Verification: Monitoring Disarmament* (Westview Press: Boulder, Colo.,1991), p. 167.

problem within the agreed procedures and at least ease political reaction in the event of ambiguous activities.

Data exchange

Agreements may provide for varying degrees of data exchange. The CFE provisions, for example, include an extensive exchange of data on the numbers and locations of TLE. These data provide a basis for additional activities to verify further compliance with an agreement. In addition to agreement on initial data exchange, including data on the numbers, locations, technical characteristics, structures, related facilities, and so on, agreement on how to update these data should also be included. An agreement for the reduction or elimination of equipment should have provisions on accounting for TLE awaiting destruction and for ensuring that TLE items are eliminated, such as: (*a*) continuous updates of the data exchanged among participants to assess the net effect of destruction activities; (*b*) restrictions on the location of TLE at agreed facilities and deployment areas declared in the data exchanges; (*c*) short-notice, on-site inspections to confirm the number of TLE items at declared sites; (*d*) advance notice each time elimination is to take place; and (*e*) destruction of equipment only at specified facilities and which is observed through mandatory on-site inspection. In general, however, the exchange leads to several questions about the validity of the data: whether initial baseline inspections permit their accuracy to be verified, whether the TLE described actually exists at described locations and whether a full account of existing TLE has been given without some items being hidden, for example, at non-declared sites.

The answers to these questions are provided by different means of verification and by intelligence sources. The exchange of data within the framework of an agreement gives more opportunity for added assurances about the precise data of another side than, for example, official exchanges of data unconnected with a particular agreement.

In order to ease problems stemming from different structures of military potentials and differences in evaluating parameters of certain categories of weapon system and units an agreement should include appropriate definitions and counting rules. Common data structures are essential for meaningful comparisons.

Intrusive arrangements allowed by an agreement to verify the data give another and very important opportunity to check their validity. At the same time, the data base created by an agreement provides a guideline for commonly agreed procedures, and information systems supporting the verification of compliance should be built upon this data base. The latter is important for timely resolution of problems such as whether a certain activity is seen as planned cheating or just a difference in the subjective interpretation of an agreement.

The readiness of states to sign an agreement reflects their assessments of their respective capabilities to check the data with greater or lesser precision and a high level of confidence that another side is sincere in providing the data. No one can be absolutely assured about the capability to check the actual numbers of TLE items, but the likelihood is certainly greater with measures additional to NTM.

The most difficult question concerns the possibility that a certain amount of TLE is hidden. The question of hidden items illustrates that verification arrangements are not a panacea for absolute confidence in the data, but it reflects one of the main verification tasks—to provide disincentives for large- and even small-scale cheating. The evaluation of this issue involves at least an analytical comparison of the size of the military potential definitely 'opened up' through NTM and intrusive verification arrangements and the magnitude of the potential which a side could conceivably hide. This raises the important issue of 'military significance'.

Militarily significant violations

If possible violations are detected, the immediate task is to assess their military significance.[18] The challenge here is that the response of any one side is ruled by their different assessments, which can result from divergent parameters according to their perceptions of threats to national security. Official statements usually evade specifications of these criteria.

In assessing the problems of militarily significant violations it should be borne in mind that their evaluation within the framework of conventional armed forces is closely connected with the data base, which details categories and types of TLE, locations and sites, organization and command structures of forces, amount of TLE, limitations, ceilings and constraints by category and level. The data base is also connected with the verification arrangements them- selves under inspection protocols, covering appropriate provisions, such as rules of conduct, terms, obligations, quotas, types of inspection, and so on.

The concept of military significance stems from the notion that the sides abide by the concept of adequacy in compliance, rather than the strictly juridi- cal approach to verification. The latter would oblige states parties to abide strictly by the terms of an agreement, with one illegal tank or aircraft represent- ing a clear violation and providing the right for an accusation of non- compliance with all the corresponding consequences. The concept of adequacy in compliance, in turn, is connected with political reality which has none the less imposed some constraints on the strict effectiveness of verification efforts.

Some approaches to enhance verification

The preferred approach of most experts for simplifying verification of reduc- tions and withdrawals requires the complete removal of military formations— divisions, brigades or regiments. The complete removal of a division is con-

---

[18] This problem is also discussed in Kokoski and Koulik (note 12), pp. 3–11.

sidered a better option than, for example, withdrawing a regiment from a division. But monitoring tasks for regimental or brigade withdrawal would be substantially easier than 'salami-type' reductions entailing, for example, removing troops and/or equipment from a company or a battalion. In general a salami-type withdrawal would require more intrusive and co-operative arrangements which may demand decisions unacceptable from the security viewpoint.

While verification tasks are complicated by the implementation of these procedures they can be facilitated by specifying that all withdrawn equipment should be removed to specially assigned storage facilities or destroyed. One safeguard on stored items suggests that key components be removed from the equipment (such as gearboxes from main battle tanks and armoured personnel carriers, or landing gear/wheels from aircraft) and stored in separate sites under verification arrangements. Such a procedure would obviously increase warning time, because reassembly takes considerable time and may be detected, especially if the parts were transferred to distant areas. Stored items could also be tagged and inspected. Another broad verification task involves close observation of main reinforcement routes, for example, allowing troops and vehicles to cross borders at specific points during the daytime only.

The effectiveness of verification can be enhanced by (a) narrowing the geographic area of application for a particular obligation under an agreement; (b) exchanging data on units with TLE, rather than simply on numbers of equipment items; (c) the presence of standard and familiar combat units, rather than new types of combat unit, reserve unit, or rear area formation; and (d) the presence of less complex units or formations.[19]

Whereas the answer to the question of what measures can be used to verify compliance is mainly technical, the answer to the question of how much verification is enough is both technical and political. Like many questions that include a political element, it is also very hard to answer fully, especially before testing of accepted arrangements. Before the CFE Treaty took shape, these debates certainly provided much food for thought and will continue to do so with respect to further conventional arms control enterprises.

All these questions can be dealt with, but they raise a final question of a different, rather subjective kind: how much certainty must a side strive for in the validity of its answers? Many experts have tried to address this question in an analytical manner and from the viewpoint of purely political considerations, but the efforts failed to satisfy everyone because many unpredictable political attitudes and assessments are also involved. John Toogood indirectly acknowledged this by stating that 'absolute certainty in any human endeavour is [a] highly unlikely characteristic and this aspect of verification, like so many other things, will have to be determined as yet another variation on the age old theme of how much is enough'.[20]

---

[19] Hirschfeld, T., *Verifying Conventional Stability in Europe: An Overview*, RAND Report N-3045-A, RAND Corporation, Santa Monica, Calif., Apr. 1990, p. 20.
[20] Hirschfeld (note 19), p. 87.

One of the most challenging constraints on successful arms control verification is that of cognitive or psychological distortion. James Macintosh explained that,

It is a way of acknowledging the significant gap that separates the unrealistic ideal of 'rational, objective assessment and judgement' and the much harsher reality of very imperfect, biased, distinctly non-rational perception and decision making that occurs in virtually every human enterprise, especially those which are subject to great uncertainty.[21]

He further illustrated the point that,

The *interpretation* of NTM material—a crucial part of the verification process—*is critically dependent upon earlier decisions made about, for instance, the character and intent of the Soviet Union. In other words, verification is the captive of existing images and interpretations.* . . . This will be true whether the simplifying images are internal to human decision makers or the artifacts of human thinking transplanted into electronic expert systems.[22]

Thus to the extent practicable negotiations should: (*a*) establish obligations as precisely as possible; (*b*) accept adequate co-operative measures to increase the ability for monitoring, including restrictions on TLE locations, on-site inspections and enhancement of national technical means; (*c*) formulate provisions which, along with the above measures, will increase problems and costs for cheating—and thereby enhancing the probability of detection; (*d*) establish reliable procedures for solving compliance problems; and (*e*) take into account possibilities to implement timely countermeasures in response to violations, if they are not resolved.

There should also be provision for increasing the likelihood of detection of clandestine TLE potential. Such a possibility is increased if there are provisions for short-notice inspection of sites previously declared as TLE sites and subsequently eliminated. These inspections help to ensure that TLE items have not been returned to the inspected sites. Agreed provisions to enhance the capability of national technical means are also desirable along with continuous portal monitoring of any final assembly facility at which TLE is produced.

Partners to the negotiation should make a technical evaluation of their available and planned resources for data collection, processing, analysis and reporting based on the limitations and constraints imposed by an agreement, and assess how these capabilities can be enhanced by specific verification provisions. Account should be taken of credible cheating scenarios and the attitudes of the party's decision makers to non-compliance.

To enhance verification effectiveness on-site inspection may be adopted, which represents the most intrusive form of verification. There are several main

---

[21] Macintosh, J., 'Further verification constraints', ed. J. O'Manique, *Proxy for Trust* (The Norman Paterson School of International Affairs, Carleton University: Ottawa, 1985), p. 121.

[22] Macintosh (note 21), p. 123.

forms of OSI which can be used in arms control and these have been discussed in conventional arms control negotiations since 1973:

1. Permanent stationing of inspectors at declared exit/entry points of reduction areas.

2. Systematic inspections to monitor locations of a specific type according to a planned schedule.

3. Random inspections defined *a priori* in general terms, as by total number per year, type of installation, and region; a given location can be visited at a given moment and the time of a visit is not disclosed in advance.

4. Challenge inspections for the purpose of analysing events or locations.[23]

It should also be kept in mind that some information about military forces may also be gathered by military attachés without disturbing normal diplomatic relations. In 1947 bilateral agreements between Soviet, US, French and British military officers established Military Liaison Missions (MLM) permitting the monitoring of military developments in the Federal Republic of Germany (FRG) and the German Democratic Republic (GDR) with complete freedom of travel other than to places where military units are located, without escort or supervision. Such routine observations increase the transparency of military activities. Also, the effectiveness of the activities of military attachés has been demonstrated many times and the experience gained by them and members of MLM was used in conducting inspections under the 1987 US–Soviet Intermediate-Range Nuclear Forces (INF) Treaty.[24]

The monitoring of exit/entry points has both strengths and weaknesses. Although it involves permanent coverage and limited physical intrusion it may be relatively easy to circumvent and have a limited range of coverage. OSI can provide highly detailed information on specific targets, permit examination of the inside of buildings, enable rapid analysis and offer the flexibility of human presence. Such inspections may be highly intrusive, however, and thus some forms may be unacceptable to the party to be inspected; they may also be limited in area of operation and duration.[25]

In addition, the options acceptable to states parties depend on the conducive nature of the current political climate to agreement on certain levels of intrusiveness. For example, for a long period in the past some participating states at the conventional armed forces negotiations rejected even the possibility of OSI. On the other hand, the final agreement to leave exit/entry point arrangements out of the Vienna negotiations can be partly explained by their having been seen as being particularly needed in the 'cold war' environment with the predominance of suspicion over trust—a situation which is rapidly disappearing.

---

[23] Altmann *et al.* (note 17), pp. 180–81.
[24] *Survival*, Nov./Dec. 1988, p. 546.
[25] Cleminson, F. R., 'Conventional arms reductions in Europe: A verification model', eds Altmann and Rotblat (note 10), p. 164.

The smooth functioning of a verification regime can, in general, be enhanced by the creation of a special bilateral, multilateral or international organization involved in analysing and discussing the implementation of compliance with an arms control agreement. At the same time non-treaty specific co-operative measures may also be put in place, incorporating monitoring arrangements which include in-country monitoring by, say, aerial means of zones or objects and activities beyond those specified in an agreement, and some type of organization which can deal with such monitoring. This type of arrangement is embodied in the Open Skies Treaty, which covers a much wider area than the CFE Treaty.

Within a treaty-specific verification regime generic monitoring tasks include: (a) counting declared inventories of treaty-limited equipment; (b) confirming ultimate force disposition, including destruction, storage and redeployments; (c) distinguishing non-prohibited but technically similar items from treaty-limited equipment; (d) detecting prohibited activities, capabilities or items; (e) detecting conversion of versatile weapon systems; and (f) monitoring qualitative limits. Within non-treaty specific co-operative monitoring regimes the tasks may also involve deterring circumvention of specific obligations of one or several treaties, but they are more importantly focused on such tasks as very early warning and the further enhancement of confidence-building. Both types of regime address the issue of transparency.

IV. About the book

This book is the second of a two-volume study. In the first volume current and emerging technological capabilities for verifying conventional arms reductions were discussed in relation to their limitations and advantages for monitoring a variety of armaments and equipment, including the possibility of counting separate TLE items.[26] The conclusions of the first volume with regard to the technological capabilities of verification were based partly on analysis of the experience gained from earlier arms control efforts. Experience has shown that the effectiveness of the technological means of verification, including NTM, could be greatly increased by positive political motivations and actions. The symbiosis of these factors has resulted in successful implementation of arms control agreements.

Nevertheless, because of the scope and specific problems of the CFE Treaty, previous arms control endeavours are in many respects not comparable with the efforts required for its implementation. Also, although the main conclusion of the first volume unambiguously supports the adequacy of the analysed array of available and emerging technologies for verifying the implementation of the November 1990 agreements, some of these technologies were excluded from the documents. They were omitted because of political and economic considerations, not to speak of the drastic changes in the European map.

[26] Kokoski and Koulik (note 12).

The present volume focuses to a greater extent on the non-technological aspects of the verification of conventional armed forces. Although no longer of the same vital importance to the CFE Treaty itself as when it was signed, the CFE verification regime together with the Treaty on Open Skies will contribute to and enhance transparency which, it can be argued, is even more important in the context of present-day Europe.

Chapter 2 includes a description and short analysis of the provisions of the CFE Treaty, the text of which is appended to this volume complete with protocols and annexes. The verification problems and opportunities presented by the CFE Treaty are analysed in chapter 3, which deals among other things with the constraints imposed by the negotiators on the verification mechanism. A short record of the MBFR and CFE negotiations which resulted in the CFE Treaty is given in chapter 4, which endeavours to shed light on both the constraints and the opportunities inherent in the Treaty. Some of the proposals or ideas put forward during the negotiations could be useful for future consideration, even though the political environment of future negotiations may be dramatically different from that of the past. In addition, the inclusion of these topics helps to place the discussion of the Treaty in its proper historical context. The new political realities and the challenges to verification of the CFE Treaty posed by the dissolution of the Soviet Union are examined in chapter 5, together with a discussion of the structural elements of conventional armed forces and the increased importance of an adequate assessment of such elements in the future. Possible methods to increase transparency in this area are suggested.

Chapter 6 is devoted to verification aspects of the 'operational approach' to arms control, as illustrated by negotiations on CSBMs and their results. These measures still promise to further expand and enhance co-operation in the military sphere in the future. The chapter examines the evolution of the CSBM verification regime within the CSCE process from the 1975 Helsinki Final Act to the Vienna Document 1992, the text of which is appended to this volume.

Chapter 7 presents some background on the concept of Open Skies and gives a brief history of the proposals and negotiations that led to the 1992 Treaty on Open Skies, the text of which is also appended. Analysis of this concept is appropriate here since it illustrates the possibility of creating a monitoring regime involving all participating states on an equal basis. Although some of the historical approaches outlined have been superseded, the core of the concept and the Treaty is very much alive for the future, particularly as a road to transparency and as a means of reducing the need to verify military structures through other arrangements.

Finally, chapter 8 reports on the lessons learned from the experience of the monitoring activity which took place leading up to and during the 1991 Persian Gulf War. Although functioning in a landscape quite different from that of Europe, and in a hostile environment, the scenario exhibits some aspects relevant to arms control in Europe.

2. The Treaty on Conventional Armed Forces in Europe

I. Introduction

The CFE Treaty, signed in Paris on 19 November 1990 and which entered into force *de facto* on 17 July 1992, is the most sweeping arms control agreement in history and marks the beginning of a new era in arms control verification. It was able in short order successfully to grapple with a revamped and still constantly changing European landscape to solidify arms limitations which at the very least greatly reduce the possibility and potential of surprise attack and large-scale offensive actions. Along with other documents signed in November 1990, the Treaty provided a basis for strengthening security and for optimism with respect to the process of eliminating military threats in Europe.

In sending the Treaty to the Senate for ratification former US President George Bush called it the most important arms control agreement ever concluded.[1] In addition to the unprecedented arms reduction measures laid down by the Treaty, a unique and far-reaching verification regime had been devised. New opportunities for on-site inspection, including very thorough and intrusive elements, were incorporated in detail in the Treaty.

The November 1990 documents

The CFE Treaty was originally signed by the 22 countries of the Warsaw Treaty Organization and the North Atlantic Treaty Organization, after 20 months of negotiations in Vienna.[2]

The following eight documents are integral parts of the Treaty:

1. Protocol on Existing Types of Conventional Armaments and Equipment with an Annex thereto;

2. Protocol on Procedures Governing the Reclassification of Specific Models or Versions of Combat-Capable Trainer Aircraft into Unarmed Trainer Aircraft;

3. Protocol on Procedures Governing the Reduction of Conventional Armaments and Equipment Limited by the Treaty on Conventional Armed Forces in Europe;

4. Protocol on Procedures Governing the Categorisation of Combat Helicopters and the Recategorization of Multi-Purpose Attack Helicopters;

---

[1] *Atlantic News*, no. 2351 (18 Sep. 1991), p. 2.
[2] The text of the Treaty on Conventional Armed Forces in Europe, Paris, 1990 is reprinted in this volume as appendix A (which includes protocols and annexes).

5. Protocol on Notification and Exchange of Information with an Annex on the Format for the Exchange of Information;

6. Protocol on Inspection;

7. Protocol on the Joint Consultative Group;

8. Protocol on the Provisional Application of Certain Provisions of the Treaty on Conventional Armed Forces in Europe.

The CFE Treaty was accompanied by three declarations:

1. The Declaration of the States Parties to the Treaty on Conventional Armed Forces in Europe with Respect to Land-based Naval Aircraft, stating that the aggregate number of land-based combat naval aircraft held by either alliance should not exceed 430. No state is to have more than 400 permanently land-based combat naval aircraft in the area of application of the Treaty; and the limitations are to apply 40 months after the entry into force of the Treaty. The problem of land-based naval aircraft was controversial during the CFE Negotiation and was resolved by this separate declaration.

2. The Declaration of the States Parties to the Treaty on Conventional Armed Forces in Europe with Respect to Personnel Strength, in which states parties commit themselves not to increase total peacetime authorized personnel during the period of the follow-on negotiations, which started on 26 November 1990.

3. The Declaration by the Government of the Federal Republic of Germany on the Personnel Strength of German Armed Forces, limiting the armed forces of the united Germany to 370 000 soldiers within three to four years. The corresponding reduction was to commence on the entry into force of the CFE Treaty. Within this ceiling no more than 345 000 troops were to belong to ground or air forces.

II. The key provisions of the CFE Treaty

The states parties

The original states parties were the 22 members of the former WTO and of NATO: Belgium, Bulgaria, Canada, the former Czechoslovakia, Denmark, France, Germany, Greece, Hungary, Iceland, Italy, Luxembourg, the Netherlands, Norway, Poland, Portugal, Romania, Spain, Turkey, the UK, the USA and the former USSR. After the dissolution of the USSR separate ratifications were made by new states parties—the Russian Federation, Armenia, Azerbaijan, Belarus, Georgia, Kazakhstan, Ukraine and Moldova.

By 30 October 1992, all 29 states parties had ratified the Treaty and the Treaty entered into force *de jure* on 9 November 1992. In 1993 the split of Czechoslovakia into two independent states, the Czech Republic and Slovakia, increased the number of states parties to 30.

Figure 1. The former Soviet military districts and the newly independent states in the ATTU zone

The area of application

The area of application of the Treaty covers the entire land territory of the states parties in Europe from the Atlantic Ocean to the Ural Mountains, including all the European island territories: the Faroe Islands (Denmark), Svalbard including Bear Island (Norway), the islands of the Azores and Madeira (Portugal), the Canary Islands (Spain), and Franz Josef Land and Novaya Zemlya (Russia). In the case of the former Soviet Union, the area of application included all territory lying west of the Ural River and the Caspian Sea—that is, the former Baltic, Byelorussian, Carpathian, Kiev, Odessa, North Caucasus, Transcaucasus, Leningrad, Moscow and Volga–Ural military districts (MDs). In the case of Turkey, it includes the territory north and west of a line extending from the point of intersection of the Turkish border with the 39th parallel to Muradiye, Patnos, Karayazi, Tekman, Kemaliye, Feke, Ceyhan, Dogankent, Gözne and thence to the sea. This area is usually referred to as the Atlantic-to-the-Urals (ATTU) zone and covers over 2.5 million square miles (over 6 million km²).

In Article IV of the Treaty three sub-zones within the ATTU area (zone IV.1) are defined—IV.2, IV.3 and IV.4. Article V defines a flank zone. Sub-zones IV.4, IV.3, IV.2 involve successively larger areas, defined so that each sub-zone includes the previous sub-zone(s). The flank zone is defined in the Treaty as an area separate from the other sub-zones with distinct limits on equipment. At the time of signature the sub-zones comprised the territories listed in table 1.

The rationale for establishing sub-zones and corresponding limits on weapons within the ATTU area was to prevent each alliance from concentrating conventional armaments and equipment close to the borders between them, thereby reducing the possibility of an attack by either side on short warning.

Since the Treaty was signed, far-reaching changes in Europe have had an impact on the criteria for the sub-zones. In particular, the disintegration of the USSR has led to the disappearance of the military districts. Independent Ukraine includes the territories of the Kiev and Carpathian MDs and a portion of the Odessa MD; Moldova plans to create its armed forces on a portion of the Odessa MD; the Volga-Urals MD has been split into the Volga MD and the Urals MD; after the dissolution of the USSR and before complete withdrawal from the Baltic states the Russian forces were included in the North-Western Group (instead of the Baltic MD), but now Russia only has the Leningrad MD and the newly established Kaliningrad Special Defence Region in its north European area; and the Transcaucasus MD formerly comprised three independent states—Georgia, Armenia and Azerbaijan. Figure 1 shows the borders of the former Soviet MDs and the newly independent states in the ATTU zone.

The strategic map of Europe has been drastically changed for the former Soviet republics. For example, Russia has found itself in a unique and totally unforeseen situation. The purely 'internal' Moscow MD is now on the external borders of independent Russia. This provoked Russian Defence Minister Pavel Grachev to put forward a plan to create a new Smolensk MD on the Russian western borders as 'the first strategic echelon'. This plan was not implemented,

Table 1. Subdivisions of the ATTU zone under the CFE Treaty

Sub-zone	Group of states	Territories
Sub-zone IV.4	NATO: WTO:	Belgium, Germany, Luxembourg, the Netherlands Czechoslovakia, Hungary, Poland
Sub-zone IV.3	Sub-zone IV.4, plus NATO: WTO:	 Denmark, France, Italy, the United Kingdom USSR (Baltic, Byelorussian, Carpathian, Kiev MDs)
Sub-zone IV.2	Sub-zone IV.3, plus NATO: WTO:	 Portugal, Spain USSR (Moscow and Volga–Ural MDs)
Flank zone	NATO: WTO:	Greece, Iceland, Norway, Turkey Bulgaria, Romania, USSR (Leningrad, North Caucasus, Odessa, Transcaucasus MDs)

Source: Treaty on Conventional Armed Forces in Europe, Paris, 1990, Articles IV and V.

however; the General complained that when the idea was introduced he faced criticism for 'aggressive intentions'.[3]

In its European part Russia now has the borders that it had 50 years ago in the north-west (with the Baltic states), 300 years ago in the west, 400 years ago in the south-west, and 150–200 years ago in the south. The large-scale 'front-line' military infrastructure, developed over these long periods, now belongs to the newly independent states. Some important strategic motivations for adherence to the CFE Treaty for the former Soviet Union are no longer relevant, and new strategic concerns for the newly independent states predominate.

During the Negotiation particular attention was paid to sub-zone IV.4, which covered Central Europe (see table 1). Much of the effort to devise a verification regime during the CFE Negotiation stemmed from concerns about the large, front-line concentration of NATO and WTO troops in that region. Subsequent Soviet military withdrawals from Czechoslovakia, Hungary, Poland and Germany have made the region of less concern, at least for NATO.

The three Baltic States, Estonia, Latvia and Lithuania, having comprised the bulk of the former Baltic MD, were excluded from the ATTU zone after they became independent in 1991. These states are now treated in the same way as the neutral and non-aligned states in the Conference on Security and Co-operation in Europe, although the treaty-limited equipment deployed there by the former Soviet Union was included in the original Soviet ceilings and remained subject to inspections under the CFE Treaty while the final Russian withdrawals took place.

The negotiators also paid much attention to the flank zone, which raised many concerns for the military stability of Europe. Moreover, the importance of the zone has increased considerably since the signing of the CFE Treaty because of several developments on the southern flank. First, there have been growing instability and military conflicts in the Balkans and the Caucasus.

---

[3] *Krasnaya Zvezda*, 1 June 1992.

Second, the barely controllable situation in the Caucasus has made the implementation of the Treaty much more difficult. Third, the North Caucasus MD of the former USSR, previously one of the least important military districts, has emerged as one of the key and strategically vital districts for Russian security. The Russian Ministry of Defence has started to strengthen the MD with new military hardware and infrastructure to meet the demands of the first defence echelon on the borders. Correspondingly, the Russian military are not satisfied with the limits for the flank zone.

The dissolution of the USSR has unexpectedly led to the inclusion of newly independent Kazakhstan among states parties to the CFE Treaty—the northwestern tip of Kazakhstan, lying west of the Ural River and the Caspian Sea, is included under the definition of the ATTU zone (see figure 1).

Despite the far-reaching political changes that have taken place in the area of application since the Treaty was signed, the sub-zones as defined in the Treaty still serve as one of the key guidelines for reduction and verification activities.

Treaty limits

Under the Treaty, each state party must limit and, as necessary, reduce its battle tanks, armoured combat vehicles (ACVs), artillery, combat aircraft and attack helicopters. ACVs include armoured personnel carriers (APCs), armoured infantry fighting vehicles (AIFVs) and heavy armoured combat vehicles (HACVs). 'Artillery' includes large-calibre systems—guns, howitzers, artillery pieces combining the characteristics of guns and howitzers, mortars and multiple-launch rocket systems (MLRS) with a calibre of 100 millimetres and above. The term 'attack helicopter' covers specialized attack helicopters (designed primarily to employ guided weapons) and multi-purpose helicopters (designed to perform multiple military functions and equipped to employ guided weapons). Agreed definitions of these systems are based on several specific technical characteristics and military functions stated in the Treaty.

The limits, to be effective 40 months after entry into force, on the TLE for each group of states within the ATTU zone and the sub-zones are shown in table 2.

Treaty-limited equipment in the ATTU zone not in active units, that is, 3500 battle tanks, 2700 ACVs and 3000 artillery pieces, must be placed in designated permanent storage sites only in sub-zone IV.2 with the permitted exception of the former Odessa MD (up to 400 battle tanks and 500 artillery pieces) and the southern part of the former Leningrad MD (up to 600 battle tanks, 800 ACVs, including no more than 300 ACVs of any type with the remaining number consisting of APCs, and 400 artillery pieces). Thus, the former Soviet Union may store up to 1000 battle tanks, 800 ACVs and 900 artillery systems in two MDs of the flank zone within the overall limits on stored TLE. Like inclusion of the former Kiev MD in zone IV.3, this exception slightly lessens the overall reductions the former USSR has been implementing in the flank zone.

Table 2. Zonal limits for each group of states (former WTO and NATO)

Zone	Battle tanks	ACVs	Artillery	Combat aircraft	Attack helicopters
ATTU zone IV.1	20 000	30 000^a	20 000	6 800	2 000
(active units)	16 500	27 300	17 000	..	..
Sub-zone IV.2	15 300	24 100	14 000	..	..
(active units)	11 800	21 400	11 000	..	..
Sub-zone IV.3^b	10 300	19 260	9 100	..	..
Sub-zone IV.4^c	7 500	11 250	5 000	..	..
Flank zone^d	4 700	5 900	6 000	..	..

^{a} Of which no more than 18 000 AIFVs and HACVs, including no more than 1500 HACVs.

^{b} Including a maximum of 2250 battle tanks, 2500 ACVs and 1500 artillery pieces in the Kiev MD as the Treaty originally prescribed.

^{c} If the aggregate treaty-limited equipment of a group of states parties in active units is less than these ceilings, and provided that no state party is thereby prevented from reaching its maximum levels for notified holdings, then the difference in each category may be located by this group in sub-zone IV.3 within ceilings for this sub-zone.

^{d} Notwithstanding these limitations, a state party or states parties may temporarily deploy additional TLE into the territory of members of the same group within the sub-zone, not to exceed 459 battle tanks, 723 ACVs and 420 artillery pieces in active units, of which no more than one-third (153 battle tanks, 241 ACVs and 140 artillery pieces) may be deployed to any one state party with territory in the sub-zone.

The Treaty also limits armoured vehicle launched bridges (AVLBs)—capable of carrying, emplacing and retrieving a bridge structure—to 740 in active units for each group of states parties. Excess AVLBs are to be placed in designated permanent storage sites. The information exchange showed that the ex-WTO states had 1580 (the USSR 976) and NATO 700 (the USA 212, Germany 299) AVLBs—the former WTO states must therefore store 840 of them.[4]

It was required that TLE to be reduced be declared present within the area of application in the exchange of information at Treaty signature. Each state was obliged to notify all other states of its reduction liability no later than 30 days after the entry into force of the Treaty.

The Protocol on Existing Types of Conventional Armaments and Equipment lists types of TLE for each category—battle tanks: 24; APCs: 49; AIFVs: 16; HACVs: 15; artillery: about 100; combat aircraft: 55; specialized attack and multi-purpose attack helicopters: 17.

It should be noted that the agreed definitions of the treaty-limited equipment supported by the Protocol constitute a very important and useful tool for relatively smooth and unambiguous reductions and verification activities—the result of truly successful negotiation.

[4] Institute for Defense and Disarmament Studies, *Arms Control Reporter (ACR)* (IDDS: Brookline, Mass.), 1990, sheet 407.B.411.

Exceptions to numerical limitations

All conventional armaments and equipment limited by the Treaty are subject to the above ceilings except (in a manner consistent with normal practices):

1. Items under manufacture or related testing;
2. Items used exclusively for research and development;
3. Items belonging to historical collections;
4. ACVs and multi-purpose attack helicopters held by organizations designed and structured to perform internal security functions in peacetime; AIFVs held by such organizations in excess of 1000 constitute a portion of the TLE while up to 600 AIFVs of a state party may be located within the flank zone;
5. Items in transit through the area of application to and from locations outside this area, if in the area for no longer than seven days;
6. Items awaiting disposal, having been decommissioned from service, provided that they are at no more than eight sites notified as declared sites and identified as holding areas for decommissioned TLE and provided that such TLE does not exceed 1 per cent of notified holdings of each state party, or a total of 250 items, whichever is greater (including no more than 200 battle tanks, ACVs and artillery pieces and no more than 50 combat aircraft and attack helicopters);
7. Items awaiting, or being refurbished for, export or re-export and temporarily retained within the area of application. Such TLE must be located elsewhere than at declared sites or at no more than 10 such declared sites notified in the previous year's annual information exchange. In the latter case they must be separately distinguishable from TLE.

There are relatively few exceptions to the Treaty limits on equipment that would permit sizeable military potentials to be maintained outside the framework of the Treaty. One of the main problems concerns the substantial numbers of TLE items held by organizations designed and structured to perform internal security functions, particularly those of the former Soviet Union. After the dissolution of the USSR, many of the TLE items on the list, belonging to the internal security ministries of the newly independent states, have been used in ethno-political conflicts on the periphery of the former Soviet Union—representing a new challenge for counting and verification activities.

The sufficiency rule

No one country can retain more than a specified amount of the total TLE in the ATTU zone. This rule is based on the political principle that 'no single state should have a dominant position in the new Europe'.[5] In other words, it was designed to allow each country to have enough weapons for its own defence, but to prevent any one country from having a military potential which might pose a threat to another alliance. To ensure that no single state party possesses

5 *Atlantic News*, 17 Nov. 1990, p. 1.

'more than approximately one-third' of the limits for NATO and ex-WTO countries within the area of application, each state party is limited to 13 300 battle tanks, 20 000 ACVs, 13 700 artillery pieces, 5150 combat aircraft and 1500 attack helicopters. This rule was aimed at limiting the potential of the former Soviet Union.

Post-CFE entitlements

The above rule notwithstanding, on 3 November 1990 foreign ministers of the six member states of the WTO agreed on TLE cuts that would have the former Soviet Union retain fewer battle tanks (13 150) and artillery systems (13 175) than specified in the Treaty two weeks later. While NATO's internal allocation of cuts was an agreement in principle, the WTO agreement was a legally binding treaty. In May 1992 the members of the Commonwealth of Independent States (CIS) managed to resolve their differences debated after the dissolution of the USSR on how to divide their forces to meet the post-CFE entitlements within the permitted ceilings for the former Soviet Union. At their summit meeting in Tashkent, the capital of Uzbekistan, they signed the Agreement on the Principles and Procedures of Implementation of the Treaty on Conventional Armed Forces in Europe (the Tashkent Document) on 15 May.[6] Taking account of these agreements, the official allocation of post-CFE entitlements for treaty-limited equipment would be as shown in table 3. (The table includes the agreed limits for the new Czech and Slovak states after the dissolution of Czechoslovakia in 1993 within the permitted ceilings for that former state.)

The Joint Consultative Group (JCG) in Vienna agreed on the necessary language changes in the CFE Treaty to accommodate the allocations of TLE among the newly independent states on 2 June 1992. At a North Atlantic Cooperation Council meeting in Oslo on 5 June the Final Document of the Extraordinary Meeting of the states parties to the CFE Treaty was signed by 29 states, formally approving the new allocations.[7]

A state party may change the maximum levels for its holdings of TLE, notifying at least 90 days in advance. However, any increase in these levels which would otherwise cause the numerical limitations in any of the four zones to be exceeded must be accompanied by a corresponding reduction in TLE holdings in one or more states parties of the same group. Such notification with regard to ACVs must also include levels for AIFVs and HACVs. Any decrease in TLE held by a state party by itself confers no right for any other state party to increase its maximum levels. Each state party is solely responsible for ensuring that its notified holdings do not exceed their maximum—states parties of the same group shall consult to ensure that the maximum holdings taken together do not exceed the Treaty's limits.

---

[6] The text of the Tashkent Document is reproduced in SIPRI, *SIPRI Yearbook 1993: World Armaments and Disarmament* (Oxford University Press: Oxford, 1993), appendix 12C, pp. 671–77.

[7] The Final Document of the States Parties to the Treaty on Conventional Armed Forces in Europe (the Oslo Document), Oslo, 5 June 1992, is reproduced in SIPRI (note 6), appendix 12C, pp. 677–82.

Table 3. Official allocation of post-CFE entitlements among states parties

Country	Battle tanks	ACVs	Artillery	Combat aircraft	Attack helicopters
NATO countries					
Belgium	334	1099	320	232	46
Canada	77	277	38	90	13
Denmark	353	316	553	106	12
France	1 306	3 820	1 292	800	352
Germany	4 166	3 446	2 705	900	306
Greece	1 735	2 534	1 878	650	18
Iceland	0	0	0	0	0
Italy	1 348	3 339	1 955	650	142
Luxembourg	0	0	0	0	0
Netherlands	743	1 080	607	230	69
Norway	170	225	527	100	0
Portugal	300	430	450	160	26
Spain	794	1 588	1 310	310	71
Turkey	2 795	3 120	3 523	750	43
UK	1 015	3 176	636	900	384
USA	4 006	5 372	2 492	784	518
NATO total	**19 142**	**29 822**	**18 286**	**6 662**	**2 000**
Ex-WTO countries					
Bulgaria	1 475	2 000	1 750	234	67
Czech Republic	957	1367	767	230	50
Hungary	835	1 700	840	180	108
Poland	1 730	2 150	1 610	460	130
Romania	1 375	2 100	1 475	430	120
Slovakia	478	683	383	115	25
USSR	13 150	20 000	13 175	5 150	1 500
Ex-WTO total	**20 000**	**30 000**	**20 000**	**6 800**	**2 000**
Former Soviet republics					
Armenia	220	220	285	100	50
Azerbaijan	220	220	285	100	50
Belarus	1 800	2 600	1 615	260	80
Georgia	220	220	285	100	50
Moldova	210	210	250	50	50
Russia	6 400	11 480	6 415	3 450	890
Ukraine	4 080	5 050	4 040	1 090	330

Source: Sharp, J. M. O., 'Conventional arms control in Europe', SIPRI, *SIPRI Yearbook 1993: World Armaments and Disarmament* (Oxford University Press: Oxford, 1993), tables 12.4 and 12.5, pp. 608–609

The timetable for the Treaty

The Treaty is of unlimited duration. Its implementation was divided into four periods:

1. *The baseline validation period* covered the first 120 days after entry into force of the Treaty for the purpose of calculating inspection quotas and for intense inspection of baseline data.

2. *The reduction period* during which TLE must be destroyed or certified was set for a 40-month period, which included the baseline validation period.

3. *The residual level validation period* covered 120 days for inspections to check new baseline data after reductions.

4. *The residual period* covers the unlimited duration of the Treaty when inspections to check data at declared and undeclared sites are to be carried out.

The reduction period consists of three phases to be completed no later than 40 months after entry into force of the Treaty. During the first 16 months after entry into force, each state party was to ensure that at least 25 per cent of its total reduction liability in each of the TLE categories had been reduced. No later than 28 months after entry into force of the Treaty, the percentage was to be raised to at least 60. The extra TLE was to be reduced during the remainder of the 40-month period.

The conversion of all battle tanks to non-military purposes was to be completed by the end of the third phase, while ACVs deemed reduced by reason of having been partially destroyed were to be fully converted to non-military purposes or destroyed no later than 64 months after entry into force of the Treaty.

Ratification of the CFE Treaty was finally completed on 30 October 1992. It entered into force *de facto* on 17 July 1992 after the original 22 signatories and seven former Soviet republics signed the Provisional Application of the CFE Treaty on 10 July. The Treaty entered into force *de jure* on 9 November, 10 days after the last signatory deposited its instrument of ratification in the Hague. Thus, the baseline validation period started on 17 July 1992 and was completed on 14 November 1992, opening the implementation of the next period, that is, of reductions. By 16 November 1993 each group of states parties had met or exceeded the 25 per cent reduction in TLE above the agreed limits. The NATO group had reduced by over 5700 TLE items and the former WTO group by over 11 500.[8]

Reductions

The reductions of conventional armaments and equipment in Europe are large-scale and unprecedented. Table 4 shows official TLE holdings of states parties in both groups as of November 1990 and the required reductions according to officially stated ceilings in each category by each state party and based on the sufficiency rule. The residual ceilings for NATO are below the Treaty limits while those for the ex-WTO countries meet the limits.

---

[8] Lachowski, Z., 'Conventional arms control and security co-operation in Europe', SIPRI, *SIPRI Yearbook 1994* (Oxford University Press: Oxford, 1994), p. 570; US General Accounting Office (GAO), *Conventional Arms Control: Former Warsaw Pact Nations' Treaty Compliance and US Cost Control*, GAO Report to Congressional Requesters, GAO/NSIAD-94-33 (GAO: Washington, DC, Dec. 1993), pp. 20–21.

It can be calculated from the November 1990 holdings shown in table 4 that the alliances had to reduce TLE categories by the following percentages, taking into account the inclusion of former GDR holdings in NATO potential and planned post-CFE ceilings:

1. NATO countries had to reduce battle tanks by 21 per cent; ACVs by 13 per cent; artillery by 12 per cent; and did not need to make reductions in combat aircraft and attack helicopters.
2. The former WTO countries had to reduce battle tanks by 37 per cent; ACVs by 28 per cent; artillery by 19 per cent; combat aircraft by 19 per cent; and did not need to reduce numbers of attack helicopters.

Comparison of the November 1990 holdings with the post-CFE entitlements indicates the scale of the required reductions. In reality the trends in allocations after the signature of the Treaty meant that a number of countries would have to make greater reductions because they had increased their holdings between the data exchanges of November 1990 and December 1992. In particular this applied to the ex-WTO states. Bulgaria increased its holdings from 6752 to 6905 TLE items, the former Czechoslovakia from 6265 to 9067 TLE items, Hungary from 4261 to 4281 items, and Romania from 10 260 to 10 551 items. Among the former Soviet republics in the ATTU zone only Belarus increased its holdings, from 6760 to 9482, while Armenia, Azerbaijan, Georgia, Moldova, Russia and Ukraine substantially or slightly reduced their TLE. As a result, beginning from 1993 the East European former WTO states had to make almost 50 per cent of the overall ex-WTO reductions, compared to their November 1990 share of about 30 per cent.

Between November 1990 and December 1992 NATO countries had slightly reduced their TLE holdings, with the exceptions of Denmark, Greece, Portugal and Turkey. Among these countries, however, only Denmark still had to reduce TLE to comply with the CFE Treaty ceilings. Greece, Portugal and Turkey had been increasing their TLE but were still below the Treaty limits at the end of 1992. Other NATO countries had decreased their TLE potentials even below the CFE limits: the USA, the UK, Spain, Norway and Canada. Besides Denmark, only Belgium, France, Germany, Italy and the Netherlands still had to make actual reductions to meet the CFE limits, as shown in table 5.

Within the overall reductions of 39 351 TLE items the share of the ex-WTO exceeds 70 per cent. Countries that have to make the greatest reductions are Germany, Russia, Romania, the former Czechoslovakia, Ukraine and Belarus. The distribution in the required reductions between the two groups of states parties did not change significantly from November 1990 to the end of 1992; the bulk of the reductions were still to be made by the ex-WTO states and the former USSR.

Table 4. Official November 1990 TLE holdings and reductions to CFE Treaty residual limits[a]

Figures are revised as of 12 August 1991 for NATO and of 28 May 1991 for ex-WTO countries.

Country	Battle tanks H	R	ACVs H	R	Artillery H	R	Combat aircraft H	R	Attack helicopters H	R
NATO countries										
Belgium	359	25	1 381	282	376	56	191	+41	0	+46
Canada	77	0	277	0	38	0	45	+45	12	+1
Denmark	419	66	316	0	553	0	106	0	3	+9
France	1 343	37	4 177	357	1 360	68	699	+101	418	66
Germany[b]	7 000	2 834	8 920	5 474	4 602	1 897	1 018	118	258	+48
Greece	1 879	144	1 641	+893	1 908	30	469	+181	0	+18
Iceland	0	0	0	0	0	0	0	0	0	0
Italy	1 246	+102	3 958	619	2 144	189	577	+73	168	26
Luxembourg	0	0	0	0	0	0	0	0	0	0
Netherlands	913	170	1 467	387	837	230	196	+34	91	22
Norway	205	35	146	+79	531	4	90	+10	0	0
Portugal	146	+154	244	+186	343	+107	96	+64	0	+26
Spain	854	60	1 256	+332	1 373	63	242	+68	28	+43
Turkey	2 823	28	1 502	+1 618	3 442	+81	511	+239	5	+38
UK	1 198	183	3 193	17	636	0	842	+58	368	+16
USA	5 904	1 898	5 747	375	2 601	109	626	+158	243	+275
NATO total	**24 366**	**5 224**	**34 225**	**4 403**	**20 744**	**2 458**	**5 708**	**+954**	**1594**	**+406**
Ex-WTO countries										
Bulgaria	2 145	670	2 204	204	2 116	366	243	8	44	+23
Former CSFR	1 797	362	2 538	488	1 566	416	348	3	56	+19
Hungary	1 345	510	1 720	20	1 047	207	110	+70	39	+69
Poland	2 850	1 120	2 377	227	2 300	690	551	91	29	+101
Romania	2 851	1 476	3 102	1 002	3 789	2 314	505	75	13	+107
Former USSR	20 725	7 575	29 890	9 890	13 938	763	6 611	1 461	1 481	+19
Ex-WTO total	**31 713**	**11 713**	**41 831**	**11 831**	**24 754**	**4 756**	**8 368**	**1 569**	**1 662**	**+338**
NATO and ex-WTO total	**56 079**	**16 937**	**76 056**	**16 235**	**45 500**	**7 214**	**14 076**	**615**	**3 256**	**+744**

[a] '+' before a number indicates that this number of TLE items may be *added* by the country in question. These figures do not take into account the obligations assumed by the USSR (outside the framework of the Treaty) which were agreed in June 1991 to resolve some final data disputes (for details see the discussion of baseline data and first disagreements in chapter 3).

[b] Including 10 674 weapons of the former GDR: 2274 tanks, 5817 ACVs, 2140 artillery pieces, 392 aircraft and 51 helicopters.

H: holdings; R: reductions

Source: Sharp, J. M. O., 'Conventional arms control in Europe', SIPRI, *SIPRI Yearbook 1993: World Armaments and Disarmament* (Oxford University Press: Oxford, 1993), tables 12.4 and 12.5, pp. 608–609.

Table 5. Required reductions in total TLE to 1995 CFE Treaty ceilings

Country	Required reduction	From Dec. 1992 holdings	To 1995 Treaty ceilings
NATO			
Belgium	188	2 219	2 031
Denmark	123	1 463	1 340
France	375	7 945	7 570
Germany	9 401	20 924	11 523
Italy	348	7 782	7 434
Netherlands	631	3 360	2 729
ex-WTO			
Bulgaria	1 379	6905	5 526
Czech Republic	2 674	6 045	3 371
Hungary	618	4 281	3 663
Poland	1 990	8 070	6 080
Romania	5 051	10 551	5 500
Slovakia	1 338	3 022	1 684
Azerbaijan	91	966	875
Belarus	3 127	9 482	6 355
Russia	8 402	36 841	28 635
Ukraine	3 615	18 205	14 590

Source: Based on Sharp, J. M. O., 'Conventional arms control in Europe', SIPRI, *SIPRI Yearbook 1993: World Armaments and Disarmament* (Oxford University Press: Oxford, 1993), tables 12.4 and 12.5, pp. 608–609.

Methods of reduction

Eight methods of TLE reduction were set by the Treaty: destruction; conversion to non-military purposes; placement on static display; use for ground instructional purposes; recategorization; use as ground targets; reclassification; and modification. These methods apply to different categories of TLE as shown in table 6. In each case, the item presented at the reduction site is to consist of a complete assembly.

Destruction. The Treaty provided for five methods of destruction: severing; explosive demolition; deformation; smashing; and use as target drones. Table 7 shows which methods may be applied to the different categories of TLE.

Conversion for non-military purposes applied to the following types of battle tank: T-54, T-55, T-62, T-64, T-72 and Leopard 1; and ACV: BMP-1, BTR-60 and OT-64. These items can be converted to: general-purpose prime movers; bulldozers; fire-fighting vehicles; cranes; power unit vehicles; mineral fine crushing vehicles; quarry vehicles; rescue vehicles; casualty evacuation vehicles; transportation vehicles; oil rig vehicles; oil and chemical spill cleaning vehicles; tracked ice-breaking prime movers; and environmental vehicles.

The states parties, within the framework of the Joint Consultative Group established to promote the objectives and the implementation of the Treaty, can

Table 6. Methods of reduction of TLE

Reduction method	Battle tanks	ACVs	Artillery	Combat aircraft	Specialized attack helicopters	Multi-purpose attack helicopters
Destruction	X	X	X	X	X	X
Conversion	X	X	0	0	0	0
Static display	X	X	X[a]	X	X	X
Ground instructional purposes	0	0	0	X	X	X
Recategorization	0	0	0	0	0	X
Ground targets	X	X	X	0	0	0
Reclassification	0	0	0	X[b]	0	0
Modification	0	X[c]	0	0	0	0

[a] Permitted only in the case of self-propelled artillery.

[b] Permitted only in the case of specific models or versions of combat-capable trainer aircraft.

[c] Permitted only in the case of one specific APC.

X - permitted

0 - not permitted

Table 7. Methods of destruction of TLE[a]

Destruction method	Tanks	ACVs	Artillery	Combat aircraft	Attack helicopters
Severing	X	X	X	X	X
Explosive demolition	X	X	X	0	X
Deformation	X	0	X[b]	X	X
Smashing	X	X	X[c]	0	0
Use as target drones	0	0	0	X[d]	0

[a] Each state party has the right to reduce its reduction liability for each category of TLE in the event of destruction by accident by an amount of no more than 1.5% of the maximum levels for holdings notified at the signature of the Treaty for that category. Destruction by accident must be notified to all other states parties within seven days and the state party should provide documentary evidence within 90 days of the notification.

[b] Only for MLRS and mortars which are not self-propelled.

[c] Only for self-propelled guns, howitzers, artillery pieces combining the characteristics of guns and howitzers or mortars.

[d] Only up to 200 per state party.

X- permitted

0- not permitted

Note: The layout of tables 5 and 6 was suggested by tables in Verification Technology Information Centre, *The VERTIC Guide to the CFE Treaty* (VERTIC: London, 1990).

make changes to the list of vehicles and the list of non-military purposes to which they may be converted. Such changes were to be considered as improvements to the viability and effectiveness of the Treaty and should only relate to minor matters of a technical nature.

The Treaty allowed each state party to convert a maximum of 5.7 per cent of its battle tanks as notified at the signature of the Treaty (not to exceed 750 battle tanks)—or 150 items, whichever is greater—and 15 per cent of ACVs as notified at signature (not to exceed 3000 ACVs)—or 150 items, whichever is greater.

Converted vehicles were not to be placed in service with the conventional armed forces of a state party.

Static display. The number of items to be reduced by static display was not to exceed 1 per cent or eight items, whichever is greater, of the maximum levels for holdings of each party declared at the signature of the Treaty. Also each state party may retain in working order two items of each existing type of TLE for static display in museums or similar sites.

Use for ground instructional purposes. The numbers of combat aircraft and attack helicopters were to be no greater than 5 per cent of the holdings of each party in each of those two categories as notified at the signature of the Treaty.

Recategorization. This method applies to multi-purpose attack helicopters—when recategorized as combat support helicopters they are no longer subject to Treaty limits. While multi-purpose attack helicopters are attack helicopters[9] designed for multiple military functions and equipped to employ guided weapons, combat support helicopters were defined as those not fulfilling the requirements of an attack helicopter but which may be equipped with a variety of self-defence and area-suppression weapons, such as guns, cannons and unguided rockets, bombs or cluster bombs, and may be equipped for other military functions. This method of reduction and the method of reclassification of combat-capable trainer aircraft are described in further detail in the appropriate protocols because they place special requirements on verification. Recategorization can be done by conversion and certification or, if helicopters do not have specified elements to be removed, by certification alone. Certification must be conducted within the area of application. Each helicopter to be recategorized must bear the original manufacturer's serial number permanently stamped in a main airframe structural member.

The Treaty stated that the former USSR could hold an aggregate total of up to 100 Mi-24R and Mi-24K helicopters equipped for reconnaissance, spotting or chemical/biological/radiological sampling outside the limits on attack helicopters. Mi-24R and Mi-24K helicopters in excess of this limit were to be categorized as specialized attack helicopters. NATO was against this provision as these versions could potentially be 'converted to attack helicopters quickly', but acknowledged that 'the actual numbers of the variants are rather small'.[10]

The Soviet Mi-26 unarmed transport helicopter was not covered by the Treaty. Some NATO countries insisted that such a heavy transport helicopter should have been covered as it was 'practically an armoured personnel carrier in the air', and even unarmed 'the soldiers it transports may be very well

---

[9] Attack helicopters are equipped to employ anti-armour, air-to-ground or air-to-air guided weapons and an associated integrated fire control and aiming system.

[10] *Vienna Fax,* 10 Sep. 1990, p. 1.

armed'. But this issue was dropped partly because of verification problems: a particular weapon site with no other TLE could become subject to OSI just because of a few Mi-26s.[11] As these transport helicopters are spread all over the former USSR the inspection teams could go everywhere in its European part where no other TLE is located. Also, if transport helicopters were included in the Treaty, TLE quotas and consequently inspections would have to have been increased.

Use as ground targets. The numbers to be reduced by this method cannot be greater than 2.5 per cent of the holdings of battle tanks and of ACVs and no more than 50 self-propelled pieces of artillery of each state party as notified at the signature of the Treaty.

Reclassification. This method allows reclassification of specific models or versions of combat-capable trainer aircraft into unarmed trainer aircraft. The following aircraft can be thus reclassified: Su-15U; Su-17U; MiG-15U; MiG-21U; MiG-23U; MiG-25U; and UIL-28. Procedures must be carried out within 40 months of the entry into force of the Treaty with resultant removal of no more than 550 such aircraft, of which no more than 130 should be of the MiG-25U model or version. Until certified as unarmed, such aircraft were to be counted against the numerical limitations on combat aircraft. Each state party can use whatever technological means it deems necessary to totally disarm the aircraft.[12]

Modification. This method applies only to the multi-purpose lightly armoured vehicle MT-LB which may be exceptionally modified within 40 months of the entry into force of the Treaty into an APC look-alike, listed as MT-LB-AT. Modification is implemented by alteration of the interior of the vehicle through the removal of the left-hand combat infantry squad seating and the welding of the ammunition racking to the side and the floor at a minimum of six points so that the vehicle is not capable of transporting a combat infantry squad. Modifications may be accomplished at locations other than reduction sites. If not modified these carriers will be reported as APCs. This Soviet combat vehicle is capable of being both an artillery tractor and an APC and the Soviet Union pledged to convert all APC models in the ATTU zone to artillery tractors.

These different procedures will of necessity place different accents on verification procedures and requirements. Each state party may use any technological means it deems appropriate to implement the procedures for reductions of TLE and to remove, retain and use those components and parts of TLE which are not themselves subject to reduction, and to dispose of debris. Additional procedures for reductions may be proposed by any state party and be deemed sufficient upon a decision to that effect by the JCG.

---

[11] *Vienna Fax,* 10 Sep. 1990, pp. 1–2.

[12] For further details see the Protocol on Procedures Governing the Reclassification of Specific Models or Versions of Combat-Capable Trainer Aircraft into Unarmed Trainer Aircraft, reproduced here in appendix A.

Permitted buildups of treaty-limited equipment

As table 4 indicates, several NATO countries were able to increase rather than decrease their TLE holdings. The sub-zone limits also permitted increases in weapons in some cases. The process of reductions in certain areas will therefore be accompanied by an increase in holdings in other areas.

NATO countries of the flank zone, plus Spain and Portugal, were allowed to increase some of their equipment and still remain within Treaty limits. For example, Portugal could more than double its tank potential and increase its major weapon holdings overall by about two-thirds; and Turkey could double its ACV holdings.

The Treaty did not reduce NATO air power, setting limits above the 1990 aircraft holdings. Germany, the only state which had to reduce aircraft, was to do so by cutting planes from the former GDR inventory. The largest increase would again take place in the flank zone.

NATO was able to substantially upgrade its ACV potential by reducing armoured personnel carriers and increasing newer and more capable AIFVs, from the current level of close to 8000 to the sub-limit of 18 000.

All states parties were able to modernize their forces—there are no restrictions on production and the Treaty did not prohibit the replacement of single-fire guns and howitzers with multiple-launch rocket systems.

Transfer of equipment

In December 1990 NATO defence ministers endorsed the plan to distribute more modern excess TLE among the members of the alliance, rather than to destroy them. This 'cascading' process is anticipated by the Treaty as a way to prevent the destruction of modern weapons if they can be substituted for older equipment which can be destroyed instead. According to the plan, the recipients were required to destroy excess equipment at their own cost. Germany, Italy, the Netherlands and the USA planned to release more than 2700 battle tanks, 1000 ACVs and 300 artillery pieces to Denmark, Greece, Norway, Portugal, Spain and Turkey. They also planned to cascade about 325 artillery systems to the flanks where about 130 of them would be offset by destruction. The NATO central region states were to export about 1075 ACVs to the flanks.[13]

However, to meet concerns of the countries in the flank zone, the Treaty limited the transfer of equipment of each group of states parties into the zone to 459 battle tanks, 723 ACVs and 420 artillery pieces and the transfer to any one country to 153 battle tanks, 241 ACVs and 140 artillery pieces. The flank states were to destroy older tanks to meet the CFE provisions.

The cascade importers (of tanks, artillery and ACVs) were to be Greece, Norway, Portugal, Spain and Turkey. In addition to cascading, net changes were to be brought about by new procurement and destruction. By November

[13] *Vienna Fax*, vol. 2, nos 6 and 7 (12 Aug. 1991), p. 7.

1993 the United States had eliminated its entire reduction liability by transferring 1993 tanks, 636 ACVs, and 180 artillery pieces to Greece, Norway, Portugal, Spain and Turkey.[14]

The substantial numbers of weapons involved in the cascading process included 917 tanks, 150 ACVs and 72 artillery pieces to Greece and 1057 tanks, 600 ACVs and 72 artillery pieces to Turkey.[15] This programme has been criticized, especially with respect to the transfer to these two countries, as significantly enhancing the military superiority of these states over their Balkan neighbours and threatening to destabilize a region which is already in crisis.[16]

By 1995 as a result of cascading Turkey will have a modern arsenal about 25 per cent larger than that it possessed in 1992. To maintain parity and political stability within the alliance NATO has provided Greece with a comparable amount of weaponry.[17]

Residual levels: a new balance

Although the Treaty limits leave enormous numbers of TLE items in place, almost 79 000 in each group of states parties, the required reductions met the goal of the negotiations, that is, the removal of the asymmetries between NATO and the former WTO in TLE. From table 4 the ratios before reductions are seen to be: battle tanks—1:1.3; ACVs—1:1.2; artillery—1:1.2; combat aircraft—1:1.5; attack helicopters—1:1.

The dissolution of the WTO (and later the USSR) produced two unexpected results in terms of new correlations in arms inventories. According to former Soviet Defence Minister Dmitriy Yazov,

the political processes in Eastern Europe and in the countries of the Warsaw Treaty Organization and the changes in the character and functions of the WTO military organization have resulted in assessment, as a rule, of armaments not of the WTO and NATO, but of the USSR and NATO. In such assessment the ratio would be correspondingly the following: in tanks and ACVs—1:1.5; in artillery, combat aircraft and attack helicopters—1:1.3. In case of reaching the limits of 20 000 artillery pieces by NATO, the ratio would further be changed to 1:1.5.[18]

The dissolution of the USSR, in turn, led to a further change in the balance. In place of the USSR, there are eight new states in the CFE area of application—Armenia, Azerbaijan, Belarus, Georgia, Kazakhstan, Moldova, Russia and Ukraine—creating a new situation as regards CFE residual limits. According to the decisions made during the Tashkent summit meeting of the CIS on

---

[14] GAO (note 8), p. 16.

[15] Kokkinides, T., 'Balkan security and the "cascading" of weapons', Analysis from the British American Security Information Council (BASIC), July 1992.

[16] Goldstein, L., Kokkinides, T. and Plesch, D., 'Fuelling Balkan fires: The West's arming of Greece and Turkey', BASIC Report 93.3 (Sep. 1993), p. 2; Kokkinides (note 15).

[17] Feinstein, L., 'CFE: Off the endangered list?', *Arms Control Today*, Oct. 1993, p. 6, Lachowski (note 8), p. 575.

[18] *Krasnaya Zvezda*, 29 Nov. 1990, p. 2.

15 May 1992, the lion's share of the residual forces will belong to Russia and Ukraine. The agreed levels for the former Soviet republics in the ATTU zone are shown in table 8.

Although the CFE negotiating concept, based on the existence of two alliances, NATO and the WTO, was undermined by subsequent events—the dissolution of the WTO and the Soviet Union—the political and technical tasks of moving down towards the agreed residual limits still exist and drive the efforts of the signatories. Moreover, the substantial residual limits in terms of military power mean that adherence to the Treaty must be closely monitored.

The former Soviet Union: reductions ahead

The Tashkent summit meeting managed to meet the challenge of dividing up the cuts and ensuring that the combined potential stays within the former Soviet share of the CFE Treaty ceilings on equipment. Comparison of the residual levels with the February 1991 data on declared Soviet TLE[19] indicates that all the former Soviet republics in the area of application of the CFE Treaty had to reduce forces in most of the categories.

According to the declared TLE as of November 1990, Latvia had 526 TLE items, Lithuania—2983, Estonia—577, Armenia—1263, Azerbaijan—2287, Belarus—7167, Moldova—795, Russia—19 552, Ukraine—18 736 and Kazakhstan—none (disputed Article III weapons were included in all these figures).[20]

Within a month of Estonia, Latvia and Lithuania becoming independent states on 18 October 1991 the Joint Consultative Group, responsible for monitoring CFE Treaty compliance, agreed to exclude these states from the ATTU zone of application of the CFE Treaty, and agreed that they should not be considered as part of the Soviet Baltic MD. Thus, the states were freed from obligations under the CFE Treaty with the exception that CFE inspectors were to be allowed on their territories until the complete withdrawal of the Russian troops.

The largest reductions were to be made by Russia, if it is considered that the groups of forces outside the former USSR and in the Baltic republics have fallen under Russian jurisdiction. Ukraine is the second in the reduction schedule.

The Tashkent Agreement also took account of protocols to the CFE Treaty concerning other forces. No state party should have more than 400 land-based aircraft, and it was agreed that Russia should have not more than 300 and Ukraine not more than 100 such aircraft. 100 Mi-24R and Mi-24K helicopters were divided as follows: Armenia—4, Azerbaijan—4, Belarus—16, Georgia—4, Moldova—4, Russia—50, Ukraine—18. As the former USSR was allowed to have no more than 462 AVLBs in active units, they were split among the

---

[19] *Arms Control Reporter*, 1992, sheet 407.E–0.12.
[20] *Arms Control Reporter*, 1992, sheets 407.E–1.64–67.

Table 8. Allocation of treaty-limited equipment entitlements among the former Soviet republics

	Main battle tanks			Armoured combat vehicles					Artillery			Aircraft	Helicopters
	Total	Active	Stored	Total	Active	Stored	AIFVs	HACVs	Total	Active	Stored		
Total for Russia	6 400	4 975	1 425	11 480	10 525	955	7 030	574	6 415	5 105	1 310	3 450	890
Total for Ukraine	4 080	3 130	950	5 050	4 350	700	3 095	253	4 040	3 240	800	1 090	330
Total for former republics in zone IV.2	10 300	8 650	1 650	17 400	16 120	1 280	..	..	9 500	8 050	1 450	..	..
Russia	5 100	4 275	825	10 100	9 945	155	..	..	4 735	3 825	910	..	..
Ukraine	3 400	2 850	550	4 700	4 000	700	..	..	3 150	2 850	300	..	..
Belarus	1 800	1 525	275	2 600	2 175	425	1 590	130	1 615	1 375	240	260	80
Total for former republics in the flank zone	2 850	1 850	1 000	2 600	1 800	800	..	..	3 675	2 775	900	..	..
Russia	1 300	700	600	1 380	580	800	..	..	1 680	1 280	400	..	..
Ukraine	680	280	400	350	350	0	..	..	890	390	500	..	..
Moldova	210	210	0	210	210	0	130	10	250	250	0	50	50
Georgia	220	220	0	220	220	0	135	11	285	285	0	100	50
Armenia	220	220	0	220	220	0	135	11	285	285	0	100	50
Azerbaijan	220	220	0	220	220	0	135	11	285	285	0	100	50
Total	**13 150**	**10 500**	**2 650**	**20 000**	**17 920**	**2 080**	**12 250**	**1 000**	**13 175**	**10 825**	**2 350**	**5 150**	**1 500**

Note: AIFVs = armoured infantry fighting vehicles; HACVs = heavy armoured combat vehicles.

Source: Sharp, J. M. O., 'Conventional arms control in Europe', SIPRI, *SIPRI Yearbook 1993: World Armaments and Disarmament* (Oxford University Press: Oxford, 1993), table 12.2, p. 597; Chairman's Summary of HLWG [High Level Working Group] Meeting on 25 May 1992, *NATO Press Release*, vol. 92, no. 50 (25 May 1992).

republics as follows: Armenia—8, Azerbaijan—8, Belarus—64, Georgia—8, Moldova—7, Russia—223, Ukraine—144.

The TLE allowed for coastal defence forces was divided between Russia and Ukraine as follows:

Russia: 542 tanks, 407 ACVs, 686 artillery pieces.
Ukraine: 271 tanks, 470 ACVs, 160 artillery pieces.

The TLE permitted for naval infantry forces was allocated as follows:

Russia: 120 tanks, 583 ACVs, 186 artillery pieces.
Ukraine: 0 tanks, 265 ACVs, 48 artillery pieces.

The former USSR was also allowed to have no more than 1701 APCs for the Strategic Rocket Forces beyond the CFE Treaty limits. These numbers were split among Belarus (585), Russia (700) and Ukraine (416).

The Agreement left two problems concerning exceptions to the TLE limits unsolved, however. First, it did not apportion the permitted 1000 AIFVs (including no more than 600 for the flank zone) among the newly independent states. These AIFVs were to be held by organizations designed and structured to perform peacetime internal security functions. Each state could therefore claim the full 1000 AIFVs (with Armenia, Azerbaijan, Georgia and Moldova each able to claim 600).

Second, each state party could have up to 550 trainer versions of combat aircraft (of which no more than 130 could be MiG-25Us) as long as these had been totally disarmed. The Agreement did not apportion combat trainer aircraft.[21]

The dissolution of the Soviet Union poses the main challenge in the implementation of the CFE Treaty. Its impact stems from the simple fact that this particular change was not anticipated by the authors of the Treaty. While in the last stages of the negotiations the possibility of the end of the WTO was taken into account, the whole set of consequences was not considered.

A new reality

The emergence of new states in place of the USSR has become an acute problem for politicians and experts in their attempts to maintain stability in Europe. The CFE Treaty provisions and their implementation have turned out to be one of the tools to 'control' the immediate restructuring process within the CIS and the sharing of the former Soviet military potential among the newly independent states.

By the end of 1993, with the implementation of the CFE Treaty still incomplete, Russia no longer enjoyed superiority in conventional armed forces. The CFE-1A Agreement strengthened this trend, limiting Russian military person-

---

[21] IISS, *The Military Balance 1992–93* (IISS: London, 1992), pp. 240, 241.

nel to 1 450 000. At the same time Ukraine has emerged as one of the most powerful military nations in Europe. It has exceeded the USA by 11 per cent and Germany by 27 per cent in TLE and possesses 450 000 troops, more than Germany (345 000), France (325 000), Italy (315 000), Spain (300 000), the UK (260 000) and the USA (250 000). In 1992 the republic had about the same TLE holdings as its neighbours—Poland, the Czech Republic, Slovakia and Hungary. In addition, the military potential of Belarus almost equalled those of France, the UK and Italy.[22]

Clearly the newly independent states have acquired substantial military potential, and they want, at least declaratively, to have as much as possible. The reassessment of their defence needs will take time—military doctrines and concepts of national security are yet to be formulated, and economic realities and financial restraints must be faced. Within this period of transformation the CFE Treaty serves as the major guideline to limiting military potential in Europe.

From quantity to quality?

The CFE Treaty left a number of important problems still to be solved, which were not completely or seriously considered by the negotiators. The first problem is that there is considerable room for technological modernization of the residual weapon stockpile and a possibility for drastic qualitative improvements of combat capabilities within the permitted quantitative ceilings. The Treaty placed no restrictions on R&D and production and thus did not limit the right of states parties to replace existing hardware with newer, more capable systems.

Also, the cascading process allowed NATO to destroy old equipment and to maintain the latest systems and types of weapon. Thereby, the CFE Treaty allows and stimulates the upgrading of the military potential. This creates further concern in the potentially volatile south-eastern flank of NATO as discussed above. While the military potentials are shrinking in quantity, therefore, they will share improved qualitative characteristics. This places an additional burden on the tasks of verification and also creates new challenges for future efforts to control arms.

---

[22] Rogov, S. (ed.), *Conventional Force Deployments within the Commonwealth of Independent States in Compliance with the CFE Treaty and the Republics' Security Requirements*, Brookings Discussion Papers (The Brookings Institution: Washington, DC, 27 Oct. 1992), p. 31.

3. The verification provisions of the CFE Treaty

I. The main verification provisions of the Treaty

Introduction

The CFE Treaty has laid out a far-reaching and intrusive verification regime which includes national and multinational technical means, a large number of several different types of on-site inspection (including the important option of challenge inspections), exchanges of detailed data about the quantity and location of forces both before and after reductions, and a Joint Consultative Group to mediate disputes. This regime was designed to operate in a dynamic environment of unprecedented reduction and removal of large numbers of weapons, each with their own specific characteristics, over a large area.

In creating a verification regime, the states parties tried to meet a number of very important requirements: clearly spelled out and detailed data were to be exchanged;[1] verification means and measures were not to be interfered with by other states parties and concealment measures were prohibited; every state party was to have an equal right to participate in verification; and maximum possible access to relevant military sites during inspections was to be provided while allowing for minimum interference with routine military activities. Cost effectiveness certainly played a role in conjunction with the related desire to make the regime as simple as possible given its inherently complex demands. These requirements had to fulfil the basic task of providing clear and convincing evidence of compliance or lack thereof.

The verification provisions did not, however, include all the measures proposed by members of both groups of states during the negotiation. The regime avoided such politically, technologically and organizationally sophisticated measures as monitoring production of TLE, using overlapping sensor systems by installing short- and medium-range sensors on the territory of a given state party, sophisticated tagging technology, permanent observation posts, portal monitoring, and so on. For inspecting reductions, the Protocol on Inspection allowed for placing 'special marks' on equipment to be reduced; these 'special marks' were not more explicitly defined but can probably be considered a simple form of tagging.

Official statements have tended to indicate that the states parties would orient their verification activities to detecting and detering militarily significant violations, rather than attempting to implement the 'effective verification' policies which require detection of any violation whatsoever. This is mainly based on

---

[1] An annex to the Protocol on Notification and Exchange of Information details the specific format the exchanged data are to adhere to. Information includes that on command organizations, holdings, location and numbers of equipment items, OOV and declared sites. See appendix A.

the new political situation in Europe, which is characterized by increased trust, on financial considerations (i.e., the need for large expenditures to even attempt to detect any and all violations) and, indeed, on understanding the practical impossibility of keeping track of every piece of conventional TLE. The negotiators did not foresee the drastic dissolution of the WTO and the Soviet Union, however. The emergence of new players which do not enjoy the same good relations as they did within the WTO and the Soviet Union complicated the verification tasks. These tasks are also aggravated by the absence of an appropriate mechanism in many of the CIS states in the ATTU zone as well as even minor co-ordinating bodies within the former WTO.

Technical means of verification

Under the terms of the Treaty a state party can use national or multinational technical means of verification at its disposal in a manner consistent with generally recognized principles of international law and must not interfere with such means of another state party. Also, it cannot use concealment measures that impede verification of compliance with the Treaty provisions by such means of another state party; this obligation does not apply to cover or concealment practices associated with normal personnel training, maintenance or operations involving TLE.

Inspections[2]

To ensure verification of compliance with the provisions of the Treaty, each state party has the right to conduct inspections within the area of application without refusal (except for challenge inspections) (a) to verify, on the basis of the information provided pursuant to provisions of the Protocol on Information Exchange, compliance with the numerical limitations; (b) to monitor the process of reduction of TLE carried out at reduction sites; and (c) to monitor the certification of recategorized multi-purpose attack helicopters and reclassified combat-capable trainer aircraft.

The states parties can inspect declared sites, witness reductions and certification, and carry out challenge inspections of undeclared sites ('specified areas'). No information obtained during inspections can be publicly disclosed without the express consent of the inspecting state party.

On-site inspections were stipulated for four specified time periods. The Treaty prescribed intensive baseline inspections for the first 120 days after entry into force (i.e., from 17 July 1992) to confirm the accuracy of the data on existing forces provided by each country. During the subsequent three years weapon reductions were to be monitored by OSI. After that OSI would validate the reduction for a further 120 days. Finally there would be a permanent inspection process to monitor compliance. There are quotas (described below) for

[2] For more details see the Protocol on Inspection, reproduced in appendix A.

each of these time periods for both declared site and challenge inspections. There are, however, no quotas for inspections of reduction or certification.

During an inspection conducted by more than one state party, one of them is responsible for the implementation of the Treaty provisions. Upon completion of the residual level validation period, each state party can conduct, and each state party with territory within the area of application must accept, an agreed number of aerial inspections within the area of application.

The stationing state party is fully responsible for compliance in respect of TLE in service with its conventional armed forces stationed on the territory of the host state party. They must co-operatively ensure compliance with the relevant provisions of the Protocol on Inspection.[3]

Objects of verification

As described in detail below, passive declared site and challenge inspection quotas for each country are calculated based on the number of objects of verification (OOV) owned by the state (passive quotas are the number of inspections of OOV a state party is obliged to accept). In general terms, OOV are elements of the military force structure with TLE. They are located at declared sites.

Because the concept of an OOV is significant, it is important to outline more strictly the definition as it appears in the Treaty itself. 'Object of verification' is defined in the following terms:

1. Any formation or unit at the organizational level of brigade/regiment, wing/air regiment, independent battalion/artillery battalion, independent squadron or equivalent as well as any separately located battalion/squadron or equivalent unit at the next level of command below the brigade/regiment, wing/air regiment level holding TLE at a notified location;

2. Any designated permanent storage site, military storage site not organic to formations or units referred to above, independent repair or maintenance unit, military training establishment or military airfield notified at which TLE are permanently or routinely present;

3. A notified reduction site for TLE;

4. In the case of units below the level of battalion holding TLE items that are directly subordinate to a unit or formation above the level of brigade/regiment or equivalent, that unit or formation to which the units below the level of battalion are subordinated is considered an OOV if it has no subordinate unit or formation at the level of brigade/regiment or equivalent.

---

[3] In case of inspection sites with only a stationing state party's TLE, and under its command, the escort team is placed under the responsibility of a representative of the stationing state party for the duration of the inspection within that inspection site where the stationing state party's TLE is located. If the TLE of both the host and the stationing state party are present in inspection sites, the escort team is composed of representatives of both parties when TLE of the stationing state party is actually inspected. During the inspection within that inspection site, the host party exercises the rights and obligations of the inspected party with the exception of those rights and obligations related to inspection of the TLE of the stationing party, which is exercised by that party. For the text of the Protocol on Inspection, see appendix A.

Table 9. Objects of verification and declared sites

State party	OOV June 1992	OOV Dec. 1992	Declared sites Dec. 1992
NATO countries			
Belgium	50	59	35
Canada	13	4	3
Denmark	64	63	2
France	257	211	16
Germany	470	255	215
Greece	60	82	71
Iceland	0	0	0
Italy	190	186	180
Luxembourg	2	0	0
The Netherlands	88	62	41
Norway	59	47	32
Portugal	28	39	37
Spain	93	95	92
Turkey	150	120	102
UK	226	180	152
USA	169	105	70
Total	**1 919**	**1 508**	**1 048**
Ex-WTO countries			
Bulgaria	93	114	94
Czechoslovakia	179	119	
Czech Republic	.	79	62
Slovakia		40	31
Hungary	59	46	35
Poland	134	149	124
Romania	127	164	130
Former Soviet republics			
Armenia	16	10	8
Azerbaijan	16	(not reported)	
Belarus	102	74	51
Georgia	16	6	6
Moldova	16	8	5
Kazakhstan	0	0	0
Russia	491	431	299
Ukraine	253	207	135
Total	**1 502**	**1 447**[*]	**980**[*]

[*] Excluding Azerbaijan

Source: Compiled from Sharp, J. M. O., 'Conventional arms control in Europe', SIPRI, *SIPRI Yearbook 1993: World Armaments and Disarmament* (Oxford University Press: Oxford, 1993), tables 12.6 and 12.7, pp. 611 and 612.

It is also noted that a formation or unit holding conventional armaments and equipment *subject* to the Treaty,[4] but not in service with the conventional armed forces of a state party is not considered an OOV.

In fulfilment of their requirements, the states parties declared their numbers of OOV in November 1990. After the dissolution of the USSR the OOV for the former Soviet Union were divided among the newly independent states parties. Some minor changes were also introduced for a few ex-WTO and NATO countries. The numbers of OOV and declared sites are shown in table 9, including those revised after the information exchange on 15 December 1992.

Quota of inspections

For a specified time period, the total number of inspections of OOV that each state party is obliged to receive is called the 'passive declared site inspection quota' and the maximum number of challenge inspections that each state party with its territory within the area of application is obliged to receive is called the 'passive challenge inspection quota'. The former is expressed as a percentage of the OOV which each state party possesses in the ATTU zone, while the latter is expressed as a percentage of the number of inspections of declared sites. These quotas are shown in table 10. This agreed rule on the number of inspections each state party is obliged to accept differs from the previously proposed rule of the passive quota as a percentage of the number of TLE items possessed by each state party.

The Treaty also provides for allotment of the inspections which each country is allowed to make, as well as the number of inspections it will be required to grant to other countries.[5] These 'active' quotas are agreed among the members of each of the two groups of states. States parties can transfer parts of their active quota to other states parties. None the less, no more than 50 per cent of a state's passive quota can be used up by a single state party in a calendar year.

No state party may conduct more than five inspections annually on the territory of a state party within the same group of states (i.e., the formerly opposing alliances). Thus, for example, ex-WTO countries can inspect each other and their passive quota for NATO inspections would be reduced accordingly and the number of such intra-alliance inspections could *in principle* be a very large portion of the total passive quota. Rights such as these may not, however, be used in order to evade the objectives of the verification regime. Thus, for example, members of the same group of states parties may not inspect each other simply with the purpose of reducing their passive quota and thereby

---

[4] Conventional armaments and equipment *subject* to the Treaty include primary trainer aircraft, unarmed trainer aircraft, combat support helicopters, unarmed transport helicopters, AVLBs, APC look-alikes and AIFV look-alikes *in addition to* conventional armaments and equipment *limited* by the Treaty (TLE).

[5] It is worth mentioning that the Western European Union regarded annual verification of 10 per cent of the declared inventory to be sufficient; Kunzendorff, V., *Verification in Conventional Arms Control*, Adelphi Papers 245 (winter 1989), p. 37.

Table 10. Passive quotas for inspections of declared and undeclared sites

	Baseline validation period	Reduction period	Residual level validation period	Residual period
Declared sites	20% of OOV	10% OOV p.a.	20% of OOV	15% OOV p.a.
Challenge inspection	15% of declared sites quota	15% of declared sites quota	15% of declared sites quota	23% of declared sites quota

reducing the number of inspections allowed by members of the other group of states parties.[6]

Joint Consultative Group

The states parties have established a Joint Consultative Group to promote the objectives and the implementation of the Treaty. It was stipulated that the first session be opened no later than 60 days after the signing of the Treaty.[7] Regular sessions were to be held twice a year and last up to four weeks each. Additional sessions may be convened at the request of one or more states parties and open no later than 15 days after the receipt of such a request by the JCG Chairman. The proceedings are confidential unless decided otherwise.[8]

Notifications and exchange of information

The CFE Treaty stated that to ensure verification of compliance with its provisions, each state party should provide notifications and exchange of information pertaining to its conventional armaments and equipment and would be responsible for its own information. This information comprises elements including:[9]

1. The structure of each state party's land, air and air defence forces within the ATTU zone;
2. The overall holdings in each TLE category;
3. The location, numbers and types of conventional armaments and equipment in service with the conventional armed forces of states parties;
4. The location and numbers of TLE within the ATTU zone but not in service with conventional armed forces;
5. The objects of verification and declared sites;
6. The location of sites from which conventional armaments and equipment have been withdrawn;
7. Timetable for the provision of information regarding the five points above;

[6] These rules may have to be revised in the light of the new political realities.
[7] This session was convened on 29 Nov. 1990.
[8] For more details see the Protocol on the Joint Consultative Group, appendix A.
[9] For more details see the Protocol on Notification and Exchange of Information, appendix A.

8. Changes in organizational structures or force levels;

9. Entry into and removal from service of TLE;

10. Entry into and exit from the area of application of TLE in service with the conventional armed forces;

11. Conventional armaments and equipment in transit through the ATTU zone;

12. Any new type, model or version of conventional armaments and equipment;

13. The number and types of armaments to be reduced by specified methods;

14. The reassignment of TLE and AVLBs to organizations not part of the conventional armed forces;

15. The location and description of the TLE within designated permanent storage sites;

16. Technical data for each model or version of existing types of conventional armaments and equipment;

17. Photographs for each existing type of TLE and of APC look-alike and AIFV look-alike;

18. Reclassification and recategorization.

The Treaty gives the timetable for provision of information about the first five of these elements: upon signature of the Treaty (for the third, fourth and fifth only); 30 days after entry into force; on 15 December of every year after entry into force; after completion of the 40-month reduction period. The timetable for provision of information on other elements is given in the Protocol on Notification and Exchange of Information.

The information to be provided thus covers not only conventional armaments and equipment *limited* by the Treaty (TLE), but in a number of cases also the broader group of conventional armaments and equipment *subject* to the Treaty. The term 'in service' applies to all conventional armaments and equipment subject to the Treaty that are within the ATTU zone, except those designed and structured to perform internal security functions in peacetime and the exceptions to numerical limitations outlined previously.

Site categories

Declared sites

A declared site is defined as a facility or precisely delineated geographic location with one or more OOV. It consists of territory within its man-made or natural outer boundary or boundaries as well as associated territory comprising firing ranges, training areas, maintenance and storage areas, helicopter airfields and railroad loading facilities at which TLE, combat support helicopters, reclassified combat-capable trainer aircraft, APC look-alikes, AIFV look-alikes or AVLBs are permanently or routinely present.[10] Inspection teams are required to be provided with diagrams of declared sites including the perimeter, major buildings and roads on the sites.

Reduction sites

The term 'reduction site' means a clearly designated location where the reduction of TLE takes place. Each state party was required to notify the locations of reduction sites, including those where the final conversion of battle tanks and ACVs to non-military purposes was to take place, upon entry into force of the Treaty. Each state party could designate as many reduction sites as it wished, revise without restriction its designation of such sites and carry out reduction and final conversion simultaneously at a maximum of 20 sites. States parties could share or collocate reduction sites by mutual agreement. Notwithstanding such rights, during the first 120 days after entry into force of the Treaty (i.e., during the baseline validation period) reduction was to be carried out simultaneously at no more than two reduction sites for each state party.

Designated permanent storage sites for TLE

TLE (and AVLBs as well) could be retained in designated permanent storage sites (DPSS) and are counted within the overall ceilings but are not subject to limitations on TLE in active units. Any TLE or AVLBs in storage other than in designated permanent storage sites are counted as being in active units.

Such storage sites are only to contain facilities for storage and maintenance, but not firing ranges or training areas associated with TLE. Each site is to be within a boundary defined by a continuous fence at least 1.5 m high, with no more than three gates for the entry and exit of armaments and equipment.

Serial numbers and special marks

The Treaty required that a working register be established at each reduction site to record the serial numbers of items undergoing reduction. It was required that this register be made available to inspectors. In addition, inspection teams have the right to record factory serial numbers from conventional arms and equipment to be reduced or to place 'special marks' on the equipment before reduction and to record these numbers or marks again at the completion of the reduction process. It was specified that each combat helicopter subject to the

[10] With regard to declared sites and OOV Julia Klare and Jeffrey Grotte noted: 'If all declared sites were treated equally, inspecting nations would almost certainly conduct most of their inspections at sites with more than one unit, maximizing the amount of information that can be gained from a single inspection. Nations that tended to concentrate units at a few locations would then be penalized by having a greater percentage of their forces subject to inspection than would nations that tended to disperse its units. Incorporating the concept of OOVs provides a leveling factor that results in a more comparable inspection burden among all signatories.' See Klare, J. L. and Grotte, J. H., 'Reducing cost while maintaining effectiveness', ed. J. Brown, *Challenges in Arms Control for the 1990s* (Vu University Press: Amsterdam, 1992), p. 155.

recategorization procedure should bear the manufacturer's serial number permanently stamped in a main airframe structural member. Both prior to and after certification, the serial numbers of helicopters and aircraft were to be provided by the certifying party, and during inspections of certification, inspectors were not to be refused the right to check these serial numbers.

Format for the exchange of information

It was required that data exchange take place in accordance with the specifics of the character and the stage of the reduction process. To avoid possible misinterpretations and ambiguities and, as a result, potential accusations, a set format for the exchange of information was agreed to by the states parties. The format is detailed according to the needs and purposes of the Treaty and includes several charts.[11]

II. On-site inspection

Introduction

The CFE verification regime involves detailed and thorough on-site inspection procedures which were deemed necessary in large part because of the multilateral nature of the Treaty. On-site inspections are intrusive co-operative measures. One of the main values of OSI stems from the relevant proximity to the object under scrutiny, increasing the likelihood of detecting a violation. In the context of CFE Treaty verification they provide an equal opportunity for every state party to participate in the verification process, regardless of its technological capabilities. They also stimulate contacts among states parties thereby introducing a new dimension—the human factor—which is considered an important element of successful verification activities. There is another advantage of OSI—fixed technical means of verification may be inflexible whereas human observation provides a more complete picture.

The Treaty provides for four types of inspection: inspections of declared sites; challenge inspections of undeclared sites—that is, within 'specified areas'; inspections to witness reductions; and inspections to witness certification. The Treaty excludes the permanent inspection activity much expected by many experts, that is, permanent manned observation posts and fixed remote sensors.[12] Table 11 shows the numbers of inspections which each state party must accept during the four implementation periods.

---

[11] The precise manner in which information is to be exchanged is outlined in the annex on the format for the Exchange of Information to the Protocol on Notification and Exchange of Information. See appendix A.

[12] See Altmann, J., 'Short distance sensors', eds R. Kokoski and S. Koulik, SIPRI, *Verification of Conventional Arms Control in Europe: Technological Constraints and Opportunities* (Westview Press: Boulder, Colo., 1990), pp. 123–38.

Table 11. Estimated passive and challenge inspections, June 1992
Figures apply after reallocation of TLE ceilings by former Soviet states.

	Inspections[a] each state must accept in:			
State party	Baseline validation period	Reduction period	Residual level valid-ation period	Residual period[b]
NATO group				
Belgium	10 (2)	5 (1)	10 (2)	8 (2)
Canada	3 (1)	1 (1)	3 (1)	2 (1)
Denmark	13 (2)	6 (1)	13 (2)	10 (2)
France	51 (8)	26 (4)	51 (8)	39 (9)
Germany	94 (14)	47 (7)	94 (14)	70 (16)
Greece	12 (2)	6 (1)	12 (2)	9 (2)
Iceland	– (1)	– (1)	– (1)	– (1)
Italy	38 (6)	19 (3)	38 (6)	28 (6)
Luxembourg	– (1)	– (1)	– (1)	– (1)
Netherlands	18 (3)	9 (1)	18 (3)	13 (3)
Norway	12 (2)	6 (1)	12 (2)	9 (2)
Portugal	6 (1)	3 (1)	6 (1)	4 (1)
Spain	19 (3)	9 (1)	19 (3)	14 (3)
Turkey	30 (4)	15 (2)	30 (4)	22 (5)
UK	45 (7)	23 (3)	45 (7)	34 (8)
USA	34 (5)	17 (3)	34 (5)	25 (6)
Total (16)	**385 (62)**	**192 (32)**	**385 (62)**	**287 (68)**
Budapest/Tashkent group				
Bulgaria	19 (3)	9 (1)	19 (3)	14 (3)
Czech/Slovak	36 (5)	18 (3)	36 (5)	27 (6)
Hungary	12 (2)	6 (1)	12 (2)	9 (2)
Poland	27 (4)	13 (2)	27 (4)	20 (5)
Romania	25 (4)	13 (2)	25 (4)	19 (4)
USSR	182 (27)	91 (14)	182 (27)	136 (31)
of which:				
Russia	98 (14)			
Ukraine	50 (6)			
Belarus	22 (3)			
Armenia	3 (1)			
Azerbaijan	3 (1)			
Georgia	3 (1)			
Moldova	3 (1)			
Total (12)	**301 (45)**	**150 (23)**	**301 (45)**	**225 (51)**

[a] Challenge inspections are in parentheses.
[b] Inspections per year.
Source: Based on Sharp, J. M. O., 'Conventional arms control in Europe', SIPRI, *SIPRI Yearbook 1993: World Armaments and Disarmament* (Oxford University Press: Oxford, 1993), table 12.6, p. 611.

During the negotiations politicians and experts discussed different options for OSI. Most attention was paid to a purely bloc-to-bloc system, a multilateral structure within a wider CSCE framework and a multilateral structure within a bloc-to-bloc framework.[13] The states parties agreed to go along with the latter option, thus choosing a regime in which the main responsibilities and capabilities involved individual countries but which was built on a bloc-to-bloc basis.

National inspectors are, for the most part, rather concerned with their own national interests. Data exchanged and verified by OSI are analysed by individual countries and they decide whether to share any information with another country even within the same group of states parties, whether a certain activity is a violation and whether to bring a violation before the JCG. At the same time, each country has the right to analyse and share results from OSI with other countries which may help in providing more reliable interpretation and judgement.

Inspection regimes can also be distinguished by the obligation associated with the OSI request. Fulfilment of the OSI request can be either mandatory, voluntary[14] or in response to challenge. The Treaty emphasizes the first of these. In the case of mandatory OSI, a state party being inspected must accept an OSI request according to stipulated procedures. The Treaty specifies that inspection of declared sites, inspection of reductions and inspection of certification may not be refused. However, the inspected state party does have the right ultimately to refuse challenge inspections within specified areas but these inspections, while important and precedent-setting, also comprise a relatively low percentage of the overall number of inspections allowed.

It should be mentioned that a specific OSI regime is a product of compromise in terms of military, political, economic and organizational considerations and interests. Besides the requirements of treaty verification *per se*, an OSI regime may be influenced by other objectives. In proposing a particular OSI package, for example, a given state or alliance may be motivated by intelligence-support considerations, its influence on current negotiating positions and other more political factors not directly related to verification.

Concern that an OSI regime could support the intelligence activities of an inspecting party might have influenced the agreement among negotiators to exclude permanent manned and remote sensor posts and to provide inspection teams with simple technical devices subject to examination by the inspected party. One can only speculate about the role of this concern in the OSI regime in comparison with other considerations, namely, the experience of the 'technologically over-designed' OSI regime with permanent inspections for the INF Treaty,[15] cost considerations, manpower requirements, and so on.

---

[13] The pros and cons of these options are thoroughly analysed in Lewis, P., 'Technological aids for on-site inspection and monitoring', eds J. Grin and H. van der Graaf, *Unconventional Approaches to Conventional Arms Control Verification. An Exploratory Assessment* (Vu University Press: Amsterdam, 1990), pp. 234–41. As the latter option is discussed below, the main characteristics of the first two options should be noted. In the first, the inspection team was planned to consist of NATO and WTO personnel. Although teams could be national or multinational, they were to be under the control of NATO and WTO verification bodies. The second option included the co-ordination of verification by a multilateral agency under the aegis of a CSCE office.

[14] A voluntary OSI regime allows each state party the option of requesting or granting OSI but places no legal requirements to oblige such a request.

[15] See Kokoski, R. and Koulik, S., 'The INF Treaty', eds Kokoski and Koulik (note 12).

Sensitive points

The Treaty uses the term 'sensitive points' to refer to any equipment, structure or location that has been designated as sensitive by the inspected state party (or the state party exercising the rights and obligations of the inspected state party through the escort teams) and to which access or overflight may be delayed, limited or refused.[16] It is worthwhile highlighting three aspects of the inclusion of such sensitive points. First is the provision, apparent from the definition, for a certain amount of room for manœuvre on the part of the inspected state party—it has more than the two choices of flat refusal or acceptance. For example, helicopter overflights above sensitive points can be delayed, limited or refused, and if permitted, photography of or above sensitive points during the overflight is permitted only with the approval of the escort team.

Second, on the other hand there are unambiguous obligations and rights. During an inspection of an OOV or within a specified area, 'inspectors shall not have the right to enter other structures or areas within structures [in which conventional armaments and equipment subject to the Treaty are permanently or routinely present], the entry points to which are physically accessible only by personnel doors not exceeding two meters in width and to which access is denied by the escort team'.[17] Such provisions are directly aimed at preventing access to areas not obviously connected with armaments and equipment subject to the Treaty.

Third, there is provision not to give unnecessary rights to the inspected party with regard to sensitive structures and areas, in order not to provoke suspicion. If, for example, the escort team declares that a sensitive point, shrouded object or container does contain certain conventional armaments and equipment covered by the Treaty, then it must display or declare them to the inspection team and take steps to satisfy the inspection team that no more than the declared amount of such conventional armaments and equipment is present.

The combination of these rights and obligations agreed to by the states parties addresses, among other things, the purpose of satisfying concerns about obtaining sufficient *access* while limiting possible acquisition of *excess* information not necessary for verification. At any rate, the trade-offs have now been made and optimal functioning of this part of the regime, of course, depends on adequate co-operation on the part of both inspecting and inspected parties. If the toughest action among different allowed options regarding sensitive areas is taken by an inspected party, this may lead to suspicions and thus hamper the co-operative OSI process.

---

[16] A few days before the Treaty was signed the USA had accepted the concept of barring inspection at sensitive points, according to a US official. 'As applied to challenge inspections, certain areas would be off-limits, and the USA wanted to protect its own sensitive points. However, it was not a serious issue. It would be serious for those states which had undeclared sites with TLE in them. The US intended to use the option for just what it was, and recognized that states had to have the option to protect areas. It would apply to, perhaps, communication facilities and national command centers.' *Arms Control Reporter*, 1990, sheet 407.B.406–407.

[17] Protocol on Inspection, VI, para. 24, see appendix A.

Political motivations and objectives

It should be borne in mind that the OSI regime can support specific political objectives. Regardless of the contribution to verification, OSI may indicate a visible commitment of a state party's intention to abide fully with the Treaty's provisions. Politicians may see the main value of this OSI regime as increased domestic confidence in the verifiability of the Treaty.

In initiating inspections at a particular site a state party can proceed from specific and non-specific motivations. Specifically, an OSI request may be aimed at resolving ambiguous situations or detecting possible violations and may be supported by information from NTM and other sources. Less specific motivations may just reflect the need to confirm data from information exchange or to deter possible violations; they might also be aimed at making the OSI process routine, enabling further training of inspectors and enhancing OSI credibility.

Such routine inspections of declared sites are important for determining the accuracy of the baseline data, although they only allow detection of violations at the declared sites and not those located elsewhere. It is not incidental that the quota of routine inspections is the largest for the 120-day baseline period before and after reductions. The other motivation with respect to the baseline period after Treaty signature may stem from intentions to make the OSI process routine from the start in order to reduce the political sensitivity of OSI, to gain more experience, to avoid different bureaucratic and political resistance, and so on.

Challenge inspections

OSI of declared sites comprise the major share of the overall inspection quota, but the most important requests could be for challenge inspections triggered, for example, by detection of ambiguous or suspicious activities. Many experts had proposed unlimited rights for challenge inspections. The negotiators found it more appropriate and adequate to limit challenge inspections by quota based on the number of declared sites as well as to conduct such inspections within the whole area of application other than at declared sites, reduction sites or sites inspected to confirm certification. The specified area of inspection may not exceed 65 km^2 with a straight line between any two points not exceeding 16 km.[18]

Unlike inspections of declared sites, an inspected party may refuse a challenge inspection as long as it provides reasonable assurance that the area does not contain TLE. Even in the case of a challenge inspection being accepted, an

---

[18] A few days before the Treaty was signed, it had been thought that challenge inspections would have applied to areas of 100 km^2. Such areas could have included facilities belonging to several countries and located in Germany. Thus inspections of these facilities could have used up an undue proportion of Germany's passive quota; *Arms Control Reporter*, 1990, sheet 407.B.407.

inspected party may deny entry by the inspecting party to certain parts of the specified area.

As noted above, some experts insisted on the need for unlimited challenge inspections (while accepting the impracticality of such proposals) though this was not included in the CFE Treaty. With a quota on inspections there is, of course, an increase in the probability that circumvention will go undetected, but if other provisions of the Treaty and of the verification regime are taken into account, the possibility of an appreciable level of such circumvention can be considered low. Also, allowing for helicopter overflight further adds to the value of inspections.

To enhance their effectiveness it is appropriate that the process of notifying an intention to carry out challenge inspections is defined in the Treaty on a bilateral basis without intervention by international bodies and with no requirement to justify such inspections. Such a procedure corresponds to the critical nature of challenge inspections with regard to the security of any state party.

An important result of the Treaty is the agreement that declared site OSI are supplemented by challenge inspections. The successful use of these methods gives a key to building confidence and confirming principle compliance with Treaty provisions.

Cued and random sampling

OSI is 'extremely useful within a very narrow set of conditions . . . but OSI is too microscopic to allow broad area searches for violations . . . [however, it is] virtually the only credible way to confirm many of the suggested qualitative arms control limits [such as] the caliber of artillery or tank guns'.[19] In addition, because they are limited in number and the only direct means of verification available to most of the CFE signatories, the manner in which inspection sites are selected is of prime importance.

The number of allotted inspections per year is much less than the number of OOV and so some way must be chosen to sample these sites. There are basically two ways in which this can be done. The first is simply a random selection, which then provides the basis for a statistical estimate of the relative probability of compliance. This is called random sampling. If, however, as is the case especially for the USA and the former USSR, there are other reliable means of ascertaining that a suspect activity is occurring, then it is possible to use this information to prompt an on-site inspection or inspections of the area in question. This is called cued sampling.

As pointed out elsewhere, it is important that, to the extent possible, both types of sampling are used.[20] Challenge inspections of undeclared sites will almost certainly always be cued by some other collateral information. Cued

---

[19] Oelrich, I., 'Conventional arms control: the limits and their verification', Occasional paper no. 8 (Center for Science and International Affairs: Harvard University, Cambridge, Mass., 1990), p. 48.

[20] Lewis, P., 'Implementation of verification methods', Kokoski and Koulik (note 12), chapter 9.

sampling should also be used so that valuable but perhaps incomplete information collected in other ways (NTM, other OSI, etc.) is made use of in the inspection process. However, various intelligence sources can often be misleading and this makes an important case for the desirability of random sampling as well. This dual sampling procedure would result in a more accurate picture of the actual state of the force structure and compliance. This would then, in turn, provide feedback to further assess and improve the manner in which intelligence is collected and analysed. To make the sampling process, and OSI in general, more effective it is desirable that groups of states co-ordinate their respective inspection site locations.

It is important to point out when considering sampling, however, that quotas for OSI do not all have to be used. Not using all of them (while certainly sampling enough to assure compliance and take advantage of the confidence-building role) will not only save money but might also convey trust. One party would in effect be saying to another that they trust in its compliance enough that such inspections are not deemed necessary. On the other hand, some states may carry out the maximum number of inspections allowed. Hopefully once the initial desire to assert their rights has been put into practice in this way they might then be bold enough to exercise their option *not* to exercise their full rights under the Treaty. The Treaty allows for this type of unilateral action.

To give an idea of the certainty which the numbers of random OSI will provide for CFE Treaty verification, the implications of a simple model can be explored. Suppose, for example, that 10 per cent of the OOV of one group of states has an excess of TLE. Then the probability that just one inspection, the location chosen at random, would turn up a violation is obviously 10 per cent.

The laws of probability[21] then imply that if X inspections are made, the probability that a violation is discovered is given by $1 - (1 - 10/100)^X$, that is, by $1 - (0.9)^X$. Five inspections allow for $1 - (0.9)^5$, that is, 41 per cent certainty. Table 12 lists the probability of detecting a violation for various numbers of random inspections. It also includes probabilities for the assumptions that only 1 per cent and 20 per cent of the OOV contain excess TLE.

Note that for the cases in which 10 per cent or 20 per cent of the OOV have excess TLE, the probability of detecting a violation increases rapidly with the number of inspections, reaching virtual certainty with the numbers of inter-alliance inspections allowed for each phase of the Treaty implementation. Thus random inspections can provide a strong deterrent to cheating. In the case that only 1 per cent of the sites have excess TLE the probability of finding such a site with OSI is not quite as high but still allows for a high probability of detection. Note also in such a situation that for a clandestine force of 10 per cent in excess of allowed TLE to be held at 1 per cent of the OOV, each of these sites

[21] See, e.g., Lewis, P., 'Implementation of verification methods', eds Kokoski and Koulik (note 12), p. 178.

Table 12. Dependence of the probability of detecting a violation on the number of inspections

Number of inspections performed	Probability of detecting a violation[a]		
	1% of OOV containing excess TLE	10% of OOV containing excess TLE	20% of OOV containing excess TLE
1	1	10	20
5	5	41	67
10	10	65	89
20	18	88	99
40	33	99	100
100	63	100	100
200	87	100	100
300	95	100	100
400	98	100	100
500	99	100	100

[a] The probability is, of course, never exactly 100%. Where 100% appears in the table it indicates that the actual probability is *at least* 99.99%.

would need to be holding, on average, 10 times their TLE allowance. Such a situation would surely be detected by other means. It can also be seen that if excess TLE are held at 10–20 per cent of OOV, these will be detected with virtual certainty with the co-ordinated conduct of 20–40 random inspections. It is hard to imagine a militarily significant amount of TLE deployed at less than this number of sites.

To use some precise numbers as an illustration, the number of declared OOV in June 1992 were 1919 and 1502 for NATO and the former WTO, respectively. The number of inspections allowed by NATO of the former WTO in the baseline phase is 20 per cent of the 1502 declared ex-WTO OOV or 300 inspections. The analogous figure for inspections by the WTO states is 384. In this phase 15 per cent of these may be challenge inspections of undeclared sites. If all of these are used this leaves 255 and 326 inspections of declared facilities which can be carried out by NATO and the former WTO, respectively. Table 12 thus indicates that, if inspections are co-ordinated within the groups of states, the probability of detecting a violation would be virtually 100 per cent if 10 per cent or 20 per cent of the OOV in fact contained excess TLE. If only 1 per cent were in violation the confidence is still quite high, although detection is further from a certainty.

Equipment will of course be in transit from one OOV to another—a factor not considered in these relatively simple calculations. In addition the five inspections annually permitted by each country of members of the same group of states have not been taken into account. These factors will lower somewhat the confidence levels predicted but probably not to an appreciable degree. Table 12 thus gives a feel for the types of confidence which can be expected, given the inspection regime which has been negotiated. Clandestine deployments also present a problem but, as stated, challenge inspections of suspect sites are allowed, the data from which can also be coupled with other means to ensure adequate compliance.

III. Steps for joint verification management

Introduction

Collection and analysis of data appropriate for verification as well as compliance determination lie within national responsibility. Nevertheless, efforts to share data on specifics of OSI, and challenge inspections in particular, among countries provide many advantages. As shown, co-ordinating activities within a group of states parties avoid redundancy and allow for the optimal application of statistical methods.

In December 1989 US Secretary of State James Baker proposed that NATO should create a NATO Arms Control Verification Staff. According to Baker, such an agency would have respected the principle that verification was a national responsibility but would have assisted NATO countries to monitor compliance with arms control agreements. This new organization could have co-ordinated inspections and other verification activities, as well as provided assistance to individual alliance governments. The idea was rejected by several NATO members. A primary concern was that US views would dominate this organization since the USA was the NATO country with the most experience in verifying arms control treaties.[22] Aside from Russia, the USA is also the only country with the full range of required technological capabilities, especially for monitoring from space.

Nevertheless, co-ordination of verification among the NATO allies has been recognized as essential. The sheer scale of the verification task makes it impractical for each individual country to perform it independently. In addition, joint efforts give the opportunity to pool expertise and partition chores, providing better information for less cost. The appropriateness of these efforts was stated in the North Atlantic Council Ministerial Communiqué of December 1990: members of the alliance 'will ensure due co-ordination of national verification efforts through new Alliance bodies'.[23]

The Verification and Information Systems Directorate

The North Atlantic Council created a Verification Coordinating Committee (VCC) in 1990, part of the NATO Verification and Information Systems Directorate. The task of the VCC is to co-ordinate verification activities among NATO's members in the arms control and verification area and particularly

---

[22] *Trust and Verify*, Feb. 1990, p. 1; *Defense News*, 2 Feb. 1990, p . 20.
[23] *Atlantic News*, 19 Dec. 1990, p. 1 (Annex).

regarding the CFE Treaty. The VCC facilitates information exchange on inspection plans of NATO members and on any verification related matters.

The VCC supervises the development and operation of a central verification data base at NATO headquarters as well as the inspection support activities of the NATO Military Authorities, including the development of common field procedures and conduct of NATO verification courses, providing guidance if necessary. Also the VCC is the forum for consultations among NATO members on compliance concerns and related issues. Finally it is the forum for consultation, co-ordination and exchange of experience on activities with regard to the implementation of the Stockholm, Vienna 1990 and Vienna 1992 CSCE documents on confidence- and security-building measures.[24]

The VCC is headed by the Director of Verification, Information Systems and Council Operations. Within the Directorate there is the Verification Support Staff (VSS) to support the VCC and deal with the operational aspects of co-ordination between the NATO members.

The creation of the North Atlantic Cooperation Council has provided another helpful structure for information exchange and an important contribution to links between ex-WTO and NATO states,[25] especially in the aftermath of the collapse of the Soviet Union.[26]

There were already models for co-operation in data acquisition and analysis within NATO before the signature of the CFE Treaty, especially in tasking and in command and control such as the NATO Airborne Warning and Control System (AWACS). The NATO Airborne Early Warning (NAEW) force is the only force owned wholly by NATO and has been in operation since 1982. It is an example of co-ordination efforts within the alliance with regard to joint funding and multinational staffing. The Boeing E-3A AWACS aircraft has become the standard for airborne early-warning systems. The NATO AWACS aircraft are manned by integrated international crews from Belgium, Canada, Denmark, Germany, Greece, Italy, the Netherlands, Norway, Portugal, Turkey and the USA.[27] It was stated by the commander of this NAEW force that the programme 'is an outstanding example of co-operation between Alliance members, of joint funding and of political and economic accommodations of

---

[24] NATO Office of Information and Press, *NATO Handbook*, Brussels, 1992, p. 78.

[25] *Jane's Defence Weekly*, 23 Mar. 1991, p. 448; Lewis, P. and Greene, O., *The CSCE, European Security and Verification: Considerations for Helsinki 1992* (VERTIC: London, Mar. 1992), pp. 9–10.

[26] Feinstein, L., 'CFE: Off the endangered list?', *Arms Control Today*, Oct. 1993, p. 5.

[27] As of 1991, the NAEW force consisted of 18 E-3A aircraft. In 1980 it was granted full NATO Command Headquarters status by the NATO Defence Planning Committee. Force Command Headquarters are located at Supreme Headquarters, Allied Powers Europe, near Mons, Belgium. The Force supports all three major NATO Commands but the Supreme Allied Commander Europe acts as the executive agent. The second component of the Force will consist of the British E-3D aircraft which will be operated by British personnel only, though under the day-to-day control of the NAEW Force Commander and assigned to the Major Commands. The main operational base of the force is located in Geilenkirche, Germany, and forward operating bases are dispersed in Italy, Greece and Turkey. There is also a forward operation location in Norway. See *Jane's NATO Handbook, 1990–91* (Jane's Information Group: Coulsdon, 1991), p. 244.

nations, resulting in the first fully integrated multinational air force in history'.[28]

As further discussed in chapter 8, such systems could in fact be useful for some verification purposes as they stand or with some readily accomplished modifications. However, after the Treaty was signed major differences have emerged within NATO regarding the incorporation of AWACS aircraft in verification activities, because some members of the alliance prefer more emphasis on national control. David Facey, NATO Air Defence Director, however, suggested that AWACS could be employed; this would involve fitting detachable pods containing radar and infrared sensors for ground surveillance to existing E-3As. Another possibility was to modify three NATO Boeing 707 aircraft currently used for AWACS training.[29]

National organizations

The main efforts, at least of several states parties which belong to NATO, however, have gone into the creation of national organizations responsible for implementing verification activities, including those for monitoring compliance with the CFE Treaty. Through their involvement in a number of arms control accords, most experience of detailed verification procedures until the CFE Treaty had been gained by two individual countries—the USA and the former USSR. As discussed below in more detail, however, with well over 1000 inspections completed by the end of 1993 many CFE states parties were gaining substantial verification experience.

France reopened an air base to accommodate the French verification centre, Unite Française de verification at the Creil air base, near Paris, also to serve as a processing centre for data from the Helios satellite.[30] Since there is a limit on the number of inspections that each country may carry out, a French official said that his country would rely on other verification measures. France has established an operational verification unit at the air base which reports to the chief of the armed forces general staff with 120 people, and which collects, processes and analyses data on CFE implementation.[31] It also established a verification unit for the CFE Treaty within the Ministry of Defence.[32]

The UK located its Joint Arms Control Implementation Group (JACIG) at RAF Scampton in Lincolnshire, with a staff of 120 commanded by an army brigadier. This tri-service unit was tasked with providing inspection, escort and interpretation duties and inspectors' training as part of verification and confidence-building activities of arms control agreements signed by the UK. The first major task of JACIG was to carry out OSI under the terms of the CFE

---

[28] Weber, A., 'Ten years of success', *NATO's Sixteen Nations*, special edition, 1990, p. 10.
[29] Hitchens, T., 'Use of AWACS for Treaty verification splits west', *Defense News*, 3 Dec. 1990, p. 31.
[30] *Jane's Defence Weekly*, 21 July 1990, p. 75. See chapter 5 for further discussion of the Helios programme.
[31] *Defense News*, 17 Dec. 1990, p. 36.
[32] *Arms Control Reporter*, 1991, sheet 407.B.448.

Treaty in WTO countries and to host inspection teams from those countries during visits to the UK.[33]

In Germany verification activities are co-ordinated by the foreign and defence ministries. The former exercises political control through a sub-division within the ministry and a 'Steering Committee' under Foreign Office chairmanship. The latter has created a special centre for verification (Zentrum für Verification Der Bundeswehr), which employs about 400 people and was put into operation on 21 May 1991. The staff of this centre are trained to verify conventional disarmament in other European countries and to escort foreign inspection missions in Germany. The centre is responsible for gathering and evaluating CFE data; exchange of information; planning, preparation and implementation of inspections; meeting, escorting and supplying foreign inspection teams and observers; co-ordination and control of measures for reducing TLE; supplying information to the government and delegations to negotiations. A further 100 people are employed in a branch office in Strausberg, east of Berlin. This office comprised the core of the former GDR's armed forces verification centre, responsible for the implementation of all verification and inspection tasks in eastern Germany, including those concerning Soviet forces and former East German armaments.[34]

The INF Treaty led to the creation of a new US Government organization, the On-Site Inspection Agency (OSIA). This agency also carries out inspections for CFE verification and 'envisions nothing generally different from INF'.[35] The basic low-technology approach has, they believe, been validated by the INF Treaty experience. With over 800 employees the OSIA combines the tasks of verifying the CFE Treaty, nuclear test limitations, START, the Open Skies regime and the Vienna Document on Confidence- and Security-Building Measures of 1992. The Director is nominated by the Secretary of Defence and has two deputies. The deputy for international affairs is responsible for international legal issues and supplies the White House, the National Security Council (NSC), the Pentagon and the US delegations to certain negotiations with information. The European Department deals with CFE issues.

After the dissolution of the USSR and the Ministry of Defence the main responsibilities for the armed forces of the CIS were inherited by the Centre for Providing for the Implementation of the Arms Reduction Treaties in the Main Staff of the Conventional Forces of the CIS. In reality, however, the responsibility for verification has generally been transferred to governmental bodies of the newly independent states, particularly to the ministries of defence. In Russia, the Directorate for Implementing the Reduction of Armed Forces and Strategic Weapons was created to supervise and support verification tasks. The Directorate works in close co-operation with other newly independent states.[36]

---

[33] *The Times*, 14 Feb. 1990; *Jane's Defence Weekly*, 5 Jan. 1991, p. 16.

[34] *Arms Control Reporter*, 1991, sheet 407.B.448.

[35] 'OSIA would remain low-tech for Start, CFE verification', *Aviation Week & Space Technology*, 6 Aug. 1990, p. 57.

[36] *Krasnaya Zvezda*, 6 Nov. 1992.

Overall, verification structures in the newly independent states mainly follow the pattern of the structures of the former Soviet Union with the responsible organizations being established within foreign offices and defence ministries. The problem is the lack of experience and professionals, traditionally concentrated in Moscow and Russia.

Indicative of the rapidly changing political situation in Europe and its effect on the verification of the CFE Treaty and perhaps also on further agreements is the eagerness expressed by some former Warsaw Pact member states to co-operate with NATO in verifying the Treaty. Hungary, Czechoslovakia and Poland were pressing in 1991 for an arrangement whereby results of on-site inspections would be shared among *all* parties to the agreement. The West reacted cautiously at first to such proposals of collaboration, stressing that any such arrangements would be of an *ad hoc* rather than a formal nature.[37]

The ex-WTO states in Eastern Europe are rather inclined to ask for technical and organizational assistance from Western states. In turn, some NATO members have already expressed their positive response to the concerns of Poland, Hungary and Czechoslovakia that they would be unable to verify CFE compliance by neighbouring states because of a shortage of financial and technical means. Johannes Bauch, Director of Security and Disarmament Policy in the German Ministry of Foreign Affairs, said that his country wanted to help the East European states with CFE verification.[38] Such an attitude partly stems from the fact that without its own potential to verify, a participating state might be discouraged from adhering to the Treaty.

An important programme has been inititated by the VCC for co-operation with the non-NATO CFE states—referred to as Co-operation Partners. Jointly conducted inspections, joint training and access to the NATO verification data base are involved. Many NATO inspection teams have been opened up to inspectors from Co-operation Partners resulting in multilateral inspections of reductions and holdings. Reasons for this programme were to acknowledge the co-operation that had been demonstrated by the Co-operation Partners during the initial CFE implementation as well as to reduce the number of inspections which they were conducting among themselves and thus increasing the number of inspections possible for NATO.[39]

Besides these verification-related co-operative measures, new arrangements are helping to enhance co-operation which, in turn, has a positive impact on the implementation of arms control agreements. The North Atlantic Cooperation Council was established in late 1991 on a more formal basis for closer relations and practical co-operation with new partners in Central and Eastern Europe and the former Soviet Union. Partnership for Peace provides another dimension in the co-operation process. It gives an opportunity for former WTO countries and former Soviet republics to increasingly align some aspects of their defence planning and organization with NATO.

[37] Hitchens, T., 'Ex-Soviet allies offer help on CFE verification', *Defense News*, 4 Mar. 1991, p. 1.
[38] *Arms Control Reporter*, 1992, sheet 407.B.470.
[39] *Disarmament Bulletin*, winter 1993/94, pp. 2, 3.

IV. Challenges for CFE Treaty verification

Notification and exchange of information

Organization and TLE holdings

Arms control specialists have long insisted that to avoid disputes over data, the exchange of which is the main first step in the effective functioning of a verification regime, exchange of aggregate data on each category of TLE must be accompanied by exchange of information on the organization, structure and disposition of forces of states parties. To make TLE counting more effective it is extremely useful to include unit structure as a basis for monitoring,[40] preferably down to brigade (NATO) or regiment (ex-WTO) level. In other words, the more detailed the information, the better the basis for verification. The CFE Treaty basically meets these requirements and covers both such data and information about command structure.[41]

In addition, as changes in military doctrines—with respect to offensive or defensive orientation in particular—can be judged from changes in the organizational structures of armed forces, information on organizational structure strengthens the co-operative environment, thus enhancing both stability and the effectiveness of the verification regime.[42]

Therefore, the organization/unit element which has been agreed upon for the CFE verification regime is an important factor in its effectiveness, especially with respect to the implementation of OSI. Through monitoring individual holdings of units one is more likely to reach an adequate assessment of the overall holdings of a state party. The Treaty's quota of inspections gives an ample opportunity to check the holdings of many individual units and reach a realistic assessment of the overall holdings.

Emphasizing the specific value of an organization/unit element, Jonathan Dean outlined the task of NATO's states parties:

What NATO will be seeking through exchange of detailed data on the strength of individual Pact units is not so much a basis for calculating Pact armament reductions. . . . The requirement of NATO's verification agencies is to have a clear understanding of unit holdings before reductions occur in order to provide a data base criterion,

[40] As aptly pointed out with respect to this point, 'every unit has a table of organization and equipment or its equivalent. It is here that the treaty-limited equipment . . . is identified in relation to personnel and other combat and combat support equipment. As a rule, Soviet and Warsaw Pact combat units had standard levels of equipment. In such a unit, the table of organization and equipment can be used in the monitoring process as a template against which every unit can be evaluated.' *Washington Quarterly*, winter 1991, p. 137.

[41] During the CFE Negotiation NATO wanted to go down to the battalion level, but the WTO insisted on going down to the regiment level. WTO regiments were the basic level of bureaucratic management, so implementing information exchange and subsequent verification of data at the battalion level would not have been easy. Thereby, some Western officials suggested that the two sides compromise by exchanging data at the regiment or brigade level, and mandating those units to provide information on their battalion level sub-units. *Arms Control Reporter*, 1989, sheet 407.B.273.

[42] This issue is extensively dealt with in Grin and van der Graaf (note 13), pp. 71–91, 131–52, 245–70.

established in advance, for verification of unit holdings after reductions take place through on-site inspection and other collection means.[43]

The value of the combination of detailed data on unit designation, location and the specific TLE contained therein[44] is indicated by the fact that it is sometimes referred to as battle intelligence. The agreement among states parties to provide this combination of data represented a breakthrough from previous traditions and thereby provided a unique opportunity to explore new pathways towards co-operation and confidence in the military sphere. In agreeing to the obligation to share this information, a state party obliges itself to provide complete and correct data and, hence, sends a message of serious commitment to abide by the terms and the spirit of the Treaty.

Definitions and counting rules

The lack of precise definitions of TLE has often created ambiguities in connection with treaty-related data exchange and the functioning of compliance mechanisms in particular. Experience with many previous arms control agreements indicates that the effectiveness of verification activities depends to a great extent on the specificity of definitions and associated counting rules for TLE agreed to among states parties. In general, the more ambiguous the definitions and counting rules, the more difficulties encountered in reaching a common position on quantitative holdings at various stages throughout the life of an agreement; and the more disagreements on data, the more problems for verification and compliance mechanisms. The detailed definitions of TLE in the CFE Treaty are oriented towards solving this problem.

However, it is always possible that some sources of ambiguity remain. For example, 'battle tanks' are tracked, heavy armoured vehicles weighing at least 16.5 tonnes and equipped with a 360-degree traverse gun of at least 75-mm calibre, but a small number of light tanks which do not correspond to this specific definition of battle tanks are included in the ACV category. On the other hand, heavily armed vehicles with wheels rather than tracks, and which 'meet all other criteria' of a battle tank, are counted as tanks.

Certainly, one would expect ambiguities in definitions to arise and to be discussed among the states parties, for example, the case of the MT-LB armoured personnel carrier. Although the Treaty contains a paragraph describing how this vehicle can be transformed into a non-combat look-alike, which would not be counted under Treaty ceilings, the two sides differed over how many MT-LBs in the Soviet arsenal were to be counted as look-alikes and how many were still

---

[43] Dean, J., 'Verifying NATO–Warsaw Pact force reductions and stabilizing measures', ed. F. Barnaby, *A Handbook of Verification Procedures* (Macmillan: London, 1990), p. 324.

[44] It is worthwhile to stress here again that not only TLE information is exchanged but in many cases also a detailed account of conventional armaments and equipment subject to the Treaty, thus including those without strict limitations but which may have important roles to play in the disposition and overall posture of a state's conventional forces. See the Protocol on Notification and Exchange of Information and the Annex on the format for the exchange of information, reprinted in appendix A.

combat-capable.[45] Because of provisions of a 1949 Geneva Convention which confers a special status on ambulances, APC ambulances may not be deemed ACVs or APC look-alikes. Thus it seems that there were problems in reaching a consensus on certain conventional armaments and equipment although, fortunately, mainly covering relatively minor TLE.

Nevertheless, it should be stressed that, more importantly, the definitions are accompanied by a list of all of the specific existing types of TLE. This combination helps to avoid some problems which might otherwise appear. The armaments and equipment are specifically named in formal lists of existing types of battle tank and ACV, and so on, and these lists are to be updated. In addition, provisions oblige states parties to provide photographs of these existing types (except those models and versions of a type that have no significant externally observable differences from the 'exemplar' of that type).

Baseline data and first disagreements

It is important that the agreement was based on carefully assessing official NATO and WTO definitions and their adequacy before Treaty signature. At the end of 1988 and in early 1989 NATO and the WTO presented official statements on their forces. These figures turned out to differ substantially in some categories and types of conventional armament, but the differences were mainly caused by differences in counting rules. For example, NATO included only artillery pieces from 100-mm calibre and above while the WTO listed artillery pieces from 75-mm and above as well as mortars from 50-mm and above in their count of artillery pieces. The same type of problem applied for counting tanks, armoured vehicles, combat aircraft and helicopters. In 1989, however, it was already unofficially acknowledged that, taking into account different counting rules, no significant divergence existed between the data tabled by the WTO in January 1989 and those tabled by NATO in November 1988.[46] Rather, the challenge was to achieve common understanding of the counting rules.

This conclusion was supported by some results obtained during the negotiations. In April 1990 the CFE negotiators took an important symbolic step, completing an informal exchange of data on artillery holdings—the one weapon category for which they had already agreed on a definition—and on the lists of specific systems covered. According to several officials, the exchange served as a successful 'dry run' for the massive official one to accompany the signing of the Treaty.[47] No divergence of the data supplied by a state party with those estimated by others was reported.

---

[45] The Treaty specifies that APC look-alikes and AIFV look-alikes are armoured vehicles based on the same chassis as, and externally similar to, APCs or AIFVs, respectively, not having a cannon or gun of 20-mm calibre or more and which have been constructed or modified in such a way as to prevent the transportation of a combat infantry squad.

[46] *Arms Control Reporter*, 1989, sheet 407.B.162.

[47] *Vienna Fax*, 18 May 1990, p. 2.

Other TLE categories had not been 'tested' before the Treaty was signed, mainly because definitions of these categories had been agreed upon within a short period of time. As a result, some substantial disagreements over data took place. Nevertheless, it should be mentioned that the agreed definitions and counting rules have had a positive impact on clearing up disagreements. On the other hand, first confusions also stemmed from a few 'objective' circumstances, primarily from Soviet redeployments beyond the Ural Mountains, the reassignment of three army divisions to coastal defence, and the Western preparations for and waging of the war in the Persian Gulf.

An initial discrepancy concerned the equipment listed by the USSR after the signature of the Treaty and NATO intelligence estimates: the Soviet data were lower than the Western estimates.[48] Several officials guessed that the discrepancies did not stem from error in estimation but were deliberate misstatements, possibly to permit continuation of the transfer beyond the Urals after the Treaty had been signed, reflecting the need to avoid high costs of destruction.[49] In the same vein, some US officials suggested that the Soviet Union intended to reach the declared levels, but failed to do so in time because of management problems. General John Galvin, NATO's Supreme Allied Commander, Europe, seemed to share the latter view.[50] Another speculation was that military commanders responsible for the transfer falsified reports because they had failed to ship equipment before the 19 November deadline. In any case later intelligence information led the USA to revise its estimates downwards, considerably narrowing the difference between the Soviet declared data and the US estimate.[51]

On the other hand, it should be mentioned that the 'Protocol on Notification and Exchange of Information' and the 'Annex on the Format for Exchange of Information' were written largely by the USA and agreed to by other states parties in the last few days before the signature of the Treaty. This might have caused some confusion in the USSR. Oleg Grinevsky, the head of the Soviet delegation to the CFE Negotiation, commented that the data had only been preliminarily analysed and corrections would also have to be made to the Western data. Germany and several other European countries corrected what one US official termed 'gross mistakes' in their own data soon after the conclusion of the Treaty.[52]

---

[48] More precisely, the US charges were based on surveillance of Soviet forces by US intelligence agencies carried out in late November. *BASIC Reports from Vienna*, 17 Dec. 1990, p. 1. It was later learned that the estimates were in fact made some time earlier.

[49] It should be noted here that by late autumn 1990, according to a letter by Soviet Foreign Minister Eduard Shevardnadze to US Secretary of State James Baker, 4000 withdrawn Soviet tanks had already been destroyed, converted or exported. Another 8000 tanks were slated for future destruction or conversion. The other 8000 of the 20 000 tanks planned for removal from the ATTU zone were being moved to the Far Eastern part of the USSR to replace ageing weapons that would in turn be destroyed. Thus, the costly process of destruction had already been started in the USSR. *BASIC Reports from Vienna*, 17 Dec. 1990, p. 2.

[50] *Arms Control Today*, Jan./Feb. 1991, p. 22.

[51] Note 50.

[52] *Arms Control Reporter*, 1990, sheets 407.B.414, 407.B.415.

The US data reflected another problem which simply stemmed from circumstances. The USA declared it had 5904 battle tanks, 5747 ACVs, 2601 artillery systems, 704 combat aircraft and 279 attack helicopters. Except for battle tanks, these data generally corresponded to earlier publicly available data. The declared number of tanks indicated that before transfers of armaments to the Persian Gulf the USA had more than 6800 tanks in active units and in storage in Europe—approximately 1000 more than expected. The US data also included the equipment sent to the Gulf, but counted against the CFE limits. This would allow it to be returned to Europe.[53] The USA transferred about 14 per cent of its tank holdings to Egypt and several other countries[54] instead of maintaining them in Europe where they would have had to be destroyed. In addition, the USA and Italy originally counted the same 630 M47 tanks stored at the designated permanent storage site at Livorno and then Italy reduced its holdings to correct the error.[55]

Another problem which cropped up immediately upon signature addressed the numbers of OOV. NATO expected approximately 1600 OOV to be declared by the USSR rather than 895[56] as included in the Soviet list. Western experts explained the discrepancy by the fact that the USSR considered each major military base as a single site, while NATO divided military complexes into several distinct sites. According to NATO officials, the counting of neighbouring sites would hinder NATO OSI, limited to 48 hours by the Treaty.[57] The Soviet data meant a substantial decrease in the numbers of inspections planned by other states parties.

This problem was discussed in the first session of the Joint Consultative Group in Vienna. The USSR put forward several explanations: the reassignment of some low-strength divisions as storage sites might represent an advantage as a large number of storage sites could be inspected as one OOV; the amalgamation of below-strength active units and consequent decrease in active units, that is, a few regiments into one divisional OOV; the reduction of numbers of training vehicles at training areas to below the threshold for declaration (30 or 12 TLE items of a single category).[58]

One other Soviet explanation is worth mentioning, at least to reflect the difficulties for counting caused by withdrawals from Eastern Europe and the process of restructuring Soviet armed forces to achieve the purposes of 'reasonable sufficiency'. Eastern and Western negotiators agreed during the final phase of negotiations not to count 120 Soviet regiments and battalions in Eastern Europe as OOV because all of their TLE had already been removed. The USSR also claimed that an additional 80 sites were removed from the list because of the withdrawals from Eastern Europe. Finally, the USSR seemed to have removed

[53] *Arms Control Today*, Dec. 1990, p. 22.
[54] Note 50, CFE supplement, p. 3.
[55] *Arms Control Reporter*, 1991, sheet 407.B.449.
[56] This number was revised to 910 in February 1991; see *Vienna Fax*, 28 Feb. 1991, p. 2.
[57] *Defense News*, 17 Dec. 1990, p. 10.
[58] *BASIC Reports from Vienna*, 17 Dec. 1990, p. 2.

all TLE from its chemical and communications and control units, thereby eliminating 360 OOV.[59]

Another NATO concern addressed the transfer of substantial portions of Soviet equipment beyond the Urals before the Treaty was signed, although it did not represent a violation of any Treaty provisions. The Soviet Union gave assurances that some of this equipment had already been destroyed and that much of the rest would be destroyed. Many items withdrawn to Siberia were reportedly left out in the open to rust (and are easily counted as long as they remain there) and would take at least two years to restore to peak condition.[60] In fact US officials stated that it was possible to monitor 'militarily significant potentials' deployed east of the ATTU zone and that, 'even if they (the USSR) do keep the stuff active in Siberia, putting them on the other side of the Urals is an important step for stability'.[61] NATO became much more concerned with another issue, however.

The dispute was sparked by the USSR transferring three motorized rifle divisions into coastal defence units[62] which it considered not limited by the Treaty (the mandate covers only ground, air and air defence forces). NATO claimed that the Treaty did not exclude ground equipment in naval units from the limits (with exceptions for internal security forces, for example). The Soviet Union in fact acknowledged the shift.[63] In total 5457 tanks, APCs and artillery pieces were reassigned to three coastal defence divisions, four naval infantry regiments, the strategic rocket forces and civil defence units.[64]

The dispute went on for eight months but was finally resolved at a meeting in Lisbon on 1 June 1991 between US Secretary of State James Baker and Soviet Foreign Minister Alexander Bessmertnykh.[65]

In a legally binding statement[66] the USSR agreed to reduce its holdings of TLE within the area of application by the number which it had in coastal defence forces and naval infantry (933 battle tanks, 1725 ACVs and 1080 artillery pieces). Of the 1725 ACVs, 972 had been destroyed or converted into civilian equipment while the remaining 753 were to be modified to APC look-alikes not covered by the Treaty. Only half of the 933 battle tanks, 972 ACVs

---

[59] Note 58.

[60] 'Soviets maneuver Warsaw Pact arms out of treaty's way', *International Herald Tribune*, 12 Nov. 1990.

[61] *Arms Control Reporter*, 1990, sheet 407.B.415.

[62] 'CFE stalls; signatories insist on Soviet compliance', *Defense News*, 18 Feb. 1991, p. 1.

[63] For example, the first deputy Chief of the Soviet General Staff, B. Omelichev, stated: 'The Soviet Union has taken measures for more reliable defence of coastal directions, taking into account the US and NATO substantial superiority in assault and mobile naval means. We started this process already in 1987. As a result, three divisions of Ground Forces have been resubordinated to the Navy as the coastal defence divisions (and not as Marine divisions). Like all naval forces, they did not become the subject of Vienna negotiations and not because of our unwillingness and thereby they cannot be considered within the framework of the Paris treaty.' See *Krasnaya Zvezda*, 16 Feb. 1991, p. 3.

[64] 'U.S. proposal could end CFE equipment dispute', *Defense News*, 8 Apr. 1991, p. 4; 'Gorbachev offers U.S. deal on arms dispute', *International Herald Tribune*, 3 Apr. 1991, p. 7.

[65] *The Economist*, 8 June 1991, p. 30; 'Breakthrough for treaty talks', *Jane's Defence Weekly*, 15 June 1991, p. 999; *Atlantic News*, 19 June, 1991, p. 1.

[66] 'Statement by the Government of the Union of Soviet Socialist Republics', reprinted in *BASIC Reports on European Arms Control*, no. 15 (17 June 1991), pp. 3, 4.

and 1080 artillery pieces were to be reduced within the area of application, however. The other half were to be withdrawn and an equivalent number (i.e., not necessarily the same equipment) were to be destroyed or converted outside the area of application. While this latter proviso did not permit the equipment destroyed or converted outside the area of application to be monitored by OSI, the conversion or destruction had to be accomplished 'in accordance with procedures which provide sufficient visible evidence that the conventional armaments and equipment have been destroyed or rendered militarily unusable. The States Parties to the Treaty shall be notified in advance, giving the location, number and types'[67] —that is, so that observations can be made using NTM. TLE within the area of application of the coastal defence forces and naval infantry are subject to challenge OSI.

As for the Strategic Rocket Forces, they would be permitted to include only APCs, the number of which cannot exceed 1701—the level on the day of the agreement. Very importantly, the Soviet declaration stated that unless otherwise specified, all TLE 'based on land within the area of application of the Treaty, *irrespective of assignment,* shall be subject to all numerical limitations of the Treaty'[68] (emphasis added).

To further assuage Western concerns, in a separate (non-legally binding) statement issued at a special session of the JCG on the same day as the statement referred to above, the USSR also promised to destroy or convert an additional 6000 tanks, 7000 artillery pieces and 1500 ACVs which had been moved east of the Urals. It also pledged that none of the equipment moved east of the Urals would be stored in unit sets or used to create new large formations.[69]

Accusations about the transfer of the three Soviet divisions point rather to the problem of compliance, that is, how to resolve disagreements about clearly detected actions of a state party. With regard to monitoring capabilities, the recent record reflects the basic fact that, while very capable, NTM are far from infallible. Moreover, as was continually stressed by experts before the signature of the Treaty, US intelligence assets continue to play a dominant role in Western monitoring activities short of OSI.

Verification of separate TLE categories

To discuss appropriately the issue of verification of the various separate categories of TLE, two important issues must be borne in mind. The first is quite straightforward in principle—the specific definition of the TLE in question. The CFE Treaty is fairly thorough in this respect. Second, while examining the effectiveness of the verification regime for each TLE item in a stabilizing mode,[70] it is necessary to attempt to understand what it is about each particular TLE category that makes it offensive (as unambiguously as possible in the set-

[67] Note 66, p. 4.
[68] Note 66, p. 4.
[69] Note 66, p. 2.
[70] Oelrich (note 19), pp. 16–17.

ting in which it will most likely be employed). This second point is of particular note for the CFE verification structure since enhanced stability is among its primary objectives.

Armoured vehicles

The Treaty defines a 'battle tank' as:

A self-propelled armoured fighting vehicle, capable of heavy firepower, primarily of a high muzzle velocity direct fire main gun necessary to engage armoured and other targets, with high cross-country mobility, with a high level of self-protection, and which is not designed and equipped primarily to transport combat troops . . . Battle tanks are tracked armoured fighting vehicles which weigh at least 16.5 metric tonnes unladen weight and which are armed with a 360-degree traverse gun of at least 75 millimetres calibre. In addition, any wheeled armoured fighting vehicles entering into service which meet all other criteria stated above shall also be deemed battle tanks. (Article II.1[C])

The definition addresses the parameters for offensive capabilities, which are a combination of mobility, firepower and armour. When an attacker is moving through a defender's lines, armour is an important factor against the defender's counter-means. After a breakthrough other parameters may increase their relative role but armour remains important. Thus, it is not incidental that the definition emphasizes armour protection, meaning weight in practical terms. As included in the definition, weight then becomes one of the criteria for verification.

More precise definitions of armour protection could have been related to weight-to-volume ratios and more elaborate definitions would have resulted. To increase armour protection and thereby tank capabilities one may also simply add armour. In terms of decreasing offensive potential, limitations on such procedures could also have been imposed. These limitations would have been essentially useless, however, since an inspected party could simply add armour after every successful inspection.[71]

Firepower is another crucial factor specified in the Treaty. Several characteristics are not mentioned, however. For example, offensive capabilities are increased with stabilized guns which allow tanks to fire on the move; but even if all states parties agreed to limitations on stabilized guns, interior access would be required to verify whether a tank had such stabilization or not and this would require a decision to allow highly intrusive inspection.[72]

Restrictions on AVLBs also limit offensive capabilities and in particular the factor of mobility. Thorough checking of the numbers of AVLBs stored thus also contributes to meeting the objectives of the Treaty. The Treaty defines an

---

[71] For example, reactive armour could add between 1.5 and 2 tonnes to some French equipment. See *Arms Control Reporter*, 1990, sheet 407.B.361.

[72] These aspects are put forward by I. Oelrich. He also mentions another possible constraint on gun effectiveness—limits on laser range-finders and similar devices. Verification in this case is not effective, even by interior access. Such devices could be added fairly quickly; see Oelrich (note 19), p. 18.

'armoured vehicle launched bridge' as 'a self-propelled armoured transporter-launcher vehicle capable of carrying and, through built-in mechanisms, of emplacing and retrieving a bridge structure. Such a vehicle with a bridge structure operates as an integrated system.' (Article II.1[I])

With regard to AVLBs and their verification, the Treaty addresses the problem adequately. AVLBs are subject to inspection if they are located at declared sites, that is, those above the limits for active units of 740 for each group of states parties. If AVLBs in active units had been included as a TLE category, the additional verification problems would have been substantial.

Much of the bridging equipment is comprised of pontoon bridges which are carried on general-purpose trucks. An attacker could thus carry the equipment inside civilian trucks and keep them in civilian storage facilities. This type of equipment would certainly be very difficult, if not impossible, to monitor. The Treaty specifies only 'armoured' vehicle launched bridges, which are not only easier to keep track of but also more effective in preparations for offensive operations. For example, scissor bridges, which are folded bridges carried on tank chassis, are large and distinctive. However, allowing for the fact that a relatively small number of AVLBs may be quite important militarily, monitoring AVLBs outside storage sites may place a proportionately large burden on the verification regime.[73] Although the Treaty does exclude AVLBs from TLE and restricts verification to keeping track of them only in storage, there does exist the *de facto* limit of 740 AVLBs per group of states parties, which does imply an additional verification burden. Nevertheless, information exchange helps to impose some restrictions on certain preparations for offensive operations with AVLBs.[74]

Unintentional violations may be expected with regard to armoured vehicles as well as other categories of TLE. These would not generally be substantial. Because of specific circumstances (moving to and from deployment areas, transferring to depot and repair facilities) the actual number may be lower or higher than declared at a particular time at a particular site (and indeed unknown to those monitoring them). Without a stand-down provision, for example, it would be difficult even for an inspected state party to be confident of the exact number of armoured vehicles within the inspected area and the given period of time. If detected, the reaction of an inspecting party to such violations can be of two types: a violator is openly accused or the issue is dealt with in a confidential atmosphere. The reaction may well depend on the perceived nature of the violation, but a low-profile reaction would seem the more appropriate. On the other hand, if an open accusation is made, it would be more likely to be politically rather than militarily motivated.

If an inspecting party detects an excess of a few tanks and treats such a violation using its 'military insignificance' criteria, a precedent may be perceived to have been set leading to an unofficial 'limit-plus-threshold' and the conse-

---

[73] *Arms Control Reporter*, 1989, sheet 407.B.161.

[74] One should keep in mind that AVLB restrictions and monitoring are of limited value as these TLE items are only capable of crossing very small water bodies and other obstacles.

quent acceptance of a 'limit-plus' as a new *de facto* limit. While the statistical nature of the process would probably lead to too few tanks being counted just as often as too many, the political nature of the process would argue that these problems be minimized by sticking to confidential discussions of non-compliance. Revealing a number of insignificant and unrelated violations may undermine an effective treaty regime.

Keeping good account of ACVs may present some formidable difficulties. One of the challenges is that the category has a large look-alike, count-alike problem. For example, in the case of the US M-113, different versions were used as command vehicles, recovery vehicles and medical vehicles. One Department of Defense official wondered whether the versions had enough observable distinctions to warrant separating them out in categories.[75]

Undeclared combat vehicles could be hard to detect. Besides tags, which are not directly included in the CFE Treaty but are referred to as 'special marks', one of the solutions is to decrease their military utility. Here an obvious link with CSBMs appears as they place certain limitations on out-of-garrison activities.

Artillery

Artillery is that TLE category whose definition was directly influenced by verification concerns. According to Canadian military advisor Colonel William Megill, 'we had this problem with the artillery. We had to go through the lists of systems with verification in the backs of our minds. So we decided that it was easier to verify systems 100mm and up. We couldn't go all over the place looking for every 81mm piece'.[76]

The term 'artillery' has been defined as 'large calibre systems' capable of engaging ground targets primarily by indirect fire:

Large calibre artillery systems are guns, howitzers, artillery pieces combining the characteristics of guns and howitzers, mortars and multiple launch rocket systems with a calibre of 100 mm and above. In addition, any future large calibre direct fire system which has a secondary effective indirect fire capability shall be counted against the artillery ceilings. (Article II.1[F])

Limits on calibre helped negotiators to agree on the specific lists of systems limited by the Treaty. Their verification requires close-up inspections, using tape measures, for example (as well as limits on tank gun calibre, weight of vehicles, etc.).

Because of the large numbers of artillery systems now deployed, both those to be reduced and those to remain, different states or groups of states may choose different priorities in verifying the various types of equipment contained in this category. If the criterion of 'military significance' is adopted, limits on

[75] *Arms Control Reporter*, 1989, sheet 407.B.271.
[76] *Arms Control Reporter*, 1989, sheet 407.B.253.

armoured artillery should be a prime focus of monitoring efforts. Also, some categories, such as *towed artillery*, are more suitable for defensive tasks and thus may not be the subject of the same concern as armoured systems.

Aircraft

The inclusion of aircraft presented the problem of 'reintroduction'. Reintroduction concerns aircraft in particular as they can be swiftly deployed over long distances from areas where their presence might be permissible to areas from which they have been banned above given allowed levels.

Counting aircraft is a complicated task, primarily because of the high mobility of this TLE category. Here again, the task could have been eased if the states parties had agreed on a stand-down provision (i.e., a halt to all aircraft flying into, out of or within a particular area for a certain period of time), whereby NTM together with on-site inspections could permit the precise number of combat aircraft to be assessed by counting all aircraft inside an area during the stand-down interval.

Even if such a provision had been included (and the logistical problems would have been immense), it would not have solved all the problems of precise counting. Another method to enhance verification of aircraft could have been permanent observation posts at main bases as a support measure to this provision. Inspectors could then have fixed a number of aircraft at different bases and exchanged data among themselves to obtain maximum coverage of aircraft potential. Again, this method was excluded from the Treaty as it required permanent presence at sensitive bases.

Even the combination of permanent monitoring posts and a stand-down provision would not be adequate to ascertain the exact aircraft potential and avoid all possibilities of circumvention. In its absence, however, the Treaty places more burdens on national technical means along with the support of less intrusive OSI schemes allowed by the Treaty. To assist the effectiveness of NTM and OSI the Treaty specifies that inspectors can freely record serial numbers or place 'special marks' on equipment before reduction and check the numbers and marks after reduction. It must be remembered here that aircraft is not a category which is to be substantially reduced and reductions are required for most of the ex-WTO countries alone (with the exception of Germany in NATO).

If the states parties agree on using specific tags, it seems less troublesome to have relatively simple inexpensive counterfeit- and transfer-resistant tags such as bar codes, now in widespread use to price and catalogue many consumer goods, rather than very sophisticated ones. First, the use of this type of tag is quite adequate and compatible with the OSI provisions of the Treaty. Second, more sophisticated tags are fraught with serious problems.[77]

---

[77] For a description of tags, see Fetter, S. and Garwin, T., 'Tags', eds Kokoski and Koulik (note 12), pp. 139–54. Some specific problems of using more sophisticated options have been analysed by L. Hansen, addressing a scenario in which each aircraft is fitted with a special transponder to transmit a unique, pre-assigned signature signal. Such a transponder is permanently set at its pre-assigned frequency.

Thus, the Treaty provisions are based on the middle ground which may be assessed as the appropriate approach for combining NTM, data exchange and on-site inspections short of permanent inspection teams and entry/exit points. This combination is expected to provide adequate knowledge of aircraft presence, although not exact potentials.

It seems that the main task for the former WTO countries, given the present large numbers of surplus NATO aircraft, is to make sure that the Treaty limits are not exceeded. This is especially true for the CIS, taking into account the NATO air force capabilities and its own persisting qualitative inferiority. For NATO the priority lies in the problems of monitoring reductions and reclassification.

The exclusion of primary trainers from TLE categories will not have a substantial impact on possibilities of circumvention or any substantial effect on the military balance.[78] They cannot easily be given combat capability and are distinguishable from true combat aircraft. The employment of L-39 primary trainers with a combat capability in the Georgia–Abkhazia conflict proves that such a capability can be introduced and could serve some military role, however. In contrast, verifying look-alike trainers does pose difficulties and needs intrusive OSI. Such OSI is allowed by the Treaty and an inspection of certification is not counted against the quotas for OSI. NATO faces the major burden in verifying look-alike trainers: most of the training facilities and hence the lion's share of training aircraft belonging to the former WTO are within the ATTU zone. On the other hand, NATO has facilities and large numbers of look-alike trainers in the USA and Canada, that is, out of the ATTU zone.[79]

Helicopters

Problems of verifying limits on helicopters have many similarities with those of verifying aircraft ceilings. Helicopters in fact presented one of the most difficult problems during negotiations as they were the one system on which a single chassis or airframe may be used for different purposes—some for military combat, some for military support and some for civilian tasks.[80]

It has to be tamper-proof, permanently affixed as a hedge against the possibility of removal or alteration and must begin to transmit whenever the aircraft is in operation. A quota of OSI to check that transponders had not been tampered with would be required. Each aircraft has its own transponder code which is catalogued for information exchange. Besides the complexity and intrusive character of this scheme, it leads to other problems: transponders break, additional maintenance is required, etc. As a result, breakdowns in the monitoring process are a real possibility. See Hansen, L., *Verifying Conventional Force Reductions,* Occasional Paper Series 1, The Henry Stimson Center, Washington, DC, Feb. 1990, pp. 28–29.

[78] According to James Woolsey, combat-capable trainers are essentially two-seater versions of single-seater combat aircraft such as the two-seater MiG-23. They can be used for combat though the range might be very slightly limited by having the added weight of an extra cockpit. *Arms Control Today,* Apr. 1990, p. 4.

[79] *Arms Control Today,* Mar. 1990, p. 16.

[80] Note 79, p. 5.

'On the other hand, modern attack helicopters do not have the internal volume to serve for transport and thus the two are quite readily distinguished.[81] Any transport helicopter can carry weapons, but its combat capabilities would be quite different from those of an attack helicopter.

Also, helicopters are more closely associated with ground forces than are aircraft. This difference should be considered when assessing the relative importance of counting individual helicopters as compared with aircraft which can operate more autonomously.

V. Implementation of the verification regime

The 120-day 'baseline validation period' began on 17 July 1992. Within this period about 370 inspections took place. The USA carried out 45 'active' inspections, while Russia conducted 80 and received 53 inspections from NATO countries. Several inspections were also carried out of Russian forces stationed in Germany and in some former Soviet republics.[82] Overall, there were some 238 NATO inspections of non-NATO sites, 128 inspections by non-NATO parties and 17 intra-NATO inspections. Comparison with the planned number of inspections for this first period, indicated in table 11, shows that overall the states parties implemented fewer inspections—which reflects a more confident environment among them after the end of the cold war. In addition, the reports of the inspection teams on the results and readiness of the inspected parties to comply with Treaty provisions were usually positive. Although minor discrepancies were reported the results of the first verification period were regarded as successful. Beginning on 15 November 1992 and lasting until 16 November 1995, the three-year reduction period is now under way. During the first phase of the reduction period (which ended on 16 November 1993) over 1000 inspections were carried out, and over 17 000 TLE items were destroyed or converted to non-military purposes.[83]

As mentioned above, the Treaty permits inspections to be carried out within the two groups of states. With only a few exceptions this right was not exercised.

The majority of inspections were of declared sites. A clear timetable laid down in the Treaty facilitated the smooth implementation of the inspection details—flight plans, destinations, membership of inspection teams, and so on. NATO states parties also set up a 'deconfliction' committee in Brussels to avoid a number of inspections from other countries converging on one site at the same time. The inspecting parties were also patient and understanding about the problems of the former Soviet republics, where the status of the forces was

[81] Oelrich (note 19), p. 25.

[82] *Focus on Vienna*, April 1993, p. 10.

[83] Lachowski, Z., 'Conventional arms control and security co-operation in Europe', SIPRI, *SIPRI Yearbook 1994* (Oxford University Press: Oxford, 1994), pp. 568–70; *Disarmament Bulletin*, winter 1993/94, p. 1.

sometimes vague and where sometimes an army had not even been officially declared by the authorities.

Western inspectors faced a problem when Russia started to redefine common areas as OOV and, accordingly, to cut the area between OOV that should be available for inspection.[84] The last report of the Bush Administration's Arms Control and Disarmament Agency also treated under-declarations of reduction obligations, inaccurate data declarations and exports of excess TLE by the former Soviet republics as violations. Reports from Western inspectors contained complaints about violations in the form of denial of inspection rights at certain cities in Russia, Ukraine and Belarus. These problems were resolved in the JCG.[85]

On the other hand the Russian side has argued that inspectors from NATO are inclined to 'see more' than needed. When inspectors visit an OOV on an inspection map they point to sensitive points and closed areas. This provokes Russian officers to suspect inspectors of 'inappropriate' interest.[86]

One of the main issues on the agenda of the JCG remains the lack of necessary information for conflict areas, such as Trans-Dniester, Georgia–Ossetia and Georgia–Abkhazia. Armed conflict between Armenia and Azerbaijan has also posed many problems.

Aside from these conflict areas in the former Soviet Union, it should be considered a success that only a few minor differences appeared during the inspections. These differences have primarily concerned interpretation regarding access to buildings, mainly 'common areas' such as mess facilities which in some cases are regarded as a good indication of the number of personnel a site is capable of supporting and therefore relevant to the CFE-1A Agreement on troop strength. The JCG has not reported 'ambiguities', that is, variations from the terms of the Treaty or differences between declared information and the findings of the inspectors. Those differences which arose were successfully resolved at a bilateral level.

After the baseline validation period was completed, the annual exchange of information took place on 15 December 1992 within the framework of the JCG. The next stage of CFE Treaty inspections was then started—to verify the actual reduction of TLE. Inspections continue, but at a slower pace.

The JCG has continued to meet in weekly plenary sessions. Several working groups deal with specific issues, for example one group discusses the evaluation of data exchange. The JCG has also discussed modification of the rules for reduction procedures so as to cut the high costs of current methods for making TLE unusable, which bear particularly heavily on East European states because of their greater reduction liabilities. Proposals to modify the procedures have been introduced by Romania, Russia and Ukraine. To be acceptable, they will have to maintain the principles on which the relevant CFE Treaty protocols are

---

[84] Sharp, J. M. O., 'Conventional arms control in Europe', SIPRI, *SIPRI Yearbook 1993: World Armaments and Disarmament* (Oxford University Press: Oxford, 1993), p. 612.

[85] Note 84.

[86] *Segodnya*, 21 Sep. 1993.

based: (*a*) that the reduction procedure will leave the TLE concerned in an irreparable condition and (*b*) that all reduction/destruction steps must be verifiable.

VI. Concluding remarks

The CFE verification regime differs substantially from the regimes of other important treaties such as the INF Treaty, the Strategic Arms Reduction (START) treaties and the Chemical Weapons Convention. Unlike the CFE Treaty, these treaties deal with weapons of mass destruction and the verification procedures are much stricter. In the cases of the INF and START treaties a baseline inventory of 100 per cent is required, in comparison with only 20 per cent for the CFE Treaty. Other differences include the percentage of sites to be inspected, the number of states parties, the use of multinational teams, the number of official languages, and so on.

A major difference is the cost of the verification activities. According to the Institute for Defence Analysis, the cost for the CFE Treaty could reach $77 million, compared with $760 million for the START treaties, $490 million for the INF Treaty and $3200 million for the 1993 Chemical Weapons Convention (CWC).[87]

In addition to the limited geographical scope of the Treaty, the CFE quota system limits the number of OOV that will actually be inspected. Inspections are also divided up among many states parties. The costs of inspections to monitor TLE elimination under the CFE Treaty are substantially lower than those for other treaties. This is partly explained by the number of states parties. As these inspections are multilateral, the three-year reduction period will require only some 10 to 20 US inspectors on a full-time basis, for example. Finally, the technical requirements for CFE inspectors are minimal, and manpower and equipment costs will, therefore, be low.[88]

Monitoring of TLE production and potential TLE production monitoring would incur substantial costs, and these tasks are excluded from the CFE verification regime. Considerable sums were spent, for example, on monitoring potential TLE production as part of the INF Treaty verification activities. The difference in approaches to monitoring illegal TLE production partly explains the difference in verification costs.

---

[87] Klare and Grotte (note 10), p. 163. Several explanations are noted here.
[88] Klare and Grotte (note 10), p. 166.

4. The debate leading up to the CFE Treaty

I. Introduction

Although the recent changes in the European geopolitical and military landscape have made many arms control and verification approaches which have been discussed more or less obsolete, this does not mean that the historical background of conventional arms control negotiations should be allowed to fade from memory. It may provide useful guidelines for possible arms control endeavours in other regions and for further advancement of verification concepts in case of future efforts to reduce military potentials of the CFE Treaty states parties.

It should be kept in mind that during the long record of the conventional arms control process in Europe a number of concepts of and approaches to verification were presented and discussed on political and academic levels. They were formulated for different situations and scenarios, ranging from the formerly confrontational environment to the present situation of growing confidence among participants.

During the negotiations the proposals dealt with several areas of application, beginning from a limited area in Central Europe and later stretching to the ATTU zone as embodied in the Treaty itelf. The problem of linking the reductions of armaments and military personnel was thoroughly evaluated and eventually solved. The role of verification in different arms control schemes and its basic purpose to ensure the successful implementation of a certain agreement was analysed. Overall, it is appropriate to examine briefly the record of the negotiations.

II. The MBFR talks

From 1973 to February 1989 the only negotiations which dealt with East–West conventional arms control and reductions were known as the Mutual and Balanced Force Reduction (MBFR) talks. They aimed at reaching an agreement on force reductions within the Central European area covering the two German states, the Benelux countries, the former Czechoslovakia and Poland. The talks involved 11 'direct' participants, including the seven countries within the area, and the USA, the USSR, the UK and Canada, all of which stationed forces there. Eight countries—Denmark, Greece, Italy, Norway, Turkey, Bulgaria, Hungary and Romania—played the role of 'indirect' participants. France refused to participate, although its forces deployed in the FRG were counted within Western totals.

After 46 rounds, the talks ended in February 1989 without concrete results. The final joint communiqué stated that 'the participants accumulated valuable experience and received a clearer notion of what will be needed in order to achieve mutually acceptable and verifiable cuts and restrictions of armed forces and armaments in Europe'.[1]

There is a widely held view that the failure of the MBFR talks stemmed primarily from substantial differences over verification problems. These problems certainly had a negative influence on the results of the negotiations, but they were subordinate to basic military and political considerations and interests that determined the positions of both sides through many years of discussions in Vienna. In turn, these considerations and interests dictated conceptual approaches to conventional arms control and reductions in Europe. As two Soviet experts noted:

The failure of the Talks was caused primarily by the conceptual differences between the Warsaw Treaty and NATO over the extent and character of reductions of the armed forces and armaments in Central Europe. Because the sides adhered to opposite positions on verification, their differences over these matters attracted obviously excessive attention and were considered by many to have caused the disruption of an agreement. However, they were in fact a secondary problem and would most likely have been overcome, if an understanding on real reductions had been reached.[2]

In an earlier SIPRI study the assessment was based on the interests of both sides: 'If the maintenance of force levels, rather than arms reductions, was NATO's first concern, then it is scarcely surprising that such little progress resulted from the MBFR talks . . . Conversely, if the Soviet Union's main aim was to get the West to participate in the CSCE, then it had no reason to make major concessions.'[3]

The failure to arrive at compromise positions on arms control arrangements stemmed from the participants' failure to compromise their overall interests. The problem of verification played a secondary role in the unsuccessful MBFR process, although it had been effectively used by both sides to excuse their lack of political preparedness for a breakthrough.

Division in interests

At the meeting in Rome in 1970 the North Atlantic Council made the first specific proposals for negotiations on mutual and balanced force reductions. This initiative was taken for several reasons. The first reason was the desire to improve *détente*. The second reason was to avoid, postpone or obtain offsetting compensations for any reductions in US forces in Europe, which at that time

---

[1] *Arms Control Reporter,* 1989, sheet 401.B.205.

[2] Kokeev, M. and Androsov, A., *Verification: the Soviet Stance. Its Past, Present and Future* (United Nations: New York, 1990), pp. 96–97.

[3] Carter, A., SIPRI, *Success and Failure in Arms Control Negotiations* (Oxford University Press: Oxford, 1989), p. 241.

seemed as imminent as they promised to be unsettling. The third was to neutralize further shifts in the military balance in Europe, which had been altered by improvements in the WTO potential that NATO—for political reasons—found difficult to match. The fourth reason was the desire to obtain some compensation for Western participation in the CSCE, which the WTO proposed in 1969 and which NATO thought presented more problems than opportunities.

The WTO responded positively to the NATO initiative for starting negotiations. It wanted to contribute to *détente* and ease the economic burden of defence; it wanted to reduce or eliminate several threats, including continued military buildup in FRG and in Western tactical nuclear capabilities; and it also considered the long-term objectives of the dissolution of NATO and the WTO, withdrawal of all nuclear weapons to the territories of the countries possessing them, the creation of nuclear weapon-free zones, an agreement on no-first-use of nuclear weapons, and reductions in armed forces west of the Soviet frontier. The Soviet Union accepted NATO's proposal in return for the West's acceptance of a conference on European security.

Gaps in initial positions

The WTO initially proposed reductions in both nuclear and conventional air and ground forces, including a reduction of 20 000 troops each in NATO and WTO ground and air forces in 1975, to be followed in subsequent years by cuts of 5 per cent and then 10 per cent. The proposal was later modified such that only US and Soviet troops would be cut initially. These reductions also applied to major weapons, such as tanks, aircraft and missile launchers, and were to be implemented in the form of comparable military units. 'Foreign troops' were to be withdrawn to their countries of origin, while 'national' units were to be disbanded, their personnel demobilized and their equipment decommissioned. Reductions in, and a subsequent freeze on, remaining ground and air forces were to be applied on a national basis. The proposal entailed the demobilization or withdrawal of about 165 000 troops for NATO and about 185 000 for the WTO, based on Western estimates, or virtually equal reductions if the WTO estimates were used. According to Western estimates of the balance, however, it could also result in a continued WTO superiority of almost 2:1 in aircraft and tanks. This was unacceptable for NATO.

NATO put forward a different conceptual approach—a package to reach equal ground forces, which would be implemented in two stages. The first envisaged the withdrawal of about 16 per cent of US and Soviet stationed forces. This would result in asymmetrical cuts of 28 500 US soldiers and 3000 airmen compared with 67 500 Soviet troops and 1700 tanks.

The second stage would establish ceilings of 700 000 on the ground forces of each side with the WTO eliminating twice as many as NATO. If reductions in weaponry during this stage were proportionate to those in manpower, the WTO would again reduce more tanks, guns and armoured personnel carriers, thus further diminishing its ability to conduct mobile operations. If the proposal was implemented, NATO could also partially offset the geographical asymmetries which it considered to be advantageous to the USSR.[4]

The factor of geographical asymmetries influenced the strategic and political interests of both sides. If Soviet forces were withdrawn and stationed in western MDs they could be rapidly redeployed back to Central Europe; if US forces stationed in Europe were withdrawn they would have to be transported across the Atlantic Ocean. NATO believed that the WTO proposition that stationed forces should remove their equipment upon redeployment was aimed at increasing this disadvantage.

Balance estimates

Because of the priorities assigned by negotiators and the context of the proposals, estimates of the military balance had to cover not only conventional forces, troops in Central Europe and combat-ready units, but also nuclear forces, reserve units and troops belonging to the Soviet Union, Western Europe, the USA and Canada. The need for consensus on estimates was considered the main starting-point for proceeding with a number of measures to reach an agreement.

NATO officials claimed that without a solution to the data problem there could be no basis for working out the requirements for unambiguous standards of compliance with an agreement or for ascertaining precise, residual levels. Without this, there could be no clear understanding of what constituted a violation.

The priorities in discussions of the 'balance problem' shifted to the manpower issue as the major focus. Such a shift stemmed largely from the NATO position on proceeding with manpower reductions. Although it narrowed the scope of discussions the manpower issue had the potential to be an unfinished enterprise, partly because of verification requirements. It had already been understood that verification of manpower limits and reductions themselves (in contrast to reductions only involving armament categories) were almost impossible if they were to satisfy sceptics in both the East and the West.

Experts from East and West acknowledged that the differences in manpower estimates had more political than military significance. Presenting its own figures for the first time in June 1976, the WTO claimed to have 150 000 ground forces fewer than the NATO estimate of 805 000. Afterwards, the disparities did not change significantly.[5]

The first, immediate requirement in resolving the difference was to clarify data ambiguities. The difference could be blamed on several factors—the WTO provided falsified data, the Western intelligence community was wrong, the real problem lay in the 'counting rules'—or a combination of these factors.

---

[4] 'Mutual force reductions: status and prospects', SIPRI, *World Armaments and Disarmament: SIPRI Yearbook 1978* (Taylor & Francis: London, 1978), p. 410.

[5] *Orbis,* vol. 27, no. 4 (winter 1984), p. 1005.

Settling these issues seemed very difficult as this required distributing data on levels which were not then acceptable to either side or changing the methods of intelligence estimates. For purely domestic reasons, this could hardly be expected, especially not in the absence of any discussion on how to validate information on a common basis.

If the differences were not resolved, the levels of armed forces in the zone could be frozen by agreement, pending further reductions. This agreement could also put in place substantial and intrusive arrangements to verify those levels. The other possible solution had to do with reaching an agreement on equal levels after reductions. The verification framework could have been agreed on accordingly with the prime task of checking residual levels. Taking into account small-scale reduction proposals on the negotiating table, all these measures would have little effect on the military balance in Europe. Thus, theoretical possibilities existed, but neither side showed a readiness for compromise.

Serious attempts to clarify ambiguities and thereby to clear a way for working out verification arrangements, for example, a discussion of counting rules or definitions, could have served as an indication that both sides wanted an agreement. Debates were limited mainly to mutual accusations, however, and did not provide an opportunity to resolve the issue.

'Forces' and 'armaments'

As indicated above, the data dispute was closely connected with the trend towards narrowing the subject of the negotiations. It should be mentioned that, from the outset, the talks were officially referred to as the Negotiations on the Mutual Reduction of Forces and Armaments and Associated Measures in Central Europe (MURFAAMCE). The later official reference to 'force reductions' only reflected preferences to limit the scope of the talks.

As the former deputy head of Canadian delegations to both the CSCE and the MBFR talks, John Toogood, recalled:

in detailed negotiations 'forces' became one subject and 'armaments' another. In a low-key fashion the East continued to advocate reductions of armaments associated with reduced forces but did not seriously attempt to describe what these armaments might be. The West, even less enthusiastically, refused to discuss armament reductions or limitations of any kind until the two sides could come to a meeting of minds on troop reductions.

The two agreed that 'forces' should be taken to mean manpower but the quarrel over existing strengths was never resolved. This data dispute blocked progress in the negotiations more or less across the board. Almost casually, though, the sides continued to discuss reductions of brigades and divisions as well as of numbers of persons.[6]

---

[6] Toogood, J., *Conventional Arms Control in Europe: Western Opening Positions*, Working Paper 15, Canadian Institute for International Peace and Security, Ottawa, Dec. 1988, p. 7.

Without counting rules the problem of verification became the subject of a political game. In fact it became a very effective tool for keeping the negotiations unsuccessful.

Soviet unilateral withdrawals

The unilateral withdrawal of 20 000 Soviet troops and 1000 tanks from the GDR announced in October and started in December 1979 provided an interesting illustration of the potential difficulties of verifying force reductions in an atmosphere of suspicion and tension. It was possible to monitor that the 6th Soviet Tank Division of about 10 000 men had left its garrisons in the GDR, but very difficult to ascertain whether or not the remaining men and tanks—taken from a number of formations—had actually left. Some speculated that they had either been brought back in smaller units or sent to Hungary.

The scope of disagreements among intelligence agencies and the political manipulation of intelligence reports showed, first, that NTM alone would clearly not be satisfactory for verifying complex troop reductions.[7] Second, it would have helped if the data ambiguities could have been resolved prior to any unilateral or mutual actions. The Western side put forward an argument that the voluntary reductions could not be considered in adjusting force levels as the Soviet reductions were not verified and the West would not agree to a stage of voluntary reductions without a data agreement. Third, at least to satisfy the Western political position, both sides needed to agree on a package of verification measures: to verify initial data, to verify withdrawal and to verify residual levels.[8] But the question of the conceptual formulation of requirements for such verification arrangements, including intrusive measures and criteria for compliance, remained untouched.

The first draft treaties

Besides the objective difficulties of dealing with verification arrangements, it was perhaps not yet realistic to discuss them broadly or specifically early on because in almost 10 years of negotiations the two sides had not even presented

---

[7] Carter (note 3), p. 238.

[8] General Wolfgang Heydrich, a member of the FRG delegation, was asked about the unilateral withdrawals of Soviet troops in 1979. He answered the question of whether this example fits into the Vienna negotiations as follows:

Conditionally it fits, because the example shows that under the proviso of the permission of unrestrained observation it is possible to ascertain that certain troop components are withdrawn. But it is far from sufficient for the MBFR requirements for verification, essentially for two reasons. First, the volume as a whole must become verifiable, and this is possible only if the entire reduction can be ascertained and added up by experts at specific points. Second, and much more important, it must be ensured that these reductions will not be balanced again through subsequent replenishments.

This means that it is absolutely necessary to ensure that there will be constant verifiability of the armed forces remaining in the area involved. The aforementioned example did not live up to these two conditions; see *Arms Control Reporter,* 1985, sheet 401.B.86. Later the West came to the conclusion that the Soviet troops had been regrouped and doubted whether their overall number was reduced.

their separate draft treaties. These drafts appeared on the negotiating table only in 1982. The first major effort to put forward verification aspects took place only in 1978, when the NATO proposal also included measures for verification of compliance with the agreement along with measures for reducing the possibility of surprise attack and for insuring against attempts to circumvent the agreement.

The Western proposals

According to the Western proposals of July 1982, as modified in April 1984, the total ground and air forces of each alliance would be reduced to common ceilings of 900 000, including 700 000 ground force personnel. Within these ceilings, the USA and the USSR would reach interim ceilings on their combat and combat support forces, later to be replaced by a numerical ceiling on their total ground force and air force potentials after completing the initial reductions. The West did not include armaments in the proposal.

Withdrawals were to be implemented in three stages within five years. The parties were obliged to share initial data on combat and combat support forces in the reduction area before the first stage. However, the West did not require an exact agreement and intended to accept WTO data which fell within an unspecified but apparently narrow range of the Western estimates. During the first stage the USA would withdraw 13 000 troops (90 per cent in unspecified units) while the USSR would withdraw 30 000 troops by divisions. The reductions were to take place over one year and then both countries would freeze the levels for the duration of the first stage. Verification of reductions was planned for the second year of this stage.

After completion and verification of the first stage a collective no-increase commitment and a data agreement on remaining forces were required. During the second and third stages all participants would reduce their forces, supported by verification activities.

Thus, the West closely linked the need for data agreement and verification activities, which included primarily an annual quota of up to 18 inspections for each side on the territory of the other side in the area of reductions (inspection teams would conduct their survey from the ground, from the air, or both) and permanent entry/exit monitoring points, with observers, for movements of forces of participants located outside the zone in and out of the area of reductions.

The Eastern proposals

The WTO supported the total ceilings for each side, but considered it important that no party's armed forces in Central Europe should exceed 50 per cent of the collective level of 900 000 after the second stage. The reductions would take place in two phases—the first by mutual example (reductions of 20 000 Soviet and 13 000 US troops) without formal agreement within one year and the second to be negotiated during the first phase of reductions. Weapons and 'combat technology' (equipment) would also be withdrawn. The detailed composition of the reduced ground forces and armaments was to be covered in a special protocol.

The main burden of verification of actual reductions was placed on withdrawals at predetermined crossing points where special representatives were invited. Among other measures the WTO proposed:

1. Mutual invitations to send observers of both sides to the withdrawals and to the reductions of the most substantial contingents of non-indigenous and indigenous troops;

2. Mutual notification of the beginning and completion of reductions;

3. Temporary monitoring posts through which withdrawing forces would pass;

4. Three or four permanent monitoring stations through which all troops would pass in entering or leaving the area of reductions;

5. On-site inspection on challenge if permitted by the host country.

In efforts to avoid data disputes the WTO put forward the idea of reducing forces to the 900 000 level and of verifying this reduction without requiring any prior agreement on data—leaving the reduction process outside the verification scheme. In this case, the bulk of activities would have been devoted to monitoring residual levels and movements into the area of reduced forces. Suggesting the intrusive measures, the Soviet side also signalled the need for political acceptance of these measures as a supplement to NTM, that is, mainly to the US and Soviet monitoring capabilities and with principle reliance on NTM after reductions.[9]

The US side did not intend to accept this plan. After exchanging draft treaties in 1982 the US Ambassador to the Vienna talks, Richard Staar, specified that satellite verification was inadequate and that NATO wanted 'permanent' observation posts not only during the reduction period but also for eight years after that. NATO's position included inspections 'on call' by low-flying aircraft, helicopter and ground teams.[10]

As the WTO demanded only temporary observation posts a compromise would seem unlikely, especially with NATO's added insistence that aerial reconnaissance on call be agreed for a certain period after reductions. Relatively little attention was paid to the fact that both sides could gain verification experience during the reduction period by detecting reintroductions of troops into the reduction area. The other opportunity could be a follow-on agreement on further reductions within the agreed reduction period and with new verification tasks and arrangements.

---

[9] *Arms Control Reporter,* 1985, sheet 401.B.84.

[10] 'Negotiations for conventional force reductions and security in Europe', SIPRI, *World Armaments and Disarmament: SIPRI Yearbook 1983* (Taylor & Francis: London, 1983), p. 602.

The emerging verification debate

In 1985 the East accepted the idea of reaching a formal agreement to reduce US and Soviet troops. The Western reaction to the 1985 WTO stance was more positive than it had been to earlier Eastern positions.

Nevertheless, the starting-point, data exchange, remained a stumbling block. To overcome the dispute Jonathan Dean suggested giving priority to verification at the negotiating table.[11] His phased plan included: temporary suspension of the Western requirement that agreement on data be resolved before any reductions occur to permit a limited first reduction of, say, 10 000 troops for the USA and 20 000 troops for the USSR. In return, the USSR, which refused to adopt verification measures until there had been actual reductions, would agree to the post-reduction exchange of detailed new information on the Soviet and US forces remaining in Central Europe and also to workable procedures for an annual quota of inspections and other verification measures to check the number of Soviet soldiers in the area. All this would be put into effect as soon as the first, limited reductions of the Soviet and US troops had taken place. Inspections could be used on a short-notice sampling basis to help verify the strength of major Soviet units selected by the West. After this first Soviet and US withdrawal the overall number of NATO and WTO troops (as well as those of the USA and the USSR) in Central Europe would be frozen for the two-year period of the agreement. Dean made a strong point that, if this approach did not succeed, there would be no risk to the security of either side through reductions of such a limited size, as the arrangement would automatically expire after two years. If it succeeded, however, further reductions could be agreed upon.

The reaction to this proposal on the part of some NATO officials followed the line that even if the West could verify that only specified Soviet units remained, the USSR could restructure units to add more personnel and filter the men in individually. They maintained that this was a possibility because of the experience with the Soviet unilateral reductions of 1979 and that the West needed the confidence to be able to point to such an increase without revealing the intelligence sources.[12] In other words, the issue of how to verify 'filtering the men in ones or twos' (even with very intrusive measures which would not force revealing the intelligence sources) could prove extremely difficult.

In December 1985 the US representative put forward a new Western proposal for a four-year agreement.[13] The relatively small number of US and Soviet troops to be reduced and redeployed to home territories within one year of the signing of the agreement—5000 and 11 500, respectively—reflected the nature of the plan which was to test verification measures before larger reductions were undertaken. Indeed, these reductions (90 per cent would be in more easily verifiable units) would not undermine NATO and WTO security.

The verification package included four elements:

[11] *Christian Science Monitor*, 11 Apr. 1985; *Arms Control Reporter*, 1985, sheets 401.C.11–12.
[12] *Arms Control Reporter*, 1985, sheet 401.B.89.
[13] *Arms Control Reporter*, 1985, sheets 401.B.96–100.

1. Conversion of observation points into permanent entry/exit points through which all forces leaving or entering the reduction area would pass;

2. The exchange of disaggregated information down to battalion level for each participating state after the completion of the initial reductions, thus providing a data base for verifying compliance with the no-increase commitment;

3. OSI to verify withdrawals as well as post-withdrawal force levels, including the right to 30 inspections per year in each of the three years following completion of initial reductions; and

4. Creation of a Consultative Commission to clarify ambiguities and settle disputes.

This time the West did not require initial agreement on data—a basic change in approach—but specified that after reductions both sides would table disaggregated data, including numbers and units, down to the battalion level for each participating state. These data would be exchanged each year. The parties would not question the tabled data but would verify the no-increase commitment of the two sides. The no-increase commitment stemmed from the proposed obligation to collectively freeze troop levels for three years after reductions, including individual commitments for the USA and the USSR. The possibility to renew the agreement was included if no significant gap appeared between declared figures and those having been verified.

It is worth mentioning the explanation given for the figure of 30 inspections by the British representative Michael Alexander: 'The West will be trying to verify force levels in the order of a million men spread over more than half a million square kilometres in more than 2000 camps and barracks in three large areas. Against that background a proposal for 30 inspections per annum is fully in accord with the nature and scope of the agreement.'[14]

None the less, given common scepticism about the possibility of stringent counting of personnel and the operational environment for verification, 30 OSI could hardly be adequate for 'effective' monitoring. Thus, the step was rather aimed at either changing the principal position of the East or at presenting another case for the lack of WTO responsiveness to accept more intrusive measures.

The West continued to remind the Conference that the fate of the proposal depended on the East's acceptance of an 'effective package of verification measures' as well as agreement to forgo an initial data agreement. Also, the requirement for the data on units was soundly justified as one of the main bases for working out a methodology of verification. Data on 'structure', including units, could improve the effectiveness of verification, but this would apply serious pressure on the WTO to expand parameters of information about its military potential.

---

[14] Quoted in Moore, J., *Conventional Arms Control and Disarmament in Europe: A Model of Verification System Effectiveness,* Arms Control Verification Papers No. 4, External Affairs and International Trade Canada, Ottawa, Mar. 1990, p. 7.

Soviet representative Mikhailov reacted immediately. Saying that the plan 'would be, naturally, carefully studied', he stressed the exclusion of reductions in armaments and the stringent verification provisions which sought 'to impose excessively inflated verification measures disregarding existing realities. All of this does not contribute to reaching a mutually acceptable agreement'.[15] Soviet spokesmen claimed that within that limited context of an agreement, 30 inspections were too many.[16]

The February 1986 WTO draft treaty specified reductions of US and Soviet troops by 6500 and 11 000, respectively, including armaments. Verification measures were added or clarified in the draft: three to four checkpoints would be set up by each side in the post-withdrawal period with joint monitoring; and all formations, units and sub-units of the land forces of the parties were to enter and leave the reduction area by these checkpoints. The proposal included advance notice of troop movements, of the call-up of reservists, and of military exercises with no more than 20 000 troops; as well as OSI 'on justified request'. The East did not accept an exchange of numerical data down to battalion level, although the information would cover the strengths of each country's army and air force. At the same time, the WTO had no objections to information on the units to be reduced being given before agreement and to creating a Consultative Commission.

According to Western criticism, data disaggregated down to division level, which the WTO supported, would not supply data for troops not in divisions or at locations of the divisions. The West strongly opposed it on the grounds of the impossibility of checking the figures provided.

In discussing verification schemes, Western experts and officials clarified some matters. An OSI would be used as a sample to count, for example, the number of beds in a garrison, rather than counting individual soldiers to determine the number of troops. Another OSI task was to uncover discrepancies. Permanent entry and exit points (PEEPs) were not the key to compliance and would not deal with the indigenous troops. The counting of troops passing through PEEPs would serve as an adjunct to the main methods, which would remain NTM.[17]

Within a short period of time both sides managed to make progress on verification issues without principal changes in the negotiation agenda. They reached basic agreement on: periodic exchanges of data after force reductions; notification of the beginning and end of reduction steps; permanent observation posts at exit/entry points of the reduction zone; and the use of OSI. They also agreed on non-interference with national technical means and the establishment of a Consultative Commission to resolve ambiguities about compliance.

[15] *Arms Control Reporter,* 1985, sheet 401.B.98.
[16] *Arms Control Reporter,* 1986, sheet 401.B.102.
[17] *Arms Control Reporter,* 1986, sheet 401.B.112.

Reshuffling the agenda

The complexion of the negotiations changed radically in April 1986 when Mikhail Gorbachev presented a new initiative. He proposed that:

agreement be reached on substantial reductions in all the components of the land forces and tactical air forces of the European states and the relevant forces of the United States and Canada deployed in Europe. The formations and units to be reduced should be disbanded and their weaponry either destroyed or stored in national territories. Geographically, reductions, obviously, should cover the entire European territory from the Atlantic to the Urals. Operational-tactical nuclear weapons could be reduced simultaneously with conventional weapons.

The question of dependable verification at every stage of this process is natural. Both national technical means and international forms of verification, including, if need be, on-site inspection, are possible.[18]

The package provided further for: exchange of data on the total numerical strength of the land forces and tactical strike forces; data on that part to be reduced and that to remain after reductions; unit designations, numerical strength, deployment and the number of the main types of armament agreed upon; and notice of the beginning and completion of reductions.

The communiqué of a summit meeting of the WTO Political Consultative Committee in May 1987 stated the readiness to verify 'the very process of reduction which would be accompanied by observation of the military activity of the troops remaining after reduction'.[19] Viktor Karpov, a high-level Soviet official, said that the whole ATTU area could be opened to inspection. The USSR would accept US military inspectors travelling in the European part of the USSR, and the Soviet inspectors would travel throughout Western Europe.[20]

The WTO countries agreed to provide data on the total numerical strength of land forces and tactical strike aviation within the area of reductions. Data on units to be reduced (unit designation and deployment, troop strength, and equipment numbers for TLE) and the units remaining after reductions would be given separately.

NATO did not respond in detail to Gorbachev's proposals. In the Brussels Declaration of December 1986 it suggested discussions on a new negotiating mandate for conventional arms control within the ATTU area to take place concurrently within two distinct negotiations—the first building upon the achievement of the Stockholm Conference on CSBMs and the second seeking to eliminate conventional force disparities between NATO and the WTO.[21]

Meetings of the 16 NATO nations and the 7 WTO nations (the 'Group of 23') on a new conventional arms control mandate began in February 1987 in Vienna. By the end of the year agreement had been reached on much of the

[18] *Pravda*, 19 Apr. 1986.
[19] *Pravda*, 30 May 1987.
[20] *Arms Control Reporter*, 1987, sheet 401.B.152.
[21] Sharp, J., 'Conventional arms control in Europe: problems and prospects', SIPRI, *SIPRI Yearbook 1988: World Armaments and Disarmament* (Oxford University Press: Oxford, 1988), p. 331.

mandate, but obstacles remained with regard to inclusion of tactical nuclear weapons and the relationship to the CSCE.

In response to the Soviet initiative NATO formed a High Level Task Force (HLTF) to formulate an Alliance approach to conventional arms control in Europe. In July 1987 the 16 Western countries presented their draft mandate which included several priorities: to eliminate the capacity for launching a surprise attack; to focus initially on classic land forces rather than air forces; exclusion of naval, chemical and nuclear forces from the first phase of the talks; a possibility to discuss limits on dual-capable artillery; asymmetrical cuts to common ceilings; and the step-by-step reductions with OSI to verify each stage. The main differences with former positions in the MBFR talks concerned the full participation of France and the inclusion of armaments in the agenda together with manpower.

Actually, the Group of 23 had already become a bloc-to-bloc forum. This was reflected in the fact that in discussing reductions each bloc would be treated as a whole and the individual states would not have to take equal shares of the reductions. Also, although forces stationed outside home territories might be treated differently, it would still be within an alliance-to-alliance framework.

In analysing a new mandate with the broader agenda the line of thinking 'data exchange–verification' and 'verification of reductions–verification of residual levels' was maintained. A US official indicated two possibilities. If tanks were reduced to equal levels of 30 000, both sides would proceed with verifying the remaining tanks by random sampling; each of the 30 inspections per year would count tanks in a battalion in which the WTO indicated it had tanks. An alternative possibility could include the exchange of information about existing forces and the further agreement on how many tanks would comprise residual levels—with subsequent verification of reductions themselves by watching exit points or destruction locations. Both possibilities were considered viable, but to implement the first one the US Government had to convince politicians and the public of its adequacy.[22]

In March 1988 the Group of 23 reached agreement with regard to verification and data exchange. Verification would be implemented by a regime of effective and strict control, including OSI as a right, and an exchange of data. The data should be sufficiently detailed to enable a specific comparison of the potential of the corresponding forces. Details would be worked out at the negotiations themselves.

The discussions were longer than many had anticipated. However, consensus was reached on the mandate and it was included as an Annex to the Concluding Document of the Vienna follow-up meeting of the CSCE, signed on 17 January 1989.[23]

---

[22] Arms Control Reporter, 1987, sheet 401.B.176.

[23] The mandate for the Negotiation on Conventional Armed Forces in Europe is reprinted in SIPRI, SIPRI Yearbook 1989: World Armaments and Disarmament (Oxford University Press: Oxford, 1989), pp. 420–26.

Some reflections

During the MBFR negotiations the verification problem encountered an obvious lack of interest in terms of formulating conceptual and detailed approaches. No serious efforts were made to provide specific analytical methods for including verification specifically within the framework of conventional arms control in Europe.

The narrowing of the agenda to primarily a manpower issue led to an obvious shortage of ideas on how to cope with the full scope of arms control challenges. Such a shortage stemmed partly from the reality that the prime subject of possible arms control measures was the most difficult to address in terms of any criteria of 'adequate verification', not to mention 'effective verification' as insisted upon by some negotiators. Some relatively simple requirements had been discussed but were turned down as politically unacceptable.[24]

Verification problems could be eased if both sides agreed to move towards limiting and reducing armaments with or without personnel, but that required substantial conceptual preparations for appropriate arrangements. Because of the lack of interest in this problem much of the time needed for applied research preparation had been lost.

The period before the CFE Negotiation could be characterized as a period with no solid conceptual framework of conventional arms control. In this regard, Michael Moodie wrote:

Problems in developing a conceptual foundation for conventional arms control are compounded by the fact that arms-control theory has been developed almost exclusively by theorists of nuclear strategy. Nuclear and conventional war, however, are very different phenomena. Nuclear warfare is defined in terms of firepower. Conventional war is a combination of firepower and maneuver. Nuclear war is fought by technology. In conventional war, technology is only one of the many factors that will determine the outcome. In nuclear war, geography is a secondary consideration and topography almost irrelevant. In conventional war, they count—sometimes dramatically.[25]

Because of the lack of serious attempts to reach a compromise, there had been a lack of readiness to formulate requirements for successful verification arrangements. The absence of appropriate criteria of 'forces' and 'armaments'

---

[24] A House Intelligence Committee (the US Congress) Report of 1987 on verification concluded that while the 'military manpower issue is one of the most difficult items to verify . . . the withdrawal or the deactivation of units required under an MBFR agreement could be monitored without significant problems'. This conclusion was also linked with the following statement: 'the general size and disposition of Warsaw Pact forces, as well as their organization and armaments, can be monitored with considerable confidence. Additionally, in a major crisis, our capability is sufficient to detect rather promptly a major mobilization and movement by Warsaw Pact forces to a war footing'. (Cited in *F.A.S. Public Interest Report,* Feb. 1988, p. 14). It should be noted that the Report took for granted a requirement of unit counting and appropriate definitions which had not been agreed upon. The Report indicated that it was the US capabilities which could cope with the problem. Extending such adequate capabilities by including other allies through verification arrangements represented another political problem.

[25] *Washington Quarterly,* winter 1989, p. 190.

to be frozen or reduced as well as the opposition to providing a necessary detailed data exchange doomed any compliance criteria to failure.

III. The CFE Negotiation

The mandate

In January 1989 NATO and WTO negotiators reached an agreement on a mandate for the new conventional arms control negotiations. The WTO also agreed to leave the problem of reducing tactical nuclear weapons for separate talks. The negotiations were to cover the land-based conventional armed forces, which include conventional armaments and equipment, of the then 23 participating states within the territory of the participants in Europe from the Atlantic to the Urals. Naval forces and chemical and nuclear weapons would not be included, but dual-capable armaments would be covered by the negotiations because of their *conventional* capability.

Although the results of the negotiations were to be determined only by the participating states, it was agreed that they would hold regular meetings with the 12 neutral and non-aligned European countries to exchange views and information.

The mandate limited the outline for exchange of information and verification to broad, but important, issues:

Compliance with the provisions of any agreement shall be verified through an effective and strict verification regime which, among other things, will include on-site inspections as a matter of right and exchanges of information.

Information shall be exchanged in sufficient detail so as to allow a meaningful comparison of the capabilities of the forces involved. Information shall also be exchanged in sufficient detail so as to provide a basis for the verification of compliance.

The specific modalities for verification and the exchange of information, including the degree of detail of the information and the order of its exchange, shall be agreed at the negotiation proper.[26]

The opening proposals

NATO presented proposals aimed at eliminating WTO superiority in tanks, artillery and armoured personnel carriers and specified overall limits for each category (40 000, 33 000 and 56 000, respectively), as well as national limits for any one country within each alliance (12 000, 10 000 and 16 500). It also wanted limits for each category in overlapping sub-zones in the ATTU zone. No one country would be permitted to have more than 30 per cent of the combined total for both alliances in these categories. Active weapons deployed by each side on allied territory would be limited to 3200 tanks, 1700 artillery pieces and 6000 armoured troop carriers.

NATO's proposals were based on several key concepts:

[26] Note 23.

1. Symmetry, or parity, and within the CFE agenda, the rule of 'sufficiency', whereby sub-limits were to be incorporated for military potentials in Europe by the biggest member of each alliance.

2. Stability, which would not be automatically guaranteed by symmetry.

3. Transparency and confidence, which would also be dealt with by the separate CSBM Negotiations.

The proposals did not include manpower, helicopters and combat aircraft and omitted the setting of a time-scale for reductions.[27]

The Warsaw Pact supported limits for the same categories without mentioning absolute figures for each limit and in addition included limits on combat aircraft, helicopters and personnel. It planned to implement reductions in three phases: first, reductions of force levels to 10–15 per cent below the lower level in each category, this phase lasting two to three years; further reductions by 25 per cent on both sides followed by a conceptual restructuring along strictly defensive lines in a third phase. The WTO also proposed a 'corridor' of reduced armaments along the line of direct contact between the two alliances. It envisaged cutting forces to equal ceilings by 1997.

Initial positions on verification

Positions on the objectives of and requirements for verification were to be determined by the positions on arms control and reduction measures and basic approaches.

Having agreed on the mandate, NATO and WTO negotiators presented official position papers in early March 1989 in which different accents on verification and verification-related tasks could be noted. The NATO paper included verification in the package 'Measures for Stability, Verification and Non-Circumvention', which specifically addressed the need for:

• stabilizing measures: To buttress the resulting reductions in force levels in the ATTU area. These could include measures of transparency, notification and constraint applied to the deployment, movement, storage and levels of readiness of conventional armed forces which include conventional armaments and equipment.

• verification arrangements: To include the exchange of detailed data about forces and deployments, with the right to conduct on-site inspection, as well as other measures designed to provide assurance of compliance with the agreed provision.

• non-circumvention provisions: *Inter alia*, to ensure that the manpower and equipment withdrawn from any one area do not have adverse security implications for any participant.

• provision for temporarily exceeding the limits . . . for prenotified exercises. [28]

---

[27] Lunn, J., 'The Conventional Forces in Europe Talks', Background Paper No. 241, House of Commons Library, 9 Feb. 1990, p. 7.

[28] *Negotiations on Conventional Armed Forces in Europe*, position paper provided by the delegations of Belgium, Canada, Denmark, the FRG, France, Greece, Iceland, Italy, Portugal, Spain, Turkey, the UK and the USA, Vienna, 6 Mar. 1989; *Arms Control Reporter*, 1989, sheet 407.D.28.

In the WTO paper verification issues were presented in a separate provision:

1. The participating States will agree on the exchange of data regarding manpower strength, number of conventional armaments and deployment of military formations and on their verification, including through on-site inspections.

2. Provision would be made for the establishment of a comprehensive and effective system of verification of compliance with agreements, including land and air on-site inspections without the right to refuse. Checkpoints would be created to monitor entry/exit both along and inside the reduced-armament-level strips (zones) and in the reduction area (at railway stations, junctions, airfields, ports). Such technical means of verification as artificial Earth satellites, aircraft, helicopters, ground automatic recording systems, including those developed through international co-operation, could also be used for the purposes of verification.

3. There would be verification of the process of reduction, elimination (dismantlement, conversion) and storage of armaments, of the disbandment of formations and units, of non-excess of the strength of armed forces and the number of armaments, and of the activities of the troops remaining after reductions.

4. An international verification (consultative) commission made up of representatives of the participating States would be set up and given wide powers (observation, inspection, consideration of disputes, etc.).

5. A prominent part in the implementation of verification and control measures should be played by the highest representative bodies—parliaments, national assemblies and the Supreme Soviet—which could act as guarantors of the reductions and redeployment of the armed forces and conventional armaments of the appropriate countries. Questions related to these decisions could be discussed within the framework of foreign and military committees and be reflected in appropriate statements to be made on behalf of the parliaments.[29]

The NATO position paper gave more detailed guidelines on information exchange, proposing that holdings of main battle tanks, armoured troop carriers and artillery pieces would be notified each year, disaggregated down to battalion level. This measure would also apply to personnel in both combat and combat support units. Any change of notified unit structures above battalion level, or any measure resulting in an increase of personnel strength in such units, would be subject to notification, on a basis to be determined in the course of the negotiations.

Discussions of official data

Agreement on data remained one of the most important and complex issues facing the negotiators in Vienna. Agreement on actual totals of personnel and now of armaments as well turned out to be less challenging in the short term than reaching agreement on counting rules and definitions used by either side. Not

---

[29] *Conceptual Framework of an Agreement on Conventional Armed Forces in Europe*, position paper submitted by the delegations of Bulgaria, Czechoslovakia, the German Democratic Republic, Hungary, Poland, Romania and the Union of Soviet Socialist Republics, Vienna, Mar. 1989.

incidentally, from the start the negotiators decided to work on the issue through exchange of 'non-papers' containing definitions of the various systems.

One important aspect of this work regarded the problem of circumvention through modernization. The circumvention of limitations through technological development was considered a serious issue for the future. Work within the alliances had already demonstrated the problem of formulating definitions that covered all types of weapon system. Thus, the task of defining a given system for identification of key characteristics on which constraints could be imposed became one of the central elements of the negotiations. Behind this, the challenge of at least managing technological pace by, among other things, verification activities, emerged.

Nevertheless, the negotiators did have a certain basis for further work on definitions. The data declared shortly before the CFE Negotiation provided important clues for analysis. NATO's unclassified assessment of the NATO/WTO balance of conventional forces in the ATTU area, which was released in November 1988,[30] showed some remarkable differences with previous assessments of 1982 and 1984.[31] In contrast with the earlier ones, the document covered only numerical comparisons of manpower, units and weapon systems, and seemed to be aimed at providing a guideline for future data exchange within the framework of negotiations, ignoring wide-ranging issues such as problems of modernization and reinforcement, regional considerations, and nuclear deterrence and the nuclear equation.

However, it did introduce figures for armoured infantry fighting vehicles and for 'other' armoured vehicles, such as light tanks, armoured personnel carriers, armoured command vehicles and military support carriers, which were given separately. NATO and WTO armoured vehicle launched bridges, often overlooked, were also included. For the first time French and Spanish forces were covered—although not part of the alliance's integrated military structure France and Spain participated fully in NATO's High-Level Task Force work to formulate an alliance position in the talks—and data on Greek and Turkish potentials were presented more carefully than before.

The document concentrated on counting conventional forces in units, as opposed to giving total inventories. For ground forces, the definition 'in units' applied to both fully and partially manned combat units and separated NATO armaments in storage and war reserve stocks. The latter assets were presented as an alliance-wide aggregate by type. As for air forces, the definition covered operational, front-line NATO squadrons and WTO regiments, excluding both combat aircraft in storage and combat-capable training aircraft.

The WTO data presented in January 1989 differed not only in numbers, but also in the method of assessment.[32] They included naval forces, thus attempting

---

[30] NATO, *Conventional Forces in Europe: The Facts,* NATO Press Service, Brussels, Nov. 1988.

[31] *Armed Forces Journal International,* Jan. 1989, pp. 47, 52.

[32] Ministers of Defence of the Warsaw Treaty Member States, 'On the relative strength of the armed forces and armaments of the Warsaw Treaty Organization and the North Atlantic Treaty Organization in Europe and adjacent water areas', *Pravda,* 30 Jan. 1989.

to give a more comprehensive picture of the military potential of both alliances, and data on civil and territorial defence forces, armaments and equipment for dual-based formations, reserves and cadre units. The two documents gave different definitions of the various weapon systems. For example, the WTO counted all tanks in the 'tank' category while NATO preferred to limit the category to main battle tanks; the WTO 'anti-tank systems' covered only anti-tank missile systems, whereas NATO also considered anti-tank artillery and recoilless rifles; the WTO divided combat aircraft of battlefield (tactical) aviation into strike aircraft and air defence fighters, whereas NATO put them into the same category.

Analysing these and other differences, some Soviet experts stressed that they reflected the need to define the cardinal criterion of the military potentials of both sides. The most important criterion to determine the potentials, they continued, is 'the number of combat-ready army divisions which are the main tactical formations capable of fighting both independently and within a larger formation. It should be borne in mind that there are three categories (A, B and C) of division in the WTO countries, subdivided according to their combat preparedness and readily available personnel and equipment'.[33] Comparison of combat-ready divisions with those of limited readiness is difficult, however, because it should involve such elements as specific conflict scenarios or factors relating to real combat experience. There was also a need to define criteria to compare different categories of combat-ready divisions of both sides, not to mention the large amounts of armaments and equipment stored for reserve units, geostrategic factors, quality of equipment, training, and so on.

One immediate problem of approaches to the data for the CFE Negotiation concerned regional arrangements within the ATTU zone. It reflected the different operational objectives of both groups of states and the complexity of combining the various factors involved (stationed and regional limits, active and stored equipment, etc.). NATO was particularly concerned about forward-deployed forces and the possibility of surprise attack. Besides its own vision of a stationing rule and proposals for stabilizing measures, its attention focused on constraining Soviet second-echelon and mobilization potential; in this respect the WTO totals for Central Europe in its regional approach were considered too high. For its part the WTO was anxious to constrain FRG forces and US Pre-positioned Material Configured to Unit Sets (POMCUS) equipment which were not affected by the NATO stationing rule.

The asymmetry of objectives also made storage a problem. The WTO was not pleased with the NATO distinction between stored and active equipment in

---

[33] USSR Academy of Sciences, Institute of World Economy and International Relations, *Disarmament and Security: 1988–1989 IMEMO Yearbook* (Novosti Press Agency: Moscow, 1989), p. 255. Category A divisions are fully combat-ready and largely deployed in the first echelons. Divisions of Category B are manned at 50–75% and equipped at 100%. They are capable of performing limited combat missions, with a 10-day time span required for full combat readiness. They are normally used in the second echelons (reserves). Divisions of Category C are manned at approximately 20% and equipped at 100%. They need 30 days for full combat readiness. As a rule they form strategic reserves; *IMEMO Yearbook*, pp. 255–56. In the West they are also referred to as Categories I, II and III.

its regional ceilings, which would permit a substantial amount of stored equipment in Central Europe; but NATO wanted to protect the US POMCUS stocks while not creating incentives for the USSR to construct Central European storage sites of its own.

Continuing disputes on the above problems not only shed light on possible priorities for a verification regime, but also indicated the amount of work which would be needed in resolving differences.

Early assessment

The first months of talks resulted in substantial progress on a number of issues. Both sides agreed on the categories to be reduced: tanks, artillery, armoured troop carriers, combat aircraft, armed helicopters, and active-duty ground and air force personnel.[34] They also agreed on reductions to equal levels of 20 000 heavy main battle tanks and 28 000 armoured troop carriers as well as limiting the armaments of Soviet forces in Eastern Europe to the equivalent of the combined holdings of NATO countries with forces stationed on the territory of other allies, mainly in the FRG. At this point, the USSR also still agreed to the figure of 30 per cent proposed by NATO for single-country holdings.[35] The sides were still apart on artillery (NATO wanted 16 500 per alliance and the WTO 24 000 by the end of round II of the negotiations in July 1989).[36]

In fact the reliability of the data provided by both sides at the end of 1988 and in early 1989 depended substantially on definitions and counting rules as well. Counting rules led to disagreements not only between the alliances, but also within NATO. Many senior NATO officials expressed doubts about the original NATO data since they could be subject to numerous interpretations. Privately, a military official told the defence ministers meeting in Brussels in June 1989 that there was a need to have a new official document with more credible data.[37] One of the divisive issues concerned methods to count aircraft and helicopters immediately after the US President's acceptance of the idea of including these categories in NATO proposals. For example, several countries resisted categorizing certain types as transport helicopters because they could be fitted with guns and rockets, or had once been so outfitted. France did not favour including training aircraft that could also be used in combat.[38]

[34] In May 1989 the US President abandoned his earlier opposition to the inclusion of combat helicopters and aircraft in the negotiations if the WTO accepted NATO's position on tanks, armoured vehicles and artillery. He called for, among other things, the reduction of attack and assault helicopters and all land-based aircraft 15 per cent below the level of the lower side and the acceleration of the CFE timetable to conclude an agreement within six months or a year and implementing it by 1992–93, four years ahead of the WTO's schedule. See *New York Times*, 30 May 1989.

[35] See Sharp, J. M. O., 'Conventional arms control in Europe', SIPRI, *SIPRI Yearbook 1991: World Armaments and Disarmament* (Oxford University Press: Oxford, 1991), p. 413. In round VI in early 1990, after agreeing to withdraw from Hungary and Czechoslovakia, they would insist on a higher figure (35–40%). See *Arms Control Reporter*, 1990, sheet 407.B.346.

[36] See Sharp, J. M. O., 'Conventional arms control in Europe', SIPRI, *SIPRI Yearbook 1990: World Armaments and Disarmament* (Oxford University Press: Oxford, 1990), table 13.6, p. 488.

[37] *Arms Control Reporter*, 1989, sheet 407.B.201.

[38] *Washington Post*, 2 July 1989.

The WTO insisted on excluding air defence aircraft. In efforts to meet NATO's concerns about this problem, Soviet representative Oleg Grinevsky, emphasizing that air defence aircraft 'have recognizable external features which make it possible to distinguish between them and the aircraft of front (tactical) aviation both from outside, that is by their silhouette, and by their weapons and equipment', stated: 'We are prepared to provide possibilities for the Western experts to see that it is really so. In particular, it can be done through on-site monitoring and appropriate notifications. Naturally, inspectors would be given the right of free access to the aircraft, of their examination including their weapon systems'.[39] In other words, the Soviet side, which had substantial numbers of 'air defence aircraft', invited other states to implement OSI procedures including examining types of armaments which would be excluded from the treaty.

Priorities of verification: some approaches

A member of the Canadian delegation expressed the priorities as follows. 'The West opposed a formal data exchange and verification at this point [i.e., two months after negotiations had started] . . . Instead data should be dealt with informally in creating the definitions and counting rules.' Canada wanted to count and verify only the residual levels after reductions.[40]

Another approach was presented during the first round of the negotiations by a Hungarian official. He advocated early data exchange and verification arrangements on their own merits—the same merits that the West saw in transparency. But he acknowledged that 'no enthusiasm for the idea exists in the two alliances'. Taking this into account, Hungary would try instead to link data exchange with the development of the categories of armaments and equipment: once a category was developed, the relevant data could be exchanged. If the data coincided, or at least no militarily significant difference appeared, no verification would be necessary. If differences occurred, two options would be available: to accept the temporary existence of differences and verify the remaining forces after reductions, or to verify the numbers at that point.[41]

The idea of concentrating verification activities on the post-reduction period had been further elaborated for counting specific categories not only before these categories had been agreed upon, but in some cases even before their inclusion was accepted by the other side. For example, a few days before President Bush gave a green light to the inclusion of 'all land-based attack aircraft' and 'attack and assault, or transport helicopters' in the NATO proposal on 29 May 1989, Soviet delegate General V. M. Tatarnikov insisted on verification of aircraft limits which could cover three main components: reciprocal information on strike aircraft and the nature of their activities; comprehensive use of NTM; and OSI with the use of inspectors. He specified that: 'After the cuts in

[39] *Arms Control Reporter*, 1989, sheet 407.B.234.
[40] *Arms Control Reporter*, 1989, sheets 407.B.158–59.
[41] *Arms Control Reporter*, 1989, sheet 407.B.160.

strike aircraft and combat helicopters are completed the sides should exchange information on these means . . . Bearing in mind the high mobility of aircraft, we should clearly not rule out the possibility of several inspection groups working in various areas at the same time'.[42]

The need to verify reductions was addressed in the context of stability. A Hungarian official stated that instability might arise if one side reduced before the other; if stability was to be taken seriously, some verification would be needed during the reduction period.[43]

Papers of autumn 1989

In September 1989 NATO produced an important list outlining collateral measures.[44] It included four specific measures: on information exchange, stabilization measures, verification and non-circumvention. Several points were of particular interest from the verification perspective.

Information by each participating state was to be provided on the command organization of its land, air and air defence forces in the ATTU zone down to the battalion and squadron level. The normal peacetime locations and holdings of TLE were to be supplied for the following: headquarters, components and units with TLE and/or AVLBs; monitored storage depots; non-unit assigned TLE not in monitored storage; other sites where TLE may be present on a regular basis, for example, repair depots, training areas, and so on; AVLBs in monitored storage and elsewhere; and equipment not subject to treaty limitation, for example, produced but not in service with national forces, or equipment held by paramilitary forces. Locations and personnel levels would be given for low-strength units, and for US and Soviet ground and air force personnel stationed on allied territory. Notification of the permanent reorganization of existing unit structures or the introduction of new units into the area of application would be required 42 days in advance. Participants would have to report changes of 10 per cent or more in unit strength or TLE holdings in the preceding annual exchange or as they occurred.

The verification regime should be capable of providing confidence that treaty provisions are being complied with, deterring violations of those provisions and, failing that, providing timely detection of the infractions. Accordingly, the tasks would be to validate the baseline data, monitor reductions and confirm compliance with the treaty after reductions. OSI were to be implemented to perform these tasks. At declared sites, inspections could be requested at short notice with no right of refusal. Quotas would be set in terms of the number of days each participant must permit inspection teams on its territory. The intensity of inspections would be greater in the first months of the treaty to validate

[42] *Arms Control Reporter,* 1989, sheet 407.B.174.

[43] *Arms Control Reporter,* 1989, sheet 407.B.160.

[44] *Measures of Information Exchange, Stabilization, Verification and Non-circumvention,* Proposal submitted by the delegations of Belgium, Canada, Denmark, France, the FRG, Greece, Iceland, Italy, Luxembourg, Netherlands, Norway, Portugal, Spain, Turkey, the UK and the USA, Vienna, 21 Sep. 1989.

the baseline data; during this period, the armed forces of the participants would not be required to stand down. The inspector would have the right to determine the sites visited and the number of days spent on the inspected state's territory, but the time spent at any one site would be limited, as would the number of teams accepted on the inspected state's territory at any given time. At non-declared sites, the inspected state would have the right of delay and ultimate refusal of a request. Inspections would be limited by quota.

Another task would involve monitoring the destruction of equipment and the withdrawal of Soviet and US personnel. Equipment in excess of treaty limits was to be destroyed according to an agreed timetable, with prior notification and OSI allowed without quotas or right of refusal. In addition to OSI, provision would be made for aerial inspection and NTM. 'Tagging' of combat aircraft and combat helicopters was also a possibility. Other measures included the creation of a joint consultative group, and general considerations regarding inspection rights, the composition of inspection teams, the transfer of unused quotas and limits to inspections accepted from the same participant.

In October 1989 the WTO tabled two working papers, one on stabilization and another on information exchange and verification measures. The proposals for data exchange differed from the Western proposals in only three respects. The WTO suggested that data be provided for land, air and air defence forces down to the regimental rather than battalion or squadron level. Whereas the West called for information on all non-naval combat aircraft, the East preferred information on front/tactical aviation only. No reference was made to the need for data on equipment not covered by the treaty, for example, equipment for export or held by paramilitary forces. It recommended that armed forces personnel levels be supplied for all participants rather than only Soviet and US stationed forces and units with TLE.

Verification measures differed only slightly. The WTO called for treaty-limited aircraft to be placed in the open for inspection upon request. Inspection teams would have the right of free access to aircraft and their weapon systems at inspected airfields. In addition, the WTO reintroduced the idea of entry/exit points established along and inside the area of application. Finally, provision was made for verifying temporary breaches of the limits because of routine replacement and other reasons.[45]

Several perceived weaknesses were pointed out in the Western proposals of September 1989. First, no relationship was foreseen with the existing verification system for CSBMs. The existence of two competing systems with a different number of participants in the same area of application would lead to a waste of money and manpower. Second, the proposals considered verification basically a national responsibility, and while this might be true for final judgements about non-compliance, it excluded the possibility of institutionalizing a multilateral verification system. Third, the proposals allowed for the possibility of refusing challenge inspection at suspected non-declared sites or installations.

[45] See Moore (note 14), pp. 14–15.

Fourth, provisions for on-site monitoring of production facilities for TLE were excluded. Finally, there was no mention of a pre-negotiation of the verification regime. In this case, the verification regime might not be operationally ready by the time of implementing a treaty.[46]

Nevertheless, the NATO paper was an impressive result of an intensive analytical effort completed within a short period of time. These preparatory efforts proved at least one thing: with a firm and directed political decision to accelerate the talks, many verification aspects long debated in the alliance could be resolved.

Divisive issues

In 1989 the USA continued insisting on monitoring production within the ATTU zone, and monitoring all of the arms shipments flowing into and out of the zone. Some other NATO states, Britain and France in particular, opposed such intrusive measures. The difference in positions was explained by one US official: 'Those who would suffer the most from Soviet inspections have taken one point of view, while those who have no territory inside the zone obviously find it easier to take another point of view'.[47]

This position explained the US concern about arguments on the part of some allies in favour of monitoring Soviet production beyond the Urals, or at least a guarantee that Soviet production would not shift to the ATTU zone. Officials saw a possibility that such a guarantee would encourage Soviet monitoring of US production and naval activities.[48]

In September the USA and the UK agreed to skirt the problem of production monitoring, and a few days later at the NATO meeting in Brussels production monitoring was side-stepped. So-called 'non-circumvention' measures were designed to prevent either side from building up forces just outside the treaty area for a surprise attack. West European allies initially wanted to mention Soviet territory behind the Urals, where aircraft might be massed without breaching the treaty; but the USA insisted on watering down this provision, believing that it could open the door to Soviet demands for constraints outside the treaty zone.

Geographical aspects inherent in the negotiations objectively highlighted the different problems concerning circumvention. If implemented, President Bush's 1989 initiative, for example, would have covered only 10 per cent of US combat aircraft and 30 per cent of US tanks—those based permanently in Europe. The plan would cut only 95 of 15 600 tanks in the US global inventory, and 120 of the 7100 aircraft. At the same time, the mandate applied to 11 of 16 military

[46] van der Graaf, H. J., 'Prospects and possible outcome of the conventional arms negotiations (CSBM's/CFE)', ed. H. G. Brauch, *Verification and Arms Control: Implications for European Security,* Results of the Sixth International AFES-PRESS Conference, Part II: Selected Papers, AFES PRESS, Mosbach, 1990, p. 83.

[47] *Washington Post,* 6 Sep. 1989, p. 1.

[48] *Arms Control Reporter,* 1989, sheet 407.B.219.

districts in the USSR, and about 70 per cent of total Soviet ground and air forces.[49] But a number of armaments and pieces of equipment could have been withdrawn beyond the Urals—this had actually been taking place before the Treaty was signed.

The other obstacle might be in the US position which did not want any measures to cover activities on its territory—measures which, however, were logically to be considered if provisions with regard to massing Soviet potential beyond the Urals were considered. As for the entry/exit issue, the USA did not want transit troops covered. It might also plan a temporary increase in the ceilings, in case of military exercises and transit movements. If this issue were included in the CFE Negotiation, a possibility to cover it in the CSBM talks could emerge. In the latter case, the USA would also have to notify non-aligned countries.

Nevertheless, the WTO position on entry/exit points was closer to the US stance than to that of some US allies. In the October 1989 working papers the WTO put forward the idea of limiting transfers of (unspecified) treaty-limited categories into or through the zone as well as of movements and concentration of troops 'across the borders of regions determined by treaty' ensured by 'agreed temporary or permanent entry/exit points'. More specifically, 'to verify the reductions, the achieving of agreed levels, consequent compliance with them as well as movements (transfers) of troops there shall be established entry/exit points both along and inside the regions and in general in the area of application, at railway junctions, ports, air force bases, and airfields'.[50]

Although the papers did not address arms storage and production limits—as NATO had expected—they did cover some touchy issues. One of the measures required ample notifications when armaments and troops were moved into and out of agreed areas in Europe and through designated locations. But the issue of notification of forces being withdrawn from the treaty zone was another cause of dispute within NATO. Britain and France, which had military responsibilities in other parts of the world, objected to having to alert the Soviet Union in the event they needed to take forces from Europe for a military operation in the Third World, for example.

The WTO proposal also described stringent measures to verify limits on aircraft. It stated that 'inspection teams shall have the right of free access to aircraft . . . including their weapons systems' and may use 'optical and electronic means of observation'. This was actually an invitation for NATO to be able to distinguish between aircraft outfitted for defensive rather than offensive missions, but it addressed a point on which NATO countries had not reached agreement. The NATO plan did not contain any requirement for continuous OSI, although the USA had urged allies to accept near-constant monitoring of key weapon transfer points.[51]

[49] Leavitt, R., 'Bush's chintzy offer at Vienna', *Bulletin of the Atomic Scientists*, vol. 45, no. 8 (Oct. 1989), p. 13.

[50] *Arms Control Reporter*, 1989, sheet 407.D.43.

[51] *Washington Post*, 20 Oct. 1989, p. 36.

These two elements—entry/exit points and measures to verify limits on aircraft—were more intrusive in the WTO verification package. Nevertheless, the proposals closely resembled each other. The WTO accepted a NATO proposal to establish quotas for inspecting designated military installations with no right of refusal to host such inspections. At the same time, it did not react to the idea of including provisions for inspection of sites not designated in the Treaty. The provisions on data exchange were very similar, including requirements to describe the location, command structure and equipment of ground force units. As described above, the differences applied mainly to the level of precision as the WTO wanted to catalogue force structures down to the regiment level while NATO preferred the battalion level.

The WTO presented the idea of monitoring the elimination of armaments and suggested that states parties inspect facilities being dismantled and so-called 'temporary armament storage sites'. The latter could serve as monitored 'way-stations' while the task was being implemented. If the West could observe the storage of equipment to be destroyed, it might be more enthusiastic about starting follow-on negotiations on conventional and tactical nuclear weapons before a CFE agreement was fully implemented.[52]

Important, although often overlooked, provisions of both sides related to stabilizing measures in their packages. The division lay primarily in the scale of exercises: NATO proposed that exercises of more than 40 000 troops be permitted once every two years, while the WTO insisted on extending this limit to three years and placing restrictions on the frequency of exercising with 25 000–40 000 troops. Among WTO stabilizing measures it is worth mentioning those which actually aimed at broadening the CFE agenda. Besides calls for exchanging data on military spending, the Pact suggested 'limitations of military activities and the number of highly mobile attack formations and units . . . in forward groupings'.

Further progress

Production monitoring

In early 1990 the USA finally dropped the idea of production and checkpoint monitoring. It had proposed that states parties reveal how many and what type of weapons were produced at a plant, as well as their destination. Once weapons were manufactured, they would be placed in the open so that satellites could observe them. Instead of these measures, which some NATO countries had rejected, the USA put forward another approach which included notification of shipments of weapons exceeding a certain threshold. Other nations could observe the shipment, by air or by ground inspections. According to a US official, air observations might be sufficient for shipments by rail, but not for those by sea.[53]

[52] *BASIC Reports From Vienna*, 6 Nov. 1989, p. 2.
[53] *Arms Control Reporter*, 1990, sheets 407.B.295 and 407.B.332.

As part of the compromise, NATO agreed on a kind of voluntary notification of some shipments and production, without any direct monitoring, and to table the proposal. A US official admitted that it would be possible to cheat under such a proposal, but insisted that US intelligence could detect covert deployment of forces large enough to be militarily significant:

In some circumstances, this could be handfuls of tanks. In others, it could be a somewhat higher number.

The United States might have been able to have an agreement . . . with the Soviet Union, but we would have [needed] . . . different allies. That [first] set of proposals [production and checkpoint monitoring] went absolutely nowhere.

We had to give up our original idea, which was to put a fence around Europe . . . and treat tens of thousands of [conventional] weapons like a small number of strategic systems—subject to absolute, round-the-clock monitoring with spy satellites or on-site inspections.[54]

The change of the US position on production monitoring directly influenced its stance on verification requirements as a whole. US representative James Woolsey summed up the change:

I think the philosophy of verification now is less one of trying to calculate each and every tank that enters, departs from, and is manufactured in Europe . . . It's more generally a philosophy of having an accurate yardstick of what is supposed to be at each declared site, so that you have a right to challenge and to have it explained if something more is there. We should have a very solid exchange of data and verification of that data and on-site observation of destruction, which is in many ways the key item for the West. Then, in the long-term steady state, we would rely on a combination of national technical means and the right to on-site inspections at declared sites—all sites where treaty-limited equipment is located. We would also have the right to challenge inspections which can be turned down, but you would have to give a satisfactory reason for this rejection.

I believe there should also be some provision for cooperative aerial inspection within the framework of CFE . . . I think one can also try to obtain some cooperative measures to enhance the effectiveness of aerial inspection and national technical means.[55]

Another reservation with regard to production concerned confidence-building measures rather than verification activities. In the March 1989 CSBM proposal, the West had already suggested the notification of the introduction of 'major conventional weapon systems' into the CSBM zone.

Objects of verification

Rejection of some intrusive methods of verification by NATO did not change its priority of making a single TLE item an object of verification. The definition

---

[54] *Arms Control Reporter*, 1990, sheet 407.B.340.
[55] 'Ambassador R. James Woolsey: closing in on a CFE treaty', *Arms Control Today*, vol. 20, no. 3 (Apr. 1990), p. 7.

of an object of verification was one of the main differences between the NATO draft treaty articles on verification and the exchange of information of 22 February 1990 and the WTO response of 12 April 1990. The NATO draft also included a proposed text for an inspection protocol.

Among other things, the NATO draft defined the rights and limitations of inspection teams, the process for listing sites at which TLE were held, such as unit garrisons, storage depots and training centres, and the procedures for exchanging information on those sites. The inspection protocols did not specify the number of annual inspections permitted, but this issue was considered as very difficult to resolve.[56]

The protocols insisted on verification by sites (the WTO also wanted a commitment by the USA and Canada to receive inspections). The WTO preferred to base the number of inspections on the number of military units, storage sites and training camps in each country. Western negotiators objected to this since force structures could be changed and a country could lower the number of inspections it hosted by consolidating its units, for example.

With regard to this aspect of the WTO approach one interesting provision dating from its October 1989 package was almost ignored in subsequent discussions. The initiative aimed at barring construction of new military bases or the expansion of existing bases within the ATTU area. This contradicted the NATO preference to give both sides the flexibility to construct or modify bases as they consolidated residual military forces. (Another initiative required an exchange of reports on restructuring the remaining military forces to reduce their offensive capability, but the US officials said they did not expect to address this until the treaty was fully implemented.[57])

Inspections

While adopting the 'military significance' criteria for verification and insisting on a 'TLE-by-TLE' approach, NATO also preferred a complex formula to count the number of inspection days. The formula presented the main advance in the NATO protocol. According to the protocol, each country within the reduction area would be obliged to accept a minimum of three inspection days per year. Beyond this, each country must accept one inspection day for every 100 combat aircraft and combat helicopters deployed, and one inspection day for every 300 tanks, ACVs and artillery pieces deployed on its territory. Also, the draft protocol included one inspection day for every 50 000 square kilometres of territory within the reduction area. This requirement specifically addressed the USSR with its large area of reduction, but left the territory of the USA and Canada untouched.

[56] A member of the Canadian delegation explained that the issue concerned two traditional questions: 'How many people do you want crawling around your country? And, how much do you want to know about the other country?' See *Defense & Disarmament Alternatives*, Mar. 1990, p. 7.

[57] *Arms Control Reporter*, 1989, sheets 407.D.43–44.

According to Eastern calculations, this meant 900 days for the WTO passive inspection quota and 400 for the NATO quota. The US Arms Control Association presented slightly different figures: the NATO countries collectively would have to accept roughly 350 inspections a year and the WTO countries roughly 800, until reductions were completed; thereafter NATO would accept about 325 a year, and the WTO about 370 a year.[58]

Closing the gap on verification provisions reflected a positive process of reaching compromises on several important and relevant problems. When NATO presented its proposals in February the two sides were close to an agreement on definitions for tanks and ACVs. The most difficult problem had been over where to draw the line between the two categories and how to structure any limits on sub-categories of these systems. The positions on aircraft were also closer than before. Both sides agreed on how to distinguish equipment in storage from items associated with active units.

One interesting development took place in early spring. Because of the converging positions on broad and major issues, attention had been focused on minor, technical arrangements, including aspects of verification. In this situation, along with the increasing involvement of technical experts, the pace of the talks slowed down, posing the danger of endless discussions of apparently unimportant questions. For example, experts debated over the parameters for equipment in storage and argued over the height requirements for fences at depot facilities. (The Eastern side favoured a minimum height of 150 cm, while NATO demanded 175 cm.) This fixation with details, however, held the danger of undermining major compromises, such as the definition of a tank.[59]

Concluding efforts

The largest part of the last-minute negotiations before Treaty signature was devoted to the verification regime and to issues of destruction. There was still a considerable gap between Soviet and US positions on the quota of OSI that a country would be required to host since the USA demanded roughly twice as many inspections of Soviet territory. Both sides had still been using different methods of calculating the number of OSI that a country was required to host (passive quota) and disagreed over the unit of measurement to be used to determine the quota. NATO maintained its negative attitude towards the Soviet concept of objects of verification on the grounds that the USSR wanted to protect its bases from full inspection by dividing them into 'objects'. Its officials also complained that the OOV being designated by the USSR were too small and numerous. At the same time the US requests could lead to roughly twice as many inspections on Soviet territory.

During discussions of new proposals tabled by NATO and the USSR in August 1990 the Soviet representative, Oleg Grinevsky, referring to the

[58] *Vienna Fax*, 21 Mar. 1990, p. 1.
[59] 'CFE talks lose steam', *BASIC Reports from Vienna*, no. 7 (11 Apr. 1990), p. 1.

estimates of Soviet experts, noted that inspection quotas covering some 7–8 per cent of the objects to be verified could assure reliability and sufficiency. But in an effort to meet NATO limits[60] he proposed: baseline data verification (120 days) covering up to 15 per cent of the OOV; verification during the reduction period covering 10 per cent of the OOV; intensive verification of residual levels of armaments and equipment covering up to 15 per cent of the OOV within 120 days; and consequent verification of compliance with the treaty envisaging annual verification of up to 10 per cent of the OOV.[61]

The situation became more complicated as a result of developments within the WTO. On 20 September 1990 Grinevsky proposed that if a country leaves an alliance other countries could fill that country's quota of TLE. Earlier he stated that 'with the unification of Germany, its inclusion in NATO, and the withdrawal of Soviet troops from Central Europe, the situation in this region having key importance for the European security is changing radically'.[62] This position was fraught with the potential for further divisions on verification, including quotas for OSI.

However, during the Washington meeting in early October 1990 between James Baker and Eduard Shevardnadze the two countries resolved differences over the conceptual framework for verification. The following numbers worked out by them were subsequently accepted by their allies:

20 per cent for baseline inspections;
10 per cent for reduction inspections;
20 per cent for the six months to monitor residual levels;
15 per cent for the indefinite future.

At the October meeting in Washington the Soviet side also explained its approach to the object of verification: 'anything contiguous to an object can be inspected, except for another object [which would count as a separate inspection under the quota] . . . [Y]ou can look at the whole site (or division) within which a regiment lies, but you have to use another inspection to look at another regiment'.[63] The USSR continued to insist on fewer inspections than the other countries would have liked. The issues of what would be inspected and the number of inspections allowed were, however, resolved but the Europeans, both NATO and other non-WTO countries, were unhappy with US acceptance of Soviet proposals to reduce inspection requirements and of what constitute objects of verification.[64]

Grinevsky revealed in August 1990 that while a three-year destruction period had been agreed upon for artillery, aircraft and helicopters, more time was

[60] According to the Soviet military official General Tatarnikov, NATO wanted to review up to 35–40% of the Soviet installations liable for inspections each year. See Arms Control Reporter, 1990, sheet 407.B.396.
[61] Arms Control Reporter, 1990, sheet 407.B.388.
[62] BASIC Reports From Vienna, 25 Sep. 1990, p. 1.
[63] Arms Control Reporter, 1990, sheet 407.B.396.
[64] See Sharp (note 35), p. 420.

needed for tanks and ACVs. By early October, however, Baker and Shevard-nadze had agreed on single-country conversion limits for these latter two TLE items.[65]

In August 1990 Baker and Shevardnadze agreed to exclude limits on man-power from the CFE Treaty. This was confirmed in October with the under-standing that this aspect be dealt with in the next stage of the negotiations.[66] October also saw the issues surrounding NATO's POMCUS stocks settled—limits were agreed for active as well as stored TLE.[67] The extremely divisive issue surrounding land-based naval aircraft was overcome by setting both alliance and single-country limits on this type.

This set the stage for the signing of the Treaty on 19 November. The road had been a long and arduous one and the final agreement could be said to have been overtaken by events to some extent. The experience gained in tackling even the thorniest verification issues, however, will remain alongside the Treaty as a lasting legacy for future constructive co-operation.

IV. The CFE-1A Negotiations

The experience of the MBFR talks, although drawn out and often frustrating, has been shown to illuminate many of the key verification issues involved with limiting and reducing numbers of troops and regulating their manner of deployment. It has become apparent for negotiators and experts that verifying the withdrawal and subsequent absence of troops is much more easily handled for relatively large contingents—including equipment—than for thinning out or other less transparent measures. In the case of withdrawal of complete units, for example, all forms of monitoring can be much more effective. This is especially true for NTM, which are of very little use in situations where most of the infrastructure of a particular troop deployment is left intact and only a small fraction of the troops are withdrawn.

The record of the CFE Negotiation shows a dramatic breakthrough in both approaches to arms control priorities and arrangements and verification con-cepts. It gives a guideline to shaping arms control agreements and to formulat-ing the agenda and the terms of an agreement with subsequent linkage to veri-fication arrangements. Any verification scheme must have a definite objective and a measure of flexibility in attaining it.

The analysis of the record of negotiations and proposals also indicates that for effective verification and for easing suspicions it is more appropriate to have a complex agreement covering major military components.

The CFE-1A Negotiations reflected that it is easier to deal with a very touchy and separate component such as military personnel once it is linked with a signed comprehensive agreement, in this case the CFE Treaty. Because the

---

[65] See Sharp (note 35), p. 417.
[66] See Sharp (note 35), p. 416.
[67] See Sharp (note 35), pp. 412–13.

Treaty covered the central militarily significant components it left little room for suspicions about possible non-compliance with the troop levels. In other words the adequate verification regime for the CFE Treaty provides more opportunities to deal with the most difficult verification challenge—compliance with troop levels. In many respects, some of the experts' debates in the past about the problems and priorities of verification have proved justified.

The Negotiations were held in a period when many of the stumbling blocks of the previous talks, including those concerning verification, were vanishing. With the complete withdrawal of the former Soviet forces from Eastern Europe underway, the NATO concerns about how to handle the thinning out of these forces were set aside. Many other problems remained, however, such as verification of force levels and redeployments inside the CIS as well as in the NATO countries.

At the same time, the new military and political situation dictated the need to reconsider the traditional guidelines for the negotiations. This took some time however, and NATO did not table a personnel proposal until July 1991. It was improved by Germany in November. Nevertheless, one of the issues on which there was general agreement almost throughout the CFE-1A talks was that of the verification requirements for personnel ceilings and reductions. In February 1992 several participants (Czechoslovakia, Hungary, Poland, Canada, France, Germany and the UK) agreed on the following in their drafts.[68]

First, the traditional concept of verification could not be applied to manpower. It was considered that one could only speak in terms of an approximate appraisal of the observance of national maximum troop levels. Strict verification of troop levels is impossible even in the new political climate. The USA still maintained, as it had in the MBFR talks, that no-one could verify personnel numbers.[69]

Second, a system of troop assessment must be built into the existing framework of the CFE Treaty, specifically, its protocol on inspections. Among other things, this agreement indicates that the optimal way of verifying troops is to link 'forces' and 'armaments'—an issue long-debated in the past. As a US official said in early 1992, 'when you visit a TLE location, you will not get a muster of troops for counting, but you will be able to sniff around and get a feel for the number of troops present'.[70]

Finally, and correspondingly, it was agreed that troop assessment should not create additional financial or organizational difficulties for any of the participating states parties. Mentioning the CFE-1A talks in 1992, a head of the Russian delegation stated that it is 'better to seek a simpler agreement that would be easier to implement. . . . The main thing is to supplement restrictions on conventional arms and equipment with corresponding restrictions on numerical strength of troops'.[71]

---

[68] *Arms Control Reporter*, 1992, sheets 410.B.17–18.

[69] *Arms Control Reporter*, 1992, sheet 410.B.19.

[70] *Arms Control Reporter*, 1992, sheet 410.B.19.

[71] *Arms Control Reporter*, 1992, sheet 410.B.17.

Table 13. CFE-1A limits on personnel

State party	Troop limit within the area of application
Belarus	100 000
Belgium	70 000
Bulgaria	104 000
Canada	10 660
Czechoslovakia	140 000
Denmark	39 000
France	325 000
Germany	345 000
Greece	158 621
Hungary	100 000
Iceland	0
Italy	315 000
Kazakhstan	0
Luxembourg	900
Netherlands	80 000
Norway	32 000
Poland	234 000
Portugal	75 000
Romania	230 000
Russia	1 450 000
Spain	300 000
Turkey	530 000
Ukraine	450 000
UK	260 000
USA	250 000

Note: Moldova, Georgia, Armenia and Azerbaijan did not present their force levels.

Source: The Concluding Act of the Negotiation on Personnel Strength of Conventional Armed Forces in Europe, Helsinki, 10 July 1992.

The draft for the CFE-1A Agreement included three parts: a definition of national ceilings, a list of participating states with their numerical ceilings and national commitments not to exceed a certain number of military personnel. Although final decisions were not made, the verification requirements had been mainly agreed upon—minimal beyond those of the CFE Treaty. Verification measures for the CFE-1A Agreement should 'provide adequate levels of overall assurance also with respect to monitoring compliance with manpower limits'.[72]

The role of verification was downgraded with the different definitions of forces and military force structures as the main factors which differentiated participants. The differences concerned what constituted reserve forces that varied widely between conscript and non-conscript armed forces. There were also disagreements on the allocation of ground support units for aviation, and the counting of police, gendarmerie and border guards.

[72] *Trust and Verify*, Jan. 1992, p. 3.

The new political realities and the expectations of the CFE Treaty's implementation made clear, at least in NATO, that personnel was not as important an indicator of military might as the 'hardware' component of military potentials. Personnel, in the context of the CFE-1A Agreement, is rather a political indicator.[73]

Another important issue on which a common understanding was reached by the majority was information exchange, agreement here also stemming from the appropriate use of corresponding provisions of the CFE Treaty.

The Concluding Act of the Negotiation on Personnel Strength of Conventional Armed Forces in Europe (the CFE-1A Agreement) signed in July 1992 specifies that 16 NATO members, 5 former East-European WTO member states and 8 newly independent states formerly part of the Soviet Union (Armenia, Azerbaijan, Belarus, Georgia, Kazakhstan, Moldova, Russia and Ukraine) decide the limits on their own armed forces. Other participating states then agreed on these set levels.

The Agreement covers the ATTU zone and a long period of implementation—40 months. The limits cover ground forces, air forces, air-defence forces and land-based naval formations but not internal security forces. The agreed levels are as shown in table 13.

The terms of this politically binding agreement indicate that the verification regime of the CFE Treaty will remain the central guarantor against possible non-compliance and for effective implementation of reduction of the military potentials in the ATTU area. At the same time it is to be supported by the verification regime under CSBM agreements.

[73] *Arms Control Reporter*, 1991, sheet 410.B.6.

5. New challenges to the verification of conventional armed forces

I. Introduction

As noted in chapter 3, adequate verification of the CFE Treaty faces a number of generic difficulties. In the previous era of East–West confrontation some of these were considered major stumbling blocks, and many problems remain even after the end of the cold war.

Despite such difficulties, the record of CFE Treaty implementation shows that the post-cold war atmosphere of confidence and the new political and strategic situation in Europe and in the international arena permit disagreements and frictions to be avoided or resolved in the preparation and conduct of on-site inspections, in making data assessments, and so on. The challenges to adequate verification seem to result not from the regime set out in the CFE Treaty, but rather from developments in the area of application that were not foreseen by those who drew up the Treaty and which have had a serious impact on the Treaty itself and, correspondingly, on verification activities.

The key challenges to the verification of conventional armed forces include: the Soviet military legacy and the CFE Treaty ceilings; the conflicts on the periphery of the former Soviet Union and the declining ability of the states in the conflict areas to control the situation; the unintentional abrogations resulting from the substantial restructuring of military potentials; and instability in a number of regions in the ATTU zone. These challenges apply mainly to the territory of the former Soviet Union.

Beyond these concerns and to a large extent in the CFE Treaty itself, it can be argued that monitoring conventional forces should be more focused on learning about the detailed *structures* of the forces—especially in the redrawn European landscape.

II. The Soviet military legacy

One of the most serious challenges for the implementation of the CFE Treaty was the need to reapportion the Soviet TLE among the newly independent states. In January 1992 almost half of the Soviet TLE was deployed outside Russia, including 49 per cent of the combat aircraft, 48 per cent of the ACVs, 43 per cent of the tanks and 35 per cent of the artillery. Excluding the Soviet forces outside the former Soviet Union, less than 30 per cent of the Soviet armaments in the ATTU zone were stationed on Russian territory, almost equal to the numbers stationed in Ukraine.[1] The Russian General Staff was concerned that the share of other republics might grow since some of the equipment to have been withdrawn from Eastern Europe was to be relocated in Ukraine and Belarus.[2] In addition, a number of TLE items were stored in Kazakhstan and Uzbekistan because of the rapid transfers of TLE from the European part of the USSR in 1990.

If the newly independent states had not accepted the CFE Treaty ceilings the strategic balance in the region could have been changed. Aside from the forces in Germany, the most combat-ready former Soviet forces were deployed in Belarus and Ukraine. At least in quantitative terms the forces on the western borders of the former Soviet Union were substantial. At the time of the dissolution of the Soviet Union Ukraine had 18 per cent of the divisions, 12.5 per cent of the battle tanks, 10 per cent of the artillery, 18 per cent of the ammunition stockpiles, 18 per cent of the combat aircraft and 32 per cent of the combat helicopters.[3]

Another immediate concern was the fate of the military potential in the Caucasus. The magnitude of deployments in this area of conflict made the region a real source of anxiety for the military and politicians in Moscow. At the time of the dissolution of the Soviet Union the Transcaucasus represented one of the most militarized areas, not only in the former Soviet Union but also in the world. The powerful infrastructure of two districts—the Transcaucasus MD and the Transcaucasus Border Guard District—plus the 19th Army of the Air Defence Forces, the Caspian Flotilla, a brigade of ships of the Black Sea Fleet and a large number of military structures of the Central Command were to be found in a strip 300-km wide and 700-km long. Such a concentration of forces would have permitted full-scale independent combat operations on the Southern Front for one month without any outside support.

The distribution of military potential among the republics in the region at the time of the dissolution of the USSR presented an acute problem. Azerbaijan possessed most of the former Soviet military resources in the area, with 15 per cent more TLE than Armenia and 27 per cent more than Georgia. The 4th Army stationed in Azerbaijan, for example, had 1310 items of 'heavy armaments', the 7th Army in Armenia had 1107 and the 31st Army Corps in Georgia had 955. In addition, Azerbaijan had enough rifles to equip 20 ground-force divisions, and clearly dominated in ammunition stockpiles.[4]

After the dissolution of the USSR the Transcaucasus republics possessed about 3500 items of heavy armaments, 260 000 rifles and 17 000 wagons of

[1] Rogov, S. (ed.), *Conventional Force Deployments within the Commonwealth of Independent States in Compliance with the CFE Treaty and the Republics' Security Requirements*, Brookings Discussion Papers (The Brookings Institution: Washington, DC, 27 Oct. 1992), p. 6.

[2] Rogov (note 1), pp. 6, 7. (The Russian authors made their calculations using data obtained from the General Staff as of 1 Jan. 1992.)

[3] *Kouranty*, 23 May 1992.

[4] The data are from the Russian General Staff, in *Novaya Ezhednevnaya Gazeta*, 10 Nov. 1993.

ammunition. This did not include aircraft ammunition, that is, about 15 000–20 000 bombs.[5]

During initial negotiations to apportion the Soviet military legacy some states did not want to reduce their nationalized or to-be nationalized armed forces to comply with the CFE Treaty ceilings, but under the pressure of NATO and Russia they had to acknowledge that it was in their interests to abide by the Treaty.

Shortly after declaring independence, Ukraine announced that it was taking over all the property of the Soviet armed forces deployed on its territory and prohibited any movement of forces 'abroad', that is, to Russia. This initiative was soon followed by Azerbaijan, Moldova and other states. The newly independent states *de facto* possessed the bulk of the Soviet military potential. In turn, in spring 1992 the Russian leadership at last decided to put the troops of the former Soviet armed forces under Russian jurisdiction. Disputes concerning the regional distribution of the Soviet TLE quotas were inevitable.

With the exception of Belarus the boundaries of the former military districts did not coincide with the borders of the new states (see figure 1). However, there were no separate CFE ceilings even for Belarus since this former Soviet republic had been part of the extended Central European zone (sub-zone IV.3). Each CFE zone included the territories of several newly independent states. The southern flank zone, for example, encompassed territories of six former Soviet republics: Armenia, Azerbaijan, Georgia, Moldova, Russia and Ukraine.

Kazakhstan posed another specific problem. The Treaty's area of application includes 'all territory lying west of the Ural river and the Caspian Sea', a definition which includes parts of the Uralsk and Guryev oblasts in Kazakhstan, formerly in the Turkestan MD.

These problems were aggravated by the failure to unify the armed forces of the Commonwealth of Independent States under the Supreme Command. Only strategic forces remained under this Command while all the newly independent states preferred to have their own fully independent armed forces. The CIS Unified Conventional Armed Forces continued to exist only on paper, except for the creation of joint peacekeeping forces.

The conclusion of the Tashkent Agreement in May 1992 represented a major breakthrough in solving the main problems of distributing the Soviet conventional military potential, but a number of challenges have remained.[6]

III. Conflicts in the former Soviet Union

The military conflicts and political instability on the periphery of the former Soviet Union in the ATTU zone have raised not only strategic and political concerns in the international community, but also many problems with regard

[5] Note 4.
[6] The text of the Tashkent Document is reproduced in SIPRI, *SIPRI Yearbook 1993: World Armaments and Disarmament* (Oxford University Press: Oxford, 1993), appendix 12C, pp. 671–77.

to the implementation and proper verification of the CFE Treaty. While the verification process is relatively smooth in the major part of the ATTU zone, it must be acknowledged that in certain regions verification cannot be controlled, at least in the short term. An immediate problem is raised by the flow of weapons to warring parties and it is important to note that this flow of weapons, particularly in the case of light armaments not covered by the CFE Treaty, is difficult to control.

The information available indicates that during the internal military struggles rival forces in the Caucasus and in Moldova have been legally or illegally supplied with armaments by 'third parties'. In late 1992 Azerbaijan insisted that Armenia had sought to purchase between 6 and 16 Mirage combat aircraft from France and allegedly had already signed a contract for six of them. Azerbaijan also accused members of the Armenian diaspora in the USA of having purchased eight F-16 planes. Taking into account that Armenia only had four Su-27 combat aircraft, such deliveries would have substantially increased the military potential of the republic,[7] however the accusations have not been confirmed.

Despite the fact that the territory of Armenia is not involved in the conflict with Azerbaijan, it is still impossible to calculate the exact number of TLE items owned by Armenia. Not incidentally, the data of the Joint Command of the CIS Armed Forces differed from those of, say, *The Military Balance*. As of autumn 1993 the former listed 180 tanks, 240 ACVs, 130 artillery pieces plus a squadron of Mi-24 and Mi-8 helicopters for Armenia. This means that the potential was lower than the CFE ceilings.[8] *The Military Balance,* however, states that there were 160 tanks, 440 ACVs, 257 artillery pieces and 20 helicopters in the country.[9]

At the same time, according to the Turkish press, in early 1993 Turkey started to supply Azerbaijan with armaments and ammunition.[10] The Armenian Foreign Ministry also protested against 'a large supply of armaments' from Ukraine to Azerbaijan in September 1993, including combat aircraft and new battle tanks. Some experts suspect Ukraine of covert supplies of weapons to other states as well.[11]

Not until November 1993, under pressure from the international community, did Azerbaijan officially acknowledge the delivery of 50 T-55 tanks from Ukraine. In addition, according to the Azerbaijani Foreign Ministry in November 1993, the republic took 286 tanks, 842 ACVs, 346 artillery pieces, 53 combat aircraft and 8 attack helicopters from the former Soviet forces deployed there under its jurisdiction in July–August 1992. The republic was said to have possessed 105 Russian ACVs and 42 artillery pieces in May 1993.[12] As a result,

---

[7] *Nezavisimaya Gazeta*, 22 Oct. 1992.

[8] *Izvestiya*, 20 Nov. 1993.

[9] International Institute for Strategic Studies, *The Military Balance 1993–1994* (Brassey's: London, 1993), p. 72.

[10] *Izvestiya*, 16 Apr. 1993.

[11] *Moscow News*, 19 Sep. 1993.

[12] *Nezavisimaya Gazeta*, 2 Dec. 1993.

Azerbaijan strengthened its military potential far beyond the CFE ceilings. The supplies also contravened international agreements banning such supplies to conflicting parties, and the Tashkent Agreement and its protocol.

It is important to bear in mind the impossibility of calculating the exact military potential of Azerbaijan. Besides the losses in the war in Nagorno-Karabakh, the above official figures have been criticized at least by Armenia. According to Armenian data, other deliveries were made before the summer of 1992, particularly between January and May 1992.[13] In contrast to its data on Armenia, the 'White Paper' of the Joint Command of the CIS Armed Forces of November 1993 does not specify the Azerbaijani military potential at all. It just states that after the withdrawal of the Russian military there remained 20 Mi-24 and Mi-8 helicopters, 70 L-29, 16 Su-24 and MiG-25 aircraft.[14] *The Military Balance* states that there are 286 tanks, 330 artillery pieces, 742 ACVs, 47 combat aircraft and 23 helicopters in Azerbaijan.[15] No one can state the exact figure.

Weapon supplies were also recorded during the conflict in Moldova. For example, Russian Minister of Defence Pavel Grachev openly accused Romania of smuggling 80 pieces of 'armoured' systems, including M-30 howitzers, to Moldova by mid-1992.[16] In late 1993 it was stated that Romania supplied T-55 tanks.[17] *The Military Balance* concluded that Moldova does not possess tanks but has 87 ACVs.[18] According to the above-mentioned CIS 'White Paper', the republic has 38 MiG-29s and a squadron of helicopters.[19]

The civil war in Georgia has raised other complicated challenges. According to preliminary data, in Abkhazia alone more than 200 armoured vehicles and tanks and 300 artillery pieces were involved in combat actions between Georgians and Abkhazians between mid-1992 and mid-1993. No information about combat aircraft has appeared so far.[20] Besides heavy losses in armaments by both sides during the Abkhazian offensive in summer–autumn 1993, some armaments were hidden deep in the mountains in so-called 'bases' by the retreating Georgian military forces. Georgians also managed to withdraw 59 tanks, 55 ACVs and 111 artillery pieces from the front line,[21] but they were immediately attacked by Georgian supporters of former President Zviad Gamsakhurdiya. This single example indicates the difficulty of calculating the amount of TLE items stationed in this troubled region.

If the above data are compared with the official information exchanges of 15 December 1992, shown in table 14, there are obvious discrepancies which

---

[13] Note 11.
[14] *Izvestiya*, 20 Nov. 1993.
[15] IISS (note 9), p. 72.
[16] *Izvestiya*, 1 June 1992.
[17] *Izvestiya*, 20 Nov. 1993.
[18] IISS (note 9), p. 72.
[19] *Izvestiya* (note 14).
[20] *Trud*, 7 Sep. 1993.
[21] *Segodnya*, 18 Sep. 1993.

Table 14. Transcaucasian and Moldovan forces as shown by the December 1992 data exchange

State	Tanks	ACVs	Artillery pieces	Aircraft	Helicopters
Armenia	77	189	160	3	13
Azerbaijan	278	338	294	50	6
Georgia	75	49	24	4	3
Moldova	0	118	108	29	0

Source: Sharp, J. M. O., 'Conventional arms control in Europe', SIPRI, *SIPRI Yearbook 1993: World Armaments and Disarmament* (Oxford University Press: Oxford, 1993), table 12.5, p. 609.

indicate that all four republics have at least increased their military potential. The selective data of the Joint Command alone show that from December 1992, despite TLE losses in combat operations, Armenia has increased its numbers of tanks and ACVs. As for the TLE of Georgia and Azerbaijan, the 'White Paper' gives no figures for tanks, ACVs or artillery, indicating an unwillingness to take responsibility for even approximate data, but the above-mentioned war episode in Abkhazia shows that the amount of artillery withdrawn from this area alone was almost five times that mentioned in the December 1992 information exchange.

According to Western data, from autumn 1992 to summer 1993 Russia transferred the following equipment (*a*) 164 tanks, 329 armoured cars and 355 artillery systems to Armenia, (*b*) 302 tanks, 267 armoured cars and 810 artillery systems to Azerbaijan, and (*c*) 109 tanks, 203 armoured cars and 13 artillery systems to Georgia.[22] These data, in turn, complicate the task of calculating the numbers. It seems that the discrepancy is not the fault of the data sources. Together with war losses and weapon transfers, the practice of stealing weapons from military bases (primarily Russian) in the region makes the task of counting TLE items even more complicated.

The issue of stolen weapons has raised serious concerns both in the West and in Russia. There are a number of reports of attacks on Russian military garrisons in the Northern Caucasus and Transcaucasus. Some of the stolen weapons in the Russian part of the Northern Caucasus were supplied to the warring parties in Armenia, Azerbaijan and Georgia. There are many accusations, at least in the mass media, that Chechnia, the 'rebellious' Russian republic, used to supply the Abkhazian army with stolen weapons: for example, it captured 42 tanks, 66 ACVs and other armaments from Russian bases on its territory.[23]

According to some Russian military experts, only about 60 per cent of the Soviet stockpiles in the region were transferred to the national armies and about 30 per cent were simply stolen or captured during attacks on military garrisons.

[22]*Arms Control Reporter*, 1993, sheets 407.E-1.127–28, 131–32.
[23] *Krasnaya Zvezda*, 1 July 1992.

These 30 per cent represent a minimum of 60 000–70 000 armaments, primarily rifles.[24]

The conflicts in the region have posed another problem. Russia (with the consent of the local governments) has had to use a quantity of armaments from the internal (police) forces for peace-keeping operations. In 1992 alone, 1400 armoured vehicles and tanks were involved in these operations, with a major portion in Abkhazia and in the Russian North Caucasian provinces.[25] Some of the armaments were lost in the operations or stolen. It will take some time for the parties involved in the conflicts in the region to calculate the losses and available military potential, even when the conflicts are over, and it will be some time before Russia can assess the amount of stolen TLE.

IV. Force reductions and restructuring in the newly independent states

Aside from the armed conflicts which have broken out, the newly independent states have also had to face a number of difficulties in dealing with the structure of the Soviet military legacy itself. First, all the former Soviet republics decided to create their own armed forces with very loose joint and mainly consultative structures, such as the Council of Defence Ministers of the CIS. Second, they still need to restructure their military potential because of economic reasons, military–industrial capabilities, their own assessments of military threats, and so on. Third, during the first two years after the dissolution of the USSR no official, unambiguous military doctrine was adopted for national forces. Finally, as a result of the Tashkent Document every newly independent state in the ATTU zone has to comply with the CFE Treaty ceilings on military equipment.

In other words, each new state in the ATTU zone has had to restructure its military forces without guidance from a military doctrine or defined concept of national security. Not even the 'Basics of the Military Doctrine of Russia', adopted in November 1993,[26] presents unambiguous guidelines for developing the armed forces. Furthermore, it officially represents a temporary document to be re-evaluated after two years.

It is becoming increasingly obvious that the prime factors that are steering the evolution of the armed forces of the newly independent states include their economic and industrial capabilities and the CFE Treaty ceilings. Other, strategic factors clearly correlate and influence developments, as indicated by Russia and Ukraine with their support for the revision of the flank zone limits, but it seems that the first two factors, in the 1990s at least, are decisive. In turn, economic factors influence the problems of implementing the CFE Treaty.

[24] *Novaya Ezhednevnaya Gazeta*, 10 Nov. 1993.
[25] *Nezavisimaya Gazeta*, 22 Apr. 1993.
[26] *Krasnaya Zvezda*, 19 Nov. 1993.

Some of the Soviet forces withdrawn from Eastern Europe are known to have been deployed in Ukraine. These are considered to have been among the most combat-ready and best-equipped forces. By October 1993, however, the Ukrainian Parliament was shocked by the statement of the new Minister of Defence, Vitaliy Radetskiy, that only 26 per cent of the armaments had a maintenance base, including spare parts, and that 75 per cent of the armaments were obsolete and in need of replacement.[27]

In the decision-making process surrounding the development of military potential the Ukrainian leadership has to cope with a number of factors: severe economic and financial crisis; overwhelming dependency for spare parts and weapon systems on other republics, particularly Russia; inability to afford spare parts and systems and unwillingness of suppliers to deliver them on privileged terms of payment; great problems in creating its own industrial base for replacing obsolete TLE; and so on. If these factors persist, the TLE potential will become more and more obsolete.

Reductions

Key factors affecting TLE reductions are the related technological and financial limitations. Not all republics have the necessary industrial capacities to destroy the prohibited tanks and ACVs. Modern tank repair plants can be used for this purpose in several former Soviet republics: six in Ukraine, two in the Baltic states and one in Georgia. Russia has two such plants: at Chita in Siberia and Ussuriysk in the Far East, outside the ATTU zone.[28] In addition Russia has converted the tank plant in St Petersburg, and tank factories in the Urals also have to eliminate some of the tanks and ACVs that were moved there from Europe before the CFE Treaty was signed.

Belarus uses three sites for the destruction of military equipment: Borisov (tanks), Stankovo (APCs) and Lesnaya (aircraft).[29] However, during the second, 60 per cent, reduction phase, it will probably also have to make use of Ukrainian and Russian facilities in order to destroy the specified number of weapons. Russia may also request Ukraine to allow its plants to be used to destroy Russian equipment. This may lead to a dispute about conversion of some tanks and ACVs (according to the CFE Reduction Protocol the USSR could convert 750 tanks and 3000 ACVs). There have been no reports of any arrangements between Belarus, Russia and Ukraine about the apportioning of the Soviet conversion quotas.

Some former Soviet TLE were successfully liquidated according to the CFE provisions at an enterprise in Winsdorf (Germany). By October 1993, 1380 TLE items had been destroyed here and there were plans to destroy another 1000 by May 1994. The Russian Western Group of Forces managed to earn DM1 million on these operations, while in Russia the destruction is considered

[27] *Nezavisimaya Gazeta*, 21 Oct. 1993.
[28] *Megapolis–Express*, no. 21 (20 May 1992), p. 13.
[29] *Arms Control Reporter*, 1993, sheet 407.E-1.111.

to be unprofitable.[30] Russia destroyed most of its tanks stationed in Germany within the country itself because of the shortage of facilities on its own territory.

Belarus announced in advance that it would have serious problems in making a 60 per cent reduction between the end of 1993 and November 1994. Because considerable resources and great efforts were required to complete the first stage of reductions, the Belarus officials proposed an international fund be organized to help in TLE destruction.[31]

Clearly, financial and economic factors, not only the CFE limits, will drive the restructuring and reductions of the conventional military potentials of the CIS and Russia as well. The process of reductions has been accompanied by a severe deceleration of military production—the result not only of the need to comply with arms control obligations, but also of the economic difficulties.

If armaments production in Russia in 1990 and 1992 are compared the trend is very indicative. The production of combat helicopters dropped by 93 per cent (from 70 to 5), artillery systems by 76 per cent (from 1900 to 450), combat fighters by 74 per cent (from 575 to 150), ACVs by 69 per cent (from 3600 to 1100) and tanks by 48 per cent (from 1300 to 675).[32] Clearly the reductions are much faster than planned.

This also applies to the reduction of military personnel. According to an official decision in 1992, the Russian armed forces were to be reduced to 2.1 million by 1995, but in fact this level was reached by the end of 1993.[33]

Obviously, the present and short-term economic and financial difficulties of the newly independent states create both problems and opportunities for the implementation and verification of the CFE Treaty. On the one hand, the timely destruction and retrofitting of TLE continues to be problematic because of the shortage of facilities and finances. On the other hand, these difficulties objectively drive the armed forces further down the road of reductions.

Restructuring

The restructuring and redeployment of forces to comply with the CFE limits represent a continuous problem, particularly for the Russian military. The recent claims of Russia supported by Ukraine to renegotiate Article V of the Treaty with regard to the flank zone illustrate the point.

The Russian military have never been satisfied with the flank zone limits, particularly taking into account the emerging importance of the North Caucasus MD and the instability in that region. As stated in chapter 3, the former Soviet leadership decided to transfer three motorized rifle divisions from the Ground Forces to the three Fleets in the ATTU zone—Northern, Baltic and Black Sea Fleets—while the fourth was transferred to the Pacific Fleet. The divisions

---

[30] *Segodnya*, 28 Oct. 1993.
[31] *Arms Control Reporter*, 1993, sheet 407.B.497.
[32] *Argumenti i Fakti*, no. 4 (Jan. 1994), p. 7.
[33] *Segodnya*, 29 Dec. 1993.

were renamed 'divisions of coastal defence' (DCD). This action was criticized by the West and later resolved.

The Tashkent Agreement revived the old concerns of the Russian military as it provided the right for Russia to deploy two active motorized rifle brigades in the flank zone. This could lead to abolishing the DCD in Archangelsk in the northern part of the European territory. The generals complained that in the Northern Flank, with the strategically important Northern Fleet and industrial centres such as St Petersburg, one active brigade and one or two additional brigades with prepositioned equipment, stored along the lines of the US Pre-positioned Material Configured to Unit Sets (POMCUS), were not enough for reliable defence.[34] The need for substantial forces in the Southern Flank has heightened the sentiments of the Russian military.

According to the limits for the North Caucasus and Leningrad MDs, Russia may have 700 tanks, 580 ACVs and 1280 artillery pieces which, in the opinion of the Ministry of Defence, is not enough for providing security, particularly in the Northern Caucasus.[35] Along with the broad concerns of reductions in the northern and southern parts of European Russia, by early 1993 these concerns led to the Russian proposal to change the flank limits.

In September 1993 President Yeltsin sent a letter to the USA, Norway, the UK, France, Denmark and Turkey with a proposal to modify the flank limits. Russia presented four reasons:

1. The Treaty was agreed and adopted under conditions which no longer exist, in which the USSR had a single powerful armed force and a sufficiently stable situation prevailed in the region. Thus the flank limitations take on a 'unilateral and discriminatory character for Russia'.

2. The existing and potential hotbeds and conflicts in the Transcaucasus, as well as spreading separatism and fundamentalism, would require a 'substantial military presence' to ensure the Russian security interests, and Russia might need more armaments than permitted by the Treaty.

3. Preservation of the flank limits would hamper an even distribution of forces, most of which would be deployed in the rear areas and the densely populated areas along Russia's western borders and in the Kaliningrad region. Thus it would petrify the East–West orientation of deployments instead of the North–South one suited to the present circumstances. Moreover—a veiled warning has been sent—such a configuration could meet the strongest resistance from the military and other political forces.

4. There were strong socio-economic reasons for settling the troops withdrawn from abroad in the south: the infrastructure for relocation already exists in the south; and harsh climate and living conditions elsewhere could give rise to social tension and unrest among the troops. This also would imply higher costs and delays in the withdrawal timetable.[36]

---

[34] Rogov (note 1), pp. 37–38

[35] *Kommersant*, 19 Nov. 1993.

[36] As summarized by Lachowski, Z., 'Conventional arms control and security co-operation in Europe', SIPRI, *SIPRI Yearbook 1994* (Oxford University Press: Oxford, 1994), pp. 572–73. Note: the Leningrad and North Caucasus MDs cover more than half the European territory of Russia. The Kaliningrad *oblast* (a small portion of the Baltic MD) is the only remnant of the former Soviet part of the CFE Expanded Cen-

The President particularly stressed that the agreement with Ukraine on the Black Sea and the future agreement with Armenia on stationing Russian troops there would minimize Russia's room for manœuvre with respect to the North Caucasus and Leningrad MDs. It would in turn, as stated further, contradict the measures aimed at strengthening stability and security in the region.

A number of the same concerns were expressed in the official statement of the Ukrainian Foreign Ministry. It particularly stressed the economic, financial and social consequences of the required redeployment of troops. Ukraine supported the Russian proposal to modify the flank limits.[37] It is reported that Russia would like to increase its quota in the southern flank zone by 2000 ACVs, 400 tanks and 500 artillery pieces.[38]

The initiative met strong resistance from most CFE states parties. Norway and Turkey were the most active opponents of the initiative. The main concern of the West seems to be not just the possible revision of flank zone limits, however, but the probable domino effect on other states parties to the CFE Treaty that might also want to introduce changes. Such concerns have been the main argument against any claims to revise the provisions of the Treaty so far.

Chief of the Russian General Staff Michail Kolesnikov noted two points. First, he has admitted that the Russian proposal has not met with 'full understanding from some states parties' and that 'we hope to convince our partners'. Second, when questioned about the possibility of Russia leaving the Treaty if the proposal is not accepted he replied that such a possibility had not been discussed even theoretically.[39]

The problems created by the dissolution of the Soviet Union and the need for the newly independent states to manage the Soviet military legacy represent the main challenge to the CFE Treaty and are not going to be easily solved. Not incidentally, the Declaration of Heads of State and Government, participating in the meeting of the North Atlantic Council held in Brussels on 10–11 January 1994, emphasized that 'we attach crucial importance to the full and timely implementation of existing arms control and disarmament agreements as well as to achieving further progress on key issues of arms control and disarmament, such as . . . ensuring the integrity of the CFE Treaty and full compliance with all its provisions.'[40]

V. Force structures and realignment: new priorities for conventional force verification

One of the key provisions associated with the CFE Treaty deals with the residual levels after the actual reductions have been made. In view of the new politi-

tral Zone which belongs to Russia. Under the CFE Treaty, Russia can and does deploy in the oblast considerable conventional forces withdrawn from eastern Germany, the Baltic states and Poland.

[37] *Kommersant*, 29 Oct. 1993.

[38] *Segodnya*, 5 Apr. 1994.

[39] *Segodnya*, 29 Dec. 1993.

[40] *NATO Review*, Feb. 1994, p. 32.

cal climate in Europe it seems that the main concerns would stem rather from changes in the structure of military potentials than from their numbers. If numbers are not consistent with the Treaty limits, this may lead to debates about compliance; but more important concerns may arise from potential changes in force structures and such changes would be the prime concern of experts and organizations dealing with the implementation of the CFE Treaty. Monitoring structures would therefore play a larger role than was expected by analysts in the late 1980s when the debates about the creation of an adequate verification regime focused primarily on actual numbers.

Security considerations inherent in the perception of whether forces are offensively or defensively structured naturally lead to the analysis of doctrines, both stated and inferred. However, as well expressed elsewhere:

doctrines cannot be discussed in isolation, separate from the consideration of force structure. In isolation, discussion would only confirm a declaratory policy without considering the other important factors which engender the perception of threat. These factors—the structures of forces, their deployment and their training—follow from and are reflected in doctrines . . . Only such an approach offers a realistic possibility of answering the question of whether or not the forces are defensively oriented.[41]

It could perhaps be argued further, especially as the conventional armed forces of Europe are being radically restructured, that force structures are the most important elements for analysis. There is inevitably a substantial time lag between the formulation (and/or explication) of doctrines and their appearance in concrete, observable structural form. When doctrinal changes were relatively minor and infrequent, it was a very fruitful exercise to examine their content (at least for what could be learned) and to attempt to connect this with actual deployments. As changing times create the necessity for re-evaluation and radically new doctrinal postures are created over relatively short periods, attempting to make appropriate connections with structures can be seen as somewhat less important. This is especially so since a new doctrine may replace an old one before the latter has had enough time to observably manifest itself.

Thus, especially as far as monitoring is concerned, it may be argued that it is the structure of forces that is the basic evidence which can and should be used reliably to evaluate threats and perceptions.

Arriving at force structures: what needs to be verified?

As conventional arms reductions and force restructuring progress in Europe, a key question arises concerning the most appropriate targets for verification and monitoring. Before the signing of the CFE Treaty this issue was discussed in detail in many forums.[42]

---

[41] Naumann, C., 'Doctrines and force structures', eds I. M. Cuthbertson and P. Volten, *The Guns Fall Silent: The End of the Cold War and the Future of Conventional Disarmament,* Institute for East-West Security Studies, Occasional Paper Series no. 17, New York, 1990, pp. 51–52.

[42] Some of what follows was discussed in particular at the Sixth International AFES-PRESS Conference in Mosbach; see Brauch, H. G. ed., *Verification and Arms Control: Implications for European Secu-*

The verification of individual TLE items and troops, for example, creates a number of problems. It would be almost impossible to obtain accurate numbers, especially where troops are concerned. Exact numbers are not necessary, however, since only militarily significant violations are important. But while a militarily significant violation in the WTO–NATO context was a large number of TLE items, this may not be the case after the disbanding of the WTO and the dissolution of the USSR, when individual states are concerned with even smaller amounts of TLE. In this case, as will become even more apparent should the new states enter into any conventional disarmament negotiations, a rather small amount of TLE may represent a large military threat to a small nation—especially one outside a protective alliance. Verifying individual TLE items piecemeal would give no measure of the structure of the armed forces, but as information accumulates and the approximate positions of a large portion of the TLE are known, and especially if the locations of all the troops are added into the picture (although this would be costly to monitor), a fairly good idea of the military structure would be obtained.

Another approach is to verify behaviour. As pointed out above, however, observing manœuvres can indicate the offensive or defensive character of the operations but does not provide clear enough evidence.

The third approach is to verify structures:

It could be advantageous to emphasize the existence of offensive and defensive structures rather than numbers. This could be done by verifying combat support elements like logistic depots and engineering units and facilities. . . . Such a verification can be done mainly by on-site inspections and on-site monitoring by technical means (tags, seals, camera's [sic] etc.).[43]

With regard to the last point, however, it would seem that much of the *large-scale* infrastructure would be quite easily verifiable using commercial satellites and aerial reconnaissance when this becomes available. This is particularly true for catching any clandestine activity involving this type of structure.

Especially for the verification of possible future agreements on conventional armed forces it has also been argued that 'adequacy will be extremely difficult to ensure . . . This will be so because the sorts of changes that need to be instituted in the military structures . . . will transcend *reduction* and will have to embrace *transformation*.'[44] Thus requirements and challenges which have so far not been a major concern for verification will become much more important.

---

rity, Results of the Sixth International AFES-PRESS Conference, Part I: Abstracts and Discussions, AFES PRESS, Mosbach, 1990; see in particular p. 127.

[43] Note 42, p. 127.

[44] Macintosh, J., 'The evolution of verification provisions in the MBFR, CCSBMDE and CFE—what next?', ed. H. G. Brauch, *Verification and Arms Control: Implications for European Security,* Results of the Sixth International AFES-PRESS Conference, Part II: Selected Papers, AFES PRESS, Mosbach, 1990, p. 91 (emphasis added).

VI. Methods of monitoring force structures

Monitoring of force structures can be carried out by all of the methods discussed with reference to the CFE Treaty. These include the now almost classical means of area surveillance: satellites. Commercial satellites are sure to play an important role here.[45] Satellite observations must, of course, be combined with other tools including those which will be available through the Open Skies Treaty and OSI, all of which are also discussed below.

The growing numbers and better resolution of commercial satellites will certainly have a profound effect on monitoring military structures, especially in the concrete sense of observing and taking note of infrastructures. This is perhaps where their limited resolution can best be put to use. Even Landsat sensors, with a resolution of 30 m,[46] are none the less able to easily point to the locations of roads and railway lines even though they may be only several metres across. This is simply because their linear structure allows them to be distinguished with these less than highly advanced systems.

Of course, commercial systems have continued to improve over the years and as this occurs—bringing increased transparency to the world—there have been calls to open up the classified systems of the USA and the former USSR. At the end of the 1980s the Director of Central Intelligence (DCI) under President Jimmy Carter, Admiral Stansfield Turner, said that: 'Openness in the world is going to be unavoidable . . . We need to adapt before it arrives'. He went on to say that one of the ways to accomplish this would be for the USA to share some of its now secret satellite photographs via an Open Skies type of agency.[47] The decision in early 1994 by the USA to allow the acquisition and sale of high resolution (as good as 1 m) satellite imagery will allow unprecedented access to high quality photographs.[48]

European satellites

Going well beyond previous statements by Europeans with regard to developing independent monitoring capabilities, French Defence Minister Pierre Joxe said on 6 May 1991 that the French Government should attach the same degree of importance to the construction of new spy satellites in the 1990s as it did to securing its independent nuclear capability in the 1960s. To reduce costs France would work in consort with other European nations to develop 'a range of

[45] See Skorve, J., 'Commercial and third-party satellites', eds R. Kokoski and S. Koulik, SIPRI, *Verification of Conventional Arms Control in Europe: Technological Constraints and Opportunities* (Westview Press: Boulder, Colo., 1990), pp. 56–88.

[46] Resolution is carefully defined in Kokoski, R., 'National technical means', eds Kokoski and Koulik (note 45), pp. 20–21. In essence, as used here a resolution of 30 m for example means that each of the individual picture elements (pixels) making up an image represents an area 30 m square on the ground. This is technically the instantaneous field of view (IFOV) definition.

[47] 'Non-superpowers are developing their own spy satellite systems', *New York Times*, 3 Sep. 1989, p. 1.

[48] Lawler, A., 'Image policy opens new market for US', *Space News*, 14–20 Mar. 1994, p. 1.

satellites to monitor arms treaty compliance and to spy on nations viewed as a threat to peace'.

Joxe said: 'Germany and Great Britain obviously would have a role. Such a system also might allow entry to nations that are not part of an alliance. After all, these programs threaten no one. Their essential goal is to maintain the peace'.[49] Capabilities would include optical, infrared and radar sensors and eventually communications interception. With regard to the latter, the value of signals intelligence (SIGINT) as outlined below would be substantial for monitoring new and differently configured deployments and, especially when combined with other information, for detecting destabilizing developments should they develop. France would reportedly have to buy the technology from the USA to develop a military radar satellite if it hopes to do so before the end of the century—this probably refers to quite high-resolution radar. This would not be necessary for the detection of large infrastructures, however, and it would probably be possible to build a somewhat more primitive, though highly useful, radar satellite much more quickly.

The Helios satellite programme, which was initiated by France and includes participation by Italy and Spain, will set a precedent in co-operative space-based verification when launched in the mid-1990s. The French Government has agreed to share information from its sensors—including high resolution visible light, infrared and signals intercept—with its allies.

Canada's Radarsat, also set for launch by the mid-1990s, will have a resolution of about 10 m, which could be very useful for detecting changes in deployments. In addition, the Western European Union (WEU) agreed in June 1991 to establish a satellite data interpretation centre in Spain which inaugurated a three-year experimental phase in March 1993. The centre will make use of data from existing satellites, including the French Système Probatoire d'Observation de la Terre (SPOT), the US Landsat and the more capable French/Spanish/Italian Helios system for verification and crisis monitoring, and make the processed data available to WEU member states.[50]

In describing the potential uses of such satellites the French Defence Minister mentioned three very important targets for observations of conventional force deployments in particular: 'early warning of potential aggression, updates on other nations' defense capabilities and a continuous flow of strategic and tactical information'.[51] Irrespective of whether or not all of the various satellite systems currently under consideration are built, a key point to be stressed here is the acknowledgement that defence officials are thinking in terms of these priorities. Though it is not explicitly stated, it is reasonable to assume that if such

---

[49] 'Joxe: Spy satellites essential for France', *Space News*, 13–19 May 1991, p. 1.

[50] de Selding, P. B., 'France confirms work on new spy satellite systems', *Space News*, 6–19 July 1992, p. 1; *Atlantic News*, no. 2521 (20 Apr. 1993), p. 4; de Selding, P. B., 'France to provide imagery to WEU', *Space News*, 3–9 May 1993, p. 9; 'WEU picks Spain to host satellite data center', *Defense News*, 25 Nov. 1991, p. 21; 'WEU to establish center to study satellite data', *Defense News*, 1 July 1991, p. 19; 'Joxe: Spy satellites essential for France', *Space News*, 13–19 May 1991, p. 1.

[51] 'Defense Minister invites French emphasis on spy satellites', *Defense News*, 13 May 1991, p. 50.

information could be obtained in a more efficient and timely manner, these means would be explored as well.

Signals collection: a valuable asset

Signals collection can play a valuable role in learning about specific aspects of and plans for particular force structures. The true functions of buildings, transportation facilities, and so on, often cannot be discerned with even the most advanced photographic techniques, whether from space or from aircraft. One method of sorting out this difficult problem is to attempt to monitor the communications to or from particular facilities or areas where suspect activity is occurring. Picking up such signals can of course occur unexpectedly when area search methods are used and would be valuable in discovering clandestine military activity—treaty-related or otherwise.

The potential for such information gathering should be stressed, in particular with respect to the smaller states in Europe, for two important and interrelated reasons. First, most if not all such states already possess the ability to receive signals[52] especially from nearby states indicating, for example, that preparations for significant military activities are occurring. Such capabilities are technologically within the reach of any country. Second, the main concern of many such countries may in fact turn out to be not large-scale offensive operations massed by large numbers of opposing states but rather the threat from smaller individual bordering nations—precisely the type of threat of which rather unsophisticated communications intercepts could be quite valuable in providing warning.

Such sensitive information may of course be encrypted, making the task of sorting out exactly what is occurring somewhat more difficult. Here it is important to realize that the mere ability to discern where a signal has originated or the priority or volume of signals activity (externals) can often provide a surprising amount of information.[53]

In a somewhat broader context, the rapidly changing environment and the nature of military force structures in Europe exacerbate problems which already exist with respect to intelligence collection methods in general. Because of the time required to develop systems and the long and increasing lifetimes of the means used to collect large amounts of intelligence, the requirements must be anticipated far in advance of the actual deployment of the systems.

On-site inspection

A great deal of information about the potential of on-site inspection for conventional force monitoring is and will be derived from experience with CFE

---

[52] Koulik, S. and Kokoski, R., SIPRI, *Verification of the CFE Treaty*, SIPRI Research Report no. 4, Stockholm, Oct. 1991.
[53] See for example Kokoski (note 46).

Treaty verification. Although it is unlikely that one or a few OSI will contribute very much to such knowledge, as more and more inspections are conducted they will certainly help the overall picture to fall into place with respect to force structures. Especially in the case of the smaller nations of Europe, with growing security concerns, the possibility of challenge inspections is especially important. Thus, such inspections without the right of refusal (under the CFE Treaty refusal is allowed with appropriate explanation) may be pressed for in any future regime.

For an effectively functioning verification system one may address a French proposal—that satellites be used to locate suspicious behaviour if and when possible, aircraft should be employed to take a closer look, and then OSI should be conducted if needed.[54] This entails moving closer and closer to a monitoring target to obtain more detailed information and is thus quite logical. However, the present reality is that most countries do not have access to high-quality space imagery nor even to aerial monitoring—although the Open Skies Treaty will hopefully soon make the latter a possibility. Neither will the time-frame of small-scale structural changes which may threaten small countries or regions allow OSI to play an important role in many situations as far as providing assurance of security is concerned. Thus it may be necessary in the interim to push forward as quickly as possible to employ aerial observations as the most practical alternative.

Aerial inspection

It is important to look at the possible contributions of aerial means to monitoring current and future force structures. As elaborated in chapter 7, the number of overflights allowed under the Open Skies regime is rather small for most of the states involved. Information-sharing considerations aside, therefore, it can probably be stated that they will be insufficient to meet all security concerns, especially those of smaller nations. Thus, as Open Skies is focused more on the broader picture, the overflights will most probably be too infrequent to assuage some of the more worrisome concerns of some smaller nations in particular, for example Hungary.

It was agreed during the CFE Negotiation that an aerial inspection regime to enhance verification of the CFE Treaty be developed and it was unclear whether such a regime would be incorporated into the Open Skies Treaty.[55] Even if they should be officially totally independent, the Open Skies regime and the CFE aerial reconnaissance provisions would overlap to a large extent. This would probably occur not only in the types of sensor allowed but perhaps also in the means by which information will be distributed. It goes without saying that the geographical areas covered would overlap to a great extent and

[54] *Defense News*, 17 Dec. 1990, p. 36.
[55] US General Accounting Office (GAO), *Conventional Arms Control: Former Warsaw Pact Nations' Treaty Compliance and US Cost Control*, GAO Report to Congressional Requesters, GAO/NSIAD-94-33 (GAO: Washington, DC, Dec. 1993), p. 16.

that the regimes would complement one another in this respect. Thus while it may be advantageous for some specific technical or operational aspects to be different, it is particularly important to avoid the case where countries are observing the same thing, not communicating the information with one another, and conducting unnecessary numbers of basically redundant flights.

VII. Changing force structures and security

Armed forces are undergoing and will undoubtedly continue to undergo substantial restructuring and realignment as a result of changing priorities. It is of the utmost importance that these changing structures do not pose undue security concerns.

Large structural changes in forces may be occurring rather quickly when measured on time-scales of the past four decades but they are still quite slow when it comes to monitoring them. Unsophisticated methods may suffice in many cases to detect that a change is taking place and to give a broad description. Motives are quite another question and would be almost impossible to surmise. Declared motives have virtually no relevance to a state which feels threatened. Thus it is important that the appropriate means be in place to detect more precisely the types of change that are taking place and the possible clues this may give to the motivations behind them.

With respect to NATO and Russia, for example, a long time would be necessary to prepare for any potential military aggression against them and the capabilities for monitoring are sufficiently wide-ranging and sophisticated to provide a lengthy warning time. These two thus have a *double advantage*. At the other extreme, for the security concerns of smaller individual states (especially those outside NATO) small force changes in neighbouring countries may be sufficient to prepare for a surprise attack and thus warning time would be shorter. Since these states do not have very sophisticated monitoring techniques to detect such changes, they are at a *double disadvantage*.

It is important to address the question of how much reassurance the monitoring regimes put in place by the CFE Treaty and Open Skies regime can contribute to satisfying these concerns. If it is not enough, what other agreements or monitoring procedures or CSBMs need to be put in place? How intrusive must they be? What is the threshold of activity which must be monitored? With respect to this last question it is becoming increasingly apparent that each individual nation will have rather different views on sufficiency. This has already been seen in the attitudes of different participants towards the CFE verification regime as they change over time.

Quantitative analysis of these problems has become much more difficult as the face of Europe changes from within. As unrest grows within and between certain states, even minor changes of force structures can have a considerable impact on the perceived security of large segments of a country's population and thus (and perhaps more importantly) on the perceived security of neighbouring states. This points to a very complex and crucial issue with which monitoring must deal: forces are restructured to perform specific missions and deal with specific contingencies. To what extent should multilateral monitoring capabilities be able to cope with detecting small changes in force structures which may have a relatively large impact on a limited area? As pointed out, it must also be considered that actions, even very small ones, provoke reactions, and conservative planners and decision makers may choose to be what they consider to be 'prudent' in dealing with a situation. One state's idea of prudence may, however, be seen by another state as over-reaction, and the cycle thus snowballs.

All of the above points to the need for a capability to deal with rather small changes in force postures so that they can be evaluated in terms of the security threats posed. Dealing with these changes means first of all monitoring them, then attempting to ascertain intentions and then, if necessary, reacting appropriately and possibly considering restructuring a country's own forces to keep its security perception at a high level. This is what had been going on since the beginning of the cold war, but the success with which the two sides were able to assess each other's postures and intentions was not always of the first order. Granted, the new openness of most of the countries in Europe, the availability of enhanced NTM, and the contribution of the CFE and Open Skies regimes will make transparency much easier to achieve. Nevertheless, it is important that these means be assessed in order that future requirements can begin to be considered and put in place *before* concerns about security arise.

Another important point in the context of smaller nations is that threatening forces which would be of concern could be deployed in a relatively short period of time. Historically, verification and CSBMs for monitoring the conventional armed forces of NATO and the WTO have usually had as their goal the detection of rather large changes in force structures in sufficiently short periods of time. Because of the large forces that were being considered, however, a few days was not considered critical, as the warning time for an alliance attack was usually seen as several weeks, even before the changes of the past few years. Today, however, when threats posed to small countries by relatively small forces are examined, such forces could be put in place in a much shorter period of time. Monitoring must be accomplished in such a way as to take into account the fact that it is conceivable that a military force of grave concern to a single state could be put in place in a matter of days. This will place very different priorities on the means of monitoring than have been examined in any detail heretofore (at least in the European theatre).

Suggestions have been made for attempts to quantify the minimum level of deployments which would need to be detected in order that all states involved are content that their security was not being put at risk. These questions are addressed in section VIII.

VIII. Quantifying threats and monitoring needs

The type of quantification needed adequately to allow for and assess appropriate monitoring methods in Europe would have been an extremely daunting task several years ago when well known alliance structures would have provided at least some basis for estimation. In the post-cold war environment, however, the problems involved are even larger.

As a point of departure an example of research on threat quantification published in 1986 is examined.[56] Formulated in terms of the then ongoing Stockholm Conference on Confidence- and Security-Building Measures and Disarmament in Europe it is appropriately set in a multilateral context. This study defends a set of reasonable monitoring measures for a reasonably defined set of activities which require verification.[57] It is argued that 'the capacity to reliably detect movements of the size and character of a "division equivalent"[58] force [is] an absolute minimum requirement'. It then goes on to clarify that,

this requirement effectively amounts to the minimum capacity to detect, with a relatively high degree of confidence, the following: a large number (perhaps as few as 25 or as many as 100, depending on the assurance demands) of tank size objects in motion (either under their own power, or the more likely instance, on even larger transporter vehicles); associated armoured and logistics vehicles (again, variable numbers but certainly in the range of at least 100 with many on road-going or rail transporters); a wide range of signals and imaging evidence indicating mass personnel movements all moving from well-known and closely-watched garrison locations.[59]

If it is not possible to detect anomalous movement of this level of equipment and personnel then it is judged that verification is not minimally adequate. Reliability is assumed to be at least a 75 per cent probability of detection of anomalous behaviour and a false alarm rate of about 5 per cent. It should be stressed here, however, that these monitoring requirements were related to those which would be in place as the result of a multilateral agreement, that is, monitoring activities 'tied to the specific measures—and *only* those measures— in a given arms control agreement',[60] and do not include open-ended intelligence gathering.

For the specific verification target dealt with above it was assumed that the monitoring regime put in place in conjunction with a multilateral accord might be expected to include third-party or other independent satellites equipped with

[56] Macintosh, J., 'The multilateralization of verification: an introduction', ed. J. O'Manique, *Multilateral Approaches to Verification*, Carleton International Proceedings, Carleton University, Ottawa, 1986, pp. 53–75.

[57] Including (*a*) notification measures, (*b*) calendar measures, (*c*) information measures, (*d*) constraint measures (including zonal), and (*e*) reduction measures.

[58] While it is realized that the use of an armoured division equivalent as a measure of the effectiveness of ground forces has some drawbacks (see, e.g., Posen, B. R., 'Measuring the European conventional balance: coping with complexity in threat assessment', *International Security*, vol. 9, no. 3 (winter 1984–85), p. 58), it has been used by many authors to assess and compare the capabilities of such forces.

[59] Macintosh (note 56), p. 66.

[60] Macintosh (note 56), p. 74.

synthetic aperture radar (SAR) as well as photo-optical sensors, radar and optical aerial monitoring capabilities, and signals intelligence (SIGINT) capabilities including space-, air- and ground-based.[61]

The likelihood of third-party or independent European satellite options materializing is discussed above and the possibilities look promising today. However, this may change, and even a somewhat rudimentary capability could be many years away. As is also discussed above, aerial monitoring will soon present new opportunities. It is argued in chapter 7 that the inclusion of a reasonably high-resolution radar capability on these aircraft makes a great deal of sense. As far as the SIGINT capability is concerned, at the present time and in the foreseeable future only the USA and Russia will have a space-based capability. Aerial SIGINT sensors were ruled out in the Open Skies Treaty. Ground-based sensors are in widespread use, although basically as intelligence-gathering means throughout Europe as has been discussed above and elsewhere.[62]

It could, in fact, be argued that not all of the above monitoring capabilities are necessary for the requirements outlined. For example, the absence of SIGINT sensors on aircraft could be compensated for to a large extent by targeting ground-based sensors to the relevant verification tasks, or by expanding them so that this is possible. As for an independent space-based monitoring capability, while this could indeed be a valuable asset, unless several well-equipped satellites were employed (at great cost), it would be difficult to keep all the parties to an agreement in Europe satisfied with enough imagery in a timely enough manner to substantially augment the verification regime. This is certainly not to argue against the concept, but only an attempt to assess the realistic contribution such systems could make to the task at hand.

Small nations worried about relatively small but threatening buildups near their borders and their timely detection also usually have small areas in which continuous monitoring is deemed a necessity. Borders between these nations may be only several hundred kilometres long or less. As stressed above signals intercepts can be valuable in such situations, but aerial reconnaissance would allow more direct confirmation of the absence of threatening situations.

Aircraft flying along such borders are capable of obtaining images of high quality to depths of hundreds of kilometres without intruding into the airspace of other countries. Such overflights could easily be conducted on a routine, perhaps even daily, basis provided the type of technology necessary was available. The cost would be minimal considering the pay-offs, as a few aircraft per country should be able to accomplish the task.

Many of the former WTO members have been looking towards possible future NATO membership. Steps such as the Partnership for Peace initiative have been taken which will bring these countries into a more co-operative relationship. As early as 1991, in efforts to decrease their technological

[61] Macintosh (note 56), p. 67.
[62] See e.g., Kokoski (note 46).

dependency on the former USSR, Hungary and the former Czechoslovakia expressed interest in acquiring Western air defence and command and control systems.[63] Such technology would be used by these countries to restructure their forces for national defence and would be a 'logical first step' in buying Western weapons.

Perhaps another step for such countries could be the purchase of reasonably sophisticated high-flying aircraft which are capable of monitoring well inside the borders of neighbouring countries while remaining within national airspace.

IX. Conclusions

The context of military structures is used as the most appropriate guideline for assessing the types of monitoring method which may prove of most relevance in a transformed Europe. The roles of various methods of verification ranging from satellite monitoring through aerial, ground-based and on-site inspections are assessed in this context.

Most of these methods were employed recently in a quite different arena during the buildup to, the fighting and the aftermath of the 1991 Persian Gulf War. In preparing for and during the actual fighting of a war it is of prime importance that the *military structures* of the opponent be adequately assessed. Knowledge of the number of weapons and troops is certainly important, but without knowing how and at what level of readiness these forces are deployed the task of war fighting would be, to say the least, vastly more difficult. The two extremes of being able to accumulate a vast quantity of information on an opponent's forces—as was the case for the Coalition—as opposed to being able to obtain very little—as with Iraq—was demonstrated in the swift and (for the Coalition) relatively painless conduct of the Persian Gulf War.

Although most of the coalition force information was obtained by US national technical means it is important to note that the basic elements of verification, involving space-based and aerial reconnaissance methods in particular, were used in a variety of operational modes. The performance of the various systems in a realistic setting can tell us a great deal about their appropriateness for verification in general and the verification of force structures in particular. In addition, it provides an opportunity to assess the various forms of camouflage, concealment and deception (CC&D) which may be employed in the deployment of conventional weapons and troops. Chapter 8 examines the elements of monitoring used in the Gulf conflict that are most relevant to the verification of conventional force agreements, with a view to identifying how the methods employed in this setting could be of use in other contexts.

---

[63] 'Czechs, Hungary look West to buy C^2', *Defense News*, 6 May 1991, p. 3.

6. Confidence- and security-building measures

I. Introduction

The concept of 'confidence-building measures' put forward at the UN in the 1950s was formalized by the Conference on Security and Co-operation in Europe (CSCE). Put forward by Belgium and Italy in 1973, during consultations to set the agenda for the CSCE, the concept initially included 'measures such as the prior notification of major military manoeuvres on a basis to be specified by the Conference, and the exchange of observers by invitation at military manoeuvres under mutually acceptable conditions'.[1]

Specific measures were formalized in the Final Act of the Helsinki Conference of the CSCE in 1975. Before this, the NATO countries viewed confidence-building measures (CBMs) in political rather than military terms, relating them to 'openness' about military activities in Europe. The WTO countries (other than Romania) could be said to have attached some importance to the military significance of CBMs. The neutral and non-aligned (NNA) countries considered them from both political and military viewpoints—a justifiable position because CBMs were introduced to provide some compensation for the NNA countries which had been sidelined by the MBFR negotiations between the two blocs.[2]

The concluding document adopted by the second CSCE follow-up meeting in Madrid in 1983 included a section on the Conference on Confidence- and Security-Building Measures and Disarmament in Europe, reflecting Yugoslavia's proposal that 'security-building measures' be added to the 'confidence-building measures' of the Helsinki Final Act.[3] The term 'confidence- and security-building measure' (CSBM) was agreed upon; inclusion of 'disarmament' in the title of the Conference was an important innovation, providing a link with disarmament measures and making it clear that CSBMs were considered as a preparatory step towards disarmament.

John Borawski distinguished three general categories of confidence- and security-building measure: (*a*) information exchange; (*b*) observation and

[1] Ghebali, V.-Y., 'Confidence-building measures within the CSCE process: paragraph-by-paragraph analysis of the Helsinki and Stockholm régimes, United Nations Institute for Disarmament Research (UNIDIR), Research Paper No. 3, Geneva, Mar. 1989, p. 3.

[2] Note 1.

[3] The document on confidence-building measures and certain aspects of security and disarmament, included in the Final Act of the Conference on Security and Co-operation in Europe, 1 Aug. 1975, is reprinted in SIPRI, *World Armaments and Disarmament: SIPRI Yearbook 1976* (Taylor & Francis: London, 1976), pp. 359–62; extracts from the concluding document adopted by the second CSCE follow-up meeting in Madrid on 6 Sep. 1983 are reprinted in SIPRI, *World Armaments and Disarmament: SIPRI Yearbook 1984* (Taylor & Francis: London, 1984), pp. 570–71.

inspection; and (c) constraints.[4] Information exchange is intended to enhance mutual knowledge about military force postures, strategies and activities. The more information that is available, the more transparent and predictable military activities become for other countries. Various forms of on-site observation and inspection allow for independent and reliable assessment of the type and character of military activities and permit verification of compliance with the agreed CSBMs. Constraints are militarily the most significant category of CSBM and refer to those measures which 'restrict military activities by directly regulating how, when, and where they are conducted beyond their notification and observation'.[5]

One of the advantages of confidence-building measures is that they reduce the likelihood of military activities being misinterpreted by other countries. Exchange of information on and observation of routine military activities make it possible to clarify or at least assess the activities and to express concerns about certain types of action. CBMs also make it more difficult for a potential attacker to hide its intentions and preparations and make it possible to establish countermeasures. Observation of activities not subject to pre-notification and verifiable restrictions on military activities and deployments also help in this respect. Even if they are violated, the restrictions hamper timely offensive preparations.

The following observation has been made on the relationship between confidence-building measures and arms control:

Analysts typically are reluctant to consider confidence-building as a type of arms control. . . . Arms control is usually understood to entail efforts to reduce the chance of war occurring, or its severity if it should occur. Thus, there appears to be no good practical or theoretical reason to exclude confidence-building measures (CBMs) from the broad range of arms control options. The fact that CBMs do not involve actual force reductions constitutes inadequate grounds for exclusion because many examples of 'arms control' also fail to eliminate weapons. The reluctance to consider confidence-building measures or agreements as examples of arms control tends to (1) improperly restrict what can count as arms control; (2) denigrate the importance of confidence-building; and (3) obscure the grey area where substantive *constraint* CBMs (for instance, limits on the placement of equipment, the composition of military unit's equipment, the types of permissible military exercise, and the size of military activities) clearly impose more 'arms control' on military forces than do modest force reductions. It is far more productive to recognize that CBMs encompass a wide range of individual measures (some very modest and 'soft', some very demanding and constraining) that properly belong to the broader category of arms control measures.[6]

In the same context, Henny van der Graaf wrote the following in 1989:

[4] Borawski, J., *Avoiding War in the Nuclear Age: Confidence-Building Measures for Crisis Stability* (Westview Press: Boulder, Colo., 1986).
[5] George, B., *Special Report on Confidence-Building Measures: Next Steps for Stability and Security*, North Atlantic Assembly: Brussels, 1988, p. 5.
[6] Macintosh, J., *Confidence-building: its Contribution to Peacekeeping*, Occasional Paper No. 11, York University, Canada, Mar. 1990, p.1.

There is a close link between CSBM's and conventional arms control. CSBM's do not reduce military capabilities, but are primarily intended to reduce the risk of unintended confrontation through openness and transparency of the military situation. CSBM's are also a logical complement to reductions of conventional forces by giving guidelines for the activities of these forces after reductions. In the future, it will be rather difficult to draw a clear distinction between CSBM's in the context of the CSCE negotiations and those which as so called stabilizing measures are to be developed in the CFE negotiations. Already now, we see that there are problems how to divide the work in the two ongoing negotiations.[7]

In the context of NATO–WTO European security two conflict scenarios were traditionally discussed: (*a*) a country or a group of countries purposefully prepares to launch an attack, and (*b*) a situation leads to a war that no country really wants. The difference is fundamental in designing concepts and frameworks for arms control and confidence-building measures.

One of the main goals for arms control and CSBMs has been to reduce the risk of an inadvertent slide into war. Because the fear of a large-scale planned attack has only recently been eliminated, the measures against inadvertent war had concentrated on lessening the threat of the first scenario, at least to win political and public support. CSBMs have not been aimed at modifying military potentials, but oriented rather towards the connection between deployments and structures (of those forces included in military activities) and the options of military planning. The direct or indirect influence of CSBMs on military planning is to ensure that military activities are at the very least non-provocative and that they are hopefully non-threatening and defence-oriented as well.

CSBMs have not traditionally been directed at preventing and eliminating internal military conflicts in Europe, but such conflicts—in the former Yugoslavia and in Moldova and Georgia, for example—have become a reality. Most of the efforts against inadvertent war during the period of CSBM negotiations were devoted to the European region, and the type of conflict witnessed between Armenia and Azerbaijan after the collapse of the USSR shows that CSCE participating states are not fully prepared to cope with such challenges. Political events clearly dictate a need for adjustments in CSBM approaches and policies.

II. The Helsinki Final Act

The 1975 Helsinki Final Act included the document on confidence-building measures and certain aspects of security and disarmament.[8] The document specified the numerical threshold for prior notification of 'major military manoeuvres' (involving more than 25 000 troops), types of military manœuvre

---

[7] van der Graaf, H. J., 'Prospects and possible outcome of the conventional arms negotiations (CSBMs/CFE)', ed. H. G. Brauch, *Verification and Arms Control: Implications for European Security,* Results of the Sixth International AFES-PRESS Conference, Part II: Selected Papers, AFES PRESS, Mosbach, 1990, p. 82.

[8] Reprinted in SIPRI 1976 (note 3), pp. 359–62.

subject to notification (independent manœuvres of land, amphibious and airborne troops, and combined manœuvres—land forces together with a naval and/or airborne component, and land forces operating with amphibious and/or airborne forces) and dealt with the zone of application for CBMs. It covered major military manœuvres on the territory, in Europe, of any participating state as well as, if applicable, in the adjoining sea area and airspace; prior notification needed to be given only of manœuvres which took place in an area within 250 km of its frontier facing or shared with any other European participating state. Prior notification of other military manœuvres was recommended on an optional basis.

The invitation of observers was recommended on a voluntary basis for military manœuvres in general, that is, irrespective of their scope. Thus, although the Helsinki Final Act did not set out arrangements for verification and inspection, and although the observation regime was very limited, it provided an important point of departure towards more substantial and intrusive arrangements[9] and was an important positive step in the process of establishing mutually acceptable principles, rules, norms and decision-making procedures to reduce the risk of war in Europe. Verification and other arrangements would have had to cope with detailed and militarily significant provisions for strengthening confidence and security.

III. The Madrid follow-up meeting: creation of a regime

At the Madrid follow-up meeting (1980–83) discussion centred upon the convening of a Conference on Disarmament in Europe, the preliminary task of which would be to negotiate a new set of CBMs. The idea of a European Disarmament Conference (EDC) emerged in the late 1970s, when slow progress in global disarmament efforts had made regional initiatives more urgent and, as mentioned in chapter 4, growing disillusion with the MBFR talks made the idea more attractive to a number of politicians and states, especially those not present at the negotiating table in Vienna.

Five delegations at the Madrid meeting (from France, Poland, Romania, Sweden and Yugoslavia) tabled proposals for an EDC. The French and Polish plans appeared to be in the forefront in representing the Western and Eastern positions.[10]

---

[9] During the implementation of the Helsinki regime, 1975–86, notifications were given by 10 of the 16 NATO members. Of 77 manœuvres notified, 39 involved between 4000 and 24 500 troops. Thirty NATO manœuvres involved between 40 000 and 132 000 troops, and 50 invitations to observers were issued. The WTO countries marked up a total of 32 notifications and 10 invitations to observers. Of the 32 manœuvres notified, 7 involved between 40 000 and 100 000 troops, and 21 manœuvres involved between 25 000 and 35 000 troops. The NNA countries gave 21 notifications and issued 12 invitations. Of the 21 manœuvres, 11 were carried out below the agreed threshold, involving between 5000 and 24 000 troops; 10 others involved between 25 000 and 51 000 troops. See UNIDIR (note 1), pp. 19–20.

[10] Extracts from the proposals for an EDC submitted by the delegations of Poland, France and the NNA countries are reprinted in SIPRI, *World Armaments and Disarmament: SIPRI Yearbook 1982* (Taylor & Francis: London, 1982), pp. 57–59.

The Polish plan suggested a gradual development from existing, voluntary CBMs towards more complex and far-reaching measures of restraint and the reduction of forces and armaments in Europe. Western delegations opposed building on existing CBMs as the starting-point because they did not represent militarily significant measures.[11]

The French proposal, while supporting a gradual approach, favoured new rather than 'second-generation' CBMs. Such a system was described by the British delegation as 'an arms control regime of openness' with the exchange of regular information on all major military formations in Europe, from the divisional level upwards, on the nature, designations and location of garrisons, and on military movements, whether for exercises or for other reasons.[12] The French proposal demanded that four criteria be agreed upon before an EDC was convened: the new CBMs should be militarily significant; they should be politically binding; appropriate arrangements should be made for verification; and the CBMs should be applicable throughout Europe, from the Atlantic to the Urals.

The concluding document adopted by the Madrid meeting in 1983 described the Conference on Confidence- and Security-Building Measures and Disarmament in Europe (CDE) as a 'process' that would be divided into 'stages'. The first stage would be devoted to the negotiation and adoption of mutually complementary CSBMs. Like the Helsinki CBMs, the CSBMs were aimed to 'reduce the risk of military confrontation in Europe', but now they were to be focused rather on military behaviour than intentions. The Document emphasized the 'military significance' of the measures. It also differed from the Helsinki Final Act by postulating a politically binding regime, excluding voluntary measures. The principle of flexible verification was added to these criteria: all CSBMs must be verifiable, and each of them must be subject to appropriate means of verification.[13]

The concluding document of the Madrid meeting resolved the differences on the area of application, an issue which was also treated as important in connection with the verification provision. According to the document, the CSBMs were to 'cover the whole of Europe as well as the adjoining sea area and air space', which meant an extension of the 250-km zone inside the western Soviet borders. The wording of the provision left many ambiguities, however, such as the interpretation of 'adjoining sea area or air space' (i.e., whether to interpret this based on a purely geographical approach, which gave equal value to the land area and sea space adjoining it, or to use a functional approach, which could imply a different value for arrangements concerning military activities on land and in the adjoining sea space).

---

[11] The NNA countries supported 'second-generation' CBMs, to include: notification of major military manœuvres and movements of troops exceeding a total of 18 000 troops, as compared with the existing threshold of 25 000 troops; and notification of naval exercises in European waters with participation of major amphibious forces comprising more than 5000 troops and 10 major amphibious vessels. Because of opposition from many Western delegations these important proposals were not discussed at the meeting.

[12] 'The CSCE and a European disarmament conference', SIPRI (note 10), pp. 53–54.

[13] Madrid concluding document (note 3), para. 6.

IV. The Stockholm Conference: regime identification

The 35-nation Conference on Confidence- and Security-Building Measures and Disarmament in Europe, the Stockholm Conference, opened in January 1984.

The Stockholm Document, signed in September 1986, can be said to have identified a CSBM regime.[14] It confirmed the principle that countries must refrain from the threat or use of force in their mutual and international relations. As a second principle it accepted the right of 'individual or collective self-defence if an armed attack occurs, as set forth in the Charter of the United Nations'. Third, it proposed that states should try to strengthen mutual confidence for the sake of international security, that is, to reduce the tension between the first two principles. The principles were based on norms which included the rights and duties of the participating states (to notify certain military activities, to exchange observers, to agree to on-site inspections, etc.). A set of explicit rules was established for every norm. Finally, the CSBM regime encompassed decision-making procedures.[15]

The Document aimed at regulating the 'activities' of military forces and required advance notification of major military activities—exercises and troop concentrations at or over 13 000 troops or 300 battle tanks—and routine observation of military activities at or over 17 000 troops, and permitted OSI upon demand by any of the 35 states. The engagement of 13 000 troops or 300 battle tanks was subject to notification only if it occurred within a divisional structure or a structure equivalent to at least two brigades or regiments, not necessarily subordinate to the same division.

The inclusion of equipment and structural thresholds and the mandatory nature of the document represented a remarkable advance on the Helsinki regime. The combination of equipment and the capacity of units has more military significance than simply the number of troops employed. This meant that verification arrangements were focused on well-defined significant military activities for the first time—and verification of tanks, divisions, brigades or regiments is in fact easier than verification of numbers of troops.

The numerical thresholds for notification were set regardless of the verification and observation requirements—they were rather the result of a compromise. The Eastern proposal suggested a threshold of 20 000 troops and the Western proposal one of 6000 troops. The compromise could also be reflected in the setting of different thresholds for notification (13 000 troops) and observation (17 000 troops).

---

[14] The Document of the Stockholm Conference on Confidence- and Security-Building Measures and Disarmament in Europe Convened in Accordance with the Relevant Provisions of the Concluding Document of the Madrid Meeting of the Conference on Security and Co-operation in Europe, Stockholm, 19 Sep 1986 is reprinted in SIPRI, *SIPRI Yearbook 1987: World Armaments and Disarmament* (Oxford University Press: Oxford, 1987), appendix 10A, pp. 353–69.

[15] Efinger, M., 'Preventing war in Europe through confidence-and security-building measures?', ed. V. Rittberger, *International Regimes in East-West Politics* (Pinter: London and New York, 1990), p.130.

Verification provisions

Verification within the Stockholm regime was largely identified with inspection. The section of the Document on compliance and verification could be regarded as a conceptual and political breakthrough. It reaffirmed the provision of the Madrid mandate that CSBMs would be provided with appropriate means of verification. Several innovations should be mentioned, however.

The Stockholm Document gave a certain multilateral dimension to the use of NTM (para. 64)—a principle that had been adopted within the framework of bilateral US–Soviet agreements on strategic arms control, although this did not mean multilateral recognition of the principle ('the participating States *recognize* that NTMs *can* be used for monitoring compliance with agreed confidence- and security-building measures' [emphasis added]). Paragraph 64 did not link the use of NTM with the generally recognized principles of international law—perhaps as a reflection of the position of the NNA countries, which did not favour multilateral legalization of means which only a few states had or could possess.

Paragraph 65 specified that 'each participating State has the right to conduct inspections on the territory of any other participating State within the zone of application for CSBMs'. It stressed the right to *conduct* and not the right to *request* inspections, thereby ruling out the possibility of refusal by the state to be inspected.

The Document permitted a state party to request an inspection when compliance is in doubt. Accordingly, an inspection could be used to check a doubt concerning a military activity, whether notified or not, that could not be observed. This provision was supported by another which required a request to be accompanied by a list of 'the reasons' to determine the admissibility of the request for inspection. Even if a state to be inspected was not satisfied with the reasons provided, it could not prevent or delay an inspection. Inspection was mandatory.

The Document gave more latitude to inspectors than to observers of notified military activities. The section on observation of certain military activities included the following arrangements: each participating state could send two observers to the military activity to be observed; observers could make requests with regard to the observation programme, to which the host state should accede if possible; a host state should provide transportation for observers to, from and within the area of the military activity to be observed; notifiable military activities could be observed in the field but the provisions allowed a host state to deny observation of restricted locations, installations and defence sites and did not limit the number or extent of such facilities; a host state was obliged to give an introductory briefing, to provide observers with a map of the area of operations (scale 1:500 000), to supply the observers with the necessary equipment (however, it was agreed that observers could use their own binoculars), to provide the observers with daily briefings, to facilitate direct observations of forces engaged, to 'guide' observers in the area of the military activity, and to provide communications between observers and the authorities which had sent them.

The functions of observers were twofold: first, to check that the notified military activity was not threatening in nature, and second to verify conformity of the activity with the information provided in the notification.

The inspection regime, on the other hand, granted inspectors the right of access, entry and unobstructed survey throughout the area specified for inspection, with exceptions for areas or sensitive points to which access is normally denied or restricted, military and defence installations, as well as naval vessels, military vehicles and aircraft. Although the restricted areas should be as limited as possible in number and extent they had no equivalent in the observation regime and indirectly represented a form of constraint. However, restricted areas were not to be designated so as to circumvent the provisions of the inspection regime.

The Document set a passive inspection quota, stating the maximum number of inspections which a participating state was obliged to accept on its territory, rather than the number of inspections it was authorized to implement. The quota specified three annual inspections for any participating state other than the USA and Canada (whose territories were exempted from the area of application). The quota of three annual inspections must each be carried out by a different participating state.

The inspection regime was arranged as follows. The state requesting the inspection may not specify an area larger than that required for an army level military activity. The state to be inspected must reply within 24 hours and the inspection team must be permitted to enter its territory within 36 hours of the request. The inspected state could select the point of entry, but it should be as close as possible to the specified area and such that an inspection team could enter the specified area without delay.

The inspection team should not exceed four members; it may divide into two parts and conduct inspection from the ground, from the air, or both simultaneously. It should be accompanied by representatives of the inspected state and the inspection must be completed within 48 hours. The inspection team was allowed to use its own maps, photo cameras, binoculars and dictaphones. Once inspections were underway it became clear that inspectors were allowed to inspect in the open terrain, including training grounds, but not within barracks, command posts or military installations surrounded by a fence.

The Stockholm Document set a precedent by allowing aerial overflights. It included several important arrangements. An inspecting state was required to specify whether aerial inspection was to be conducted using an aeroplane, a helicopter, or both, but the type of aircraft was to be chosen by mutual agreement between the inspecting and inspected states. The provisions enabled inspectors to deviate from the flight plan to make specific observations—on request and on condition that the activity would not breach the provisions on prohibited or restricted areas. Inspectors were granted additional rights to observe data on flight equipment at any time, as well as topographical maps to determine the exact position of the aircraft, and to return to the specified area as many times as necessary during the inspection period (this was also valid for ground inspectors).

One of the main flaws of the Stockholm regime as regards the effectiveness of observation and inspections was that it did not contribute much to reducing the risk of short-warning attack. This important shortcoming stemmed from the failure to agree on a number of relevant arrangements, such as establishing zones of restricted military potentials or limitations on alertness activities.

V. Implementation of the Stockholm Document

The implementation of the Stockholm Document was widely accepted as a positive experience. As of 15 June 1990, 117 military activities had been notified and 50 observed,[16] and over the period 1987–90, 44 inspections were conducted—23 by NATO and 21 by the WTO countries.[17] No NNA country had conducted or hosted inspections.

The experience reflected several basic requirements for an inspected party: (*a*) some personnel should be on permanent alert, ready for inspections at any time; (*b*) the host state should provide an interpreter for an inspection team and one or several liaison officers; (*c*) several vehicles and a minimum of two helicopters and certain reserve transportation means should be available for inspection and escort teams (this added to manpower requirements for drivers and pilots); (*d*) the presence of doctors and other arrangements for medical care is needed; and (*e*) several additional personnel are required to fulfil communication requirements. In all, some 50 people are needed to support and accompany four inspectors, excluding personnel for providing food, accommodation, and so on. The substantial costs of hosting inspections are clearly largely associated with manpower.

The costs of implementing the OSI provisions were underestimated on conclusion of the Document. In 1987 several states began to set up inspection agencies. This entailed heavy expenditures for qualified personnel and equipment and the cost factor was an important one behind the reluctance of smaller states, particularly NNA countries, to carry out OSI.[18]

The Document assigned tasks including verifying numbers of troops and certain *matériel* involved in military exercises; the engagement of formations of forces in the exercise under a single operational command or otherwise; the number and types of divisions participating; and the number of sorties of the air forces within a certain notified military activity. The task of verifying this information was to be carried out within specific parameters, including those mentioned above: the interval between a request for inspection and its commencement; duration of an inspection; the number of inspection teams; con-

---

[16] *Jane's NATO Handbook, 1990–91* (Jane's Publishing Co: Coulsdon, UK, 1990), p. 173.
[17] *Jane's NATO Handbook, 1991–92* (Jane's Publishing Co: Coulsdon, UK, 1991), p. 125.
[18] Efinger (note 15), pp.142–43.

straints on inspections; information to be provided by a receiving state; and equipment allowed for an inspection team.

According to the rules, a four-person inspection team had to count notified personnel and some equipment, such as tanks on the move, in an area of about 15 000 square km within 48 hours. Because of these constraints an inspection team had to rely mainly on information provided by a host state through briefings and questions and was, therefore, dependent on the intentions of the inspected state to provide correct information.

The existence of sensitive points closed to inspection could provide a loophole for circumvention, for example, if headquarters were located at these points. Furthermore, the maximum number of forces involved in an exercise potentially exceeding the notification threshold of 13 000 troops or 300 tanks at any time could be reached during one day of an exercise which might last two weeks. If an inspection team was absent on that particular day, there would be no opportunity to verify the actual largest numbers. There were arguments that counting aircraft in the sky at any given moment was militarily irrelevant and thereby notification and observation of air activities would be merely symbolic. Because of the speed and range of aircraft their withdrawal from border areas as a possible confidence-building measure was also considered irrelevant. Proposals to establish a ceiling on the number of main operating bases as a way to restrict the sortie-generation capability were met with the counter-argument that it would make the remaining bases more vulnerable to pre-emption, which would hardly be stabilizing.[19]

Thus, the effectiveness of observation and inspection depended to a great extent on the good will of the inspected state, especially in providing inspectors and observers with wider access to certain activities and installations rather than giving extensive briefings which need to be checked anyway. In the latter case frequent references to the possibility of checking Western information by reading Western open literature were certainly valid in terms of the relatively less open Eastern literature about Eastern capabilities. In either case, however, the information required checking.

The opportunities lie rather in the more intrusive standards of observation and inspection. If arrangements for the observation of manœuvres are extensive, particularly with helicopter overflights, there is a marginal difference between inspection and observation in highly militarized areas or small countries. All installations (except those behind walls) could be photographed subsequently. Such installations could be the subject of inspections under the CFE Treaty provisions, which also extend the territory for verification to the European part of the former Soviet Union. The observation and inspection provisions of the CSBM regime permit a wide range of activities and items to be monitored.

---

[19] Palmisano, S. and Fernau, H. (eds), *Military Confidence- and Security-Building Measures in Europe at Present and in Future* (Institute for Military Security Policy: Vienna, 1988), p. 84.

It was argued that a threshold had been reached in observations of certain military activities. Manœuvres illustrate specific features of command structure and troop behaviour, which differ from country to country. In order to extract information that could facilitate assessment of the threatening character of military activities knowledge of a standard pattern of activities is needed that might be achieved through observing at least two exercises of the same type in the same country. Two ways to ease this task were considered appropriate: to establish continuity, by sending the same observers to the same exercise every year, and/or to establish a data base of the particular features of at least the regularly observed exercises. Such a data base could help to assess any tendency towards exercises of a more or less threatening character.[20]

The Stockholm Document reflected greater openness from the Eastern side, in comparison with initial arrangements and earlier standards. Some hurdles, for example allowing helicopter overflights, were overcome, but others, though perhaps minor at first glance, none the less remained. One of the problems which faced Western observers was the lack of appropriate unclassified military maps or detailed civilian maps of Eastern countries. The publication of documents related to verification and the exchange of maps and basic material for inspection can be seen as important steps to enhance the verification regime. The argument has been that more precise maps can be used to assess the tactical characteristics of a landscape, in preparation for artillery fire and for flight profiles of missiles, for example.[21]

The CDE regime was designed to implement low-level verification tasks and mainly aimed at greater openness and transparency as a confidence-building measure. In practice, the lion's share of the monitoring of relevant activities was still borne by national technical means, but the technologies available and access to them varied substantially within both alliances. Only one aspect of the regime required co-ordination—the quota of three inspections per year whenever several countries were interested in inspecting a particular country (particularly in the case of the USSR and the GDR).

Another message for the negotiators of the agreements which followed the Stockholm Document, including the CFE Treaty, was the cost of a verification regime with extensive on-site inspection. A certain amount of co-operation among states could reduce the costs and also rule out the need for individual states to attempt to sample the entire area of application continuously. Such co-operation would substantially reduce the intensity of inspections, and with more detailed information a less intrusive regime could perhaps be envisaged.

---

[20] Clausen, H-C., 'Some thoughts on improving confidence-and security-building measures', Palmisano and Fernau (note 19), pp. 59–60.
[21] This argument was stated by the head of the topographical service of the Soviet Armed Forces, General Alexey Losev. He also said that in 1986 the Ministry of Defence declassified maps at a scale of 1 : 1 000 000. Later they declassified maps at 1 : 500 000 and 1 : 200 000, but by 1989 they had not considered declassifying maps at 1 : 100 000 or less (*Krasnaya Zvezda,* 22 July 1989).

VI. The Vienna Document 1990

The Vienna CSBM Negotiations

Having been the centre-piece of the CSCE agenda in the military area confidence-building measures started to play a lesser role at the third CSCE follow-up meeting in Vienna (1986–89), partly because more importance was attached to conventional arms control, and also because there were fewer disagreements in the area of CSBMs. The NATO, WTO and NNA countries agreed, however, that the Stockholm measures had not exhausted the potential of further CSBMs for European security. The only remaining problem concerned how to formulate the negotiating mandate for future CSBMs.

Four drafting groups were set up in February 1990, based on working groups established in 1989. They covered the following areas:

1. Verification and information, to deal with static military data[22] and their evaluation, including random evaluation visits and inspections.

2. Communication, consultation, and military contacts, to cover diplomatic communication, review meetings on implementation of measures, and military contacts.

3. Notification and observation, to focus on improving the Stockholm agreement, mostly by lowering the notification and observation thresholds.

4. Constraints and annual calendars.[23]

In February 1990 FRG Foreign Minister Hans-Dietrich Genscher called for pan-European institutions in the CSCE framework, including a European conflict management centre and a European verification centre. In June the GDR, Czechoslovakia and Poland discussed their proposal for institutionalizing the CSCE. Among the issues in the draft document they included the creation of a centre for confidence building, arms control and verification in Berlin and a centre for the prevention of conflicts. In June, US Secretary of State James Baker presented his ideas on the future shape of the CSCE, which included the establishment of mechanisms for conflict resolution and for greater military openness.[24]

The NATO summit meeting in July 1990 called for a CSCE Centre for the Prevention of Conflict 'that might serve as a forum for exchanges of military information, discussion of unusual military activities, and the conciliation of disputes involving C.S.C.E. member states'.[25]

The CFE and CSBM negotiations posed similar problems in terms of information exchange and verification activities. Not every participant rejected the value of the mutual exchange of information, but the acceptable level of infor-

---

[22] Static military data are data not directly related to military activities but dealing with military structures and installations such as peace-time location of units, headquarters, depots, and command and control facilities.

[23] *Arms Control Reporter,* 1990, sheet 402.B.257.

[24] *Arms Control Reporter,* 1990, sheet 402.B.262.2.

[25] *Arms Control Reporter,* 1990, sheet 402.B.262.5.

mation was the subject of substantial and in many cases principle differences. Each participant, although to a different extent, was concerned with the level of uncertainty in assessing compliance with the provisions to be accepted. Narrowing the positions in order to reach compromise agreements represented a serious political challenge, but this was eventually overcome.

The Vienna Document 1990 of the Negotiations on Confidence- and Security-Building Measures Convened in Accordance with the Relevant Provisions of the Concluding Document of the Vienna Meeting of the Conference on Security and Co-operation in Europe integrated a set of new confidence- and security-building measures with measures adopted in the Stockholm Document.[26]

Unlike the Stockholm Document, the Vienna Document did not contain a lengthy section on refraining from the threat or use of force and, while the 1986 Document called for CSBMs 'to reduce the dangers of armed conflict and of misunderstanding or miscalculation of military activities', the 1990 Document simply stated that the new set of mutually complementary CSBMs is 'designed to reduce the risk of military confrontation in Europe'. In principle, however, it was an innovative document. The main points of departure from the Stockholm Document are listed in this section.

Annual exchange of military information

One of the most important innovations concerned annual exchange of military information. Section I covered information on military forces, on plans for the deployment of major weapon and equipment systems, and on military budgets.[27] Information on military forces in the zone of application was specified as follows:

1. Information on the command organization of land and amphibious forces specifying the designation and subordination of all formations (armies, corps, divisions and equivalents) and units (brigades, regiments and equivalents) at each level of command down to and including brigade/regiment or equivalent.

2. Information for each formation and combat unit of land forces down to and including brigade/regiment or equivalent, and for each amphibious formation and amphibious combat unit permanently located in the zone of application down to and including brigade/regiment or equivalent, on: designation and subordination; active or non-active status;[28] the normal peacetime location of its

---

[26] The Vienna Document 1990 is reprinted in SIPRI, *SIPRI Yearbook 1991: World Armaments and Disarmament* (Oxford University Press: Oxford, 1991), appendix 13B, pp. 475–88.

[27] Information on military budgets requires the annual exchange of information on military budgets of the participating states for the forthcoming fiscal year, itemizing defence expenditures on the basis of the categories set out in the United Nations 'Instrument for Standardised International Reporting of Military Expenditures' adopted on 12 Dec. 1980. Each state may ask for clarification from any other participating state of the budgetary information provided.

[28] Non-active formations or combat units are those at 0–15 per cent of their authorized combat strength. In the Chairman's Statement (Annex V), it is stated that 'it is understood that in the continuing

headquarters indicated by exact geographic terms and/or co-ordinates; the peacetime authorized personnel strength; the major organic weapon and equipment systems, specifying numbers of each type of battle tank, helicopter, ACV, anti-tank guided missile launcher permanently/integrally mounted on armoured vehicles; and self-propelled and towed artillery pieces, mortars and multiple rocket launchers (100-mm calibre and above) and AVLBs.

3. Information for each air formation and air combat unit of the air forces, air defence aviation and naval aviation permanently based on land down to and including wing/air regiment or equivalent on: designation and subordination; the normal peacetime location of the headquarters indicated by exact geographic terms and/or co-ordinates; the normal peacetime location of the unit by the air base or military airfield on which it is based, specifying the designation or, if applicable, name of the air base or military airfield and its location indicated by exact geographic terms and/or co-ordinates; the peacetime authorized personnel strength; and the numbers of each type of combat aircraft and helicopter organic to the formation or unit.

Information exchange on deployment plans for major weapon and equipment systems was to cover plans for the following year: the type and name of the weapon/equipment systems to be deployed; total number of each weapon/equipment system; whenever possible, the number of each weapon/equipment system planned for allocation to each formation or unit; and the extent to which the deployment will add to or replace existing weapon/equipment systems.

Risk reduction

The section on risk reduction, another innovation of the Vienna Document, contained a sub-section on a mechanism for consultation and co-operation as regards unusual military activities.[29] If a participating state was concerned about unusual and unscheduled activities, it could request an explanation and later a meeting with the state concerned—in all cases within 48 hours. Either state could invite other interested participating states to attend. The Conflict Prevention Centre could serve as a forum for such meetings.

Contacts

The Document included new provisions on visits to air bases. Observers were to have an opportunity to view activities at the air base, including preparations to carry out the functions of the air base, and to gain an impression of the approximate number of sorties and type of missions being flown. The quota made this measure largely symbolic—no participating state would be obliged to arrange more than one such visit in any five-year period, involving up to two

---

negotiations an adequate solution will be found to evaluate non-active formations and units which are activated for routine training purposes'.

[29] Another sub-section covered co-operation as regards hazardous incidents of a military nature.

visitors from each participating state for 24 hours, and the invitation should be extended 42 days or more in advance.[30]

Prior notification

The provisions on prior notification of certain military activities were unchanged except for the sub-section on information on different types of notifiable military activity. The provision of the Stockholm Document on the 'number and type of divisions participating for each state' was expanded in the Vienna Document to read: 'the designation, subordination, number and type of formations and units participating for each State down to and including brigade/regiment or equivalent level'. This was a very substantial change, broadening the information about formations and units in the same exercise.

Observation of certain military activities

The most important changes in this section were as follows: observers were to be provided with a more precise map at 1 : 250 000, depicting the area of the notified military activity and the initial tactical situation in this area, with a possibility of smaller-scale maps showing the entire area (besides a requirement of a scale of 1 : 500 000, the Stockholm Document only permitted 'a sketch indicating the basic situation'); observers were to be allowed to use (subject to examination and approval by the host state) a wider range of equipment, such as their own binoculars, maps, photo and video cameras, dictaphones and hand-held passive night-vision devices; a host state was to be encouraged to provide an aerial survey, preferably by helicopter, of the area of the military activity, allowing at least one observer to monitor the disposition of forces engaged in the activity from the air; the observers were to be given the opportunity to observe combat and support units of all participating formations of a divisional or equivalent level and, whenever possible, to visit units below divisional or equivalent level and communicate with commanders and troops (the Stockholm Document only permitted observation of 'major combat units of the participating formations at a divisional or equivalent level'); at the close of each observation the observers should be able to meet together and with host state officials to discuss the course of the observed activity; the participating states are encouraged to permit media representatives from all participating states to attend observed activities and be provided with equal access to those facets of the activity open to them.

---

[30] A sub-section on military contacts is also important for strengthening the process of CSBMs. It included exchanges and visits between senior military/defence representatives; contacts between relevant military institutions; attendance by military representatives of other participating states at courses of instruction; exchanges and contacts between academics and experts in military studies, etc. This type of communication can also be used for discussing verification and compliance problems and the appropriate ways to overcome difficulties in implementing corresponding activities.

Annual calendars

The Vienna Document 1990 contained important new arrangements for the exchange of annual calendars: a participating state which was to host military activities subject to prior notification conducted by any other participating state(s) would include these activities in its annual calendar; a participating state should inform all other participating states if it did not forecast any military activity subject to prior notification; the area of the military activity should be 'indicated by geographic features where appropriate and defined by geographic co-ordinates'; and information should be provided on the planned duration of the military activity, indicating the envisaged start and end dates. Each state should give information on: the envisaged total number of troops engaged in the military activity and, for activities involving more than one state, the host state should provide such information for each state involved; the envisaged level of the military activity; and the designation of direct operational command under which the activity will take place.

Constraining provisions

In contrast to the Stockholm Document, which included verification provisions in the section on constraining provisions, the Vienna Document divided constraining and verification provisions into two separate sections. Aside from the absence of provisions on inspection (see below) the section on constraining provisions differed from the Stockholm Document only in lowering the threshold of military activities subject to prior notification, unless they have been the object of communication, from 75 000 to 40 000 troops.

Compliance and verification

The section on compliance and verification started with the same language as the Madrid Mandate (CSBMs 'will be provided with adequate forms of verification which correspond to their content') and stated that participating states recognized that NTM 'can play a role in monitoring compliance with agreed' CSBMs. The lion's share of provisions on *inspection* and corresponding arrangements and requirements were identical in both documents, but the Vienna Document contained several additions. These included: the right for inspection teams to use their own charts, video cameras and hand-held passive night vision devices (among these three means the Stockholm Document allowed only their 'own aeronautical charts'); a requirement for the inspection team to show the equipment to the representatives of the inspected state upon arrival in the specified area; and a requirement for the inspected state to provide the team with access to appropriate telecommunications equipment for the purpose of continuous communication between the sub-teams (the Stockholm Document limited the arrangement by allowing the inspection teams access to this equipment of the inspected state, 'including the opportunity for continuous communication between the members of an inspection team in an aircraft and those in a land vehicle employed in the inspection').

The Vienna Document set new arrangements for inspection. Inspectors would be entitled to request and receive briefings at agreed times by military representatives of the inspected state. At the inspectors' request, such briefings were to be given by commanders of formations or units in the specified area. Another arrangement applied to 'ensure that no action is taken by the representatives of the inspected state which could endanger inspectors and, if applicable, auxiliary personnel'. Whereas these inspection arrangements were not principal innovations, permission to use extra technical means does help to enhance the effectiveness of verification.

A rather more important contribution of the Vienna Document was the separate set of provisions in the new sub-section on *evaluation*. Each state was obliged to accept a quota of one annual evaluation visit for every 60 units, or portion thereof, reported in the annual exchange of military information, but no more than 15 visits per calendar year, or one-fifth of its quota of visits, was to be from the same participating state. No formation or unit was to be visited more than twice during a calendar year or more than once by the same participating state during a calendar year. No participating state would be obliged to accept more than one visit at any given time on its territory.

If a participating state had formations or units stationed on the territory of other participating states in the zone of application of CSBMs, the maximum number of evaluation visits permitted to its forces in each of the states concerned was to be proportional to the number of its units in each state.

Requests for such visits were to be submitted with five days' notice. The reply was to be given within 48 hours of the receipt of the request and to indicate whether the formation or unit would be available for evaluation on the proposed date at its formal peacetime location. If formations or units are unavailable for evaluation, although in their normal peacetime location, a state may refuse a visit, and the reasons, along with the number of days that a formation or unit is unavailable for evaluation, are to be stated in the reply. Each state will be entitled to invoke this provision up to a total of five times for an aggregate of no more than 30 days per calendar year. If a formation or unit was absent from the normal peacetime location, a requested state would indicate the reasons for and the duration of its absence. This state might offer a visit to the formation or unit outside its normal location, otherwise the requesting state would be able to visit the normal peacetime location; but the Vienna Document indirectly cast doubt upon the usefulness of the action by stating that 'the requesting State may however refrain in either case from the visit'.

The evaluation team would have up to two members and might be accompanied by an interpreter as auxiliary personnel. The visit was to take place in the course of a single working day, last up to 12 hours and start with a briefing by an officer commanding the formation or unit, or his deputy, in the headquarters of the formation or unit, concerning the personnel as well as major weapon and equipment systems reported upon. The team was to be accompanied at all times by representatives of the receiving state.

In case of a visit to a unit (a brigade, regiment or equivalent), the inspected state was to provide the possibility to observe personnel and the major weapon and equipment of the unit reported in the information exchange in their normal locations. It is to provide the same for a visit to a formation (an army corps, division or equivalent), but not to 'any of its formations or units'. Access would not have to be granted to sensitive points, facilities and equipment, and the visit should not interfere with activities of the formation or unit.

Annual implementation assessment meetings

The Vienna Document created a procedure for an annual implementation assessment meeting for which the newly established Conflict Prevention Centre would serve as the forum. Discussions would cover the present and future implementation of agreed CSBMs and might extend to: clarification of questions arising from such implementation; operation of agreed measures; and implications of all information originating from the implementation of any agreed measures for the CSBM process in the framework of the CSCE.

VII. The Vienna Document 1992

The three-year negotiations on CSBMs were concluded on 4 March 1992 with the adoption of the Vienna Document 1992.[31] By the final stages of the negotiations the number of participating states had grown to 48. The Document was signed by several new states—Albania, Armenia, Azerbaijan, Belarus, Estonia, Kazakhstan, Kyrgyzstan, Latvia, Lithuania, Moldova, the Russian Federation, Tajikistan, Turkmenistan, Ukraine and Uzbekistan. The Document came into force on 1 May 1992, by which time Georgia, Slovenia and Croatia had also signed.

The Vienna Document 1992 encompassed all the CSBMs agreed since the beginning of the Helsinki process and, for the first time, addressed the real limitations on military activities at the same time as it included new measures to enhance transparency.

Many provisions repeated the corresponding sections and provisions of the Vienna Document 1990: the Preamble, Annual exchange of military information, Information on plans for the deployment of major weapon and equipment systems, Information on military budgets, Mechanism for consultation and co-operation as regards unusual military activities, Co-operation as regards hazardous incidents of a military nature, Visits to air bases, Military contacts, Prior notification of certain military activities, Observation of certain military activities, Annual calendars, Constraining provisions, Compliance and verifica-

---

[31] For the text of the Vienna Document 1992 see appendix B.

tion, Evaluation, Communications, Annual Implementation Assessment Meeting.

The Document also contained a few new sections: Data relating to major weapon and equipment systems, Voluntary hosting of visits to dispel concerns about military activities, Demonstration of new types of major weapon and equipment systems. In addition, several new paragraphs were added to the sections from the 1990 Document.

Annual exchange of military information

This section included a new provision on the exchange of information on armoured personnel carrier look-alikes and armoured infantry fighting vehicle look-alikes (para. 11.2.5.4), thereby extending coverage of this type of equipment to states not party to the CFE Treaty and indicating the concern with these types both from a verification point of view and from possible ambiguities which might arise in dealing with them.

The Document included an important new provision on exchange of information on planned increases in personnel strength above the authorized peace-time level for more than 21 days by more than 1500 troops for each active combat unit and by more than 5000 troops for each active formation, excluding personnel increases in the formation's subordinate formations and/or combat units subject to separate reporting under paragraph 11.2, which specifies information for each formation and combat unit of land forces down to and including brigade/regiment or equivalent level (para. 11.3.1).

The next paragraph (11.3.2) prescribed information for each non-active formation and non-active combat unit which was planned to be temporarily activated for routine military activities or for any other purpose with more than 2000 troops for more than 21 days.

Data relating to major weapon and equipment systems

The Document went beyond the Vienna Document 1990 by specifying in detail the data to be supplied on major weapon and equipment systems, with specific additional data on new types and versions. The data to be exchanged should include:

Battle tanks: type; national nomenclature/name; main gun calibre; unladen weight; in addition, on new types and versions—night vision capability; additional armour; track width; floating capability; snorkelling equipment.

ACVs (APCs, AIFVs and HACVs): type; national nomenclature/name; type and calibre of armaments; data on new types and versions—night vision capability; seating capability (for APCs); additional armour (on AIFVs and HACVs); floating capability; snorkelling equipment.

APC look-alikes and AIFV look-alikes: type; national nomenclature/name; type and calibre of armaments, if any.

Anti-tank guided missile launchers permanently/integrally mounted on armoured vehicles: type; national nomenclature/name.

Self-propelled and towed artillery pieces, mortars and multiple rocket launchers (100 mm calibre and above) (artillery pieces, mortars and multiple launch rocket systems): type; national nomenclature; calibre. Data on new types or versions of MLRS will, in addition, include number of tubes.

AVLBs: type; national nomenclature/name; data on new types and versions—span of the bridge and carrying capacity/load classification.

Combat aircraft: type; national nomenclature/name; data on new types or versions—type of integrally mounted armaments, if any.

Helicopters: type; national nomenclature/name.

Along with the data, each participating state was to be provided with photographs showing the right or left side, and top and front views for each of the types of major weapon and equipment system concerned. Additionally, photographs of APC and AIFV look-alikes were to include a view clearly showing their internal configuration to illustrate the specific characteristic which distinguishes each vehicle as a look-alike (paras 12–13.11).

Voluntary hosting of visits

Another important new section dealt with the voluntary hosting of visits to dispel concerns about military activities (paras 19–19.2). It specified that participating states might, at their discretion, invite other participating states to designate personnel accredited to the host state or other representatives to take part in visits to areas on the territory of the host state in which there might be cause for such concerns. The host state can communicate to all other participating states its intention to conduct the visit, indicating the reasons for the visit, the area to be visited, the states invited and the general arrangements to be adopted.

Demonstration of new types of major weapon and equipment system

This innovative section obliged the first participating state which deployed a new type of major weapon and equipment system in the zone of application to arrange at the earliest opportunity, for example, during an observation, a demonstration for representatives of all other participating states. Invitations were to be extended to all participating states 42 days or more in advance of visits. Replies, indicating whether or not the invitation is accepted, were to be given no later than 21 days after the issue of invitation (paras 35–35.4).

Prior notification of certain military activities.

The new agreement went further than the Vienna Document 1990 by lowering the level at which activities should be notified to those involving 9000 troops, including support troops, or at least 250 battle tanks. The same limits were set for forces being transferred from outside or being concentrated within the area of application if they were organized into a divisional structure or at least two brigades/regiments, not necessarily subordinate to the same division (paras 38.1.1, 38.3.1).

Observation of certain military activities

As in the case of prior notification, the Document lowered the level of the activities to be observed. Military activities would be subject to observation where the number of troops engaged meets or exceeds 13 000 or where the number of battle tanks engaged meets or exceeds 300, except in case of either an amphibious landing or a parachute assault by airborne forces, which would be subject to observation whenever the number of troops engaged meets or exceeds 3500 (para. 45.4).

Constraining provisions

The section included several new obligations. First, no participating state was to carry out within two calendar years more than one military activity subject to prior notification involving more than 900 battle tanks or 40 000 troops (para. 71.2). A maximum of six military activities subject to prior notification involving over 13 000 troops or 300 battle tanks might take place within a calendar year. Of these six, no participating state was to carry out more than three such activities involving more than 25 000 troops or 400 battle tanks (para. 71.2.1). No participating state was to carry out simultaneously more than three military activities subject to prior notification each involving more than 13 000 troops or 300 battle tanks (para. 71.3). Information should be provided to all states parties by 15 November each year concerning military activities subject to prior notification involving more than 40 000 troops or 900 battle tanks which are planned to be carried out or hosted in the second subsequent calendar year (para. 72).

Inspection

The main difference from the 1990 Document regarded the right of the inspecting state to invite other participating states to take part in an inspection (para. 77). The section added to the list of requests for inspection of the inspecting state to the receiving state other participating states participating in the inspection, if applicable (para. 90.9). In this case, the inspection team would be headed by a national of the inspecting state, which would have at least as many inspectors in the team as any invited state. The inspection team would be under the responsibility of the inspecting state, against whose quota the inspection is counted (para. 96).

Evaluation

This section contained a new provision. Non-active formations and temporarily activated combat units were to be made available for evaluation during the period of temporary activation and in the area/location of activation. In such cases the provisions for the evaluation of active formations and units would be applicable, *mutatis mutandis*. Evaluation visits conducted under this provision would count against the quotas of one evaluation visit per calendar year for every 60 units, or portion thereof (para. 113.1). However, no participating state would be obliged to accept more than 15 visits per calendar year (para. 114).

Some observations

The Vienna Document 1992 led to further reductions in the numbers and scale of military activities in every participating state. It expanded the inspection regime and established multinational inspections. The option of inviting accredited personnel (for example, military attachés) to the inspected areas of the host country may be quite useful as it provides more flexible methods to encourage confidence.

One of the most important features of the Document was the inclusion of new participating states and the introduction of new measures dealing with major weapon and equipment systems and their observation. Being a partial solution to the strict verification guidelines, the latter provided an opportunity to limit the scope for cheating. The former presented the possibility for more difficulties for inspections and evaluation, particularly taking into account the absence of qualified personnel and experience in many of the new states and the conflict situations in or among some of these states.

There has been a clear downward trend in the level of military activities since 1989 with six military exercises subject to notification conducted in 1992 and only four in 1993.[32] At the third Annual Implementation Assessment Meeting (AIAM) held in May 1993 it was suggested that since the changed politico-military situation was giving rise to a reduction in large military manœuvres and an increase in smaller ones, a lower threshold should be considered for notification and invitation to observers.

It was also proposed at the AIAM that the maximum area to be visited in any single inspection be more precisely defined and the number of inspections and inspectors be increased. Concerning evaluation visits to active formations it was proposed that increases be made in the minimum number of visits any country must receive (from the current maximum of 15 per year), the general quota for such visits, their duration and the size of the evaluation teams.

---

[32] Lachowski, Z., 'The Vienna confidence- and security-building measures in 1992', SIPRI, *SIPRI Yearbook 1993: World Armaments and Disarmament* (Oxford University Press: Oxford, 1993), appendix 12A; and Lachowski, Z., 'The Vienna confidence- and security-building measures', SIPRI, *SIPRI Yearbook 1994* (Oxford University Press: Oxford, 1993), appendix 14A.

It was further recommended that international courses on inspections and other verification mechanisms be organized along with the development of other modalities to bring together on an international level personnel involved in national verification. This would facilitate a common understanding of the aims and operation of CSBMs.[33]

As was often expressed at the AIAM the CSBMs so far agreed upon are still 'fair weather instruments' which are not well equipped for resolving crises, and mechanisms for conflict prevention and crisis management should also be established.[34] The conflicts in the former Yugoslavia and on the territories of the former Soviet Union serve to point out that present measures to enhance confidence and security remain out of step with rapidly changing and unpredictable crises.[35] None the less the CSBM regime experience was positively assessed by delegations to the third Annual Implementation Assessment Meeting, who noted that while the regime needed to be strengthened it remains an indispensable element for the successful continuation of the CSCE process.[36]

---

[33] *Focus on Vienna*, no 30 (Aug. 1993), p. 8.
[34] Note 33, p. 7.
[35] Lachowski in *SIPRI Yearbook 1994* (note 32), appendix 14A.
[36] Note 33, p. 9.

7. Open Skies

I. Introduction

On 12 May 1989 US President George Bush relaunched the 'Open Skies' proposal for an agreement that would allow flights by unarmed reconnaissance aircraft over the territory of the USA, the USSR and their allies. This culminated on 24 March 1992 in the Open Skies Treaty which promised to open up a new era in transparency for the 27 states that had signed by the end of 1993.[1] The idea of Open Skies was first put forward by President Dwight D. Eisenhower on 21 July 1955 at the Geneva Conference of Heads of Government.

President Bush made a short and rather broad proposal, urging that it be discussed with other countries in detail later. He linked his plan directly to that of his predecessor:

Now let us again explore that proposal, but on a broader, more intrusive and radical basis—one which I hope would include allies on both sides. We suggest that those countries that wish to examine this proposal meet soon to work out the necessary operational details, separately from other arms control negotiations. Such surveillance flights, complementing satellites, would provide regular scrutiny for both sides. Such unprecedented territorial access would show the world the true meaning of the concept of openness. The very Soviet willingness to embrace such a concept would reveal their commitment to change.[2]

The explicit reference to the US initiative of 1955 that was rejected by Moscow, and to Soviet acceptance in principle of the revival of an Open Skies concept 'on a broader, more intrusive and radical basis', reflected the new political and military environment and dramatic domestic changes in the USSR and its allies. The opportunity to negotiate the issue seriously, and the possibility of a detailed and substantial negotiating process being undertaken after the Bush initiative, also indicated a different reality from that of the 1950s—the idea could be closely, though not directly, linked with other developments in arms control, confidence- and security-building measures and verification.

II. The 1950s: some reflections

In May 1955 the Soviet Union presented a document on international control over the reduction of armaments, the prohibition of atomic weapons and the elimination of the threat of a new war, proposing that the International Disar-

---

[1] For the text of the Treaty on Open Skies, Helsinki, 24 Mar. 1992, see appendix C.
[2] *Congressional Quarterly Weekly Report*, 20 May 1989, p. 1210.

mament Commission draft an international convention on these matters.[3] The document explicitly linked different measures of 'control', including inspections and the establishment of an 'international control organ' which would also 'require from States parties any necessary information on the execution of measures for the reduction of armaments and armed forces', with 'the fulfilment by States of their obligations under the convention (treaty) on the reduction of armaments and the prohibition of atomic weapons'.

Although the document lacked detailed references to the 'reduction of armaments and armed forces', and even covered the possibility of 'unimpeded access to records relating to the budgetary appropriations of States for military purposes' by an 'international control organ', it explicitly linked 'control' measures with preventing a surprise attack and with the prohibition of nuclear weapons. For this purpose it allowed for 'control posts at large ports, at railway junctions, on main motor highways and in aerodromes'. Also, for inspectors of all states signatories, it permitted 'unimpeded access at all times within the limits of the supervisory functions they exercise, to all objects of control'.

The USA quickly reacted with its own reservations about this proposal which left many ambiguities and unknowns with regard to inspections. The main problem was seen to be that: 'international control and inspection still appear to fall short of the minimum safety requirements. It is not clear that the control organ's inspectors can go everywhere and see everything necessary to make sure that forbidden munitions are not being manufactured or that nuclear weapons are not being secreted.'[4] These reservations were certainly warranted, especially concerning the adequacy of the inspection regime for disarmament purposes, but the Soviet document proposed a regime which gave priority to measures against the danger of surprise attack.

The US reaction included a vision of how to cope with the danger of such an attack by confidence-building and inspection arrangements, and it was especially for this purpose that President Eisenhower shared his 'Open Skies' plan with the participants at the Geneva Conference.

The Eisenhower initiative addressed the need to reduce 'the fears and dangers of surprise attack' and supported limited reconnaissance flights over the USA and the USSR as well as exchange of a 'complete blueprint of our military establishments'.[5] These measures were aimed at lessening suspicion and tension.

On the other hand, as Allan Krass judged from the US documents,

[3] UN document DC/SC. I/26/Rev.2, 10 May 1955.

[4] Statement by the Deputy United States Representative on the Disarmament Subcommittee (Wadsworth) Regarding the New Soviet Proposals, 11 May 1955, reprinted in US Department of State, *Documents on Disarmament 1945–1959, Vol. I: 1945–1956* (US Government Printing Office: Washington, DC, 1960), p. 473.

[5] Statement by President Eisenhower at the Geneva Conference of Heads of Government: Aerial Inspection and Exchange of Military Blueprints, 21 July 1955, in *Documents on Disarmament* (note 4), p. 487.

In 1955 the United States possessed all the necessary weapons for a counterforce nuclear attack against the Soviet Union. The major obstacle to confidence that such an attack could be carried out without a massive Soviet counter-attack was the lack of accurate and complete targeting data. The US Strategic Air Command was faced with a rapidly expanding target list . . . In this context the Open Skies plan can be seen as a military intelligence measure of the highest importance, one which would strengthen the weakest link in US nuclear war-fighting plans.

The Open Skies plan was, of course, unacceptable to the Soviet Union mainly for this latter reason . . . Given good intentions on both sides, an Open Skies agreement would have indeed reduced tension and fear of surprise attack and could have contributed to real disarmament. But given a continued commitment to military competition, a hostile political atmosphere and a clear imbalance of military forces, such an arrangement could in fact be dangerous to the weaker party and is obviously unacceptable.[6]

The political and military environment at the time was unfavourable to the proposal. The USA was not only far ahead in nuclear potential and nuclear research, but also in nuclear delivery capabilities.[7] Moscow was constantly reminded of the geostrategic vulnerability of the USSR by the US flights from West European and Turkish bases over Soviet territory. Nevertheless, the Soviet Union did have one clear 'advantage'—a highly secret regime which provided vast opportunities for bluff. The Soviet leadership insisted, among other things, on 'reliable air defence', but the question of how reliable Soviet air defence really was against US strategic bombers remained. Under these conditions the Soviet leadership considered that secrecy played an important role in deterrence, although it encouraged the strategic buildup of the USA and an atmosphere of suspicion and tension.

It is now widely accepted that the White House did not expect Soviet acceptance of the proposal. Later Eisenhower himself acknowledged this by emphasizing his confidence in a negative result.[8] The US documents show that Eisenhower had also been informed about the coming breakthrough in surveillance capabilities to be brought by a high-altitude aircraft (the U-2), that would 'open skies' with or without Soviet acceptance, and gave approval to the U-2 programme.[9]

As noted above, Krass presented an interesting and widely shared notion that with *good intentions* an Open Skies agreement 'would have indeed reduced tension and fear of surprise attack and could have contributed to real disarmament'. One key question in connection with the outcome is whether an Open Skies agreement would have been limited to that as defined by Eisenhower in the initiative.

[6] Krass, A. S., SIPRI, *Verification: How Much Is Enough?* (Taylor & Francis: London, 1985), p. 118.

[7] See, for example: *International Security*, winter 1979/80, pp. 193, 195; Talbott, S. (ed.), *Khrushchev Remembers: Vol. 1. The Last Testament* (Deutsch: London, 1974), pp. 39–40.

[8] Interview with D. Eisenhower on 28 July 1964; cited in *SShA: ekonomika, politika, ideologiya*, no. 1 (1990), p. 54.

[9] Ambrose, S., *Eisenhower: The President, vol. II* (Simon & Schuster: New York, 1984), p. 278; Beshloss, M., *Mayday, Eisenhower, Khrushchev and U-2 Affair* (Harper & Row: New York, 1986), p. 92.

Eisenhower concentrated attention at the Geneva Conference on 'the fears and dangers of surprise attack'. Within this context he put forward a two-step approach for an exclusively US–Soviet Open Skies 'arrangement':

These steps would include:

To give to each other a complete blueprint of our military establishments, from beginning to end, from one end of our countries to the other; lay out the establishments and provide the blueprints to each other.

Next, to provide within our countries facilities for aerial photography to the other country—we to provide you the facilities within our country, ample facilities for aerial reconnaissance, where you can make all the pictures you choose and take to your own country to study, you to provide exactly the same facilities for us and we to make these examinations, and by this step to convince the world that we are providing as between ourselves against the possibility of great surprise attack, thus lessening danger and relaxing tension.[10]

The proposal was quite broad and invited more questions than it provided answers. One can speculate that the US President meant some kind of full information exchange about the military potential of the two countries, and certainly the exclusion of other countries from these arrangements. The next step assumed that the information would be checked exclusively through aerial surveillance. There was one important constraint: it was the inspected side that was to select the facilities to be inspected and not the inspecting side or, at least, both countries should be involved in aerial inspections on a 'reactive basis', that is, one country was to take the initiative to inspect certain facilities and the other had to inspect 'exactly the same facilities' even though it might be interested in other categories of objects of inspection.

The main line of military confrontation was located along the division in Central Europe and a year later, in 1956 when the WTO was created, along the NATO/WTO border. The Western concern with a large-scale WTO conventional offensive presupposed the area neighbouring this line to be the prime target of monitoring, preferably including the Western military districts of the USSR. The Soviet Union was preoccupied with the possibility of a US nuclear first strike by bomber forces taking off from West European bases. Accordingly, its main concerns logically included inspections in that region—which were not part of the US initiative.

To meet these concerns about surprise attack, overflights could be applied to the European theatre. Both sides had agreed on some measures as 'a beginning', and the Soviet leadership did accept this type of inspection in 1956. Referring specifically to Eisenhower's initiative, the Soviet Declaration Concerning the Question of Disarmament and Reduction of International Tension clearly stated that,

---

[10] Statement by President Eisenhower, reprinted in *Documents on Disarmament* (note 4), pp. 487–88.

this proposal does not decide either the problem of controlling disarmament or preventing aggression.

Considering, however, that the proposal for aerial photography is presented as a condition for reaching agreement on disarmament questions, which creates serious obstacles for achieving such an agreement, the Soviet Government for the purpose of facilitating the quickest achievement of agreement is prepared to consider the question of using aerial photography in the area in Europe where basic military forces of the North Atlantic Pact are located and in countries participating in the Warsaw Pact to a depth of 800 kilometers to the East and the West from the line of demarcation of the above-mentioned military forces, if there is agreement of the appropriate states.

... the Soviet Government considers that after their implementation it is necessary to raise the question about the complete liquidation of armed forces and armaments of all types with retention by states of only such contingents of militia (police) which are necessary for assuring internal security and the security of frontiers.[11]

This approach had two principal flaws from the Western point of view. It did not cover Soviet territory and also made a direct link to proceeding with disarmament in Europe. Both points seemed to be unacceptable. But the provisions indicated that Moscow was ready to start first with confidence-building measures unrelated to arms control and definitely related to the problem of a surprise attack. In other words, it accepted the idea of Open Skies, which, under the Eisenhower (and later the Bush) formula, allowed overflights separately from arms control agreements. Certainly, within the context the proposal was not without a propaganda intent; none the less an approach for applying overflights was outlined.

Aside from the failure of the Open Skies proposal to address the problem of surprise attack, also as compared with other proposals, it can be asked what level of confidence an Open Skies proposal could have provided with respect to a transparent regime for the USA and the USSR. The Soviet side mentioned important loopholes. According to an address by Soviet Premier N. Bulganin to the Supreme Soviet,

During unofficial talks with the leaders of the United States Government we straightforwardly declared that aerophotography cannot give the expected results, because both countries stretch over vast territories in which, if desired, one can conceal anything. One must also take into consideration the fact that the proposed plan touches only the territories belonging to the two countries, leaving out the armed forces and military constructions situated in the territories of other states.[12]

During discussions with Eisenhower in the wake of the summit meeting he presented another important argument:

---

[11] Declaration of the Soviet Government Concerning the Question of Disarmament and Reduction of International Tension, 17 Nov. 1956, in *Documents on Disarmament* (note 4), p. 726.

[12] Address by the Soviet Premier (Bulganin) to the Supreme Soviet, 4 Aug. 1955, extracted in *Documents on Disarmament* (note 4), p. 496.

Judge for yourself, Mr. President: what would the military leaders of your country do if it were reported to them that the aerophotography showed that your neighbor had more airfields? To be sure, they would order an immediate increase in the number of their own airfields. Naturally, our military leaders would do the same in a similar case. It is not difficult to understand that the result would be a further intensification of the armaments race.[13]

This argument was clearly valid as it raised the problem of guarantees. Taking into account at least two factors—the absence of any arms control regime in the main categories of armaments and a limited aerial overflight regime—what guarantees could the leaders of either side give to direct this confidence-building measure to lessening the military competition and denying the military establishments any possibility to 'react' or, more important, possibly 'overreact' militarily to the data gained via overflights?

One of the logical solutions for domestic checks and balances (also in a co-operative environment) would certainly be arms control and reduction arrangements. They could provide certain assurances against unavoidable claims from the military. Unfortunately, these two aspects were separated in the President's statement that, 'The United States is ready to proceed in the study and testing of a reliable system of inspections and reporting, and when that system is proved, then to reduce armaments with all others to the extent that the system will provide assured results'.[14]

The Open Skies discussion finally closed after the Soviet shooting down of the US U-2 reconnaissance aircraft in 1960, and with the achievements of satellite programmes reconnaissance from space, which needed no permission, has since become the prime means for the task.

Open Skies represents a means of enhancing the monitoring and intelligence capabilities of the states involved. Because of this clear assignment and because it does not connect explicitly with verification activities, a functional definition of the requirements is very important. References to 'confidence' and 'openness' may not be enough, either for political or for management reasons.

In his analysis, Rostow recalls two propositions that emerged during further discussions on overflights in the late 1950s and early 1960s:

1. No serious arms control agreement was possible without reliable inspection, and aerial inspection was less intrusive than serious inspection (not fixed control points) on the ground.

2. Even without arms control agreements, mutual aerial inspection provided a means for avoiding excessive U.S. reactions to Soviet military strength . . .[15]

With regard to the first point, the proposals on far-reaching arms reductions and disarmament lacked such intrusive measures. As for the second proposition, it was valid under one condition: that both sides favoured the channelling

[13] Cited in Rostow, W. W., *Open Skies: Eisenhower's Proposal of July 21, 1955* (University of Texas Press: Austin, Tex., 1982), p. 80.
[14] Statement by President Eisenhower, in *Documents on Disarmament* (note 4), pp. 487–88.
[15] Rostow (note 13), pp. 80–81.

of military competition so as to avoid destabilizing overreaction. Whether the intrusive measures within a confidence-building process, theoretically possible even during military buildups, could cope with the competition at the time could be considered somewhat doubtful.

The efforts to define requirements for different inspection concepts and confidence-building, including overflights, continued much later at the independent conference of experts for a study of possible measures for the prevention of surprise attack (the Surprise Attack Conference, Geneva, November 1958).[16] Principal differences with regard to arms control and disarmament, however, meant that the results were inconclusive.

The Western side (experts from Canada, France, Italy, the UK and the USA) favoured the analysis of methods and objects of monitoring and the assessment of the results of implementing those measures to reduce the danger of surprise attack. The Eastern side (experts from Albania, Czechoslovakia, Poland, Romania and the USSR) linked the practicality of recommendations on measures for preventing surprise attack with definite disarmament steps.

The West considered the objects of monitoring to be missiles, long-range and tactical aircraft, ground forces, missile-launching submarines and other naval forces. These objects would be monitored by aerial and ground inspection, sea-based surveillance techniques, long-range radar capability, other instruments of long-range detection, satellite inspection, and so on.

The East proposed the prohibition of flights by aircraft carrying nuclear weapons over the territories of foreign states and the open seas, the establishment of 54 ground control posts on the territories of NATO and of the Baghdad Pact, 28 ground control posts on WTO territory, and areas for aerial photography extending 800 km east and west of the NATO/WTO borderline as well as on Greek, Turkish and Iranian territories. Aerial photography could also be carried out on equal parts of the eastern territories of the USSR and western areas of the USA, and over Japan, including Okinawa. The Eastern side suggested two air groups, each of which would photograph its own territory in the presence of liaison officers of the other side. The Soviet approach to on-site inspection could thus be seen rather as a form of self-inspection. As OSI *per se* could not lessen the danger of surprise attack to any substantial extent, it could, according to the proposal, be linked with a reduction of at least one-third of the foreign troops stationed in Europe and an understanding not to have nuclear weapons in the two German states.

The Conference did not reach consensus because of differences in the two approaches. As Henny van der Graaf concludes, 'The West sought to promote technical military analysis of the problems and the evaluation of the effects of various monitoring systems. They considered the analysis of disarmament measures not within the terms of reference of the Conference. The Eastern delega-

---

[16] van der Graaf, H., 'Past experience with verification', eds J. Grin and H. van der Graaf, *Unconventional Approaches to Conventional Arms Control Verification. An Explanatory Assessment* (Vu University Press: Amsterdam, 1990), p. 28.

tions sought discussion of a selection of political proposals for the most part not susceptible of technical assessment'.[17]

III. The NATO Basic Elements paper

The 1989 Bush initiative was put forward without large-scale consultations within the Alliance. This could explain the fact that in the Brussels Declaration made at the end of May 1989 the NATO leaders only characterized the announcement as 'an important initiative'.[18] The Open Skies idea was not present in the NATO position paper in the CFE Negotiation of 21 September, although it appealed to the delegates to 'consider cooperative measures to enhance aerial inspection'.

An important impetus for the idea appeared during the meeting between Soviet Foreign Minister Eduard Shevardnadze and US Secretary of State James Baker at Jackson Hole, Wyoming, in September 1989. Soviet support of the general idea, although not without their own reservations, made it possible to begin to work out a detailed programme. On 23 September 1989 a joint statement was issued which in part called for an international conference on Open Skies. The first part of the conference was held in Ottawa, Canada, in February 1990 and the second part in Budapest, Hungary, in April–May of that year.

In fact, in summer 1989 the USA was already discussing constraints on the Open Skies proposal for the purpose of concealing sensitive items, including advance notification of overflights and the designation of zones where overflights were off-limits. At the same time one US official suggested that since the USA and the USSR already had satellites, the overflights would not have added much useful intelligence data.[19]

After the US intelligence community made a net assessment of the pros and cons of maximum openness, President Bush in summer 1989 decided to go further with this policy. The Pentagon and the intelligence community had come to the conclusion, for example, that 'with sufficient advance notice, one Warsaw Pact overflight per week would not pose an unacceptable security risk to sensitive U.S. programs and installations, although shutting down entire facilities before an overflight would be costly'.[20] The outlines of the US proposal were as follows.

US aircraft with a US crew and equipment would be used by the USA. Before an overflight it would be subject to Soviet inspection to check whether it carried armaments and unauthorized equipment—primarily to ensure that SIGINT equipment, none of which would be permitted, was not being carried. (A prohibition on loitering over a particular area was also included to further limit the possibilities for SIGINT collection.) The crew would file its flight plan

[17] van der Graaf (note 16), p. 28.
[18] *New York Times*, 31 May 1989.
[19] *Washington Times*, 18 July 1989.
[20] Tucker, J. B., 'Back to the future: the Open Skies talks', *Arms Control Today*, Oct. 1990, p. 21.

24 hours before its mission. There would be no restrictions on the flight plan other than those national and international flight restrictions which apply to private and commercial air traffic. An aircraft could therefore fly over any military installation (within the limits of national and international flight rules and bearing in mind that standard rules restrict flying over certain military installations when this is hazardous to air safety). The standard operating procedure would have host country escorts on overflights. The US Administration expected to conduct two to three flights per week over the USSR, and the USSR could conduct one flight per week over the USA (because the land mass of the Soviet Union was two and one-half times larger than that of the USA). There would be one flight by one aircraft at a time and repeated flights over the same area were possible.

Such a proposal could be aimed at monitoring military activities that cannot be hidden within 24 hours. These activities would include massing tank battalions or significant naval activity. The USA did not consider a centralized processing organization to be necessary or appropriate.

There were several reasons for the 24-hour waiting period: the need to review the flight plan to ensure compliance with national and international flight regulations; to inspect the aircraft; to have an opportunity for the crew to rest; and to allow some security precautions to be taken at very sensitive facilities by an overflown country.

Canada had its own reservations: it envisioned Open Skies eventually being open to European countries. Canada preferred to encourage 'any two countries' to create their own Open Skies regime.[21] This position was rejected at the meeting of NATO foreign ministers in December 1989 where they agreed on 'basic elements' for Open Skies which aimed at covering the entire territories of the European region, Canada, the USA and the USSR. France did not want to use the treaty to freeze the alliance structure and encouraged the idea that the organization be based on individual states and the participation of the 12 European neutral and non-aligned states.

One of the main divisions among the positions of the NATO member states concerned the types of quota for a regime. The USA and Canada preferred passive quotas with the active quotas to be determined within NATO, rather than in the negotiations with the WTO. The allies could determine themselves how to share the data and to pool the means of aerial missions.

On the other hand, France, along with Spain, Italy and other countries, favoured active quotas, assuming that without them the Soviet Union would take a substantial portion of overflights of NATO territory. An active quota could rather emphasize the national status and not the *de facto* arrangements on an alliance basis. Also, as France sympathized with the inclusion of non-allied CSCE participating countries, an active quota regime was preferred since even though these states might not be full participants they should have the opportunity to participate in some overflights. As for the USA and Canada, they were

---

[21] *Arms Control Reporter*, 1990, sheet 409.B.4.

not opposed to participation by the non-aligned countries but preferred that it wait until later stages.[22]

The French position was oriented towards some kind of linkage with a CFE Treaty—a line opposed by other NATO countries. Open Skies, according to French officials, should rather be treated as a national or multinational technical means, though these means were included in the CFE position paper on information exchange, stabilization, verification and non-circumvention. Also, they wanted to use this linkage to open up the opportunity of expanding participation in the CFE Negotiation to all CSCE states.

The difference in positions could be partly explained by the hopes surrounding the kind of regime that would be implemented. The USA and Canada insisted on its confidence-building character. Several other states tended to look upon Open Skies as enabling them to acquire their own national technical means in this area. This position was reflected in the fact that NATO's European members preferred a shorter request-delay period for a 'surprise' overflight, while the USA favoured a 24-hour period for advance notification of an overflight plus 6 hours for filing the flight plan. It has been speculated that France may have raised difficulties at least in part to stimulate the interest of other countries in its Helios satellite programme.[23]

The Open Skies agenda was being set during the emergence of a more fundamental tension among NATO allies which was defined by a Pentagon official as allied concern over potential lack of verification. He said that the French and British, for example, were alarmed that the CFE Negotiation would lead to 'permanent limits on their power' but have less effect on the USA and the Soviet Union.[24]

The NATO Basic Elements paper agreed to in December 1989 represented an effort to arrive at compromise positions within the Alliance. Among these elements it is worth noting the following.

1. The stated *purpose* of the regime was to strengthen confidence and transparency with respect to military activities:

The basic purpose of Open Skies is to encourage reciprocal openness on the part of the participating states and to allow the observation of military activities and installations on their territories, thus enhancing confidence and security. Open Skies can serve these ends as a complement both to national technical means of data collection and to infor-

---

[22] Among the reasons for this cautious attitude different views of non-aligned countries on transparency and openness and potential problems with the zones should be mentioned. As an Open Skies regime applies to the non-European part of the USSR and the North American territory, this could have influenced both CFE and CSBM negotiations if the participation of all CSCE states was accepted.

[23] Borawski, J., 'NATO Europe and Open Skies', eds M. Slack and H. Chestnutt, *Open Skies: Technical, Organizational, Legal and Political Aspects* (Centre for International and Strategic Studies, York University: Toronto, 1990), p. 124.

[24] *Aerospace Daily*, 7 Dec. 1989, p. 379.

mation exchange and verification arrangements established by current and future arms control agreements.[25]

Although arms control agreements in general naturally require their own verification regimes, often highly intrusive in nature:

It seems useful . . . particularly in the prevailing context of improved East–West relations, to reflect on other ways of creating a broadly favourable context for confidence-building and disarmament efforts.

In this context, the Open Skies concept has a very special value. The willingness of a country to be overflown is, in itself, a highly significant political act in that it demonstrates its availability to openness; aerial inspection also represents a particularly effective means of verification, along with the general transparency in military activities . . .

This double characteristic of an Open Skies regime would make it a valuable complement to current East–West endeavours, mainly in the context of the Vienna negotiations but also in relation to other disarmament efforts (START, chemical weapons).[26]

2. *Participation* would initially be open to all members of NATO and the WTO:

It would seem desirable to focus now on the European region, while also including the entire territories of the Soviet Union, the United States, and Canada. Accordingly, we will be ready to consider at an appropriate time the wish of any other European country to participate in the Open Skies regime.[27]

3. *A quota regime* would be established in order to limit the number of overflights. 'The quotas will be derived from the geographic size of participating countries. The duration of flights can also be limited in relation to geographic size. For larger countries, the quota should permit several flights a month over their territory. All parties will participate in such observation flights on a national basis, either individually or jointly in co-operation with their allies.'[28] The document emphasized that a country would not undertake flights over the territory of any other country of the same alliance. Quota totals should be arranged so as to ensure a rough correspondence between those for NATO and the WTO and, within these totals, between the USSR and the USA plus Canada. All countries would be obliged to accept a minimum quota of one overflight per quarter. Smaller nations (those subject to the minimum quota) would be allowed to group themselves into one unit to host overflights and jointly accept the quota that would apply to the geographical area of this larger unit.

[25] Open Skies Basic Elements paper, agreed by the North Atlantic Council meeting in Ministerial Session at NATO Headquarters, Brussels, on 14 and 15 Dec. 1989, reprinted in *Arms Control Reporter*, 1990, sheet 409.D.2.
[26] Open Skies Basic Elements paper (note 25), sheet 409.D.1.
[27] Open Skies Basic Elements paper (note 25), sheet 409.D.2.
[28] Open Skies Basic Elements paper (note 25), sheet 409.D.2.

4. *Aircraft and sensors*: the participants would use 'unarmed, fixed-wing civilian or military aircraft capable of carrying host country observers.'[29] A wide variety of sensors would be allowed, with the limitation that sensors used for SIGINT purposes would not be allowed.

5. *Technical co-operation:* either multilateral or bilateral arrangements within alliances for the sharing of aircraft or sensors, or conducting joint overflights, would be permitted.

6. *Mission operation and results:* provision was allowed for 16 hours notice by the observing state of arrival at the point of entry and filing of a flight plan within a subsequent 6 hours. Thereafter a 24-hour pre-flight period would allow for safety, servicing and inspection. The members of each alliance would determine among themselves how the information acquired would be shared with each party deciding how the information would be used.

7. *Consultative body:* the participating states would 'establish a body to resolve questions of compliance with the terms of the treaty and to agree upon such measures as may be necessary to improve the effectiveness of the regime'.[30]

Thus, the document did not directly link Open Skies with verification of the CFE Treaty. It did not use the terms of active and passive quotas directly and called for annual updating of a list of prohibited sensors.

The US and allied governments agreed on a number of different sensor types that might be included in Open Skies missions, although specifics had not been set. The list covered photographic cameras, infrared imagers and imaging radar, with sensors capable of detecting nuclear materials and chemical weapons manufacture possible as well.[31]

One of the main challenges to reaching an agreement which came to light from the start was the determination of appropriate overflight quotas. As mentioned above, NATO's original plan included the quotas derived from the geographic size of participating countries. This meant that on the alliance-to-alliance basis the distribution of passive quotas was almost equal. For example, allowing one overflight for every 10 000, 50 000 or 100 000 square miles, the numbers of overflights accepted by NATO and the WTO would be correspondingly 872 and 894, 172 and 176, and 85 and 87. Within the total for the WTO, however, the Soviet Union would have to accept the lion's share of overflights, on the one hand, as well as a disproportionate distribution when compared with the US quota. Using the above example, the passive quotas for the USSR and the USA would be 857 and 361, 171 and 72, and 85 and 36.[32]

---

[29] Open Skies Basic Elements paper (note 25), sheet 409.D.3.

[30] Open Skies Basic Elements paper (note 25), sheet 409.D.4.

[31] A US official said that if sensors were shared among all parties to an agreement, the 'transparency' of the other side would be diminished because the most sophisticated sensors would have to be withheld from Open Skies missions to avoid technology loss. While total sensor sharing would result in 'lowest common denominator' sensors, even under the NATO position the USA would probably withhold its most advanced sensors. See *Aerospace Daily*, 11 Jan. 1990, pp. 56–57.

[32] These figures are from Jones, P., 'The determination of overflight quotas for an Open Skies regime', Slack and Chestnutt (note 23), p. 69.

Taking into account the larger territory of Canada, the Warsaw Pact countries would be allowed to conduct more overflights there than over the United States. This situation would obviously not be to the liking of the Soviet Union as they would be interested in much more extensive flights over the USA. The NATO document limited itself to the declaration of a rough correspondence in quotas, within the total, between the USSR and the North American members of NATO.

Another problem stemming from using the geographical criterion was the consequent implementation of relatively few overflights of the non-Soviet ATTU area. Again using the above three area bases of 10 000, 50 000 and 100 000 square miles, NATO's European territory would be subject to 15, 13 and 13 per cent of the total overflights, while the non-Soviet WTO member states would be subject to only 4, 3 and 2 per cent. Finally, this formula would also have resulted in a larger number of flights over Western Europe than over East European territories. These problems show that the method of apportioning overflights on a bloc-to-bloc basis did not adequately address the requirements of political or practical confidence-building or the size of the military force potential concentrated in this part of the ATTU area.

Alternatively, overflight quotas based on the total armed forces of each country could have been considered.[33] This would also provide an overall balance of passive quotas between the alliances. If one inspection were allowed per 10 000 or 25 000 troops, for example, the passive quotas for NATO and the WTO would be correspondingly 533 and 540 or 211 and 215. In addition, the distribution of overflights of the ATTU zone, excluding the Soviet territory, would come out somewhat more equal, although quite far from parity: 312 and 115; or 122 and 45. At the same time, however, the number of overflights of Soviet territory would still have been roughly twice as great as those of the USA: 212 and 425; or 85 and 170.[34]

This formula would probably also have needed to take into account in some manner the presence of foreign troops in European countries in defining quotas in a more representative manner. One further problem with this formula came potentially from the reductions of troops under way in the European territory, which could increase the number of flights over the non-ATTU area.

On the other hand, the geographical size criterion accepted by NATO could mean that a basic objective was to monitor the Soviet non-ATTU territory as it comprised the major part of the USSR. If the overflight numbers for the ATTU area were obviously high, one could conclude that these flights comprised the *de facto* aerial monitoring for a CFE verification regime. Correspondingly, it could lead to less burden on overflight arrangements possibly made within the CFE framework.

---

[33] Jones (note 32), p. 72.

[34] These calculations were presented by Jones (note 32), p. 72. The numbers of troops are based on IISS, *The Military Balance 1989/90* (International Institute for Strategic Studies: London, 1989).

A still different scenario could have been to have the overflight quotas linked in some way with the TLE which each nation is allowed to keep under the CFE Treaty, for example. This has the advantage that the number of overflights would be based on a number which has already been negotiated and is a good measure of the proportionate number of flights over areas likely to need monitoring. A possible problem with this approach, however, is assigning an appropriate weight to the importance of different types of weapon—for example, whether a tank should count as much as an attack aircraft or more than a piece of artillery.

There is also the question of monitoring non-conventional weapons. The possession or non-possession of nuclear weapons, for example, should perhaps also be factored into the equation to determine such quotas.

One way of maximizing political acceptability would have been to use a formula for quotas which was directly linked to more than one variable. For example, it could have included dependence on geographical size *and* the number of troops in order to create a more fairly proportioned surveillance regime.

The NATO document itself also linked geographic area to the duration of flights, but the quotas were not expressed in terms of total overflight hours for, say, a year or a month. This option would have provided more flexibility for the overflying state. If, for example, a state wanted to inspect a certain area or object and thereby to avoid lengthy examination of other areas, the time period for such a short overflight could be deducted from the total time quota. This approach could lead to complications for the host party, however, because it would have to carry out substantial preparations for organizing a short overflight—almost the same as for a long overflight.

It is also worth mentioning that the NATO document presented a specific plan, mainly in broad terms but more precise than NATO's position on aerial monitoring in the CFE Negotiation up to that time. In the CFE package put forward on 21 September 1989 the provision on this issue was limited to the message that 'a CFE regime will include provisions for aerial inspection. Modalities and quotas require further study. The parties shall consider co-operative measures to enhance aerial inspection'.[35] In the subsequent NATO draft CFE treaty of 15 December 1989 this broad provision remained unchanged, and the WTO draft text presented in October did not elaborate on the problem.

Trial overflight

On 6 January 1990 a Canadian Forces Lockheed C-130 conducted a test overflight of Hungary. The aircraft did not carry any sensors and it was primarily a test of technical details such as air traffic control and aircraft inspection proce-

---

[35] *Measures of Information Exchange, Stabilization, Verification and Non-circumvention*, Proposal submitted by the delegations of Belgium, Canada, Denmark, France, the FRG, Greece, Iceland, Italy, Luxembourg, Netherlands, Norway, Portugal, Spain, Turkey, the UK and the USA, Vienna, 21 Sep. 1989.

dures. For 3.5 hours the aircraft flew in a 'figure eight' pattern on a route chosen by Canadian military officers over a large area of the country at altitudes ranging from 4500 to 14 700 feet (about 1370 to 4480 metres). In doing so it overflew facilities including both Hungarian and Soviet army bases and airfields, as well as two Soviet fighter bases.[36]

One of the potential difficulties became during an inspection of the aircraft to ascertain whether any sensors had been hidden. Certain important aircraft components had to be disassembled, which raised the issue of the crew's subsequent faith in the safety of the aircraft. This then led to agreement that, in order to aid in familiarization with the aircraft beforehand, appropriate technical information would be exchanged before any agreement entered into force.

Hungary was offered the right to conduct a reciprocal flight over Canada but was unable to do so because an appropriate aircraft was not available. The fielding of appropriate aircraft would apparently also be a problem for many of the other former WTO members as well as some of the smaller members of NATO. Given a similar offer the USSR expressed its feeling that the flight was premature before the first Open Skies conference in Ottawa.[37]

IV. Negotiations: the Ottawa and Budapest conferences

Ottawa

In the opening statement at the February 1990 Ottawa Conference Soviet Foreign Minister Eduard Shevardnadze put forward several important points which were valuable not only for analysing the Soviet position, but also for highlighting some of the issues associated with Open Skies. Having presented a formula calling for 'sufficiency in armaments and redundancy in verification (monitoring) methods' and again accepting the Open Skies concept, he stated,

This formula also is dictated by the trends and perspectives of the current situation in Europe. We are witnessing the emergence of a Europe which consists of not three–four groups of states, but as an area with a more complicated political composition. Unfortunately, there is hardly anyone who is ready to insist that this new composition would not create new problems and new local complications . . . Under these conditions an 'Open Skies' regime could be a quite necessary and effective means of maintaining and strengthening confidence, a means of eliminating emerging suspicion and concerns.[38]

---

[36] 'Canadians fly over Hungary in first test of "open skies"', *Toronto Star*, 7 Jan. 1990, p. 1; 'Alliances to discuss inspections from the air', *New York Times*, 11 Feb. 1990, p. 16; 'Open Skies treaty will give 23 nations surveillance rights', *Aviation Week & Space Technology*, 19 Feb. 1990, p. 20; *Aerospace Daily*, 22 Jan. 1990, p. 113; 'Canada and Hungary to fly military aircraft over each other's land', *The Globe and Mail*, 4 Jan. 1990, p. 1.

[37] *Aerospace Daily*, 9 Feb., 1990, p. 260.

[38] *Vestnik*, Apr. 1990, p. 60.

One of the main requirements for the elimination of suspicion and concerns, and also in connection with redundancy in monitoring and verification methods, he continued, would be to extend the Open Skies idea to include measures on 'Open Space' and 'Open Seas'. Shevardnadze stated that the easiest way to launch a surprise attack at the time would be from the sea. More specifically, the Soviet side proposed an Open Seas regime which would include information exchange on naval potentials, notifications of large-scale naval exercises and redeployments of troops closer to the borders of other countries, and invitation of inspectors to exercises and manœuvres. As a confidence-building measure, such a regime would thus not require very intrusive arrangements.

The idea of Open Space presupposed a more intrusive inspection regime because it was aimed at the prohibition of weapons in space. Accordingly, Shevardnadze urged the creation of an inspection system to monitor cargoes before they were launched into space, including an international inspectorate and an international space monitoring agency. These two additional proposals were rejected by the USA and the attention of the Conference and further discussion were concentrated on Open Skies, rather than on the whole Soviet package.

Although an Open Skies agreement was considered as a separate, independent document, the Soviet side emphasized 'the need to connect it in substance' with arms control and disarmament agreements. This need was justified on the grounds that 'the implementation of an agreement would contribute to prevent possible non-compliance with other international agreements and treaties and thereby would in a certain degree affect them'. Hence, it stated the requirement to allow for the possibility of moulding an agreement bearing in mind its correspondence to obligations of the participants with respect to arms control and disarmament agreements and to monitoring and verification mechanisms.[39] NATO's initial proposals did not include any possibility of this type of connection but treated an agreement as a valuable complement to arms control accords.

Another element in the Soviet proposal concerned 'the principle of comprehensive and complete equality' which included: equality in acquiring and in access to information, which could not be used at the expense of any participant; equality with regard to the area of application, covering military activities of states not only on their own territory, but abroad as well; and equality with regard to overflight quotas, to aircraft use, surveillance technology and data processing.[40] By putting forward this principle, the Soviet Union let its concerns in this area be known and also indicated its readiness to focus attention on specific arrangements and technical details during the work on an agreement.

In the communiqué on Open Skies presented by the 16 NATO and 7 WTO foreign ministers in Ottawa it was noted that, while it would not be an arms control or verification measure *per se*, the successful implementation of an

[39] *Vestnik* (note 38), p. 61.
[40] *Vestnik* (note 38), p. 61.

Open Skies agreement would encourage reciprocal openness among the states involved. In addition, it would strengthen confidence, lessen the risk of conflict and add to the predictability of military activities. It would also contribute to existing monitoring capabilities and further the process of arms control and reduction. Thus, while recognizing the relationship between Open Skies and the CFE Negotiation, the communiqué avoided any explicit linkage.

The Ministers agreed on the following:

The 'Open Skies' regime will be implemented on a reciprocal and equitable basis which will protect the interests of each participating state, and in accordance with which the participating states will be open to aerial observation.

The regime will ensure the maximum possible openness and minimum restrictions for observation flights.

Each participating state will have the right to conduct, and the obligation to receive, observation flights on the basis of annual quotas which will be determined in negotiations so as to provide for equitable coverage.

The agreement will have provisions concerning the right to conduct observation flights using unarmed aircraft and equipment capable in all circumstances of fulfilling the goals of the regime.

The participating states will favourably consider the possible participation in the regime of other countries, primarily the European countries.[41]

The declaratory guideline accepted by the participants was thus chosen so as to base Open Skies on a confidence-building principle, separating it from a verification mechanism. Although its verification role was not rejected, it was placed secondary to the confidence-building function. In this regard, James Macintosh emphasized that 'because our understanding of the underlying nature of confidence-building (the "hidden process") is still imperfect, the insight that might be carried to an examination of the Open Skies approach is somewhat limited'.

Nevertheless, he characterized Open Skies as a monitoring CBM with the objective of providing information on military activity within a large region not specific to any treaty. He accounted for the sudden acceptance of the Open Skies proposal as resulting from the pre-existence of a 'process of psychological transformation' and indicated that its eventual acceptance rested on a 'pre-existing and expanding *process* of confidence-building' in the absence of which the Open Skies idea could not have been considered. He also made the important distinction between the function of an Open Skies regime as a CBM and as a set of verification measures. Although the monitoring techniques involved may be virtually identical, Open Skies would stand on its own, apart from the political judgements inherent in a verification process. The information acquired should be adequate to assure the nations involved that they correctly perceive the military deployments and activities of one another and to provide warning of preparations for aggressive activity. He saw the main purpose of

[41] *Disarmament Bulletin*, spring 1990, p. 9.

Open Skies as being 'to support—and promote the continued growth of—the positive psychological transformation of the East–West international security environment'.[42]

During the Ottawa Conference the parties were able to reach compromises on a number of specific issues, but many problems remained unsolved, the divisions indicating the potential difficulties in reaching an agreement.

NATO countries favoured permitting any country to use its own aircraft for overflights with a provision for the host country to inspect the aircraft. The USSR preferred options which would provide more control by the host country which could be implemented through a common fleet of aircraft or through aerial inspection in aircraft of the host country piloted by its crew.

The Soviet preference for a common fleet of aircraft and sharing among all parties of all data acquired during overflights was not met with enthusiasm by many participants: a common fleet presented problems related to acquiring the aircraft and providing crews; problems would also arise with data-sharing arrangements. The USSR thus dropped the earlier proposal for a multinational fleet of aircraft but continued to insist on the inspected country being allowed to choose whose aircraft would be selected for overflights.[43]

Concerning the sharing of data, even French officials who had supported the idea of broadly shared data acquired from commercial satellites opposed such sharing of information within an Open Skies regime. Greece and Turkey were not sympathetic to data sharing, while the USA feared that sharing data would compromise NTM. The difficulties in deciding whose equipment to use for data processing and ensuring appropriate analysis were also raised.

Concerning geographical scope NATO, along with all the East European countries, favoured allowing overflights of all regions except where flight safety prohibited. To allow this, nations might have to re-examine national airspace procedures (for example, the FRG had large portions of airspace closed to civil traffic). The Soviet Union on the other hand defended the position that flights should not be allowed over the USSR in three different categories of restricted airspace. According to the head of the Soviet delegation, Viktor Karpov, the USSR objected to surveillance below 10 000 m of chemical and nuclear plants and of densely populated areas because of fear of aircraft crashes.[44] In addition, the USSR insisted on the right to overfly bases of NATO nations in countries not part of the Open Skies talks. This was acceptable to the USA only for its bases in island territories such as Guam and Puerto Rico.

With regard to specific sensors, NATO gave preference to having each nation provide the suite of sensors it wanted to use. The WTO countries, however, wanted a common sensor suite to be made available to all participants. The USSR insisted on using visible-light cameras only, which would only be suitable for use in daytime conditions, and also wanted to allow resolutions no bet-

[42] Macintosh, J., 'Open Skies as a confidence-building process', Slack and Chestnutt (note 23), pp. 55–56.

[43] Tucker, J. B., 'Back to the future: the Open Skies talks', *Arms Control Today*, Oct. 1990, p. 23.

[44] *Trust and Verify*, Mar. 1990, p. 1.

ter than 2–3 m. NATO would allow a day–night, all-weather sensor suite, including some form of optical, electro-optical, infrared and synthetic aperture radar (SAR) equipment. At the same time, all participants agreed on the exclusion of any signals intelligence equipment on board aircraft and on the condition that any data obtained during an overflight should stay on the aircraft until landing and not be transmitted to the ground, to other aircraft or to satellites.

Towards the conclusion of the Ottawa Conference NATO endorsed a quota system which would be based not on a bloc-to-bloc structure (the WTO was becoming more obviously moribund) but on a nation-to-nation basis. It drew up a matrix to illustrate the concept only, not yet willing to endorse specific numbers. The WTO was proposing a quota of 30 overflights per alliance per year with the added stipulation that no more than 15 of these be over any single country.[45]

In five key areas—type of aircraft, data sharing, sensors to be used, geographical scope and quotas—there still remained substantial differences at the close of the Ottawa Conference.

Budapest

Unfortunately the Budapest Conference, held from late April until mid-May 1990, did not see substantial progress on any of the important unresolved issues. Nevertheless there was some moving together, mainly in the areas of the particular sensors which could be used and the quota arrangements.

In between the Ottawa and Budapest conferences the USSR had indicated a willingness to allow SAR on the aircraft. This was affirmed in Budapest, but the USSR wanted to limit the SAR resolution to no better than 10 m. They were, however, also willing to allow cameras with resolutions down to 30 cm, much greater than the 2–3 m resolution they had insisted upon in Ottawa. This was still quite far from the position of most Western countries who deemed a SAR resolution of 3 m and resolution of at least 15 cm for optical cameras to be appropriate.[46]

The East European countries had been particularly interested in a far-reaching regime as it could provide more independence from the Soviet Union in acquiring information. This thrust was encouraged by NATO whose negotiators indicated their willingness to relax restrictions on the export of relevant sensors so that sensors comparable to those used by the West would be commercially available to Open Skies participants.[47] In allaying East European fears of tech-

---

[45] *Arms Control Today*, Oct. 1990, p. 22; *Arms Control Reporter*, 1990, sheet 409.B.12.

[46] *Arms Control Today*, Oct. 1990, p. 24.

[47] According to the information by 'one source familiar with export control policy' to *Aerospace Daily* at the end of 1989, the USA was then moving towards a loosening of certain export controls on sales of aerospace products to the Eastern bloc that could allow sales of commercial aircraft or engines. Although initial exports would probably be in the commercial area, there was some potential for limited military-related exports as well. 'Surveillance and verification' were among areas in which East European governments might want to 'diversify their sourcing'. Taking into account that 'in so far as our (verification) stuff is better than the Soviets', the USA might also have to sell them some of this equipment. 'If you

nological inferiority, this served effectively to isolate the USSR on the issues of restricted use of sensors and the necessity of data sharing.

On quotas, before the Conference the USSR was willing to accept about 15 overflights per year. This figure was increased to 25 in Budapest but this was still not close to the NATO position: NATO was requesting 106 overflights of the Soviet Union per year of which 46 could be conducted by the USA. All countries but the USSR were in agreement that the flight duration should be proportional to the geographical area of the country being overflown. The USSR, however, was proposing a 10-hour or 5000-km limit, with the added proviso that sensors could be operated for no more than three hours.[48]

Some East European participants indicated that they were just as interested as NATO countries in overflying Soviet territory. In one overflight quota discussion during the Budapest Conference the sub-group decided that it would be useful if all states would just note down on an anonymous basis the countries they were interested in overflying. 'When they tallied up the totals . . . the totals for the Soviet Union were just astronomical, and the numbers for other states in Europe were minimal except for Germany, and nobody much wanted to overfly the United States'.[49]

While it had initially been hoped that an Open Skies agreement could be signed at the Budapest Conference, the meeting concluded without agreement even on a date for resumption of talks. At this time it was still unclear how the issue of aerial inspections would be settled at the CFE Negotiation. After the signing of the CFE Treaty in November 1990, it was proposed at the CFE-1A Plenary that the Open Skies talks be resumed in Vienna in February 1991. It was pointed out that this could be useful in two ways. First, some involved in the CFE Negotiation were looking to Open Skies to aid in the completion of a CFE aerial regime and, second, those involved in the Open Skies deliberations could perhaps use the experience gained by CFE delegations.[50] The proposed resumption of talks in February 1991 was not to take place and further Open Skies initiatives would not be put forward until several months later, as discussed in section VI.

---

move to open skies you may well see them wanting to use some of our stuff, for example C-130 [aircraft]'. East European countries had apparently made requests for either the C-130 transports or their L-100 civilian model counterparts (*Aerospace Daily*, 6 Dec. 1989, p. 370). The Lockheed C-130 and the Canadair Challenger 600 were later mentioned in the West for overflights (*Aerospace Daily*, 9 May 1990, p. 228). The sensor equipment on the *Challenger* was valued at 27 million Canadian dollars (*Aviation Week & Space Technology*, 2 Apr. 1990, p. 41).

[48] *Arms Control Today*, Oct. 1990, p. 24.

[49] *Aerospace Daily*, 9 May 1990, p. 228.

[50] *Arms Control Reporter*, 1990, sheet 409.B.18.

V. Important general considerations

Open Skies and the CFE Treaty

For its part the United States clearly indicated a prime interest in having aerial access both to the European part of the Soviet Union and to the area beyond the Urals. Despite disagreements in Ottawa on specific issues and joint statements of only indirect linkage with the CFE verification measures, the US Administration in spring 1990 intended to present a CFE verification package with inclusion of Open Skies missions and flights specifically targeted for areas of suspected violations. Simultaneously, it strongly urged a link of CFE verification with monitoring out of the ATTU zone in order to be confident of Soviet non-circumvention.

According to explanations of the two types of overflight made by a senior US official, Open Skies flights would be 'a little bit giving each country its own national technical means'.[51] Just as the USA uses NTM 'to look at arms control verification issues from time to time but also to do other things, so a country having an (Open Skies) aircraft able to fly over East Germany or Poland or the Soviet Union (could) use it to look at what it wants to look at'. CFE-oriented flights, he continued, would be

somewhat different . . . It seems that there is a potentially important role for rather specific types of aircraft tied rather closely to specific measures to be monitored— flights in certain regions of a country, flights perhaps with small, slow, low flying air- craft, flights set up to work with stabilizing measures such as leaving doors of build- ings open or shed tops open on certain days—all sorts of rather useful things one can do with aerial inspection that is geared to enforcing a specific agreement.

Responding in the negative to the question of whether these and other means would make it impossible to cheat, he added:

But most people (in the US government) will tell you that if all of this works out, the only area in which it would make any sense to try to build up large numbers of military forces would probably be east of the Urals (in the Soviet Union), and that would have been possible even with the original concept of entries and exits and production monitoring . . . because east of the Urals is unconstrained.

The issue, however, was formally divided into aerial overflights for CFE verification and Open Skies flights including other regions of the CFE partici- pants' territories. Canadian officials pointed out that if in a CFE regime only certain sensors were used, they could not imagine that the USSR would accept more intrusive sensors in Open Skies which was 'only' a confidence-building regime.[52]

---

[51] *Aerospace Daily*, 14 Mar. 1990, p. 450.
[52] *Arms Control Reporter,* 1990, sheet 409.B.18.

In the First Mountbatten Lecture at Southampton University on 9 May 1990 Oleg Grinevsky welcomed aerial inspection for the CFE regime and said he did not think that the Open Skies stalemate would affect aerial overflights for CFE Treaty verification. He pointed out that it was worth remembering that the zone of application was more limited than that for Open Skies and that the CFE verification task was more specific.[53]

Legal elements

With respect to the legal aspects of aerial monitoring it has been stated in the context of Open Skies that:

To engage in aviation is to be subjected to a plethora of rules and regulations both municipal and international. Although they are of differing importance, the neglect to comply with even an apparently minor one, may have devastating consequences . . . A treaty duly ratified by all the relevant nations in which they permit overflight pursuant to a 'verification for arms limitation' scheme is the only safe and incontrovertibly legal means to proceed.[54]

The principle of state sovereignty according to traditional international law specifies the complete jurisdiction of states over their land territory, their territorial seas and their airspace. It is reflected in the main international convention for aviation—the 1944 Convention on International Civil Aviation (the 'Chicago Convention')—which states that 'The contracting States recognize that every State has complete and exclusive sovereignty over the air space above its territory'. Article 3 of the Convention reiterates the prohibition against overflights by state aircraft of foreign territory without authorization.[55]

However, it also provides for the common right of 'flights into or in transit non-stop across' the territory of contracting states for non-scheduled civilian aircraft (including charters and small recreational aircraft) '*without* the necessity of obtaining prior permission'. Thus, as Jason Reiskind writes,

we see that the key international convention in the field amends the general rule of exclusive state sovereignty, to allow for theoretically free overflights of private foreign aircraft not engaged in scheduled service. This would seem to give substantial opportunities to interested persons to gather all sorts of information by overflying foreign states. It would appear that all one need do is obtain an adequate aircraft and photographic equipment, file a flight plan with the authorities of states to be overflown and take off. In fact, this is not the case because the Chicago Convention gives overflight rights with one hand, with the other it gives states a whole series of excuses to return to the classical rule of exclusive sovereignty.[56]

[53] *Trust and Verify*, May 1990, p. 1.

[54] Banner, A. V., Young, A. J. and Hall, K. W., *Aerial Reconnaissance for Verification of Arms Limitation Agreements: An Introduction*, UNIDIR (UN: New York, 1990), p. 21.

[55] Reiskind, J., 'Open Skies: Overview of relevant legal instruments', Slack and Chestnutt (note 23), p. 85.

[56] Reiskind (note 55), p. 85.

Article 9 of the Chicago Convention allows the whole or part of a country to be made temporarily off limits to overflights in 'exceptional circumstances or during a period of emergency, or in the interest of public safety'; Article 36 enables states to prohibit or regulate the use of photographic apparatus in aircraft over its territory; and Article 89 specifies that the provisions of the Convention do not apply to the activities of states in the case of war or declared national emergency. The Convention requires special permission for scheduled carriers to enter the airspace of a foreign state, while the 1944 International Air Services Transit Agreement and related Transport Agreement, 'provide common overflight "privileges" to scheduled international air services of contracting states, but here too there are limitations regarding routings, military airports and the application of Chicago Convention rules.'[57]

The Convention gives limited overflight rights to private non-commercial aircraft, charters and scheduled aircraft of states parties. As for government/military aircraft (which are to be used for aerial surveillance), it defines them as 'state aircraft' and maintains that the Convention applies only to 'civil aircraft'. It simultaneously maintains the prohibition against overflights by state aircraft 'without authorization by special agreement or otherwise'. Although the definition of state aircraft is quite vague ('State aircraft are understood to mean aircraft on special missions for a national State'), it would certainly include aircraft which could be used in an Open Skies regime, or aircraft belonging to or loaned by an international agency.[58] Thus, the functioning of an Open Skies regime requires explicit permission for overflights by foreign states or international aircraft.[59]

Some historical cases may illustrate the legal aspects of flights over sovereign territories. During the discussion in the Security Council of the shooting down of the US U-2 reconnaissance aircraft while overflying Soviet territory, no participant questioned the right to fly a reconnaissance mission. The subject of discussion rather centred on denouncing the violation of Soviet national air sovereignty. The Sinai agreements between Egypt and Israel cast light on the possibility of international arrangements for surveillance missions, including those involving a third party, in this case the USA.[60] The agreements, including such arrangements for verification, represented an important example of the possibility of allowing, in certain instances, such flights over sovereign territory. In this case it also included the sharing of the data acquired from the missions with Egypt, Israel and elements of the UN peace-keeping missions.

---

[57] Reiskind (note 55), p. 86.

[58] Reiskind (note 55), p. 86.

[59] During the discussions in 1989 and early 1990 there was another problem with regard to the FRG. The Status of Forces Agreements which governed stationed forces permitted the Allies to control the airspace over their own facilities. There was also the Four Power Berlin Air Safety Centre. Because of this, Poland, for example, was concerned with an Open Skies regime affecting Four Power rights in the FRG and the GDR.

[60] See Koulik, S., 'The Sinai experience', eds R. Kokoski and S. Koulik, SIPRI, *Verification of Conventional Arms Control in Europe: Technological Constraints and Opportunities* (Westview Press: Boulder, Colo., 1990), pp. 217–28.

This precedent was followed by the 1986 Stockholm Document which included the following paragraphs:

(89) The inspecting State will specify whether aerial inspection will be conducted using an airplane, a helicopter, or both. Aircraft for inspection will be chosen by mutual agreement between the inspecting and receiving States. Aircraft will be chosen which provide the inspection team a continuous view of the ground during the inspection.

(90) After the flight plan, specifying, *inter alia*, the inspection team's choice of flight path, speed and altitude in the specified area, has been filed with the competent air traffic control authority the inspection aircraft will be permitted to enter the specified area without delay. Within the specified area, the inspection team will, at its request, be permitted to deviate from the approved flight plan to make specific observations provided such deviation is consistent with paragraph (74) as well as flight safety and air traffic requirements. Directions to the crew will be given through a representative of the receiving State on board the aircraft involved in the inspection.

(91) One member of the inspection team will be permitted, if such a request is made, at any time to observe data on navigational equipment of the aircraft and to have access to maps and charts used by the flight crew for the purpose of determining the exact location of the aircraft during the inspection flight.

(92) Aerial and ground inspectors may return to the specified area as often as desired within the 48-hour inspection period.[61]

The Document also stated that:

In the specified area the representatives of the inspecting State accompanied by the representatives of the receiving State will be permitted access, entry and unobstructed survey, except for areas or sensitive points to which access is normally denied or restricted, military and other defence installations, as well as naval vessels, military vehicles and aircraft. The number and extent of the restricted areas should be as limited as possible. Areas where notifiable military activities can take place will not be declared restricted areas, except for certain permanent or temporary military installations which, in territorial terms, should be as small as possible, and consequently those areas will not be used to prevent inspection of notifiable military activities. Restricted areas will not be employed in a way inconsistent with the agreed provisions on inspection.[62]

The Document did not contain provisions with regard to the dissemination and use of the data, however. With respect to aerial monitoring, it is worth mentioning that the provisions of the Vienna Document of 1990 are identical with the above passages from the Stockholm Document.

---

[61] The Stockholm Document is reprinted in SIPRI, *SIPRI Yearbook 1987: World Armaments and Disarmament* (Oxford University Press: Oxford, 1987), appendix 10A, pp. 355–69.

[62] Note 61, p. 365 (para. 74).

Geographical constraints

An important problem, especially for the former Soviet Union, was third-party involvement. Within an Open Skies regime the USSR was interested in having overflight access to US bases in foreign countries. Under the Vienna Convention on the Law of Treaties, a third state is any state not a party to any particular treaty. Thus it does not have any obligations under the treaty.

For NATO, it was important that maximum openness of the then Soviet territory be assured. In the USA there are a few military installations which are frequently out of bounds for aircraft overflights, but there are virtually no areas in the USA which are constantly closed to overflights under Federal Aviation Administration (FAA) regulations.

Sensors

SIGINT sensors

US representatives at a NATO meeting in late 1989 insisted that sensors capable of collecting signals intelligence be prohibited on Open Skies aircraft purely on Fourth Amendment grounds: 'Under Open Skies the Soviets will be able to photograph almost anything in the United States from above, but they won't be able to intercept telephone calls.'[63]

This is of course a very real concern no matter how much openness Open Skies would attempt to achieve. It is perfectly legitimate that SIGINT sensors be prohibited and this should not be seen as any restriction on full openness but only as a protection of the private rights of individuals. There is of course the added and growing worry on the part of the more technologically advanced countries that other countries will not just increasingly attempt to acquire military secrets but will also engage in more extensive industrial espionage activities. Permitting SIGINT sensors would certainly also allow some of this type of activity to take place. The constitutional questions pose significant difficulties, not only in the USA but also in other countries. The use of SIGINT equipment has, therefore, continued to be ruled out.

In addition, the original US proposal included measures to minimize the chance that SIGINT could be conducted, such as pre-flight inspections and, importantly, a ban on loitering.[64] The ability to loiter over a specific area of interest for an extended period of time is an important advantage that aircraft have over space-based image collection. That consideration was given to sacrificing this advantage as a result of the political unacceptability of the collection of SIGINT information points to the importance attached to restricting such activity.

---

[63] *Aerospace Daily,* 22 Jan. 1990, p. 113.
[64] Tucker, J. B., 'Back to the future: the Open Skies talks', *Arms Control Today*, Oct. 1990, p. 21.

Other sensors

One issue which complicates an aerial inspection regime is the connection between the choice of sensors and other aspects. In Open Skies, for example, agreement on a relatively short notification period is important since this adds to the confidence that activities which may be of interest cannot be hidden. However, the usefulness of a short notification period is substantially diminished if weather or lighting considerations do not allow the areas of interest to be imaged. Parties may be tempted to carry out illegal activities when weather forecasts are for cloud for days or even weeks on end. Thus it would seem appropriate to allow for relatively high-resolution radar to be employed to take maximum advantage of the short-notification provisions.

An on-site inspection or NTM, for example, might indicate that an aerial reconnaissance mission is desirable within a short period of time. If only visible-light sensors are available then there could be a great deal of difficulty in seeing what is desired. Low-altitude flights under the cloud ceiling would be necessary—but this would limit a broad area coverage which might be the option that the inspecting side deems necessary to see what it wants to. In addition it might be suspected that evasion would take place at night. Infrared sensors have capabilities that would be useful in this context and the additional information provided by radar would also certainly add to the openness of the regime.[65]

At the Ottawa Conference the USSR wanted to restrict sensors to visible-light cameras with 2–3 m resolution. There is a problem associated with this type of proposal in general since for these types of sensor the resolution decreases in direct proportion to the distance of the target from the aircraft. The former USSR of course recognized this and in connection with its 30-cm resolution proposal in Budapest suggested that to maintain this resolution would necessitate the aircraft flying at a constant altitude.[66] Problems would probably arise from the inflexibility thus built into each overflight. This particular problem would not exist for SAR equipment since theoretically its resolution does not depend on the aircraft altitude but solely on the radar characteristics.[67]

In addition, whether the resolution of the SAR would be limited to 10 m as proposed by the USSR or 3 m or less as argued by most Western countries[68] might have important implications. If the inspecting party is interested only in large-scale infrastructure, clandestine deployments of non-trivial size, and so on, then the lower resolution would suffice—if some types of activity were detected with the lower resolution radar imagery, other higher resolution sensors might be used in a good weather, daytime overflight at a later stage to get a better picture if necessary. If, however, more detailed information is deemed

[65] See e.g., Banner, Young and Hall (note 54), p. 91.

[66] *Arms Control Reporter*, 1990, sheet 409.B.16.

[67] The resolution of less advanced real aperture radar does depend however on the relative location of aircraft and target. See, e.g., Banner, Young and Hall (note 54), pp. 92–97; Elachi, C., *Introduction to the Physics and Techniques of Remote Sensing* (Wiley: New York, 1987), pp. 204–205.

[68] *Arms Control Today*, Oct. 1990, p. 24.

necessary and/or a quick-response capability is necessary, then it is difficult to imagine this being acquired on a timely basis with the lower resolution SAR.

According to a Canadian official, using only electro-optical sensors would mean that countries with better weather would 'take more of a beating'.[69] To the extent that allowed SAR resolution is closer to the allowed optical resolution, then the different types of weather make less of a difference—placing all countries on a more equal footing.

Using a common suite of sensors is certainly not without advantages. Even among NATO countries themselves, the differing sensor capabilities could lead to the same types of difficulty as with data acquired through NTM. Different types of sensor used by different countries could also complicate the quota system. The types of sensor which a country like the USA could employ would permit it to acquire a great deal more information than those used by a less technologically advanced country in the same type of overflight. This would be an unfair advantage since each overflight-hour would be much more valuable for some countries than for others. This could in turn lead to disputes about quotas.

VI. Completion of the Open Skies Treaty

For quite some time after the conclusion of the Budapest Conference the prospects for a swift conclusion of an Open Skies agreement remained somewhat dim. A US official saying that Open Skies 'seems to have self-destructed' blamed Soviet intransigence.[70] Towards the end of 1990, however, there were indications that the USA would make an effort to revive the stalled talks.[71] Early in 1991 Hungary and Romania agreed to institute a bilateral Open Skies agreement.[72] In April 1991 compromise proposals were offered by NATO to the USSR which appeared to go a long way in allaying many of the Soviet concerns. NATO agreed to a standard package of sensors, restricted to those available for open trade, and agreed to permit the inspected country to demand that it provide flights for the inspecting side and that the information collected be shared with the country which is inspected.[73]

A Soviet reply was received in August which prompted one official to state: 'In general terms, we seem to be talking the same language for the first time'.[74] This led to a reconvening of the talks in Vienna in September 1991. At that time differences still remained, however, over territorial restrictions, quotas and choice of equipment. September saw the resolution of several important issues and by the time the talks were to reconvene towards the end of 1991 negotiators

---

[69] *Arms Control Reporter,* 1990, sheet 409.B.10.

[70] 'Soviets close door on Open Skies talks, U.S. diplomats say', *Defense News,* 1 Oct. 1990, p. 20.

[71] 'U.S. begins effort to revive Open Skies talks with Soviet Union', *Defense News,* 10 Dec. 1990, p. 27.

[72] *Defense News,* 25 Mar. 1991, p. 35.

[73] *Defense News,* 10 June 1991, p. 2; 'NATO offers Soviets new "Open Skies" plan', *Aviation Week & Space Technology,* 10 June 1991, p. 27.

[74] 'NATO to reopen negotiations on Open Skies', *Defense News,* 19 Aug. 1991, p. 1.

were expecting to complete an agreement in time for the follow-up meeting of the CSCE scheduled for March 1992. They were to be proven correct. Meeting continuously from 13 January 1992 until well into March, the negotiatiors completed the final 100-page document (including extensive annexes).[75]

Noting its potential 'to improve openness and transparency, to facilitate the monitoring of compliance with existing or future arms control agreements and to strengthen the capacity for conflict prevention and crisis management in the framework of the Conference on Security and Co-operation in Europe and in other relevant institutions',[76] the Treaty on Open Skies was signed on 24 March 1992. The Treaty had been initialled on 21 March by the 16 members of NATO, the five former members of the WTO (Bulgaria, Czechoslovakia, Hungary, Poland and Romania), as well as Belarus, Russia and Ukraine. The admission of Georgia to the CSCE during the opening of the Helsinki follow-up meeting brought the total number of signatories to 25.[77]

Covering the area from Vancouver to Vladivostok, the Treaty on Open Skies represents 'the most wide ranging international effort to date to promote openness and transparency in military forces and activities'.[78]

Quotas

The largest passive quotas (42 inspections) were allocated to the USA and Russia/Belarus combined. Germany, Canada, France, the UK, Italy, Turkey and Ukraine will accept up to 12 inspections each; Norway 7; Benelux,[79] Denmark, Poland and Romania 6 each; Portugal 2; and the remaining countries 4 each. Quotas of new signatories are to be considered in the Open Skies Consultative Commission (OSCC).

It was stipulated that the total active quota of a party must not exceed its passive quota, but the first distribution of active quotas was set up such that no party must accept more than 75 per cent of its passive quota. The first distribution of active quotas is specified in detail in Annex A to the Treaty—for example Germany is allowed three overflights of Russia/Belarus and one over Ukraine; Ukraine is allowed one flight over Czechoslovakia, two over Turkey and one each over Hungary, Poland and Romania. The active quota distribution is subject to annual review and upon full implementation[80] of the Treaty the distribution of active quotas may be such that the full passive quotas are attained.

Active quotas are transferable to other states parties but the number of overflights of one state party by another is limited to 50 per cent of the active quota

---

[75] The text of the Treaty is reprinted in appendix C. The annexes are listed.

[76] Treaty on Open Skies preamble, see appendix C.

[77] White, D., 'Old enemies agree to surveillance flights', *Financial Times,* 21 Mar. 1992, p. 2; Agence France Presse, 24 Mar. 1992.

[78] Statement by US State Department spokesman Richard A. Boucher quoted in 'Agreement will open skies to reconnaissance flights', *New York Times,* 21 Mar. 1992.

[79] For most purposes the Treaty considers Belgium, Luxembourg and the Netherlands as a single state party (Article XIV.1).

[80] The phasing of implementation of the Treaty is discussed in section VII.

of the observing party or the passive quota of the observed party, whichever is less. Provision is made for two or more states to form a group of states parties, co-operating with respect to quotas.

Maximum distances of the observation flights are also set out in detail for each state party and for each individual airfield which may be used.

Sensors and data

Sensors to be provided on Open Skies aircraft are stipulated in Article IV as (a) optical panoramic and framing cameras, (b) video cameras with real-time display, (c) infrared line scanning devices, and (d) sideways-looking synthetic aperture radar. Recording media are specified in Article IX for each sensor type as respectively (a) black-and-white photographic film, (b) magnetic tape, (c) black-and-white photographic film or magnetic tape, and (d) magnetic tape. The sensors must be commercially available to all states parties.

The data collected from each overflight are available to all states parties. Data collected during sensor certification using calibration targets are jointly examined and analysed but there is no provision for analysing any other data. Sensors are subject to very strict performance limits including ground resolutions no better than 30 cm for optical panoramic and framing cameras, 50 cm for infrared sensors and 3 m for radar. Annex B to the Treaty details the substantial degree of technical information which must be provided on all sensors and the manner in which data must be annotated to, among other things, aid in interpretation.

It is important to note that the possibility of addressing improvements in the capabilities of these sensors and the addition of other categories exists within the Open Skies Consultative Commission. Collection, processing, retransmission or recording of SIGINT are all prohibited, a restriction which will doubtless remain.

Before use each aircraft type and its sensors must be certified. Each state party may participate in this certification, which entails examination of the aircraft and sensors on the ground and in-flight. The ground examination allows complete access to the entire aircraft, its sensors and associated equipment including the opening of compartments and removal of panels or barriers as required. An in-flight examination includes the determination of the ground resolution of each sensor making use of well-defined calibration targets on the ground. For sensors, the resolution of which is altitude-dependent, this also includes the determination of the minimum altitude from which the sensors may be operated in keeping with ground resolution limits.

Covers or other devices inhibiting operation of the sensors must be provided so that data cannot be collected while travelling to points of entry or from points of exit or during transit flights.

Aircraft

All states parties have the right to designate one or more types or models of aircraft for use in observation flights and detailed information on the aircraft so designated must be provided. It was agreed that the observed state has the right to provide the observation aircraft. If it chooses not to exercise this right, the observing party will provide an aircraft designated by itself or another state party. Moscow's previous insistence on territorial limits and the right to fly over US bases outside US territory was dropped in exchange for this option of a party to provide aircraft for overflights of its own territory.[81]

Preparation for and conduct of observation flights

A minimum notification of 72 hours must be given prior to the arrival of the observing party. After arrival of the observing party at the appropriate Open Skies airfield and at least 24 hours prior to the observation flight itself, a mission plan must be submitted. This means that at least four full days must pass from the initial notification to the actual conduct of the flight—leaving open the possibility that the observed nation may have sufficient time to curtail important activity or make effective use of some CC&D techniques.

Importantly, however, all points on the territory of the observed party may be observed provided only that International Civil Aviation Organization (ICAO) standards and practices for flight safety are complied with. Height above ground level must be such as to ensure that ground resolution limitations are not exceeded and the flight-path must not cross the same point more than once, nor can a single point be circled—unfortunately these limitations restrict several advantages discussed above that aircraft have over satellite observations. The maximum flight distances allowed vary greatly with the size of each country and are specified for each designated Open Skies airfield.

A pre-flight inspection of the sensors and associated equipment (and the aircraft if it is being provided by the inspecting party) lasting no longer than eight hours may be carried out to confirm that they are in conformity with allowed types. This may be followed, if so requested, by a demonstration flight lasting for no more than two hours in order to observe operation of the sensors and confirm their capability.

From the time of arrival the observation flight must be completed within 96 hours (24 hours may be added to this time if the observed state party has requested a demonstration flight).

The Consultative Commission

An Open Skies Consultative Commission is established by Article X of the Treaty to consider compliance questions, resolve ambiguities which may arise,

---

[81] White, D., 'Old enemies agree to surveillance flights', *Financial Times,* 21 Mar. 1992, p. 2.

consider applications for and agree to technical and administrative measures upon accession by other states. It may also propose amendments to and agree on improvements to the Treaty. At least four regular meetings per year are to be held.

Other salient elements

The Treaty is of unlimited duration but states parties have the right to withdraw on six months' notice. A conference to review implementation of the Treaty is to be convened three years after entry into force and every five years thereafter.

The Treaty is to be implemented in phases. From entry into force until 31 December of the third year following the year of entry into force infrared line-scanning devices may not be used, and in addition no state party is obliged to provide an aircraft equipped with sensors from each of the four categories as long as it is equipped with one optical panoramic camera or at least a pair of optical framing cameras. Therefore, unless agreed to by the observing and observed parties, the advantages made possible by infrared imaging will await full implementation. Also during this period the distribution of active quotas discussed above will remain such that no party must accept more than 75 per cent of its passive quota.

States parties may also agree among themselves to conduct observation flights over each other's territory and, unless they agree otherwise, the resulting data will be made available to the OSCC. The Commission will also consider requests from bodies of the CSCE and other international organizations to conduct overflights of a state party with its consent. In either of the above situations the overflights will not count against quotas.

The Treaty is open for signature to all of the other former members of the Soviet Union at any time. Six months after it enters into force any other CSCE state may apply for accession and the Consultative Commission may also consider accession of any state willing and able to contribute to the Treaty's objectives.

VII. Implementation

Implementation of the Treaty has been proceeding at a smooth but rather slow pace. By the end of 1993, only 13 states had ratified and documents of ratification had been deposited by only 12 states. With the signing of Kyrgyzstan and the split of Czechoslovakia, the number of signatories increased to 27.[82]

---

[82] Lachowski, Z., 'The Treaty on Open Skies', SIPRI, *SIPRI Yearbook 1994* (Oxford University Press: Oxford, 1994), appendix 14B.

The Consultative Commission

The OSCC has already shown itself capable of operating effectively by eliminating some of the issues involving costs and sensors left for it to resolve at the time the Treaty was signed.

During 1992 two meetings of the Consultative Commission were held in Vienna (2 April–17 July and 21 September–17 December). The first session sought to resolve issues related to sensor calibration and various cost considerations. Decisions included types of camera and film to be used, film processing methods and minimum requirements for camera operations.[83] The second meeting discussed sensor calibration mechanisms using the results of the test overflights which occurred in November 1992. Cost issues were also discussed and agreement was reached on a number of points including which countries would pay for such items as fuel, oil and servicing under various circumstances. In addition, a method of calibration for synthetic aperture radar resolution was agreed to. An environmental seminar was also held to explore ways in which Open Skies could contribute to monitoring such phenomena as ozone levels, global warming, water and air pollution and deforestation.[84]

Weekly meetings held during 1993 focused on technical issues related to resolution for infrared and video sensors, elaboration of standards for calibrating image-processing equipment, the certification of observation equipment, flight rules and procedures, notifications and agreement on sensor data format. Progress has been quite slow, however, and with delays in ratification meetings were planned only on a monthly basis for 1994.[85]

Trial overflights

Among the many trial overflights conducted during 1992 after the signing of the Treaty the first was made over Poland in April by a Belgian Air Force C-130 Hercules aircraft. Primary sensors for the flight were a panoramic camera as well as a FLIR (forward-looking infrared) sensor. The latter, while not strictly allowed by the Treaty at present, was none the less employed to perfect procedures for the future. Operating at an altitude of between 600 and 2000 metres, the aircraft was used for observation of two Polish air bases, an army training ground, a chemical plant and three Russian facilities.[86] A reciprocal flight was made by the aircraft over the Benelux countries on behalf of Poland in April.

---

[83] *Disarmament Bulletin*, no. 19 (winter 1992/93) p. 15; *Arms Control Reporter*, 1992, sheet 409B.33; 1993, sheet 409.A.2.

[84] Jones, P., 'Open Skies: events in 1992', *Verification Report 1993: Yearbook on Arms Control and Environmental Agreements* (VERTIC: London, 1993); *Arms Control Reporter*, 1992, sheets 409.B.32–35, 37.

[85] Lachowski (note 82).

[86] Participating observers (in addition to the three-person crew) were from Belgium, Canada, Czechoslovakia, France, Germany, Hungary, Italy, Luxembourg, the Netherlands, Poland, Portugal, Spain, the UK and the USA. See *Arms Control Reporter*, 1992, sheets 409.B.32–33.

In June 1992 flight tests took place from Boscombe Down in the UK in order to settle issues relating to sensor resolution.[87] The flights aided in reaching the previously discussed agreement during the first OSCC on film and camera types and processing methods.

In September 1992 overflights of Russia and Belarus were conducted by an Andover aircraft from the UK and a Russian An-30. Three flights were made involving approximately 10 hours of flying time in total. The exercise tested procedures which included ensuring that sensors were sealed while overflying countries other than those slated for inspection. In addition to the British and Russian crews, observers from all the Western European Union countries as well as from Sweden and the USA were present. The series of flights was considered a success.[88]

In October 1992 three aircraft, provided by Canada, Denmark and Russia, tested synthetic aperture radars over specially designed targets in Hungary in order to demonstrate calibration of three very different SAR sensors. This successful experiment was hailed as 'a milestone in technical co-operation among parties to the Open Skies Treaty' and it was noted that the 'monumental task of negotiating such complicated issues as SAR parameters was a vivid example of the confidence-building intent of the Treaty at work'.[89]

A reciprocal flight to the 1992 overflights by the UK in Russia and Belarus was conducted in June 1993 by a Russian Air Force An-30. This was the first trial foreign overflight of the UK. The two main components involved management of air traffic control and translation of technical limits on camera capabilities into operational procedures. Although cloudy weather proved a problem the planning and procedural aspects were deemed a success.[90] Further overflights in 1993 were carried out by the USA and Hungary over Hungary, by Russia over Germany and by Germany over Russia.[91]

In 1993 Belgium, the Netherlands and Luxembourg (which has no aircraft of its own) concluded a co-operative agreement on joint observation flights. They will originate from the Belgian Air Force base at Melsbroeck using Belgian and Dutch C-130 Hercules aircraft.[92]

Modification and testing of the first of the converted WC-135 aircraft (designated OC-135B) to be used by the USA for Open Skies overflights was completed in 1993. The sensor suite included two KS-87B oblique-mounted framing cameras plus a vertical-mounted KS-87 for use in low (3300–8600 ft or about 1000–2600 m) altitude and a KA-91B panoramic camera for taking photographs above 26 000 ft (almost 8000 m). A full sensor suite including SAR, an infrared line scanner and a video camera are to be installed from

---

[87] *Trust and Verify*, no. 28 (May 1992), p. 4; *Arms Control Reporter*, sheet 409.B.33, 1992.
[88] *Atlantic News*, no. 2543 (9 Sep. 1992) p. 4; *Trust and Verify*, no. 32 (Oct. 1992), p. 3.
[89] *Disarmament Bulletin*, no. 19 (winter 1992/93), p. 15.
[90] *Trust and Verify*, no. 39 (July/Aug. 1993), p. 2.
[91] Lachowski (note 82).
[92] *Trust and Verify*, no. 42 (Nov. 1993), p. 2.

November 1995. Current plans are for one or two additional aircraft to be procured. [93]

VIII. Conclusions

The unnecessarily long stalemate over an Open Skies regime reflected a paradoxical situation. While the political purposes, including openness and transparency, were agreed upon, the lengthy discussions of technical details meant that both sides failed to display sufficient trust to reach an agreement for quite some time.

Another problem stemmed from the lack of precise definitions of the basic purposes of an agreement—no one tried to categorize or list activities or military installations which could be addressed. The USSR was perhaps not forthcoming enough in this area since NATO insisted on less specified surveillance. Accordingly, it was almost impossible to specify 'limits' on confidence-building activities.

It seems that for the former Soviet Union geostrategic factors played more of a role than would appear at first glance. Soviet unwillingness to allow full use of national capabilities has stemmed less from the fear of technological inferiority than from its geostrategic inequality. The specifics of force infrastructure which do not have analogues, say, in the USA, for example in air-defence complexes, may also play a role.

While, as pointed out above, some shortcomings remain, the Treaty on Open Skies has substantial potential to add to the increasing trust which is now emerging among all European nations. The inclusion of all the territory of the former USSR and the USA and Canada, plus the potential full participation of all CSCE states, will promote the type of transparency which is essential for new reductions of conventional armaments to be negotiated in an optimal manner.

The Treaty on Open Skies remains an important and wide-ranging multilateral Treaty which has the potential to increase transparency and openness on an unprecedented scale. The Open Skies Consultative Commission has already shown that it can function in an effective manner, raising hopes that the implementation of the agreement will proceed efficiently. Ratification of the agreement has been proceeding rather slowly, however, and this may at least in part be the result of the changed security concerns resulting from the demise of the Soviet Union. However, while the restructured map of Europe has certainly led to the diminution of certain fears, other security concerns have been created and the potential for increased instability remains in many areas. The monitoring capability provided by the Open Skies regime can be a valuable asset in addressing and helping to alleviate such concerns.

---

[93]Kandebo, S., 'USAF to modify second 'Open Skies' WC-135 in 1994', *Aviation Week & Space Technology*, 25 Oct. 1993, p. 59.

The costs associated with carrying out aerial inspection have also proved to be an issue, particularly for the smaller, less wealthy nations involved. However, the Open Skies Treaty has the potential to provide the greatest benefit particularly for these states which do not have access to other even more costly means of acquiring comparable information, such as satellite reconnaissance. The resultant transparency created throughout the area of application promises to be invaluable in alleviating many of their security concerns.

Open Skies also has the potential to provide valuable lessons, both in its content and through its eventual implementation for the negotiation of aerial inspection regimes in other regions of the world where this particular type of monitoring capability could go a long way to further enhance security, such as the Middle East.

8. Verification lessons of the Persian Gulf War

I. Introduction

The Iraqi invasion of Kuwait and the subsequent response of the allied Coalition provided opportunities to learn about the capabilities of various weapon systems, their performance, modes of operation, interoperability, and so on. The analysis of the data acquired will continue for years and perhaps decades to come. Called the 'first space war',[1] the Persian Gulf War has provided a unique opportunity to evaluate space-based reconnaissance in particular. In the present context there are many lessons which have relevance in the areas directly and indirectly related to the monitoring and verification of military force structures, weapons and troops.

II. Intelligence estimates

Lessons learned from the conflict with respect to troop counts, intelligence gathering, and so on, are all relevant to monitoring and verification of conventional forces in particular. Much has been reported in the press about the inadequacy of some elements of intelligence collection. Of course, one of the main problems was to quickly refocus intelligence resources over a relatively short period of time.

In fact, it seems likely that one important gap in US intelligence estimates was with respect to accurate figures for Iraqi troop deployments. The estimates may have been off by as much as 50 per cent.[2] The Coalition allies may also have overestimated Iraqi battlefield fortifications. Evidence points to the danger in assuming that units are at full strength as was often the case with such estimates in the Gulf.[3] From log-books and debriefings it now appears there were only about 350 000 troops in the Kuwaiti Theater of Operations (KTO)—far fewer than the earlier official Pentagon figure of 540 000. One of the reasons for this was that many of the front-line units were only at 50 per cent strength. Not until Christmas 1990 did the presence of Special Forces teams near the border (and even in holes inside Iraqi-held territory—i.e., a type of 'clandestine OSI') begin to allow revisions to be made in the force estimates. Part of the problem was the ability of the monitoring system to cover only a portion of the area at a time which 'made it difficult to fix the table of organization of some

[1] 'War tests satellites prowess', *Space News*, 21 Jan.–3 Feb. 1991, p. 1.
[2] Smith, J., R., 'Congress to probe intelligence gaps', *International Herald Tribune*, 19 Mar. 1991, p. 3.
[3] Moore, M., 'Desert mirages: In the war, things weren't always what they seemed', *International Herald Tribune*, 18 Mar. 1991, p. 1.

Iraqi units, led to over-counting of Iraqi troops and rendered the allied forces incapable of totally eliminating mobile threats'.[4]

It has been stated that 'the main ammunition and supply depot for the Iraq Army corps . . . apparently went undetected by allied intelligence and remained well stocked and intact until marine forces overran it'.[5] Of course there was no information exchange concerning how many troops and how much equipment should have been in a given area as would be the case under an arms control agreement such as the CFE Treaty, for example. This type of data allows focusing NTM (or OSI and aerial overflights if allowed under an agreement) more locally to try to detect discrepancies. None the less, the area of the KTO was extremely small when compared to the ATTU zone.

With respect to information exchange within NATO, it is important to note that the Joint Operational Intelligence Centre (JOIC), established in order to make information from US intelligence sources available, 'proved to be invaluable in intelligence exchanges, as well as in the planning, co-ordination and execution of operations'.[6]

There are of course different views on the efficacy of the various forms of intelligence gathering used. For example, there has been discussion of the adequacy of tactical intelligence (used, among other things, to determine the location of forces and selected targets) during the Persian Gulf War. Senator David Boren, Chairman of the Senate Select Committee on Intelligence, said it was excellent, while Senator John Glenn said he found complaints that aerial reconnaissance was inadequate.[7]

This related specifically, for example, to the problem that the numbers of Scud missiles were underestimated. After the War, General Norman Schwarz-kopf said that intelligence gathered during the War indicated that there may have been as many as 10 times the number indicated by the pre-war intelligence estimates—citing evidence that estimates of the number of launchers 'were either grossly inaccurate or our pilots [who have seen more launchers than were estimated] are lying through their teeth'.[8]

The amount declared to be left after the War suggested that US intelligence had also underestimated Iraq's arsenal of chemical weapons, and an immense effort by Iraq to develop nuclear weapons was not detected until the UN-sanctioned on-site inspections were undertaken.

These facts indicate how far off estimates can be from some sources, and how much more accurate they become when different methods (in this case close-up aerial views or OSI) are used. However, in the case of the Scud missiles, for example, they became a much greater priority once the Iraqi forces began to fire them, and it is not precisely clear to what extent intelligence resources were being focused on them before this time.

[4]'Key military officials criticize intelligence handling in the Gulf war', *Aviation Week & Space Technology*, 24 June 1991, p. 83.

[5] *International Herald Tribune*, 18 Mar. 1991, p. 1.

[6] Howe, J. T., 'NATO and the Gulf crisis', *Survival*, vol. 23, no. 3 (May/June 1991), p. 250.

[7] 'Spy efforts in Gulf debated', *Defense News*, 25 Mar. 1991, p. 2.

[8] 'DOD to redesign tactical intelligence', *Defense News*, 4 Mar. 1991, p. 13.

Details about the information received through US NTM on Iraqi force postures prior to the invasion of Kuwait certainly provide an indication of the capabilities of these systems. More important in the context of verification of conventional forces in Europe, however, they indicate the type of information and warning which may be necessary. While detailed satellite photographs may not be available to most parties to conventional arms accords in Europe, aerial reconnaissance—whether through the Open Skies Treaty or other arrangements—may provide equivalent information in the years to come. It is instructive, therefore, to examine the manner in which the Iraqi force buildup was monitored and analysed.

About two weeks before the invasion a Defense Intelligence Agency (DIA) analyst saw from satellite photographs the first signs of a brigade of an Iraqi T-72 tank division—a division which he could identify from the photographs and one of the most potent of those Iraq possessed.[9] By the next day the entire division of 300 tanks and in excess of 10 000 men were in place close to the Kuwaiti border and a second division was appearing; by the third day there was another division and by 19 July there were over 35 000 men from three divisions close to the border. However, because the Iraqis had always had the practice of rehearsing operations during the war with Iran and as no such rehearsals had been noted for this type of movement, the intelligence summary 'stressed the extraordinary nature of the troop movements but did not forecast that they would be used'.[10] General Schwarzkopf's evaluation at this time was that at most Iraq was poised for a limited punitive strike into Kuwait.

Within 11 days a total of eight divisions and 100 000 troops were in place. On 30 July, two days before the invasion, a DIA analyst, noting movement of artillery, logistics and aircraft, advised that the force would in fact be used. Although the assessment was passed to Colin Powell, he considered it to be an 'educated guess'. Even when on 1 August three divisions had moved forward to within three miles of the border and all communications and logistics were deployed Powell knew that 'the only way to be sure of *intent* was to know what was in the leader's mind'[11] and no good human sources within the Iraqi Government were available. A credible bluff would have to include all of the manœuvring which had taken place, but by then Powell no longer believed that the moves were a bluff.

This experience points to a number of factors of general relevance in the verification context. First, the best monitoring capabilities are only as good as the analysis which accompanies them. The satellite photographs were detailed enough to allow recognition of the fact that the most competent elements of Iraq's forces were being redeployed, for example, but it took a trained analyst to identify these units and realize the significance of their movement. Second, even with good information and competent analysis, the warning time when a

---

[9] This and the summary of events that follows is based on the account in Woodward, B., *The Commanders* (Simon & Schuster: New York, 1991), pp. 206–22.

[10] Woodward (note 9), p. 207.

[11] Woodward (note 9), p. 219, emphasis added.

dedicated foe is involved can be very short, even for a large and potent force. In the case of Iraq the USA obviously could not respond by putting forces which it did not have in the region on increased alert or redeploying them in return. In Europe such moves would be possible and feasible, but only if the situation was known. In the absence of sophisticated satellite monitoring this points directly to the value of aerial monitoring in particular and on a not infrequent basis. Third, unmasking the *intent* of force movements and changing force structures—an extremely valuable but also very difficult task—can be aided through appropriate notifications and other CSBMs within the European context.

III. The UN Special Commission on Iraq

UN Security Council resolution 687 signalled both the end of the Persian Gulf War and the beginning of, among other things, far-ranging access to Iraqi territory by international inspectors. Iraq was obliged by the resolution to accept 'urgent on-site inspection' of its nuclear, biological, chemical and missile capabilities as well as future continuous monitoring and verification of its compliance with aspects of the resolution.

To carry out these tasks the resolution called for the creation of a Special Commission (UNSCOM) which would carry out its mission based upon both 'Iraq's declarations and the designation of any additional locations by the Special Commission itself'.[12] These latter designations have been based on Iraq's declarations and information supplied by UN member states, as well as on aerial reconnaissance data including those from helicopters and a United States U-2 aircraft which was put at the disposal of the Commission, flying regular missions over Iraqi territory. Information gathered in earlier inspections was of course also used to cue and enhance the effectiveness of those following. UNSCOM would also oversee the 'destruction, removal or rendering harmless' of much of Iraq's weapon capability.

In the case of Iraq's nuclear potential, the International Atomic Energy Agency (IAEA) was given primary responsibility for carrying out on-site inspections, with the assistance and co-operation of UNSCOM.

Particularly in its initial declarations in the nuclear area, Iraq was far from forthcoming. It was therefore largely up to the inspectors to uncover the true extent of the Iraqi weapon programme. This led to unexpected results.

Iraq's nuclear capability

Although a great deal of highly specialized intelligence-gathering equipment had been focused on Iraq up to and during the conflict, not until the occurrence of inspections on the ground did the extent of the nuclear programme begin to become apparent. Perhaps the biggest surprise was the extensive uranium

---

[12] Resolution 687 (1991) adopted by the Security Council at its 2981st meeting on 3 Apr. 1991 (United Nations Security Council document S/RES/687, 8 Apr. 1991).

enrichment programme using the electromagnetic isotope separation (EMIS) process (used by the USA during the Manhattan Project but soon thereafter abandoned). A full-scale plant designed for 90 separators was perhaps 18–36 months away from full operation with an identical 'backup' facility being constructed at a separate location.

Information from an Iraqi defector on EMIS enrichment activity was reportedly corroborated by intelligence information on file in the USA including satellite photographs taken months before the defector's revelations. These photographs were originally thought to show a military facility unrelated to the nuclear programme in Iraq but, when reviewed in light of the defector's statements, its true purpose was more clearly apparent.[13] This points to the value and potential synergistic effects in using multiple resource types—while one source of information may be of limited use in a given situation, information from another source or sources may greatly enhance its value in identifying a particular facility or activity.

Other information which only came to light as a result of persistent efforts by inspectors concerned the extensive centrifuge enrichment programme which relied much less on indigenous production and involved a very well organized international procurement effort. It also became apparent that Iraq had been working on, although had subsequently abandoned, gaseous diffusion technology and was also exploring chemical separation techniques for uranium enrichment. Iraq had also produced small quantities of plutonium in a safeguarded reactor and had engaged in reprocessing activity.

Inspections were therefore instrumental in the UN Security Council's Resolution 707, condemning Iraq's non-compliance with its safeguards obligations and further declaring that this violated Iraq's commitments as a party to the NPT.[14]

The dramatic results of the inspections have strengthened the case for the use of IAEA Special Inspections of undeclared facilities in other countries. The Director General of the IAEA has stated that 'a high degree of assurance can be obtained that the Agency can uncover clandestine nuclear activities if three major conditions are fulfilled: First, that access is provided to information obtained, *inter alia* through national technical means, regarding sites that may require inspection; second, that access to any such sites, even at short notice, is an unequivocal right of the Agency; and third, that access to the Security Council is available for backing and support that may be necessary to perform the inspection'.[15] Lessons learned in the Iraqi inspections will doubtless be invaluable for planning potential future inspections to other countries.

However, a great deal of the information on the specifics of the nuclear programme in Iraq was obtained from the many documents which were also seized

---

[13] Hibbs, M. and Seneviratne, G., 'U.S. believes Iraq has built magnetic isotope enrichment plant', *Nucleonics Week*, vol. 32, no. 25 (20 June 1991), p. 2.

[14] Resolution 707 (1991) adopted by the Security Council at its 3004th meeting on 15 Aug. 1991 (United Nations Security Council document S/RES/707, 15 Aug. 1991).

[15] Quoted in IAEA Press Release, PR/91 24 (18 July 1991).

by inspectors. Iraq did obstruct the inspectors—preventing them from gathering all of the material they would have liked—but a great wealth of classified documents was obtained.[16] This again highlights the special nature of the Iraqi case—no future verification regime currently envisioned is likely to allow inspectors to pry into and carry away whatever information files they might desire.

Other capabilities

With respect to chemical weapons, inspectors found fewer discrepancies between declared capabilities and what they actually found on the ground. None the less, an Australian inspector pointed out the usefulness of the inspections for the future: 'We have inspected declared storage and production sites, and undeclared storage and production sites. In doing this, we have accumulated a lot of practical experience about the conduct of "routine" and "challenge" inspections, which will, I hope, be of assistance to those charged with drawing up the verification regime for the CWC.'[17]

While Iraq initially denied that it possessed biological weapons, subsequent UNSCOM inspections, while failing to uncover evidence of weaponization, have shown conclusively that advanced military biological research was being conducted.

Concerning Iraq's ballistic missile capability, relevant declared missiles have been found and destroyed along with additional launchers and other support equipment found by the inspection teams. Substantial uncertainty remains, however, over the existence of additional missiles.[18]

Security Council resolution 715 provides plans for future monitoring of Iraq.[19] To ensure that Iraq will not pose a threat in the future, the plan calls for the continued right of UNCSOM to continued any-time, anywhere inspections and aerial overflights and requires the provision of detailed data on weapons, equipment and facilities.

Experience gained

The basic functioning of UNSCOM—entailing declarations of holdings by Iraq and their subsequent verification through methods including on-site inspections and followed by a longer-term monitoring process—is inherent in the process of much of present and likely future arms control efforts. Because the inspectors associated with UNSCOM have operated basically with *carte blanche* with

[16] Report on the sixth IAEA on-site inspection in Iraq under Security Council resolution 687 (S/23122, Nov, 1991).

[17] Interview with Dr John Gee appearing in 'Confessions of an on-site inspector', *Pacific Reseach*, Nov. 1991, p. 3.

[18] Ekéus, R., 'The United Nations Special Commission on Iraq', SIPRI, *SIPRI Yearbook 1992: World Armaments and Disarmament* (Oxford University Press: Oxford, 1992).

[19] United Nations Security Council document S/RES/715, 11 Oct. 1991.

the full backing of the Security Council, however, drawing direct lessons for other regimes carried out under different conditions is not an easy task.

It is most important to point out that even with the virtually unlimited access it none the less took a large number of inspections and extremely persistent staff to acquire reasonable confidence that an accurate picture of Iraqi military potential emerged. The wide-ranging access allowed for decisions to be made in the field as to how best to proceed with the inspection process. Of course in the future, in other circumstances and other states, the inspected country may prove more co-operative, facilitating the tasks of future inspection teams. In addition, inspectors in other situations will be unlikely to encounter difficulties associated with heavily damaged structures and equipment as well as clearing and removal operations which had been carried out at several locations and thus often severely hindered the inspection process in Iraq. Certainly the wealth of experience gained by hundreds of inspectors of many different nationalities is very valuable in itself.

The use of data from the U-2 aircraft put at the disposal of UNSCOM and operating in co-operation with the inspection teams on the ground will provide valuable lessons for the future. As recently pointed out the positive results in this area have already in fact drawn on past experience: 'The commission has few doubts about the importance of aircraft to their mission. Its long-term monitoring plans, approved by the Security Council, include the right to overfly at any time, without hindrance, any area, site, or facility in Iraq, in fixed- or rotary-wing aircraft equipped with appropriate sensors. The commission's insistence on aerial inspection is the result of first-hand U.N. experience' [in the Sinai, Angola, the Western Sahara, Cambodia and other areas].[20]

It is important to note that valuable experience has been and, at the time of writing, continues to be gained in Iraq in acquiring and analysing intelligence and then assessing the results through inspections with, if not an uncooperative, certainly a less than forthcoming state. The many-tiered approach of space-based, aerial- and ground-based sensors, coupled with OSI, was employed.

A full analysis of the many specific lessons would require access to classified information, but it has been aptly summarized that UNSCOM 'has a wealth of experience, organizational, political and technical, to offer Europe in the future. This experience covers decisions on where to make on-site inspections (using information from a variety of sources), the on-site inspections themselves, missiles destruction, warhead (chemical) destruction, removal of nuclear materials and handling of biological agents'.[21]

For conventional forces, the UNSCOM experience points in particular to the special role which on-site inspections must necessarily play in any future comprehensive verification regime which aims at a high degree of transparency.

---

[20] Smithson, A. E., 'Open skies ready for takeoff', *Bulletin of the Atomic Scientists*, vol. 48, no. 1 (Jan/Feb. 1992), p. 17.

[21] Lewis, P. M. and Greene, O., *The CSCE, European Security and Verification: Considerations for Helsinki 1992*, Verification Technology Information Centre, London, Mar. 1992, p. 14.

While in future cases it may not be possible to use one or more of the methods employed by UNSCOM immediately (or at all), it is certain that the methods which are to be available will, as a result of UNSCOM activities, be able to provide much more useful information than they would have otherwise.

IV. European satellites

The prospects of the development of a European satellite monitoring capability have certainly fluctuated in the past few years, but several important developments have occurred since and often as a result of events in the Gulf.

The Parliamentary Assembly of the WEU[22] had already issued two reports recommending the development of a European satellite system specifically for verification. France had proposed the formation of a joint processing and interpretation centre which is now in operation in Spain to train photo-interpreters using commercially available SPOT and Landsat images.[23] The need for the capabilities such a system would provide have not been universally accepted, however. With respect to information already flowing from the USA, opinion has been divided. The chief spokesman for the FRG Defence Minister remarked that the amount of intelligence flowing from the USA did not justify the costs that would be involved in a European reconnaissance satellite.[24] Prior to the Gulf operations similar sentiments were also voiced by Britain's Minister for Defence Procurement, stressing cost considerations and the 'good deal from the United States' that Britain is getting in terms of intelligence acquired from space.[25] Along with France, however, Spain, Italy, Belgium and the Netherlands were all agreed on an independent European surveillance system.[26]

Satellite surveillance technology was identified by defence ministers from 13 European countries in a mid-November 1990 meeting as among 11 priority areas in which Europeans could benefit from co-operation under the Euclid (European Cooperation for the Long Term in Defence) programme. Projects agreed upon included satellite surveillance technology, high-resolution optical sensors, advanced SAR data processing and ground-based systems.[27]

Shortly after the invasion of Kuwait it was still being reported, for example, that, although it served to remind West European governments of their dependence on the USA for space-based imagery 'the volume and quality of intelligence available from other sources make it unlikely that Europe will decide that the benefits of an independent reconnaissance satellite justify its development

---

[22] Member countries include Belgium, Britain, France, Germany, Italy, Luxembourg, the Netherlands, Portugal and Spain.

[23] *Military Space,* 14 Jan. 1991, p. 7; de Selding, P. B., 'France to provide imagery to WEU', *Space News,* 3–9 May 1993, p. 9.

[24] 'Mideast crisis deflates arguments favouring European spy satellite', *Space News,* 27 Aug.–2 Sep. 1990, p. 3.

[25] 'U.K. minister balks at call for European spy satellite', *Space News,* 16–22 July 1990, p. 1.

[26] 'Allies, U.S. explore space cooperation', *Military Space,* vol. 7, no. 24 (19 Nov. 1990), p. 1.

[27] 'Europe keen on spy satellite network', *Space News,* 26 Nov.–2 Dec. 1990, p. 2; *Military Space,* vol. 7, no. 24 (19 Nov. 1990), p. 5; 'Europeans launch cooperative R&D effort to bolster industries, gain technology', *Aviation Week & Space Technology,* 24 Dec. 1990, p. 67.

and operating costs'.[28] None the less, the President of the WEU (which had voted 7 June 1990 in support of a 'large-scale European system of satellite verification') said on 23 August that 'the effectiveness of the deployment of [European] air and naval forces to the Gulf will suffer from the lack of sufficient information sources'.[29] In the same spirit a senior French military officer voiced concern that the data which they did obtain from the USA were already processed, but that the raw data were needed so that they could come to their own conclusions.[30] In this same context it is interesting to note that Israel may have accelerated its programme to launch a remote sensing satellite as a result of the conflict. Defence Minister Moshe Arens said that it should come as no surprise if a satellite with 'intelligence gathering capability'[31] were launched. Like many European nations Israel, which has already launched experimental satellites, has not been very happy about the need to rely on the USA for satellite data.

French Defence Minister Pierre Joxe pointed to the role played by observation satellites in the quick allied victory and noted that this should encourage France and other nations to develop satellite systems for arms control verification as well as for keeping track of weapon and troop movements in a more general context. 'Space is very important for war, as we have seen in recent days, but it also can be very important for peace, for monitoring arms control through these observation techniques. One of the great lessons of [the Gulf War] is that, for the future—if the international community is willing—we should employ space technology to assure disarmament, and to verify compliance'.[32] By 6 May 1991, in calling in strong terms for European space-based imaging systems, he pointed out that reliance on US technology was not satisfactory for Europe. He stated that 'Our extreme dependence on American sources . . . was flagrant, particularly in the initial phase. [It] was the United States that provided, when and how it wanted, the essential information necessary for the conduct of the conflict'.[33]

Thus, based on the performance of US military intelligence satellites, claims made in the months after the end of the War by European officials both in government and industry that 'Western European governments are on the verge of establishing a pan-European satellite-verification capability' should perhaps now be taken more seriously. Reportedly, the capabilities may include a radar-equipped satellite expressly for the purpose of arms control monitoring.'[34] A 1993 WEU study points to the possibility of a European intelligence capability by 2000, and officials have noted that such a system for treaty verification and

---

[28] Note 25.
[29] Note 25, p. 3.
[30] Note 25, p. 3.
[31] 'Israel hints at plans to launch spy satellite', *Defense News*, 11 Mar. 1991, p. 6.
[32] 'Gulf war spurs call for European spy satellites', *Space News*, 11–17 Mar. 1991, p. 3.
[33] 'Defense Minister invites French emphasis on spy satellites', *Defense News*, 13 May 1991, p. 50.
[34] 'European eye spy satellite', *Defense News*, 8 Apr. 1991, p. 2.

crisis management will, in fact, ultimately be necessary.[35] The opening of the WEU interpretation centre in 1993 represents a firm first commitment.

The stated willingness of France to share the information acquired by its Helios satellite programme with countries of the Western European Union is a very positive development. Because the resolution of Helios will be about 1 m, high enough to detect and distinguish among many conventional force elements including weapons, this is a highly significant development. The decision was announced by the French Defence Minister, who assumed office in the middle of the Gulf crisis and who 'has stressed repeatedly that France and Europe required a major investment in military space assets so as not to be dependent on American satellites'.[36] A 1993 WEU study points to the possibility of a European intelligence satellite capability by 2000 and officials have noted that such a system for treaty verification and crisis management will, in fact, ultimately be necessary.[37] This may also well pave the way for future further information exchange structures.

As a further consequence of the Persian Gulf War a proposal has been made to expand the Helios programme to include three generations, the first consisting of the two satellites already authorized. Two second-generation spacecraft equipped with visual and infrared sensors would follow. The next decade would then see third-generation satellites equipped with advanced sensors as well as radar.[38]

V. Use of commercial satellites

The Persian Gulf crisis also showed, however, that there are limits to the 'openness' of commercial satellites. Possible future problems with commercial satellites for verification were made apparent in that a precedent was set at the onset of the crisis in restricting the images from SPOT—only orders for archived images of the area were taken and orders for new images would not be accepted.[39] Post-invasion Landsat images were openly distributed, although not to Iraq; however, it would have been easy for Iraq to obtain these images through third parties.[40]

Just as free and open access was (some might argue justifiably) limited during the crisis—this could lead to fears that relying heavily on this type of verification means for monitoring conventional forces in Europe could result in denial of previously available information. This would probably occur at just the time that the information was needed most, that is, at time of crisis.

[35] de Braganti, G., 'WEU study group envisions spy satellite program', *Space News,* 1–7 Feb. 1993, p. 3.

[36] 'Joxe: France to share Helios images with WEU', *Space News*, 10–16 June 1991, p. 22.

[37] de Braganti, G., 'WEU study group envisions spy satellite program', *Space News*, 1–7 Feb. 1993, p. 3.

[38] 'Matra Marconi space proposes expanded program for Helios reconnaissance satellite', *Aviation Week & Space Technology*, 20 May 1991, p. 63.

[39] *Space News*, 13–19 Aug. 1990, pp. 15–16.

[40] *Trust & Verify,* no. 14 (Oct. 1990), p. 3.

At present the Russian firm Soyuzkarta provides the most finely detailed commercially available satellite images. While the quality can be uneven, resolution has been known to be better than 5 m. One image of Saudi Arabia, for example, was good enough 'to permit the clear identification of US transport aircraft and to see the sites of infantry, armoured and transport facilities' as well as to identify individual vehicles and was estimated to have 3-m resolution.[41] Fighter jets have also been identified on Soviet commercial images taken with the KFA-1000 camera.[42] These images are obtained with photographic film, thus they must be digitized before they can be further processed by computer and also, since the film capsules must be returned to earth for processing, the time required to obtain the images can be somewhat longer than for SPOT or Landsat images which are transmitted electronically. None the less, the best of these images could be very useful in monitoring conventional forces and force structures in Europe.

The War has pointed again to the importance of multispectral imagery which was obtained from the US Landsat satellites for mapping and terrain analysis. Multispectral imagery can also be important for detecting certain forms of camouflage. General Donald Kutyna, chief of US Space Command, has also endorsed new versions of the Landsat satellites with higher resolution sensors.[43] Current maximum Landsat resolution is 30 m, but future systems will doubtless feature improvements. The multispectral imaging capabilities of the SPOT satellite also saw extensive use for planning, map updates and sensor fusion. This has reportedly led the Air Force to see the need for a follow-on to present Landsat imaging technology for increased self reliance.[44]

VI. New monitoring methods

Of the monitoring methods which made their first appearance in the Persian Gulf War, that most reported on was the Joint Surveillance Target Attack Radar System (JSTARS), which was also suggested by some analysts for CFE Treaty verification. It was originally designed to use side-looking radar flown on a modified Boeing 707 and to be sophisticated enough to distinguish individual ground targets amid the often hilly European landscape at a range of over 250 km. Its moving target indicator (MTI) was designed to differentiate between tracked and wheeled vehicles. For verification purposes, it could be effectively employed in an NTM role as well as perhaps in a co-operative aerial reconnaissance agreement. With respect to the latter, there were, however, US concerns

[41] Zimmerman, P., 'Intelligence for the asking: civil remote sensing's ripe commercial potential', *Space News*, 3–9 Dec. 1990, p. 24.

[42] 'Firm sells sharp Soviet space data of Mideast to all but Iraqi agents', *Space News*, 19–25 Nov. 1990, p. 4.

[43] *Military Space*, 6 May 1991, p. 5.

[44] 'Military leaders say GPS success in Gulf assures tactical role for satellites', *Aviation Week & Space Technology*, 13 May 1991, p. 89.

about the sensitive technologies involved and whether they could be shared with all the other CFE Treaty signatories.[45]

Two prototype aircraft were undergoing testing when they were deployed to Saudi Arabia just days before the commencement of the air offensive on 17 January 1991. JSTARS reportedly provided 'an extraordinary reconnaissance and battlefield management capability', and the deployed aircraft were also useful in locating mobile missile launchers.[46] One of the aircraft kept up a 12-hour mission schedule every day it was in the region.[47] By the end of 1993, performance verification testing had been completed on two J-STARS with 20 of the aircraft to be built.[48] The aircraft is being considered for potential use as a peacekeeping instrument in situations such as the Bosnian conflict to detect troop movements or removal of weapons from storage areas.[49]

An airborne signals intelligence platform was hurriedly made ready and deployed by the US Marines in January 1991. The 'Senior Warrior' system marries a C-130 transport with a computerized SIGINT system named 'Senior Scout'. Complementing the 'Rivet Joint' RC-135 SIGINT aircraft and other means, this signals intelligence asset was used 'to determine the location of Iraqi weapons and units, their organizations and technical qualities'.[50] These capabilities point towards the often understated capabilities of signals intelligence to provide valuable information on structural aspects of conventional weapon deployments. This is especially important in the European context where most of the countries involved in the CFE Treaty, for example, do have some form of SIGINT capability.[51]

NATO considered the use of some of its multinational fleet of 18 E-3A Airborne Early Warning and Control System (AWACS) aircraft, modified with radar and infrared sensors, for CFE aerial reconnaissance. This would allow the aircraft, originally designed primarily to track aircraft (moving targets can be detected at distances of hundreds of kilometres), to operate in a ground-surveillance role. This type of multilateral approach would have obvious appeal to the smaller and less wealthy members of the alliance.[52] Hurried upgrades of some of the US AWACS aircraft brought about by the War in the Persian Gulf included a non-cooperative target recognition system which can be used to identify specific aircraft using their radar signature.[53]

An interesting example of a system which could be employed for verification purposes and the effect which the Persian Gulf War had upon it is the French

[45] 'A new market takes off', *Jane's Defence Weekly*, 24 Nov. 1990, p. 1039; 'While congress debates Joint STARS' future, system demonstration shows success in Europe', *Aviation Week & Space Technology*, 15 Oct. 1990, p. 104; 'U.S. pushes verification role for JSTARS', *Defense News*, 22 Oct. 1990, p. 1.

[46] 'Planners eye JSTARS results', *Defense News*, 15 Apr. 1991, p. 23.

[47] 'Joint STARS "was 100% reliable"', *Jane's Defence Weekly*, 30 Mar. 1991, p. 466.

[48] 'E-8As complete performance testing', 3 Jan. 1994, p. 53.

[49] *Aviation Week & Space Technology*, 10 Jan. 1994, p. 21.

[50] 'Airborne Senior Warrior helped U.S. snoop on Iraqis', *Defense News*, 29 Apr. 1991, p. 22.

[51] Koulik, S. and Kokoski, R., *Verification of the CFE Treaty*, SIPRI Research Report no. 4, Stockholm, Oct. 1991.

[52] 'Use of AWACS for treaty verification splits West', *Defense News*, 3 Dec. 1990, p. 31.

[53] Munro, N., 'Improved AWACS, allied air control reduce aircraft ID mishaps', *Defense News*, 25 Feb. 1991, p. 32.

Orchidee battlefield surveillance radar. Its capabilities include the detection of land vehicles and discrimination between armoured vehicles and trucks. Configured for use on helicopters its range is more limited than systems like JSTARS because of its lower operating altitude—but it is still in excess of 60 km allowing for monitoring of some of a neighbouring country's military activities even in a non-cooperative environment. Its capability to communicate through a data link with a JSTARS ground station has also been demonstrated.[54] Development and production were cancelled in August 1990 before the Gulf War, a victim of budgetary constraints.[55] However, field tests of a simplified version of the system named Horizon were carried out for a number of reconnaissance missions during the War and reportedly performed very well. As a result of this experience a decision was taken to deploy Horizon in the latter half of the 1990s.[56]

VII. The technology race and monitoring implications

The impressive performance of a wide array of sophisticated weaponry during the Persian Gulf War has served to accentuate the importance of the qualitative aspects of conventional arms. The increasing sophistication of conventional weapons in general will necessitate that qualitative factors take on increased importance on the arms control agenda.

The use of F-117A stealth aircraft, for example, has provided direct evidence of the limitations of 'bean counting' when attempting to limit capabilities of forces. Also important and perhaps even more so is the *type* of weapon (in the case in point, aircraft) which is deployed and its capabilities—including smart munitions capabilities, for example. Specifically,

Air Force documents provided to congressional armed services committees [in Mar. 1991] show an ability to use only eight F-117As to do the same bombing job as 16 conventional aircraft . . . the eight F-117As—each equipped with two 2000-pound precision bombs—would require the support of only two tankers, as opposed to a conventional force package that would require the support of 11 tankers, 12 radar-killing planes and gunships to depress enemy air defenses, and about 16 F-16 fighters that would escort the planes to and from their target objectives.[57]

Thus the need to verify not only aircraft ceilings in the future but perhaps ceilings on certain types of obviously more capable aircraft will create a more difficult challenge. If limitations on various types of high technology weapon

[54] 'France discloses technical details of Orchidee surveillance system', *Aviation Week & Space Technology*, 27 Aug. 1990, p. 84; 'Gulf war test may save Orchidee', *Jane's Defence Weekly*, 23 Mar. 1991, p. 423.
[55] 'French end development of Orchidee radar', *Aviation Week & Space Technology*, 24 Sep. 1990, p. 22.
[56] 'Gulf war test may save Orchidee', *Jane's Defence Weekly*, 23 Mar. 1991, p. 423; Blake, B. (ed.), *Jane's Radar and Electronics Warfare Systems 1992–93*, 4th edn (Jane's Information Group: Coulsdon, Surrey, 1992), p. 220.
[57] 'Air force sticks to its stealth plans', *Defense News*, 1 Apr. 1991, p. 6.

which may be available to some parties and not others are not included, then overall totals lose much of their meaning.

Even without stealth, the same type of problem also exists with more advanced stand-off missile technology, for example—only here the verification problems are even more difficult since the same types of aircraft may or may not employ these types of weapon. Sufficiently intrusive on-site inspection would appear to be one of the few ways to handle these difficulties.

The US Navy will not have a new attack aircraft until well past the turn of the century, for example, and 'as a result the fielding of improved generations of long-range air-to-air and air-to-ground missiles will assume greater importance in order to increase the ranges at which the Navy's aging aircraft can successfully engage enemy aircraft and installations'.[58] As Edward Luttwak has stated, 'future conflicts will likely involve aggressive entry by air into enemy territory through the use of increasingly long-range aircraft that exploit stealth and advanced electronic combat technologies.' Put in a more colloquial manner, 'the one who shoots first is going to win. But it's not only a matter of who shoots first, but of how fast your bullet is'.[59]

The US Air Force will reportedly place new emphasis on guided bombs and specialty weapons as a result of the successful performance of precision guided munitions during the War. F-111Fs outfitted with Pave Tack laser guidance pods were able to destroy 77 pieces of Iraqi armour in one night, for example.[60] Here again the War will doubtless have a very large impact on the qualitative aspects of arms development and deployment. The inherent difficulties and subtleties surrounding these aspects will necessitate new ways of thinking about arms control and verification.

The use of aircraft in general, one of the most difficult of conventional weapons to monitor effectively because of their high mobility, may see a surge as a result of the effectiveness with which they were employed in the Persian Gulf War. As affirmed by Colonel Dennis M. Drew of the USAF Center for Aerospace Doctrine, 'We're seeing the maturity of airpower after 80 years . . . There were lots of things that hindered the early airmen: darkness, bad weather, speed and range. Now we can fly virtually anywhere at any time and deliver any load with enormous precision . . . Technology has caught up with doctrine'. Although there may not be complete agreement with his subsequent remarks that the Persian Gulf War provided 'clear evidence to all the doubters of airpower in warfare . . . airpower now dominates land warfare',[61] increased emphasis on development and deployment of aircraft could create incentives for countries to concentrate efforts to protect these assets more carefully in future arms control regimes. They would, therefore, want to be more

[58] 'Navy to offset aging aircraft with improved standoff missiles', *Defense News*, 1 Apr. 1991, p. 9.

[59] 'AF planners advocate quick-strick doctrine', *Defense News*, 8 Apr. 1991, p. 4.

[60] 'Desert Storm success renews USAF interest in specialty weapons', *Aviation Week & Space Technology*, 13 May 1991, p. 85.

[61] 'Catching up with doctrine', *Jane's Defence Weekly*, 29 June, 1991, p. 1174.

assured that other countries were abiding by limitations on these weapons, thus creating new and potentially difficult problems for future verification regimes.

With respect to C³I and its relationship to force operability, US Air Force Lieutenant-General James Cassidy, director of command, control and communications for the Joint Chiefs of Staff, said on 26 March 1991, 'In the first 90 days [of operation in the Persian Gulf] we put in more communications connectivity than we have had in Europe over the past 40 years'.[62] This gives an indication that, while the force levels may be decreasing, the ease with which they can be controlled, reinforced and become a potent threat in a short period of time must be appropriately considered.

VIII. Camouflage, concealment and deception

Iraq was thought to have used camouflage to a large extent during the Persian Gulf crisis, having learned a great deal from the Soviet Union and further tailored the methods for their particular needs in the eight-year war with Iran. In addition, Iraq had become somewhat familiar with the capabilities of US intelligence systems through information passed to it by the USA during the Iraq–Iran War. This enabled it to employ CC&D techniques more effectively.[63] Means and methods reportedly included inflatable tanks and aircraft and painted 'bomb craters' on aircraft runways. Evidence that some of these tactics are becoming more and more sophisticated includes the suspected use of decoy missiles outfitted with transmitters giving off signals to attempt to further mimic the real thing. Although good decoys were hard to recognize in many circumstances, highly trained analysts assisted by computers to fuse photographic and other information were said to be able to 'tell in two seconds if this stuff is a fake', according to a US Defense Department analyst.[64]

The Coalition forces employed techniques such as electronic emissions to make it appear that units were remaining stationary when in fact they were moving under radio silence in the large flanking attack manoeuvre. The USSR used satellites to image the area, accumulating data in part to aid its efforts to learn as much as possible about possible intelligence evasion techniques.[65]

Allied forces were also able to descramble some of the encoded message systems used by the Iraqis (purchased from Britain, France and the USSR, for example). Much communication was, in fact not scrambled at all. Also the organization and location of units could often be determined simply by examining the patterns of the communications traffic without necessarily understanding the contents of the messages themselves.[66]

[62] Kiernan, V., 'Cooper lifts veil of secrecy to applaud DSP', *Space News*, 1–7 Apr. 1991, p. 6.

[63] Ball, D., *The Intelligence War in the Gulf*, Canberra Papers on Strategy and Defence No. 78 (Strategic and Defence Studies Centre, Research School of Pacific Studies, The Australian National University: Canberra, 1991), pp. 76–77.

[64] 'With fakes, Iraqis make a mockery of warfare', *International Herald Tribune*, 25 Jan. 1991, p. 5.

[65] Gen. John A. Wickham, Jr, USA (Ret.), 'The intelligence role in Desert Storm', *Signal*, Apr. 1991, p. 2.

[66] 'Allied forces cracked Iraqi scrambling systems', *Defense News*, 15 Apr. 1991, p. 19.

Although secretly researched since the mid-1980s, the success of stealth technology in the War has sped-up efforts to develop ground combat vehicles less visible to sensors. Methods being investigated to 'give fighting vehicles the signature of a light bulb' include 'composite armour, exhaust reduction measures, sensor-jamming equipment and deception techniques'.[67] The flexibility inherent in composite materials would not only make the vehicles less visible to enemy radar, for example, but would allow for a tank's height to be reduced, thus making it easier for it to make use of natural camouflage as well. Such developments will of course make it more difficult for certain forms of verification monitoring systems, especially space- and aerial-based systems, to detect them. This would tend to imply a greater role for OSI, for example, if reasonably precise estimates of, say, the number of tanks were deemed necessary. As such developments and the location of weapons employing these types of technology would undoubtedly not be widely announced, it again highlights the fact that all of the rungs on a monitoring ladder will need to be employed to some extent.

IX. Conclusions

As data are further analysed many more lessons concerning the monitoring of conventional forces in particular will be extracted from the experience of the Persian Gulf War. As the above demonstrates, however, much can already be gleaned regarding the advantages and shortcomings of various monitoring methods of relevance to the verification of conventional forces.

The experience pointed in particular to the important information which could be acquired by commercial satellites, especially as far as infrastructure is concerned, provided distribution is not prohibited in times of crisis, and to the advantages of using several means of monitoring together with NTM—including aerial reconnaissance as a vital component.

It should be noted that the monitoring tasks were being carried out in a highly non-cooperative environment. The various methods employed would be that much more effective if employed in the framework of arms control agreements and other co-operative arrangements, as in the case in Europe.

---

[67] 'Gulf success prods efforts to develop stealth tank', *Defense News*, 20 May 1991, p. 1.

9. Conclusions

Arms control and disarmament have always been about *change*—change in the number of weapons, setting or redefining ceilings, altering the structure of forces and the overall strategic balance, and so on. The verification provisions of arms control agreements have had to deal with these changes and have been structured to do so with a minimum of controversy and a maximum of assured compliance. These provisions have rarely performed perfectly, but neither could they be expected to do so.

Change in the political world is now much more difficult to anticipate. The current situation ensures that arms control agreements and the verification structures and CSBMs which help them along must now deal with this new and most importunate type of change. The agreements which have come about are important, and the manner in which the agreements are able to cope with the changing atmosphere in which they must be implemented is what will determine their success or failure.

Measures to monitor the changes and enhance transparency are already in existence and will continue to evolve. At the same time, the verification of arms control agreements presents new challenges, perhaps most prominently in attempting to provide a true perspective on the amount and type of monitoring that is really necessary for them to succeed. National security is a function of threat perception. Adequate knowledge is the key to providing an accurate assessment of threats, and acquiring this knowledge in the most efficient and timely manner is fundamental. An important issue which must be faced now in a drastically altered and changing environment is to identify the appropriate forums to address the tasks at hand.

The CFE Treaty seems likely to be one of the last 'politicized' arms control agreements within the 'East–West context' and it has become an important document for the process of restructuring military potentials in Europe. It is clear that the burden of political demands and ambitions which have had a definite impact on the terms of the CFE and CSBM agreements will figure less prominently in the future.

It can also be predicted that the previously justified political race in the past to involve certain weapon categories and types in the arms control agreements will be replaced by other approaches and agreements which deal with the problems of how to shape and maintain a desired and acceptable strategic situation on the continent. These factors would have an impact on the role of verification and monitoring as well as on the possibility to put more burden on agreed monitoring arrangements.

Nevertheless, the successful implementation of the CFE Treaty is an important task. It serves as a testing ground for exploring and choosing the best combination of verification and monitoring techniques in the changing situation.

Given the dynamic political climate in which it operates, the CFE Treaty itself has been shown to present a number of challenges to and opportunities for the effective operation of the verification regime. As illustrated in the explication and analysis of the Treaty presented here, new and important breakthroughs in verification have occurred with its signature. The Treaty has seen the ground-breaking introduction of challenge on-site inspection of undeclared sites. Although such inspection may be refused, appropriate assurances must then be forthcoming. Multinational technical means to further improve monitoring and solidify co-operation among many of the signatories appear quite probable in the years ahead. The multilateral nature of the regime, including countries without the sophisticated NTM available to the USA and Russia, makes these measures particularly necessary.

Detailed information exchange, including data not only on numbers and locations of TLE items but also on overall force structures, provides a breakthrough in transparency, substantially aiding the overall verification process as well as contributing to the reinforcement of a positive political climate in which to resolve any ambiguities or problems which may arise. Importantly, such information will continue to be exchanged in a periodic manner throughout the lifetime of the Treaty. Moves towards the defensive orientation of forces have been included through such measures as zonal constraints and quantitative limits on bridging equipment, for example. These elements will, of course, place a burden on the monitoring and verification structure, but their inclusion plays an important role in ensuring that the objectives of the mandate will be met and, as discussed in this book, the verification regime has been defined to deal effectively with these measures.

The political and security framework established by the CFE Treaty offers an equitable participation of all states, both old and new, within the zone of application. The exercise of the inherent rights of nations to self-determination ought to be beneficial and not detrimental to co-operative security building in Europe. With the changes in the European landscape, quantitative elements embodied in the Treaty have already taken on less relevance. However, functional elements, including the verification structure and its future implementation, will continue in importance.

Although resolution of the increasingly important qualitative elements associated with conventional weaponry was not the subject of this agreement and was thus not dealt with, it must be recognized that this aspect should be given high priority in the near future.

While perhaps not accomplishing all that it could have, the CFE Treaty, together with its verification regime, has dealt in an effective manner with a large and complex array of weaponry. Of course, the different types of equipment limited by the Treaty pose inherent individual problems associated with the appropriate monitoring of their location and movements, and these are discussed in this book.

In light of the overall analysis, it is concluded that the CFE Treaty verification regime is adequate to detect militarily significant violations, defined in terms of the original aims of the Treaty, in time to make possible an appropriate response. In terms of achieving the priority objectives of the mandate, namely the elimination of the capability for launching a surprise attack and initiating large-scale offensive action, the vast ongoing restructuring of conventional forces implies that the monitoring regime will provide more than adequate warning of the redeployments which would be necessary.

One of the main challenges for the verification regime will involve implementation arrangements associated with the multilateral character of the Treaty. States parties are not yet fully prepared for the information management which is necessary, but care should be taken to optimize appropriate structures towards the goal of a smoothly functioning verification regime. In particular, methods should be directed towards minimizing potential difficulties in communication between national and multinational verification bodies. The initial problems with respect to ambiguities associated with such communications with the former Soviet Union could perhaps be seen in a positive light as giving a breathing space and preventing rushing ahead with hastily prepared procedures. Further challenges may involve surfacing ambiguities in the Treaty and associated differences in interpretation such as those which have already surfaced. In this respect the idea of proceeding towards the creation of a joint verification organization for the European continent should not be ignored.

However, with the breakup of the WTO and the dissolution of the USSR, concerns that were not imagined at the outset of the CFE Negotiation have come to the fore. The provision of adequate monitoring of relatively small military movements or buildups that may threaten individual states has become an important issue. To address such concerns, monitoring of conventional forces will be required on a much smaller scale than that for which the verification structure put in place by the CFE Treaty has been designed.

The Open Skies Treaty has the potential to play a prominent role as the structure of Europe continues to evolve. Making available capabilities to provide transparency at a reasonable cost to all CSCE states will certainly also be useful in the context of CFE, not least in view of the large amount of equipment which has been moved east of the Urals. More important, however, as unilateral arms reductions and restructuring become increasingly common, Open Skies can provide the ready-made means to aid in providing adequate security assurances. The Open Skies Consultative Commission has shown itself to be a valuable instrument for resolving the difficulties leading up to implementation of the Treaty. In addition to the important role the Treaty is certain to play in enhancing the security of the signatories, the experience gained may prove to be invaluable for such aerial monitoring arrangements in other areas of the globe where they could aid in furthering security.

In tandem with the CFE Treaty and the Treaty on Open Skies, the comprehensive CSBMs already in place have further increased transparency and facilitate the ongoing CSCE process. While they have yet to demonstrate the ability to keep pace with and deal with crisis situations which continue to unfold with the fast-changing geopolitical situation, useful improvements are being discussed. Tailoring inspections to the increasingly smaller military exercises now taking place and working towards an international community of verification experts are among the changes which will contribute to enhanced results of CSBM efforts.

This raises the dialectics: history is evolving through a spiral development in which some old ideas are being shaped to fit the new situation and in which the latter gives an opportunity to revive, re-examine and implement these ideas in updated form. Specifically, therefore, one should not be surprised that some agreements meet the old formula 'verification for the sake of verification'—this time, however, as an element of the process towards increased transparency. What was completely unacceptable in the quite recent past could be desirable and even necessary in the future.

Appendix A. The Treaty on Conventional Armed Forces in Europe

Paris, 19 November 1990

The Kingdom of Belgium, the Republic of Bulgaria, Canada, the Czech and Slovak Federal Republic, the Kingdom of Denmark, the French Republic, the Federal Republic of Germany, the Hellenic Republic, the Republic of Hungary, the Republic of Iceland, the Italian Republic, the Grand Duchy of Luxembourg, the Kingdom of the Netherlands, the Kingdom of Norway, the Republic of Poland, the Portuguese Republic, Romania, the Kingdom of Spain, the Republic of Turkey, the Union of Soviet Socialist Republics, the United Kingdom of Great Britain and Northern Ireland and the United States of America, hereinafter referred to as the States Parties,

Guided by the Mandate for Negotiation on Conventional Armed Forces in Europe of January 10, 1989, and having conducted this negotiation in Vienna beginning on March 9, 1989,

Guided by the objectives and the purposes of the Conference on Security and Cooperation in Europe, within the framework of which the negotiation of this Treaty was conducted,

Recalling their obligation to refrain in their mutual relations, as well as in their international relations in general, from the threat or use of force against the territorial integrity or political independence of any State, or in any other manner inconsistent with the purposes and principles of the Charter of the United Nations,

Conscious of the need to prevent any military conflict in Europe,

Conscious of the common responsibility which they all have for seeking to achieve greater stability and security in Europe,

Striving to replace military confrontation with a new pattern of security relations among all the States Parties based on peaceful cooperation and thereby to contribute to overcoming the division of Europe,

Committed to the objectives of establishing a secure and stable balance of conventional armed forces in Europe at lower levels than heretofore, of eliminating disparities prejudic-

ial to stability and security and of eliminating, as a matter of high priority, the capability for launching surprise attack and for initiating large-scale offensive action in Europe,

Recalling that they signed or acceded to the Treaty of Brussels of 1948, the Treaty of Washington of 1949 or the Treaty of Warsaw of 1955 and that they have the right to be or not to be a party to treaties of alliance,

Committed to the objective of ensuring that the numbers of conventional armaments and equipment limited by the Treaty within the area of application of this Treaty do not exceed 40 000 battle tanks, 60 000 armoured combat vehicles, 40 000 pieces of artillery, 13 600 combat aircraft and 4 000 attack helicopters,

Affirming that this Treaty is not intended to affect adversely the security interests of any State,

Affirming their commitment to continue the conventional arms control process including negotiations, taking into account future requirements for European stability and security in the light of political developments in Europe,

Have agreed as follows:

Article I

1. Each State Party shall carry out the obligations set forth in this Treaty in accordance with its provisions, including those obligations relating to the following five categories of conventional armed forces: battle tanks, armoured combat vehicles, artillery, combat aircraft and combat helicopters.

2. Each State Party also shall carry out the other measures set forth in this Treaty designed to ensure security and stability both during the period of reduction of conventional armed forces and after the completion of reductions.

3. This Treaty incorporates the Protocol on Existing Types of Conventional Armaments and Equipment, hereinafter referred to as the Protocol on Existing Types, with an Annex thereto; the Protocol on Procedures Governing the Reclassification of Specific Models or

Versions of Combat-Capable Trainer Aircraft into Unarmed Trainer Aircraft, hereinafter referred to as the Protocol on Aircraft Reclassification; the Protocol on Procedures Governing the Reduction of Conventional Armaments and Equipment Limited by the Treaty on Conventional Armed Forces in Europe, hereinafter referred to as the Protocol on Reduction; The Protocol on Procedures Governing the Categorisation of Combat Helicopters and the Recategorisation of Multi-Purpose Attack Helicopters, hereinafter referred to as the Protocol on Helicopter Recategorisation; the Protocol on Notification and Exchange of Information, hereinafter referred to as the Protocol on Information Exchange, with an Annex on the Format for the Exchange of Information, hereinafter referred to as the Annex on Format; the Protocol on Inspection; the Protocol on the Joint Consultative Group; and the Protocol on the Provisional Application of Certain Provisions of the Treaty on Conventional Armed Forces in Europe, hereinafter referred to as the Protocol on Provisional Application. Each of these documents constitutes an integral part of this Treaty.

Article II

1. For the purposes of this Treaty:

(A) The term 'group of States Parties' means the group of States Parties that signed the Treaty of Warsaw* of 1955 consisting of the Republic of Bulgaria, the Czech and Slovak Federal Republic, the Republic of Hungary, the Republic of Poland, Romania and the Union of Soviet Socialist Republics, or the group of States Parties that signed or acceded to the Treaty of Brussels** of 1948 or the Treaty of Washington*** of 1949 consisting of the Kingdom of Belgium, Canada, the Kingdom of Denmark, the French Republic, the Federal Republic of Germany, the Hellenic Republic, the Republic of Iceland, the Italian Republic, the Grand Duchy of Luxembourg, the Kingdom of the Netherlands, the Kingdom of Norway, the Portuguese Republic, the Kingdom of Spain, the Republic of Turkey, the United Kingdom of Great Britain and Northern Ireland and the United States of America.

(B) The term 'area of application' means the entire land territory of the States Parties in Europe from the Atlantic Ocean to the Ural Mountains, which includes all the European island territories of the States Parties, including the Faroe Islands of the Kingdom of Denmark, Svalbard including Bear Island of the Kingdom of Norway, the islands of Azores and Madeira of the Portuguese Republic, the Canary Islands of the Kingdom of Spain and Franz Josef Land and Novaya Zemlya of the Union of Soviet Socialist Republics. In the case of the Union of Soviet Socialist Republics, the area of application includes all territory lying west of the Ural River and the Caspian Sea. In the case of the Republic of Turkey, the area of application includes the territory of the Republic of Turkey north and west of a line extending from the point of intersection of the Turkish border with the 39th parallel to Muradiye, Patnos, Karayazi, Tekman, Kemaliye, Feke, Ceyhan, Dogankent, Gözne and thence to the sea.

(C) The term 'battle tank' means a self-propelled armoured fighting vehicle, capable of heavy firepower, primarily of a high muzzle velocity direct fire main gun necessary to engage armoured and other targets, with high cross-country mobility, with a high level of self-protection, and which is not designed and equipped primarily to transport combat troops. Such armoured vehicles serve as the principal weapon system of ground-force tank and other armoured formations.

Battle tanks are tracked armoured fighting vehicles which weigh at least 16.5 metric tonnes unladen weight and which are armed with a 360-degree traverse gun of at least 75-millimetres calibre. In addition, any wheeled armoured fighting vehicles entering into service which meet all the other criteria stated above shall be deemed battle tanks.

(D) The term 'armoured combat vehicle' means a self-propelled vehicle with armoured protection and cross-country capability. Armoured combat vehicles include armoured personnel carriers, armoured infantry fighting vehicles and heavy armament combat vehicles.

The term 'armoured personnel carrier' means an armoured combat vehicle which is designed and equipped to transport a combat infantry squad and which, as a rule, is armed with an integral or organic weapon of less than 20-millimetres calibre.

---

* The Treaty of Friendship, Cooperation and Mutual Assistance signed in Warsaw, 14 May 1955

** The Treaty of Economic, Social and Cultural Collaboration and Collective Self-Defence signed in Brussels, 17 March 1948

*** The North Atlantic Treaty signed in Washington, 4 April 1949

The term 'armoured infantry fighting vehicle' means an armoured combat vehicle which is designed and equipped primarily to transport a combat infantry squad, which normally provides the capability for the troops to deliver fire from inside the vehicle under armoured protection, and which is armed with an integral or organic cannon of at least 20 millimetres calibre and sometimes an antitank missile launcher. Armoured infantry fighting vehicles serve as the principal weapon system of armoured infantry or mechanised infantry or motorised infantry formations and units of ground forces.

The term 'heavy armament combat vehicle' means an armoured combat vehicle with an integral or organic direct fire gun of at least 75 millimetres calibre, weighing at least 6.0 metric tonnes unladen weight, which does not fall within the definitions of an armoured personnel carrier, or an armoured infantry fighting vehicle or a battle tank.

(E) The term 'unladen weight' means the weight of a vehicle excluding the weight of ammunition; fuel, oil and lubricants; removable reactive armour; spare parts, tools and accessories; removable snorkelling equipment; and crew and their personal kit.

(F) The term 'artillery' means large calibre systems capable of engaging ground targets by delivering primarily indirect fire. Such artillery systems provide the essential indirect fire support to combined arms formations.

Large calibre artillery systems are guns, howitzers, artillery pieces combining the characteristics of guns and howitzers, mortars and multiple launch rocket systems with a calibre of 100 millimetres and above. In addition, any future large calibre direct fire system which has a secondary effective indirect fire capability shall be counted against the artillery ceilings.

(G) The term 'stationed conventional armed forces' means conventional armed forces of a State Party that are stationed within the area of application on the territory of another State Party.

(H) The term 'designated permanent storage site' means a place with a clearly defined physical boundary containing conventional armaments and equipment limited by the Treaty, which are counted within overall ceilings but which are not subject to limitations on conventional armaments and equipment limited by the Treaty in active units.

(I) The term 'armoured vehicle launched bridge' means a self-propelled armoured transporter-launcher vehicle capable of carrying and, through built-in mechanisms, of emplacing and retrieving a bridge structure. Such a vehicle with a bridge structure operates as an integrated system.

(J) The term 'conventional armaments and equipment limited by the Treaty' means battle tanks, armoured combat vehicles, artillery, combat aircraft and attack helicopters subject to the numerical limitations set forth in Articles IV, V and VI.

(K) The term 'combat aircraft' means a fixed-wing or variable-geometry wing aircraft armed and equipped to engage targets by employing guided missiles, unguided rockets, bombs, guns, cannons, or other weapons of destruction, as well as any model or version of such an aircraft which performs other military functions such as reconnaissance or electronic warfare. The term 'combat aircraft' does not include primary trainer aircraft.

(L) The term 'combat helicopter' means a rotary wing aircraft armed and equipped to engage targets or equipped to perform other military functions. The term 'combat helicopter' comprises attack helicopters and combat support helicopters. The term 'combat helicopter' does not include unarmed transport helicopters.

(M) The term 'attack helicopter' means a combat helicopter equipped to employ antiarmour, air-to-ground, or air-to-air guided weapons and equipped with an integrated fire control and aiming system for these weapons. The term 'attack helicopter' comprises specialised attack helicopters and multi-purpose attack helicopters.

(N) The term 'specialised attack helicopter' means an attack helicopter that is designed primarily to employ guided weapons.

(O) The term 'multi-purpose attack helicopter' means an attack helicopter designed to perform multiple military functions and equipped to employ guided weapons.

(P) The term 'combat support helicopter' means a combat helicopter which does not fulfill the requirements to qualify as an attack helicopter and which may be equipped with a variety of self-defence and area suppression weapons, such as guns, cannons and unguided rockets, bombs or cluster bombs, or which may be equipped to perform other military functions.

(Q) The term 'conventional armaments and equipment subject to the Treaty' means battle tanks, armoured combat vehicles, artillery, combat aircraft, primary trainer aircraft, unarmed trainer aircraft, combat helicopters, unarmed transport helicopters, armoured vehicle launched bridges, armoured personnel carrier look-alikes and armoured infantry fighting vehicle look-alikes subject to information exchange in accordance with the Protocol on Information Exchange.

(R) The term 'in service', as it applies to conventional armed forces and conventional armaments and equipment, means battle tanks, armoured combat vehicles, artillery, combat aircraft, primary trainer aircraft, unarmed trainer aircraft, combat helicopters, unarmed transport helicopters, armoured vehicle launched bridges, armoured personnel carrier look-alikes and armoured infantry fighting vehicle look-alikes that are within the area of application, except for those that are held by organisations designed and structured to perform in peacetime internal security functions or that meet any of the exceptions set forth in Article III.

(S) The terms 'armoured personnel carrier look-alike' and 'armoured infantry fighting vehicle look-alike' mean an armoured vehicle based on the same chassis as, and externally similar to, an armoured personnel carrier or armoured infantry fighting vehicle, respectively, which does not have a cannon or gun of 20 millimetres calibre or greater and which has been constructed or modified in such a way as not to permit the transportation of a combat infantry squad. Taking into account the provisions of the Geneva Convention 'For the Amelioration of the Conditions of the Wounded and Sick in Armed Forces in the Field' of 12 August 1949 that confer a special status on ambulances, armoured personnel carrier ambulances shall not be deemed armoured combat vehicles or armoured personnel carrier look-alikes.

(T) The term 'reduction site' means a clearly designated location where the reduction of conventional armaments and equipment limited by the Treaty in accordance with Article VIII takes place.

(U) The term 'reduction liability' means the number in each category of conventional armaments and equipment limited by the Treaty that a State Party commits itself to reduce during the period of 40 months following the entry into force of this Treaty in order to ensure compliance with Article VII.

2. Existing types of conventional arma-ments and equipment subject to the Treaty are listed in the Protocol on Existing Types. The lists of existing types shall be periodically updated in accordance with Article XVI, paragraph 2, subparagraph (D) and Section IV of the Protocol on Existing Types. Such updates to the existing types lists shall not be deemed amendments to this Treaty.

3. The existing types of combat helicopters listed in the Protocol on Existing Types shall be categorised in accordance with Section I of the Protocol on Helicopter Recategorisation.

Article III

1. For the purposes of this Treaty, the States Parties shall apply the following counting rules:

All battle tanks, armoured combat vehicles, artillery, combat aircraft and attack helicopters, as defined in Article II, within the area of application shall be subject to the numerical limitations and other provisions set forth in Articles IV, V and VI, with the exception of those which in a manner consistent with a State Party's normal practices:

(A) are in the process of manufacture, including manufacturing-related testing;

(B) are used exclusively for the purposes of research and development;

(C) belong to historical collections;

(D) are awaiting disposal, having been decommissioned from service in accordance with the provisions of Article IX;

(E) are awaiting, or are being refurbished for, export or re-export and are temporarily retained within the area of application. Such battle tanks, armoured combat vehicles, artillery, combat aircraft and attack helicopters shall be located elsewhere than at sites declared under the terms of Section V of the Protocol on Information Exchange or at no more than 10 such declared sites which shall have been notified in the previous year's annual information exchange. In the latter case, they shall be separately distinguishable from conventional armaments and equipment limited by the Treaty;

(F) are, in the case of armoured personnel carriers, armoured infantry fighting vehicles, heavy armament combat vehicles or multi-purpose attack helicopters, held by organisations designed and structured to perform in peacetime internal security functions; or

(G) are in transit through the area of application from a location outside the area of application to a final destination outside the area of application, and are in the area of application for no longer than a total of seven days.

2. If, in respect of any such battle tanks, armoured combat vehicles, artillery, combat aircraft or attack helicopters, the notification of which is required under Section IV of the Protocol on Information Exchange, a State Party notifies an unusually high number in more than two successive annual information exchanges, it shall explain the reasons in the Joint Consultative Group, if so requested.

Article IV

1. Within the area of application, as defined in Article II, each State Party shall limit and, as necessary, reduce its battle tanks, armoured combat vehicles, artillery, combat aircraft and attack helicopters so that, 40 months after entry into force of this Treaty and thereafter, for the group of States Parties to which it belongs, as defined in Article II, the aggregate numbers do not exceed:

(A) 20 000 battle tanks, of which no more than 16 500 shall be in active units;

(B) 30 000 armoured combat vehicles, of which no more than 27 300 shall be in active units. Of the 30 000 armoured combat vehicles, no more than 18 000 shall be armoured infantry fighting vehicles and heavy armament combat vehicles; of armoured infantry fighting vehicles and heavy armament combat vehicles, no more than 1 500 shall be heavy armament combat vehicles;

(C) 20 000 pieces of artillery, of which no more than 17 000 shall be in active units;

(D) 6800 combat aircraft; and

(E) 2000 attack helicopters.

Battle tanks, armoured combat vehicles and artillery not in active units shall be placed in designated permanent storage sites, as defined in Article II, and shall be located only in the area described in paragraph 2 of this Article. Such designated permanent storage sites may also be located in that part of the territory of the Union of Soviet Socialist Republics comprising the Odessa Military District and the southern part of the Leningrad Military District. In the Odessa Military District, no more than 400 battle tanks and no more than 500 pieces of artillery may be thus stored. In the southern part of the Leningrad Military District, no more than 600 battle tanks, no more than 800 armoured combat vehicles, including no more than 300 armoured combat vehicles of any type with the remaining number consisting of armoured personnel carriers,

and no more than 400 pieces of artillery may be thus stored. The southern part of the Leningrad Military District is understood to mean the territory within that military district south of the line East–West 60 degrees 15 minutes northern latitude.

2. Within the area consisting of the entire land territory in Europe, which includes all the European island territories, of the Kingdom of Belgium, the Czech and Slovak Federal Republic, the Kingdom of Denmark including the Faroe Islands, the French Republic, the Federal Republic of Germany, the Republic of Hungary, the Italian Republic, the Grand Duchy of Luxembourg, the Kingdom of the Netherlands, the Republic of Poland, the Portuguese Republic including the islands of Azores and Madeira, the Kingdom of Spain including the Canary Islands, the United Kingdom of Great Britain and Northern Ireland and that part of the territory of the Union of Soviet Socialist Republics west of the Ural Mountains comprising the Baltic, Byelorussian, Carpathian, Kiev, Moscow and Volga–Ural Military Districts, each State Party shall limit and, as necessary, reduce its battle tanks, armoured combat vehicles and artillery so that, 40 months after entry into force of this Treaty and thereafter, for the group of States Parties to which it belongs the aggregate numbers do not exceed:

(A) 15 300 battle tanks, of which no more than 11 800 shall be in active units;

(B) 24 100 armoured combat vehicles, of which no more than 21 400 shall be in active units; and

(C) 14 000 pieces of artillery, of which no more than 11 000 shall be in active units.

3. Within the area consisting of the entire land territory in Europe, which includes all the European island territories, of the Kingdom of Belgium, the Czech and Slovak Federal Republic, the Kingdom of Denmark including the Faroe Islands, the French Republic, the Federal Republic of Germany, the Republic of Hungary, the Italian Republic, the Grand Duchy of Luxembourg, the Kingdom of the Netherlands, the Republic of Poland, the United Kingdom of Great Britain and Northern Ireland and that part of the territory of the Union of Soviet Socialist Republics comprising the Baltic, Byelorussian, Carpathian and Kiev Military Districts, each State Party shall limit and, as necessary, reduce its battle tanks, armoured combat vehicles and artillery so that, 40 months after the entry into force of

this Treaty and thereafter, for the group of States Parties to which it belongs the aggregate numbers in active units do not exceed:

(A) 10 300 battle tanks;

(B) 19 260 armoured combat vehicles; and

(C) 9100 pieces of artillery; and

(D) in the Kiev Military District, the aggregate numbers in active units and designated permanent storage sites together shall not exceed:

(1) 2250 battle tanks;

(2) 2500 armoured combat vehicles; and

(3) 1500 pieces of artillery.

4. Within the area consisting of the entire land territory in Europe, which includes all the European island territories, of the Kingdom of Belgium, the Czech and Slovak Federal Republic, the Federal Republic of Germany, the Republic of Hungary, the Grand Duchy of Luxembourg, the Kingdom of the Netherlands and the Republic of Poland, each State Party shall limit and, as necessary, reduce its battle tanks, armoured combat vehicles and artillery so that, 40 months after entry into force of this Treaty and thereafter, for the group of States Parties to which it belongs the aggregate numbers in active units do not exceed:

(A) 7500 battle tanks;

(B) 11 250 armoured combat vehicles; and

(C) 5000 pieces of artillery.

5. States Parties belonging to the same group of States Parties may locate battle tanks, armoured combat vehicles and artillery in active units in each of the areas described in this Article and Article V, paragraph 1, subparagraph (A), up to the numerical limitations applying in that area, consistent with the maximum levels for holdings notified pursuant to Article VII and provided that no State Party stations conventional armed forces on the territory of another State Party without the agreement of that State Party.

6. If a group of States Parties' aggregate numbers of battle tanks, armoured combat vehicles and artillery in active units within the area described in paragraph 4 of this Article are less than the numerical limitations set forth in paragraph 4 of this Article, and provided that no State Party is thereby prevented from reaching its maximum levels for holdings notified in accordance with Article VII, paragraphs 2, 3 and 5, then amounts equal to the difference between the aggregate numbers in each of the categories of battle tanks, armoured combat vehicles and artillery and the specified numerical limitations for that area

may be located by States Parties belonging to that group of States Parties in the area described in paragraph 3 of this Article, consistent with the numerical limitations specified in paragraph 3 of this Article.

Article V

1. To ensure that the security of each State Party is not affected adversely at any stage:

(A) within the area consisting of the entire land territory in Europe, which includes all the European island territories, of the Republic of Bulgaria, the Hellenic Republic, the Republic of Iceland, the Kingdom of Norway, Romania, the part of the Republic of Turkey within the area of application and that part of the Union of Soviet Socialist Republics comprising the Leningrad, Odessa, Transcaucasus and North Caucasus Military Districts, each State Party shall limit and, as necessary, reduce its battle tanks, armoured combat vehicles and artillery so that, 40 months after the entry into force of this Treaty and thereafter, for the group of States Parties to which it belongs the aggregate numbers in active units do not exceed the difference between the overall numerical limitations set forth in Article IV, paragraph 1 and those in Article IV, paragraph 2, that is:

(1) 4700 battle tanks;

(2) 5900 armoured combat vehicles; and

(3) 6000 pieces of artillery;

(B) notwithstanding the numerical limitations set forth in subparagraph (A) of this paragraph, a State Party or States Parties may on a temporary basis deploy into the territory belonging to the members of the same group of States Parties within the area described in subparagraph (A) of this paragraph additional aggregate numbers in active units for each group of States Parties not to exceed:

(1) 459 battle tanks;

(2) 723 armoured combat vehicles; and

(3) 420 pieces of artillery; and

(C) provided that for each group of States Parties no more than one-third of each of these additional aggregate numbers shall be deployed to any State Party with territory within the area described in subparagraph (A) of this paragraph, that is:

(1) 153 battle tanks;

(2) 241 armoured combat vehicles; and

(3) 140 pieces of artillery.

2. Notification shall be provided to all other States Parties no later than at the start of the deployment by the State Party or States Parties conducting the deployment and by the recipi-

ent State Party or States Parties, specifying the total number of each category of battle tanks, armoured combat vehicles and artillery deployed. Notification also shall be provided to all other States Parties by the State Party or States Parties conducting the deployment and by the recipient State Party or States Parties within 30 days of the withdrawal of those battle tanks, armoured combat vehicles and artillery that were temporarily deployed.

Article VI

With the objective of ensuring that no single State Party possesses more than approximately one-third of the conventional armaments and equipment limited by the Treaty within the area of application, each State Party shall limit and, as necessary, reduce its battle tanks, armoured combat vehicles, artillery, combat aircraft and attack helicopters so that, 40 months after entry into force of this Treaty and thereafter, the numbers within the area of application for that State Party do not exceed:

(A) 13 300 battle tanks;
(B) 20 000 armoured combat vehicles;
(C) 13 700 pieces of artillery;
(D) 5150 combat aircraft; and
(E) 1500 attack helicopters.

Article VII

1. In order that the limitations set forth in Articles IV, V and VI are not exceeded, no State Party shall exceed, from 40 months after the entry into force of this Treaty, the maximum levels which it has previously agreed upon within its group of States Parties, in accordance with paragraph 7 of this Article, for its holdings of conventional armaments and equipment limited by the Treaty and of which it has provided notification pursuant to the provisions of this Article.

2. Each State Party shall provide at the signature of this Treaty notification to all other States Parties of the maximum levels for its holdings of conventional armaments and equipment limited by the Treaty. The notification of the maximum levels for holdings of conventional armaments and equipment limited by the Treaty provided by each State Party at the signature of this Treaty shall remain valid until the date specified in a subsequent notification pursuant to paragraph 3 of this Article.

3. In accordance with the limitations set forth in Articles IV, V and VI, each State Party shall have the right to change the maxi-

mum levels for its holdings of conventional armaments and equipment limited by the Treaty. Any change in the maximum levels for holdings of a State Party shall be notified by that State Party to all other States Parties at least 90 days in advance of the date, specified in the notification, on which such a change takes effect. In order not to exceed any of the limitations set forth in Articles IV and V, any increase in the maximum levels for holdings of a State Party that would otherwise cause those limitations to be exceeded shall be preceded or accompanied by a corresponding reduction in the previously notified maximum levels for holdings of conventional armaments and equipment limited by the Treaty of one or more States Parties belonging to the same group of States Parties. The notification of a change in the maximum levels for holdings shall remain valid from the date specified in the notification until the date specified in a subsequent notification of change pursuant to this paragraph.

4. Each notification required pursuant to paragraph 2 or 3 of this Article for armoured combat vehicles shall also include maximum levels for the holdings of armoured infantry fighting vehicles and heavy armament combat vehicles of the State Party providing the notification.

5. Ninety days before expiration of the 40-month period of reductions set forth in Article VIII and subsequently at the time of any notification of a change pursuant to paragraph 3 of this Article, each State Party shall provide notification of the maximum levels for its holdings of battle tanks, armoured combat vehicles and artillery with respect to each of the areas described in Article IV, paragraphs 2 to 4 and Article V, paragraph 1, subparagraph (A).

6. A decrease in the numbers of conventional armaments and equipment limited by the Treaty held by a State Party and subject to notification pursuant to the Protocol on Information Exchange shall by itself confer no right on any other State Party to increase the maximum levels for its holdings subject to notification pursuant to this Article.

7. It shall be the responsibility solely of each individual State Party to ensure that the maximum levels for its holdings notified pursuant to the provisions of this Article are not exceeded. States Parties belonging to the same group of States Parties shall consult in order to ensure that the maximum levels for holdings notified pursuant to the provisions of this

Article, taken together as appropriate, do not exceed the limitations set forth in Articles IV, V and VI.

Article VIII

1. The numerical limitations set forth in Articles IV, V and VI shall be achieved only by means of reduction in accordance with the Protocol on Reduction, the Protocol on Helicopter Recategorisation, the Protocol on Aircraft Reclassification, the Footnote to Section I, paragraph 2, subparagraph (A) of the Protocol on Existing Types and the Protocol on Inspection.

2. The categories of conventional armaments and equipment subject to reductions are battle tanks, armoured combat vehicles, artillery, combat aircraft and attack helicopters. The specific types are listed in the Protocol on Existing Types.

(A) Battle tanks and armoured combat vehicles shall be reduced by destruction, conversion for non-military purposes, placement on static display, use as ground targets, or, in the case of armoured personnel carriers, modification in accordance with the Footnote to Section I, paragraph 2, subparagraph (A) of the Protocol on Existing Types.

(B) Artillery shall be reduced by destruction or placement on static display, or, in the case of self-propelled artillery, by use as ground targets.

(C) Combat aircraft shall be reduced by destruction, placement on static display, use for ground instructional purposes, or, in the case of specific models or versions of combat-capable trainer aircraft, reclassification into unarmed trainer aircraft.

(D) Specialised attack helicopters shall be reduced by destruction, placement on static display, or use for ground instructional purposes.

(E) Multi-purpose attack helicopters shall be reduced by destruction, placement on static display, use for ground instructional purposes, or recategorisation.

3. Conventional armaments and equipment limited by the Treaty shall be deemed to be reduced upon execution of the procedures set forth in the Protocols listed in paragraph 1 of this Article and upon notification as required by these Protocols. Armaments and equipment so reduced shall no longer be counted against the numerical limitations set forth in Articles IV, V and VI.

4. Reductions shall be effected in three phases and completed no later than 40 months after entry into force of this Treaty, so that:

(A) by the end of the first reduction phase, that is, no later than 16 months after entry into force of this Treaty, each State Party shall have ensured that at least 25 percent of its total reduction liability in each of the categories of conventional armaments and equipment limited by the Treaty has been reduced;

(B) by the end of the second reduction phase, that is, no later than 28 months after entry into force of this Treaty, each State Party shall have ensured that at least 60 percent of its total reduction liability in each of the categories of conventional armaments and equipment limited by the Treaty has been reduced;

(C) by the end of the third reduction phase, that is, no later than 40 months after entry into force of this Treaty, each State Party shall have reduced its total reduction liability in each of the categories of conventional armaments and equipment limited by the Treaty. States Parties carrying out conversion for non-military purposes shall have ensured that the conversion of all battle tanks in accordance with Section VIII of the Protocol on Reduction shall have been completed by the end of the third reduction phase; and

(D) armoured combat vehicles deemed reduced by reason of having been partially destroyed in accordance with Section VIII, paragraph 6 of the Protocol on Reduction shall have been fully converted for non-military purposes, or destroyed in accordance with Section IV of the Protocol on Reduction, no later than 64 months after entry into force of this Treaty.

5. Conventional armaments and equipment limited by the Treaty to be reduced shall have been declared present within the area of application in the exchange of information at signature of this Treaty.

6. No later than 30 days after entry into force of this Treaty, each State Party shall provide notification to all other States Parties of its reduction liability.

7. Except as provided for in paragraph 8 of this Article, a State Party's reduction liability in each category shall be no less than the difference between its holdings notified, in accordance with the Protocol on Information Exchange, at signature or effective upon entry into force of this Treaty, whichever is the greater, and the maximum levels for holdings it notified pursuant to Article VII.

8. Any subsequent revision of a State

Party's holdings notified pursuant to the Protocol on Information Exchange or of its maximum levels for holdings notified pursuant to Article VII shall be reflected by a notified adjustment to its reduction liability. Any notification of a decrease in a State Party's reduction liability shall be preceded or accompanied by either a notification of a corresponding increase in holdings not exceeding the maximum levels for holdings notified pursuant to Article VII by one or more States Parties belonging to the same group of States Parties, or a notification of a corresponding increase in the reduction liability of one or more such States Parties.

9. Upon entry into force of this Treaty, each State Party shall notify all other States Parties, in accordance with the Protocol on Information Exchange, of the locations of its reduction sites, including those where the final conversion of battle tanks and armoured combat vehicles for non-military purposes will be carried out.

10. Each State Party shall have the right to designate as many reduction sites as it wishes, to revise without restriction its designation of such sites and to carry out reduction and final conversion simultaneously at a maximum of 20 sites. States Parties shall have the right to share or co-locate reduction sites by mutual agreement.

11. Notwithstanding paragraph 10 of this Article, during the baseline validation period, that is, the interval between entry into force of this Treaty and 120 days after entry into force of this Treaty, reduction shall be carried out simultaneously at no more than two reduction sites for each State Party.

12. Reduction of conventional armaments and equipment limited by the Treaty shall be carried out at reduction sites, unless otherwise specified in Protocols listed in paragraph 1 of this Article, within the area of application.

13. The reduction process, including the results of the conversion of conventional armaments and equipment limited by the Treaty for non-military purposes both during the reduction period and in the 24 months following the reduction period, shall be subject to inspection, without right of refusal, in accordance with the Protocol on Inspection.

Article IX

1. Other than removal from service in accordance with the provisions of Article VIII, battle tanks, armoured combat vehicles, artillery, combat aircraft and attack helicopters within the area of application shall be removed from service only by decommissioning, provided that:

(A) such conventional armaments and equipment limited by the Treaty are decommissioned and awaiting disposal at no more than eight sites which shall be notified as declared sites in accordance with the Protocol on Information Exchange and shall be identified in such notifications as holding areas for decommissioned conventional armaments and equipment limited by the Treaty. If sites containing conventional armaments and equipment limited by the Treaty decommissioned from service also contain any other conventional armaments and equipment subject to the Treaty, the decommissioned conventional armaments and equipment limited by the Treaty shall be separately distinguishable; and

(B) the numbers of such decommissioned conventional armaments and equipment limited by the Treaty do not exceed, in the case of any individual State Party, one percent of its notified holdings of conventional armaments and equipment limited by the Treaty, or a total of 250, whichever is greater, of which no more than 200 shall be battle tanks, armoured combat vehicles and pieces of artillery, and no more than 50 shall be attack helicopters and combat aircraft.

2. Notification of decommissioning shall include the number and type of conventional armaments and equipment limited by the Treaty decommissioned and the location of decommissioning and shall be provided to all other States Parties in accordance with Section IX, paragraph 1, subparagraph (B) of the Protocol on Information Exchange.

Article X

1. Designated permanent storage sites shall be notified in accordance with the Protocol on Information Exchange to all other States Parties by the State Party to which the conventional armaments and equipment limited by the Treaty contained at designated permanent storage sites belong. The notification shall include the designation and location, including geographic coordinates, of designated permanent storage sites and the numbers by type of each category of its conventional armaments and equipment limited by the Treaty at each such storage site.

2. Designated permanent storage sites shall contain only facilities appropriate for the storage and maintenance of armaments and equip-

ment (e.g., warehouses, garages, workshops and associated stores as well as other support accommodation). Designated permanent storage sites shall not contain firing ranges or training areas associated with conventional armaments and equipment limited by the Treaty. Designated permanent storage sites shall contain only armaments and equipment belonging to the conventional armed forces of a State Party.

3. Each designated permanent storage site shall have a clearly defined physical boundary that shall consist of a continuous perimeter fence at least 1.5 metres in height. The perimeter fence shall have no more than three gates providing the sole means of entrance and exit for armaments and equipment.

4. Conventional armaments and equipment limited by the Treaty located within designated permanent storage sites shall be counted as conventional armaments and equipment limited by the Treaty not in active units, including when they are temporarily removed in accordance with paragraphs 7, 8, 9 and 10 of this Article. Conventional armaments and equipment limited by the Treaty in storage and other than in designated permanent storage sites shall be counted as conventional armaments and equipment limited by the Treaty in active units.

5. Active units or formations shall not be located within designated permanent storage sites, except as provided for in paragraph 6 of this Article.

6. Only personnel associated with the security or operation of designated permanent storage sites, or the maintenance of the armaments and equipment stored therein, shall be located within the designated permanent storage sites.

7. For the purpose of maintenance, repair or modification of conventional armaments and equipment limited by the Treaty located within designated permanent storage sites, each State Party shall have the right, without prior notification, to remove from and retain outside designated permanent storage sites simultaneously up to 10 percent, rounded up to the nearest even whole number, of the notified holdings of each category of conventional armaments and equipment limited by the Treaty in each designated permanent storage site, or 10 items of the conventional armaments and equipment limited by the Treaty in each category in each designated permanent storage site, whichever is less.

8. Except as provided for in paragraph 7 of this Article, no State Party shall remove con-

ventional armaments and equipment limited by the Treaty from designated permanent storage sites unless notification has been provided to all other States Parties at least 42 days in advance of such removal. Notification shall be given by the State Party to which the conventional armaments and equipment limited by the Treaty belong. Such notification shall specify:

(A) the location of the designated permanent storage site from which conventional armaments and equipment limited by the Treaty are to be removed and the numbers by type of conventional armaments and equipment limited by the Treaty of each category to be removed;

(B) the dates of removal and return of conventional armaments and equipment limited by the Treaty; and

(C) the intended location and use of conventional armaments and equipment limited by the Treaty while outside the designated permanent storage site.

9. Except as provided for in paragraph 7 of this Article, the aggregate numbers of conventional armaments and equipment limited by the Treaty removed from and retained outside designated permanent storage sites by States Parties belonging to the same group of States Parties shall at no time exceed the following levels:

(A) 550 battle tanks;
(B) 1000 armoured combat vehicles; and
(C) 300 pieces of artillery.

10. Conventional armaments and equipment limited by the Treaty removed from designated permanent storage sites pursuant to paragraphs 8 and 9 of this Article shall be returned to designated permanent storage sites no later than 42 days after their removal, except for those items of conventional armaments and equipment limited by the Treaty removed for industrial rebuild. Such items shall be returned to designated permanent storage sites immediately on completion of the rebuild.

11. Each State Party shall have the right to replace conventional armaments and equipment limited by the Treaty located in designated permanent storage sites. Each State Party shall notify all other States Parties, at the beginning of replacement, of the number, location, type and disposition of conventional armaments and equipment limited by the Treaty being replaced.

Article XI

1. Each State Party shall limit its armoured vehicle launched bridges so that, 40 months after entry into force of this Treaty and thereafter, for the group of States Parties to which it belongs the aggregate number of armoured vehicle launched bridges in active units within the area of application does not exceed 740.

2. All armoured vehicle launched bridges within the area of application in excess of the aggregate number specified in paragraph 1 of this Article for each group of States Parties shall be placed in designated permanent storage sites, as defined in Article II. When armoured vehicle launched bridges are placed in a designated permanent storage site, either on their own or together with conventional armaments and equipment limited by the Treaty, Article X, paragraphs 1 to 6 shall apply to armoured vehicle launched bridges as well as to conventional armaments and equipment limited by the Treaty. Armoured vehicle launched bridges placed in designated permanent storage sites shall not be considered as being in active units.

3. Except as provided for in paragraph 6 of this Article, armoured vehicle launched bridges may be removed, subject to the provisions of paragraphs 4 and 5 of this Article, from designated permanent storage sites only after notification has been provided to all other States Parties at least 42 days prior to such removal. This notification shall specify:

(A) the locations of the designated permanent storage sites from which armoured vehicle launched bridges are to be removed and the numbers of armoured vehicle launched bridges to be removed from each such site;

(B) the dates of removal of armoured vehicle launched bridges from and return to designated permanent storage sites; and

(C) the intended use of armoured vehicle launched bridges during the period of their removal from designated permanent storage sites.

4. Except as provided for in paragraph 6 of this Article, armoured vehicle launched bridges removed from designated permanent storage sites shall be returned to them no later than 42 days after the actual date of removal.

5. The aggregate number of armoured vehicle launched bridges removed from and retained outside of designated permanent storage sites by each group of States Parties shall not exceed 50 at any one time.

6. States Parties shall have the right, for the purpose of maintenance or modification, to remove and have outside the designated permanent storage sites simultaneously up to 10 percent, rounded up to the nearest even whole number, of their notified holdings of armoured vehicle launched bridges in each designated permanent storage site, or 10 armoured vehicle launched bridges from each designated permanent storage site, whichever is less.

7. In the event of natural disasters involving flooding or damage to permanent bridges, States Parties shall have the right to withdraw armoured vehicle launched bridges from designated permanent storage sites. Notification to all other States Parties of such withdrawals shall be given at the time of withdrawal.

Article XII

1. Armoured infantry fighting vehicles held by organisations of a State Party designed and structured to perform in peacetime internal security functions, which are not structured and organised for ground combat against an external enemy, are not limited by this Treaty. The foregoing notwithstanding, in order to enhance the implementation of this Treaty and to provide assurance that the number of such armaments held by such organisations shall not be used to circumvent the provisions of this Treaty, any such armaments in excess of 1000 armoured infantry fighting vehicles assigned by a State Party to organisations designed and structured to perform in peacetime internal security functions shall constitute a portion of the permitted levels specified in Articles IV, V and VI. No more than 600 such armoured infantry fighting vehicles of a State Party, assigned to such organisations, may be located in that part of the area of application described in Article V, paragraph 1, subparagraph (A). Each State Party shall further ensure that such organisations refrain from the acquisition of combat capabilities in excess of those necessary for meeting internal security requirements.

2. A State Party that intends to reassign battle tanks, armoured infantry fighting vehicles, artillery, combat aircraft, attack helicopters and armoured vehicle launched bridges in service with its conventional armed forces to any organisation of that State Party not a part of its conventional armed forces shall notify all other States Parties no later than the date such reassignment takes effect. Such notification shall specify the effective date of the reassignment, the date such equip-

ment is physically transferred, as well as the numbers, by type, of the conventional armaments and equipment limited by the Treaty being reassigned.

Article XIII

1. For the purpose of ensuring verification of compliance with the provisions of this Treaty, each State Party shall provide notifications and exchange information pertaining to its conventional armaments and equipment in accordance with the Protocol on Information Exchange.

2. Such notifications and exchange of information shall be provided in accordance with Article XVII.

3. Each State Party shall be responsible for its own information; receipt of such information and of notifications shall not imply validation or acceptance of the information provided.

Article XIV

1. For the purpose of ensuring verification of compliance with the provisions of this Treaty, each State Party shall have the right to conduct, and the obligation to accept, within the area of application, inspections in accordance with the provisions of the Protocol on Inspection.

2. The purpose of such inspections shall be:

(A) to verify, on the basis of the information provided pursuant to the Protocol on Information Exchange, the compliance of States Parties with the numerical limitations set forth in Articles IV, V and VI;

(B) to monitor the process of reduction of battle tanks, armoured combat vehicles, artillery, combat aircraft and attack helicopters carried out at reduction sites in accordance with Article VIII and the Protocol on Reduction; and

(C) to monitor the certification of recategorised multi-purpose attack helicopters and reclassified combat-capable trainer aircraft carried out in accordance with the Protocol on Helicopter Recategorisation and the Protocol on Aircraft Reclassification, respectively.

3. No State Party shall exercise the rights set forth in paragraphs 1 and 2 of this Article in respect of States Parties which belong to the group of States Parties to which it belongs in order to elude the objectives of the verification regime.

4. In the case of an inspection conducted jointly by more than one State Party, one of them shall be responsible for the execution of the provisions of this Treaty.

5. The number of inspections pursuant to Sections VII and VIII of the Protocol on Inspection which each State Party shall have the right to conduct and the obligation to accept during each specified time period shall be determined in accordance with the provisions of Section II of that Protocol.

6. Upon completion of the 120-day residual level validation period, each State Party shall have the right to conduct, and each State Party with territory within the area of application shall have the obligation to accept, an agreed number of aerial inspections within the area of application. Such agreed numbers and other applicable provisions shall be developed during negotiations referred to in Article XVIII.

Article XV

1. For the purpose of ensuring verification of compliance with the provisions of this Treaty, a State Party shall have the right to use, in addition to the procedures referred to in Article XIV, national or multinational technical means of verification at its disposal in a manner consistent with generally recognised principles of international law.

2. A State Party shall not interfere with national or multinational technical means of verification of another State Party operating in accordance with paragraph 1 of this Article.

3. A State Party shall not use concealment measures that impede verification of compliance with the provisions of this Treaty by national or multinational technical means of verification of another State Party operating in accordance with paragraph 1 of this Article. This obligation does not apply to cover or concealment practices associated with normal personnel training, maintenance or operations involving conventional armaments and equipment limited by the Treaty.

Article XVI

1. To promote the objectives and implementation of the provisions of this Treaty, the States Parties hereby establish a Joint Consultative Group.

2. Within the framework of the Joint Consultative Group, the States Parties shall:

(A) address questions relating to compliance with or possible circumvention of the provisions of this Treaty;

(B) seek to resolve ambiguities and differences of interpretation that may become apparent in the way this Treaty is implemented;

(C) consider and, if possible, agree on measures to enhance the viability and effectiveness of this Treaty;

(D) update the lists contained in the Protocol on Existing Types, as required by Article II, paragraph 2;

(E) resolve technical questions in order to seek common practices among the States Parties in the way this Treaty is implemented;

(F) work out or revise, as necessary, rules of procedure, working methods, the scale of distribution of expenses of the Joint Consultative Group and of conferences convened under this Treaty and the distribution of costs of inspections between or among States Parties;

(G) consider and work out appropriate measures to ensure that information obtained through exchanges of information among the States Parties or as a result of inspections pursuant to this Treaty is used solely for the purposes of this Treaty, taking into account the particular requirements of each State Party in respect of safeguarding information which that State Party specifies as being sensitive;

(H) consider, upon the request of any State Party, any matter that a State Party wishes to propose for examination by any conference to be convened in accordance with Article XXI; such consideration shall not prejudice the right of any State Party to resort to the procedures set forth in Article XXI; and

(I) consider matters of dispute arising out of the implementation of this Treaty.

3. Each State Party shall have the right to raise before the Joint Consultative Group, and have placed on its agenda, any issue relating to this Treaty.

4. The Joint Consultative Group shall take decisions or make recommendations by consensus. Consensus shall be understood to mean the absence of any objection by any representative of a State Party to the taking of a decision or the making of a recommendation.

5. The Joint Consultative Group may propose amendments to this Treaty for consideration and confirmation in accordance with Article XX. The Joint Consultative Group may also agree on improvements to the viability and effectiveness of this Treaty, consistent with its provisions. Unless such improvements relate only to minor matters of an administrative or technical nature, they shall be subject to consideration and confirmation in accordance with Article XX before they can take effect.

6. Nothing in this Article shall be deemed to prohibit or restrict any State Party from requesting information from or undertaking consultations with other States Parties on matters relating to this Treaty and its implementation in channels or fora other than the Joint Consultative Group.

7. The Joint Consultative Group shall follow the procedures set forth in the Protocol on the Joint Consultative Group.

Article XVII

The States Parties shall transmit information and notifications required by this Treaty in written form. They shall use diplomatic channels or other official channels designated by them, including in particular a communications network to be established by a separate arrangement.

Article XVIII

1. The States Parties, after signature of this Treaty, shall continue the negotiations on conventional armed forces with the same Mandate and with the goal of building on this Treaty.

2. The objective for these negotiations shall be to conclude an agreement on additional measures aimed at further strengthening security and stability in Europe, and pursuant to the Mandate, including measures to limit the personnel strength of their conventional armed forces within the area of application.

3. The States Parties shall seek to conclude these negotiations no later than the follow-up meeting of the Conference on Security and Cooperation in Europe to be held in Helsinki in 1992.

Article XIX

1. This Treaty shall be of unlimited duration. It may be supplemented by a further treaty.

2. Each State Party shall, in exercising its national sovereignty, have the right to withdraw from this Treaty if it decides that extraordinary events related to the subject matter of this Treaty have jeopardised its supreme interests. A State Party intending to withdraw shall give notice of its decision to do so to the Depositary and to all other States Parties. Such notice shall be given at least 150 days prior to the intended withdrawal from this Treaty. It shall include a statement of the extraordinary events the State Party regards as having jeopardised its supreme interests.

3. Each State Party shall, in particular, in

exercising its national sovereignty, have the right to withdraw from this Treaty if another State Party increases its holdings in battle tanks, armoured combat vehicles, artillery, combat aircraft or attack helicopters, as defined in Article II, which are outside the scope of the limitations of this Treaty, in such proportions as to pose an obvious threat to the balance of forces within the area of application.

Article XX

1. Any State Party may propose amendments to this Treaty. The text of a proposed amendment shall be submitted to the Depositary, which shall circulate it to all the States Parties.

2. If an amendment is approved by all States Parties, it shall enter into force in accordance with the procedures set forth in Article XXII governing the entry into force of this Treaty.

Article XXI

1. Forty-six months after entry into force of this Treaty, and at five-year intervals thereafter, the Depositary shall convene a conference of the States Parties to conduct a review of the operation of this Treaty.

2. The Depositary shall convene an extraordinary conference of the States Parties, if requested to do so by any State Party which considers that exceptional circumstances relating to this Treaty have arisen, in particular, in the event that a State Party has announced its intention to leave its group of States Parties or to join the other group of States Parties, as defined in Article II, paragraph 1, subparagraph (A). In order to enable the other States Parties to prepare for this conference, the request shall include the reason why that State Party deems an extraordinary conference to be necessary. The conference shall consider the circumstances set forth in the request and their effect on the operation of this Treaty. The conference shall open no longer than 15 days after receipt of the request and, unless it decides otherwise, shall last no longer than three weeks.

3. The Depositary shall convene a conference of the States Parties to consider an amendment proposed pursuant to Article XX, if requested to do so by three or more States Parties. Such a conference shall open no later than 21 days after receipt of the necessary requests.

4. In the event that a State Party gives notice of its decision to withdraw from this Treaty pursuant to Article XIX, the Depositary shall convene a conference of the States Parties which shall open no later than 21 days after receipt of the notice of withdrawal in order to consider questions relating to the withdrawal from this Treaty.

Article XXII

1. This Treaty shall be subject to ratification by each State Party in accordance with its constitutional procedure. Instruments of ratification shall be deposited with the Government of the Kingdom of the Netherlands, hereby designated the Depositary.

2. This Treaty shall enter into force 10 days after instruments of ratification have been deposited by all States Parties listed in the Preamble.

3. The Depositary shall promptly inform all States Parties of:

(A) the deposit of each instrument of ratification;

(B) the entry into force of this Treaty;

(C) any withdrawal in accordance with Article XIX and its effective date;

(D) the text of any amendment proposed in accordance with Article XX;

(E) the entry into force of any amendment to this Treaty;

(F) any request to convene a conference in accordance with Article XXI;

(G) the convening of a conference pursuant to Article XXI; and

(H) any other matter of which the Depositary is required by this Treaty to inform the States Parties.

4. This Treaty shall be registered by the Depositary pursuant to Article 102 of the Charter of the United Nations.

Article XXIII

The original of this Treaty, of which the English, French, German, Italian, Russian and Spanish texts are equally authentic, shall be deposited in the archives of the Depositary. Duly certified copies of this Treaty shall be transmitted by the Depositary to all States Parties.

———

PROTOCOL ON EXISTING TYPES OF CONVENTIONAL ARMAMENTS AND EQUIPMENT

The States Parties hereby agree upon: (*a*) lists, valid as of the date of Treaty signature, of existing types of conventional armaments and equipment subject to the measures of limitation, reduction, information exchange and verification; (*b*) procedures for the provision of technical data and photographs relevant to such existing types of conventional armaments and equipment; and (*c*) procedures for updating the lists of such existing types of conventional armaments and equipment, in accordance with Article II of the Treaty on Conventional Armed Forces in Europe of November 19, 1990, hereinafter referred to as the Treaty.

Section I. Existing types of conventional armaments and equipment limited by the Treaty

1. Existing types of battle tanks are:

M-1	T-34
M-60	T-54
M-48	T-55
M-47	T-62
Leopard 1	T-64
Leopard 2	T-72
AMX-30	T-80
Challenger	TR-85
Chieftain	TR-580
Centurion	
M-41	
NM-116	
T-54	
T-55	
T-72	

All models and versions of an existing type of battle tank listed above shall be deemed to be battle tanks of that type.

2. Existing types of armoured combat vehicles are:

(A) Armoured Personnel Carriers:

YPR-765	BTR-40
AMX-13 VTT	BTR-152
M113	BTR-50
M75	BTR-60
Spartan	OT-62 (TOPAS)
Grizzly	OT-64 (SKOT)
TPz-1 Fuchs	OT-90
VAB	FUG D-442
M59	BTR-70
Leonidas	BTR-80

VCC1	BTR-D
VCC2	TAB-77
Saxon	OT-810
AFV 432	PSZH D-944
Saracen	TABC-79
Humber	TAB-71
BDX	MLVM
BMR-600	MT-LB*
Chaimite V200	
V150S	
EBR-ETT	
M3A1	
YP 408	
BLR	
VIB	
LVTP-7	
6614/G	
BTR-152	
BTR-50	
BTR-60	
BTR-70	
MT-LB*	

All models and versions of an existing type of armoured personnel carrier listed above shall be deemed to be armoured personnel carriers of that type, unless such models and versions are included in the armoured personnel carrier look-alike list in Section II, paragraph 1 of this Protocol.

(B) Armoured Infantry Fighting Vehicles:

YPR-765 (25mm)	BMP-1/BRM-1
Marder	BMP-2
AMX-10P	BMP-23
Warrior	MLI-84
M2/M3 Bradley	BMD-1
AFV 432 Rarden	BMD-2
NM-135	BMP-3
BMP-1/BRM-1	
BMP-2	

---

* This multi-purpose lightly armoured vehicle may be exceptionally modified within 40 months of entry into force of the Treaty into an armoured personnel carrier look-alike listed in Section II, paragraph 1 of this Protocol as MT-LB-AT by alteration of the interior of the vehicle through the removal of the left-hand combat infantry squad seating and the welding of the ammunition racking to the side and the floor at a minimum of six points so that the vehicle is not capable of transporting a combat infantry squad. Such modifications may be accomplished at locations other than reduction sites. MT-LB armoured personnel carriers that have not been modified shall be reported in accordance with the Protocol on Information Exchange as armoured personnel carriers.

All models and versions of an existing type of an armoured infantry fighting vehicle listed above shall be deemed to be armoured infantry fighting vehicles of that type, unless such models and versions are included in the armoured infantry fighting vehicle look-alike list in Section II, paragraph 2 of this Protocol.

(C) Heavy Armament Combat Vehicles:

AMX-l0RC	PT-76
ERC 90 Sagaye	SU-76
BMR-625-90	SU-100
Commando V150	ISU-152
Scorpion	
Saladin	
JPK-90	
M-24	
AMX-13	
EBR-75 Panhard	
PT-76	

All models and versions of an existing type of heavy armament combat vehicle listed above shall be deemed to be heavy armament combat vehicles of that type.

3. Existing types of artillery are:

(A) Guns, Howitzers and Artillery Pieces Combining the Characteristics of Guns and Howitzers:

105mm:
105 Light Gun
M18
105 Krupp Gun
105 R Metal Gun
105 Pack How
M 56 Pack How
M 101 Towed How
M 102 Towed How
Abbot SP Gun
M 108 SP How
M 52 SP How
105 HM-2 How
M-38 Gun (Skoda)
105 AU 50 How
R58/M26 Towed How

100mm:
BS-3 Field Gun
Model 53 Field Gun
Skoda How (Model 1914/1934, 1930, 1934)
Skoda How (Model 1939)

105mm:
Schneider Field Gun (Model 1936)

120mm:
2B16 How
2S9 SP How

122mm:
122/46 Field Gun
D30 How
M 30 How
2S1 SP How

122mm:
D30 How
M-30 How
D74 How
2S1 SP How
A19 Gun (Model 31/37)
Model 89 SP How

130mm:
M 46 Gun

140-mm:
5.5" (139.7mm) Towed How

150mm:
150 Skoda Gun

152mm:
D20 Gun-How
2S3 SP How

155mm:
M 114 Towed How
M 114/39 (M-139) Towed How
FH-70 Towed How
M 109 SP How
M 198 Towed How
155 TRF1 Gun
155 AUF1 Gun
155 AMF3 Gun
155 BF50 Gun
M44 SP How
M59 Towed Gun
SP70 SP How

175mm:
M 107 SP Gun

203mm
M115 Towed How
M110 SP How
M55 SP How

(B) Mortars

107mm:
4.2" (ground mounted or on M106 armoured vehicle)

120mm:
Brandt (M 60, M-120-60; SLM-120-AM-50)
M120 RTF 1
M120 M51
Soltam/Tampella (ground mounted or on M 113 armoured vehicle)
Ecia Mod L (ground mounted M-L or mounted on either the BMR-600 or M 113 armoured vehicle)
HY12 (Tosam)
2B11 (2S12)

130mm:
Gun 82
M-46 Gun

150mm:
Skoda How (Model 1934)
Ceh How (Model 1937)

152mm:
D1 How
2S3 SP How
2A65 How
ML20 How-Gun
D20 Gun-How
Gun 81
2A36 Gun
Dana SP Gun-How
M77
2S5 SP Gun
2S19 SP How
Gun-How 85
How Model 1938
How 81

203mm:
B4 How
2S7 SP Gun

107mm:
Mortar M-1938

120mm:
2B11 (2S12)
M 120 Model 38/43
Tundzha/Tundzha Sani SP Mortar (mounted on MT-LB)
Mortar Model 1982
B-24

160mm:
M160

240mm:
M240
2S4 SP Mortar

(C) Multiple Launch Rocket Systems:

110-mm:	122-mm:
LARS	BM-21 (BM-21-1, BM-21V)
122-mm:	RM-70
BM-21	APR-21
RM-70	APR-40
140-mm:	130-mm:
Teruel MLAS	M-51
	RM-130
227-mm:	BM-13
MLRS	R.2
	140-mm:
	BM-14
	220-mm:
	BM-22/27
	240-mm:
	BM-24
	280-mm:
	Uragan 9P140
	300-mm:
	Smerch

All models and versions of an existing type of artillery listed above shall be deemed to be artillery of that type.

4. Existing types of combat aircraft are:

A-7	IAR-93
A-10	IL-28
Alpha Jet A	MiG-15
AM-X	MiG-17
Buccaneer	MiG-21
Canberra	MiG-23
Draken	MiG-25
F-4	MiG-27
F-5	MiG-29
F-15	MiG-31
F-16	SU-7
F-18	SU-15
F-84	SU-17
F-102	SU-20
F-104	SU-22
F-111	SU-24
G-91	SU-25
Harrier	SU-27
Hunter	TU-16
Jaguar	TU-22
Lightning	TU-22M
MiG-21	TU-128
MiG-23	Yak-28
MiG-29	
MB-339	
Mirage F1	
Mirage III	
Mirage IV	

Mirage V
Mirage 2000
SU-22
Tornado

All models or versions of an existing type of combat aircraft listed above shall be deemed to be combat aircraft of that type.

5. Existing types of attack helicopters are:

(A) Specialised Attack Helicopters:

A-129 Mangusta	Mi-24
AH-1 Cobra	
AH-64 Apache	
Mi-24	

Subject to the provisions in Section I, paragraph 3 of the Protocol on Helicopter Recategorisation, all models or versions of an existing type of specialised attack helicopter listed above shall be deemed to be specialised attack helicopters of that type.

(B) Multi-Purpose Attack Helicopters:

A-109 Hirundo	IAR-316
Alouette III	Mi-8/Mi-17
BO-105/PAH-1	
Fennec AS 550 C-2	
Gazelle	
Lynx	
Mi-8	
OH-58 Kiowa/AB-206/CH-136	
Scout	
Wessex	

Subject to the provisions in Section 1, paragraphs 4 and 5 of the Protocol on Helicopter Recategorisation, all models or versions of an existing type of multi-purpose attack helicopter listed above shall be deemed to be multi-purpose attack helicopters of that type.

Section II. Existing types of conventional armaments and equipment not limited by the Treaty

1. Existing types of armoured personnel carrier look-alikes are:

YPR-765	MILAN
	CP
	PRCOC1
	PRCOC2
	PRCOC4
	PRCOC5
	PRMR
AMX-13 VTT	MILAN
	PC
M113	MILAN
	A1/A2 (ATGW)

Vehicle	Variants	Vehicle	Variants
	E/W TOW		PWAT
	ARTFC		PWRDR
	ARTOBS		PWV
	FACONT	BTR-50	
	MORTFC		PU
	A1E		PK (MRF)
	Mortar Carrier		PK (B)
	SIG	BTR-60	PU-12/PA PU-12
	HFTRSM		BBS
	CP		ABS
	CPSVC		R-137B
	A1CP		R-140 BM
	A1ECP		R-145
	4.2"/M106 A1 4.2"		R-156
	M106 81mm		R-409 BM
	M-125 81mm		P-238 BT
	M125 A1 81mm		P-240 BT
	M125 A2 81mm		P-241 BT
	NM-125 81mm		B
TPz-1 FUCHS	HFTRSM	MT-LB	PI
	AD CP		MP-21-25
	CP		1W-13-16
	ENGRCP		AFMS
	ELOKA		R-381 T
	NBC		R-330 P
	RASIT		Beta 3M
M59	CP		MTP-LB
LEONIDAS	1	BTR-40	CP
VAB	PC	BTR-50	PU
BMR-600	SIG		PUM
	PC		P
	81 mm		PUR 82
			PK (MRF)
SPARTAN	STRIKER		UR-67
	SAMSON		PK (B)
	CP		MTP-1
	JAVELIN		
	MILAN	BTR-152	CP
SAXON	AD	BTR-60	PU
	CP		PU-12/PA PU-12
	MAINT		PAU
			BBS
AFV 432	CP/RA		ABS
	81 mm		R-137 B
	CYMB		R-140 BM
	AFV 435		R-145
	AFV 436		R-156
	AFV 439		R-409 BM
HUMBER	SQUIRT		P-238BT
SARACEN	SQUIRT		P-240BT
	CP		P-241BT
	ADR		E-351BR
			R-975
YP 408	PWMR		MTP-2
	PWCO		1V18, 1V19

	1V118		Beta 3M
	B		SPR-l
BTR-70	KShM		WPT/DTP
	SPR-2		BREM
	BREM		TRI
	ZS-88		MTP-LB
	Kh		BRM Sova/BRM 30
BTR-80	1V119	TAB-71	A
	RCHM-4		TERA-71-L
			AR
BTR-D	ZD	TAB-77	A
	RD		TERA-77-L
OT-62 (TOPAS)	CP		RCH-84
	WPT/DPT-62		PCOMA
	BREM	TABC-79	AR
	R-2M		A-POMA
	R-3M		
	R-3MT	TAB	TCG-80
	R-4MT	MLVM	AR

2. Existing types of armoured infantry fighting vehicle look-alikes are:

OT-64 (SKOT)	CP		
	R-3Z		
	R-2M	WARRIOR	RA
	R-3MT		REP
	R-4		REC
	R-4MT	BMP-l	MTP
	R-2AM		MP-31
	PROPAGANDA		
	R-4M	BMP-l	KSh
	R-6		9S743
	WPT/DR-64		PRR-3, -4
	BREM		MP-31
	S-260 inz.		B
	S-260 art.		SVO
OT-810	OT-810/R-112		DTB-80
			VPV
OT 90	VP 90		IRM
FUG D-442	VS		MTP
	MRP		BREM-4, -2, -D
	OT-65/R-112	BMD-1	KSh
	OT-65 DP	BRM-1	KSh
	OT-65 CH		

3. Existing types of primary trainer aircraft which are designed and constructed for primary flying training and which may possess only limited armament capability necessary for basic training in weapon delivery techniques are:

PSZH D-944	CP		
MT-LB	AT		
	KShM-R-81	Alpha Jet E	I-22
	R-80	C-101 Aviojet	IAR-99
	9S743	Fouga	L-29
	PI	Hawk	L-39
	IW-13-16	Jet Provost	TS-11
	IW-21-25	L-39	
	IW-12	MB-326	
	MP-21-25		
	AFMS		
	R-381T		
	R-330P		

PD-808
T-2
T-33/CT-133
T-37
T-38

4. Existing types of combat support helicopters are:

A-109 Hirundo	IAR-316
AB-412	IAR-330
Alouette II	Mi-2
Alouette III	Mi-6
Blackhawk	Mi-8/Mi-17
Bell 47/AB 47/Sioux	
BO-105	
CH 53	
Chinook	
Fennec AS 555 A	
Hughes 300	
Hughes 500/OH-6	
Mi-8	
OH-58 Kiowa/AB-206/CH-136	
Puma	
Sea King	
UH-lA/lB/AB-204	
UH-lD/lH/AB-205	
UH-lN/AB-212	
Wessex	

5. Existing types of unarmed transport helicopters which are not equipped for the employment of weapons are:

AB 47	Mi-2
AB-412	Mi-26
Alouette II	SA-365N Dauphin
CH 53	W-3 Sokol
Chinook	
Cougar AS 532 U	
Dauphin AS 365 Nl	
Hughes 300	
NH 500	
Puma	
Sea King/H-3F/HAR 3	
SH-3D	
UH-lD/lH/AB-205	
UH-1N/AB-212	

6. Existing types of armoured vehicle launched bridges are:

M47 AVLB	MTU
M48 AVLB	MT-20
M60 AVLB	MT-55A
Centurion AVLB	MTU-72
Chieftain AVLB	BLG-60
Brueckenlegepanzer	BLG-67M
Biber/Leopard	BLG-67M2
1 AVLB	

Section III. Technical data and photographs

1. Technical data, in accordance with the agreed categories in the Annex to this Protocol, together with photographs presenting the right or left side, top and front views for each of its existing type of conventional armaments and equipment listed in Sections I and II of this Protocol shall be provided by each State Party to all other States Parties at the signature of the Treaty. In addition, photographs of armoured personnel carrier look-alikes and armoured infantry fighting vehicle look-alikes shall include a view of such vehicles so as to show clearly their internal configuration illustrating the specific characteristic which distinguishes this particular vehicle as a look-alike. Photographs in addition to those required by this paragraph may be provided at the discretion of each State Party.

2. Each existing type of conventional armaments and equipment listed in Sections I and II of this Protocol shall have a model or version of that type designated as an exemplar. Photographs shall be provided for each such designated exemplar pursuant to paragraph 1 of this Section. Photographs shall not be required of models and versions of a type that have no significant externally observable differences from the exemplar of that type. The photographs of each exemplar of a type shall contain an annotation of the existing type designation and national nomenclature for all models and versions of the type that the photographs of the exemplar represent. The photographs of each exemplar of a type shall contain an annotation of the technical data for that type in accordance with the agreed categories in the Annex to this Protocol. In addition, the annotation shall indicate all models and versions of the type that the photographs of the exemplar represent. Such technical data shall be annotated on the side view photograph.

Section IV. Updates of existing types lists and obligations of the States Parties

1. This Protocol constitutes agreement by the States Parties only with respect to existing types of conventional armaments and equipment as well as with respect to the categories of technical data set forth in Sections I and II of the Annex to this Protocol.

2. Each State Party shall be responsible for the accuracy of technical data for only its own conventional armaments and equipment provided in accordance with Section III of this

Protocol.

3. Each State Party shall notify all other States Parties, upon the entry into service with the armed forces of that State Party within the area of application, of: (*a*) any new type of conventional armaments and equipment which meets one of the definitions in Article II of the Treaty or which falls under a category listed in this Protocol, and (*b*) any new model or version of a type listed in this Protocol. At the same time, each State Party shall provide all other States Parties with the technical data and photographs required by Section III of this Protocol.

4. As soon as possible, and in any case no later than 60 days following a notification pursuant to paragraph 3 of this Section, the States Parties shall initiate update actions, in accordance with the provisions set forth in Article XVI of the Treaty and the Protocol on the Joint Consultative Group, for the lists of existing types of conventional armaments and equipment in Sections I and II of this Protocol.

Annex to the Protocol on Existing Types of Conventional Armaments and Equipment

Section I. Agreed categories of technical data

The following are agreed categories of technical data for each model and version of existing types of conventional armaments and equipment:

1. Battle tanks
    Existing Type
    National Nomenclature
    Main Gun Calibre
    Unladen Weight

2. Armoured Combat Vehicles

    Armoured Personnel Carriers
    Existing Type
    National Nomenclature
    Type and Calibre of Armaments, if any

    Armoured Infantry Fighting Vehicles
    Existing Type
    National Nomenclature
    Type and Calibre of Armaments

    Heavy Armament Combat Vehicles
    Existing Type
    National Nomenclature
    Main Gun Calibre
    Unladen Weight

3. Artillery
    Guns, Howitzers and Artillery Pieces Combining the Characteristics of Guns and Howitzers
    Existing Type
    National Nomenclature
    Calibre

    Mortars
    Existing Type
    National Nomenclature
    Calibre

    Multiple Launch Rocket Systems
    Existing Type
    National Nomenclature
    Calibre

4. Combat Aircraft
    Existing Type
    National Nomenclature

5. Attack Helicopters
    Existing Type
    National Nomenclature

6. Armoured Personnel Carrier Look-Alikes
    Existing Type
    National Nomenclature
    Type and Calibre of Armaments, if any

7. Armoured Infantry Fighting Vehicle Look-Alikes
    Existing Type
    National Nomenclature
    Type and Calibre of Armaments, if any

8. Primary Trainer Aircraft
    Existing Type
    National Nomenclature
    Type of Armaments, if any

9. Combat Support Helicopters
    Existing Type
    National Nomenclature

10. Unarmed Transport Helicopters
    Existing Type
    National Nomenclature

11. Armoured Vehicle Launched Bridges
    Existing Type
    National Nomenclature

Section II. Specifications for photographs

Photographs provided pursuant to Section III of this Protocol shall be in black and white. The use of flash and lighting equipment shall be allowed. The object being photographed shall contrast with the background of the photograph. All photographs shall be of high definition, with continuous tone and in sharp focus. Photographs measuring 13 centimetres by 18 centimetres, not including a border, shall be provided. For aspects other than over-head, all photographs shall be taken from the same level as the equipment being photographed, with the camera placed along or perpendicular to the longitudinal axis of the object being photographed; for the top view, photographs shall show the top and may show the rear aspects of the equipment. The object being photographed shall fill at least 80 percent of the photograph in either horizontal or vertical aspect. A reference gauge shall be included in each photograph together with the object. The gauge shall have alternating half-metre sections in black and white. It shall be long enough to provide accurate scaling and shall be placed on or against the object or in close proximity to it. Each photograph shall be labelled to provide the information required by Section III, paragraph 2 of this Protocol as well as the date when the photograph was taken.

PROTOCOL ON PROCEDURES GOVERNING THE RECLASSIFICATION OF SPECIFIC MODELS OR VERSIONS OF COMBAT-CAPABLE TRAINER AIRCRAFT INTO UNARMED TRAINER AIRCRAFT

The States Parties hereby agree upon procedures and provisions governing total disarming and certification of the unarmed status of specific models or versions of combat-capable trainer aircraft in accordance with Article VIII of the Treaty on Conventional Armed Forces in Europe of November 19, 1990, hereinafter referred to as the Treaty.

Section I. General provisions

1. Each State Party shall have the right to remove from the numerical limitations on combat aircraft in Articles IV and VI of the Treaty only those specific models or versions of combat-capable trainer aircraft listed in Section II, paragraph 1 of this Protocol in accordance with the procedures set forth in this Protocol.

(A) Each State Party shall have the right to remove from the numerical limitations on combat aircraft in Articles IV and VI of the Treaty individual aircraft of the specific models or versions listed in Section II, paragraph 1 of this Protocol that have any of the components set forth in Section III, paragraphs 1 and 2 of this Protocol only by total disarming and certification.

(B) Each State Party shall have the right to remove from the numerical limitations on combat aircraft in Articles IV and VI of the Treaty individual aircraft of the specific models or versions listed in Section II, paragraph 1 of this Protocol that do not have any of the components set forth in Section III, paragraphs 1 and 2 of this Protocol by certification alone.

2. Models or versions of combat-capable trainer aircraft listed in Section II of this Protocol may be disarmed and certified, or certified alone, within 40 months after entry into force of the Treaty. Such aircraft shall count against the numerical limitations on combat aircraft in Articles IV and VI of the Treaty until such aircraft have been certified as unarmed in accordance with the procedures set forth in Section IV of this Protocol. Each State Party shall have the right to remove from the numerical limitations on combat aircraft in Articles IV and VI of the Treaty no more than 550 such aircraft of which no more than 130 shall be of the MiG-25U model or version.

3. No later than entry into force of the Treaty, each State Party shall notify all other States Parties of:

(A) the total number of each specific model or version of combat-capable trainer aircraft that the State Party intends to disarm and certify in accordance with Section I, paragraph 1, subparagraph (A), Section III and Section IV of this Protocol; and

(B) the total number of each specific model or version of combat-capable trainer aircraft that the State Party intends to certify alone, in accordance with Section I, paragraph 1, subparagraph (B) and Section IV of this Protocol.

4. Each State Party shall use whatever technological means it deems necessary to implement the total disarming procedures set forth in Section III of this Protocol.

Section II. Models or versions of combat-capable trainer aircraft eligible for total disarming and certification

1. Each State Party shall have the right to remove from the numerical limitations on combat aircraft in Articles IV and VI of the Treaty in accordance with the provisions of this Protocol only the following specific models or versions of combat-capable trainer aircraft:

SU-15U	MiG-23U
SU-17U	MiG-25U
MiG-15U	UIL-28
MiG-21U	

2. The foregoing list of specific models or versions of combat-capable trainer aircraft is final and not subject to revision.

Section III. Procedures for total disarming

1. Models or versions of combat-capable trainer aircraft being totally disarmed shall be rendered incapable of further employment of any type of weapon system as well as further operation of electronic warfare and reconnaissance systems by the removal of the following components:

(A) provisions specifically for the attachment of weapon systems, such as special hardpoints, launching devices, or weapon mounting areas;

(B) units and panels of weapon control systems including weapon selection, arming and firing or launching systems;

(C) units of aiming equipment and weapon guidance systems not integral to navigation and flight control systems; and

(D) units and panels of electronic warfare and reconnaissance systems including associated antennae.

2. Notwithstanding paragraph 1 of this Section, any special hardpoints which are integral to the aircraft, as well as any special elements of general purpose hardpoints which are designed for use only with the components described in paragraph 1 of this Section, shall be rendered incapable of further employment with such systems. Electrical circuits of the weapon, electronic warfare, and reconnaissance systems described in paragraph 1 of this Section shall be rendered incapable of further employment by removal of the wiring or, if that is not technically practicable, by cutting out sections of the wiring in accessible areas.

3. Each State Party shall provide to all other States Parties the following information, no less than 42 days in advance of the total disarming of the first aircraft of each model or version of combat-capable trainer aircraft listed in Section II of this Protocol:

(A) a basic block diagram portraying all major components of weapon systems including aiming equipment and weapon guidance systems, provisions designed for the attachment of weapons as well as components of electronic warfare and reconnaissance systems, the basic function of the components described in paragraph 1 of this Section, and the functional connections of such components to each other;

(B) a general description of the disarming process including a list of components to be removed; and

(C) a photograph of each component to be removed illustrating its position in the aircraft prior to its removal, and a photograph of the same position after the corresponding component has been removed.

Section IV. Procedures for certification

1. Each State Party that intends to disarm and certify, or certify alone, models or versions of combat-capable trainer aircraft shall comply with the following certification procedures in order to ensure that such aircraft do not possess any of the components listed in Section III, paragraphs 1 and 2 of this Protocol.

2. Each State Party shall notify all other States Parties in accordance with Section IX, paragraph 3 of the Protocol on Inspection of each certification. In the event of the first certification of an aircraft that does not require total disarming, the State Party that intends to conduct the certification shall provide to all other States Parties the information required in Section III, paragraph 3, subparagraphs (A), (B) and (C) of this Protocol for an armed model or version of the same aircraft type.

3. Each State Party shall have the right to inspect the certification of combat-capable trainer aircraft in accordance with Section IX of the Protocol on Inspection.

4. The process of total disarming and certification, or certification alone, shall be deemed completed when the certification procedures set forth in this Section have been completed regardless of whether any State Party exercises the certification inspection rights described in paragraph 3 of this Section and Section IX of the Protocol on Inspection, provided that within 30 days of receipt of the notification of completion of the certification and reclassification provided pursuant to paragraph 5 of this Section no State Party has notified all other States Parties that it considers that there is an ambiguity relating to the certification and reclassification process. In the event of such an ambiguity being raised, such reclassification shall not be deemed complete until the matter relating to the ambiguity is resolved.

5. The State Party conducting the certification shall notify all other States Parties in accordance with Section IX of the Protocol on Inspection of completion of the certification.

6. Certification shall be conducted in the area of application. States Parties belonging to

the same group of States Parties shall have the right to share locations for certification.

Section V. Procedures for information exchange and verification

All models or versions of combat-capable trainer aircraft certified as unarmed shall be subject to information exchange in accordance with the provisions of the Protocol on Information Exchange, and verification, including inspection, in accordance with the Protocol on Inspection.

PROTOCOL ON PROCEDURES GOVERNING THE REDUCTION OF CONVENTIONAL ARMAMENTS AND EQUIPMENT LIMITED BY THE TREATY ON CONVENTIONAL ARMED FORCES IN EUROPE

The States Parties hereby agree upon procedures governing the reduction of conventional armaments and equipment limited by the Treaty as set forth in Article VIII of the Treaty on Conventional Armed Forces in Europe of November 19, 1990, hereinafter referred to as the Treaty.

Section I. General requirements for reduction

1. Conventional armaments and equipment limited by the Treaty shall be reduced in accordance with the procedures set forth in this Protocol and the other protocols listed in Article VIII, paragraph 1 of the Treaty. Any one of such procedures shall be deemed sufficient, when conducted in accordance with the provisions of Article VIII of the Treaty or this Protocol, to carry out reduction.

2. Each State Party shall have the right to use any technological means it deems appropriate to implement the procedures for reducing conventional armaments and equipment limited by the Treaty.

3. Each State Party shall have the right to remove, retain and use those components and parts of conventional armaments and equipment limited by the Treaty which are not themselves subject to reduction in accordance with the provisions of Section II of this Protocol, and to dispose of debris.

4. Unless otherwise provided for in this Protocol, conventional armaments and equipment limited by the Treaty shall be reduced so as to preclude their further use or restoration for military purposes.

5. After entry into force of the Treaty, additional procedures for reduction may be proposed by any State Party. Such proposals shall be communicated to all other States Parties and shall provide the details of such procedures in the same format as the procedures set forth in this Protocol. Any such procedures shall be deemed sufficient to carry out the reduction of conventional armaments and equipment limited by the Treaty upon a decision to that effect by the Joint Consultative Group.

Section II. Standards for presentation at reduction sites

1. Each item of conventional armaments and equipment limited by the Treaty which is to be reduced shall be presented at a reduction site. Each such item shall consist, at a minimum, of the following parts and elements:

(A) for battle tanks: the hull, turret and integral main armament. For the purposes of this Protocol, an integral main armament of a battle tank shall be deemed to include the gun tube, breech system, trunnions and trunnion mounts;

(B) for armoured combat vehicles: the hull, turret and integral main armament, if any. For the purposes of this Protocol, an integral main armament of an armoured combat vehicle shall be deemed to include the gun tube, breech system, trunnions and trunnion mounts. For the purposes of this Protocol, an integral main armament shall be deemed not to include machine guns of less than 20 millimetre calibre, all of which may be salvaged;

(C) for artillery: the tube, breech system, cradle including trunnions and trunnion mounts, trails, if any; or launcher tubes or launcher rails and their bases; or mortar tubes and their base plates. In the case of self-propelled pieces of artillery, the vehicle hull and turret, if any, shall also be presented;

(D) for combat aircraft: the fuselage; and

(E) for attack helicopters: the fuselage, including the transmission mounting area.

2. In each case, the item presented at the reduction site in accordance with paragraph 1 of this Section shall consist of a complete assembly.

3. Parts and elements of conventional armaments and equipment limited by the Treaty not specified in paragraph 1 of this Section, as well as parts and elements which are not affected by reduction under the procedures of this Protocol, including the turrets of armoured personnel carriers equipped only with

machine guns, may be disposed of as the State Party undertaking the reduction decides.

Section III. Procedures for reduction of battle tanks by destruction

1. Each State Party shall have the right to choose any one of the following sets of procedures each time it carries out the destruction of battle tanks at reduction sites.

2. Procedure for destruction by severing:

(A) removal of special equipment from the chassis, including detachable equipment, that ensures the operation of on-board armament systems;

(B) removal of the turret, if any;

(C) for the gun breech system, either:

(1) welding the breech block to the breech ring in at least two places; or

(2) cutting of at least one side of the breech ring along the long axis of the cavity that receives the breech block;

(D) severing of the gun tube into two parts at a distance of no more than 100 millimetres from the breech ring;

(E) severing of either of the gun trunnions and its trunnion mount in the turret;

(F) severing of two sections from the perimeter of the hull turret aperture, each constituting a portion of a sector with an angle of no less than 60 degrees and, at a minimum, 200 millimetres in radial axis, centred on the longitudinal axis of the vehicle; and

(G) severing of sections from both sides of the hull which include the final drive apertures, by vertical and horizontal cuts in the side plates and diagonal cuts in the deck or belly plates and front or rear plates, so that the final drive apertures are contained in the severed portions.

3. Procedure for destruction by explosive demolition:

(A) hull, hatches and cornerplates shall be open to maximise venting;

(B) an explosive charge shall be placed inside the gun tube where the trunnions connect to the gun mount or cradle;

(C) an explosive charge shall be placed on the outside of the hull between the second and third road wheels, or between the third and fourth road wheels in a six road wheel configuration, avoiding natural weaknesses such as welds or escape hatches. The charge must be located within the radius of the turret casting. A second charge shall be placed on the inside of the hull on the same side of the tank,

offset and opposite to the external charge;

(D) an explosive charge shall be placed on the inside of the turret casting in the area of the main armament mounting; and

(E) all charges shall be fired simultaneously so that the main hull and turret are cracked and distorted; the breech block is stripped from the gun tube, fused or deformed; the gun tube is split or longitudinally cut; the gun mount or cradle is ruptured so as to be unable to mount a gun tube; and damage is caused to the running gear so that at least one of the road wheel stations is destroyed.

4. Procedure for destruction by deformation:

(A) removal of special equipment from the chassis, including detachable equipment, that ensures the operation of on-board armament systems;

(B) removal of the turret, if any;

(C) for the gun breech system, either:

(1) welding the breech block to the breech ring in at least two places; or

(2) cutting of at least one side of the breech ring along the long axis of the cavity that receives the breech block;

(D) severing of the gun tube into two parts at a distance of no more than 100 millimetres from the breech ring;

(E) severing of either of the gun trunnions; and

(F) the hull and turret shall be deformed so that their widths are each reduced by at least 20 percent.

5. Procedure for destruction by smashing:

(A) a heavy steel wrecking ball, or the equivalent, shall be dropped repeatedly onto the hull and turret until the hull is cracked in at least three separate places and the turret in at least one place;

(B) the hits of the ball on the turret shall render either of the gun trunnions and its trunnion mount inoperative, and deform visibly the breech ring; and

(C) the gun tube shall be visibly cracked or bent.

Section IV. Procedures for the reduction of armoured combat vehicles by destruction

1. Each State Party shall have the right to choose any of the following sets of procedures each time it carries out the destruction of armoured combat vehicles at reduction sites.

2. Procedure for destruction by severing:

(A) for all armoured combat vehicles, removal of special equipment from the chassis, including detachable equipment, that ensures the operation of on-board armament systems;

(B) for tracked armoured combat vehicles, severing of sections from both sides of the hull which include the final drive apertures, by vertical and horizontal cuts in the side plates and diagonal cuts in the deck or belly plates and front or rear plates, so that the final drive apertures are contained in the severed portions;

(C) for wheeled armoured combat vehicles, severing of sections from both sides of the hull which include the front wheel final gearbox mounting areas by vertical, horizontal and irregular cuts in the side, front, deck and belly plates so that the front wheel final gearbox mounting areas are included in the severed portions at a distance of no less than 100 millimetres from the cuts; and

(D) in addition, for armoured infantry fighting vehicles and heavy armament combat vehicles:

(1) removal of the turret;

(2) severing of either of the gun trunnions and its trunnion mount in the turret;

(3) for the gun breech system:

(*a*) welding the breech block to the breech ring in at least two places;

(*b*) cutting of at least one side of the breech ring along the long axis of the cavity that receives the breech block; or

(*c*) severing of the breech casing into two approximately equal parts;

(4) severing of the gun tube into two parts at a distance of no more than 100 millimetres from the breech ring; and

(5) severing of two sections from the perimeter of the hull turret aperture, each constituting a portion of a sector with an angle of no less than 60 degrees and, at a minimum, 200 millimetres in radial axis, centred on the longitudinal axis of the vehicle.

3. Procedure for destruction by explosive demolition:

(A) an explosive charge shall be placed on the interior floor at the mid-point of the vehicle;

(B) a second explosive charge shall be placed as follows:

(1) for heavy armament combat vehicles, inside the gun where the trunnions connect to the gun mount or cradle;

(2) for armoured infantry fighting vehicles, on the exterior of the receiver/breech area and lower barrel group;

(C) all hatches shall be secured; and

(D) the charges shall be detonated simultaneously so as to split the sides and top of the hull. For heavy armament combat vehicles and armoured infantry fighting vehicles, damage to the gun system shall be equivalent to that specified in paragraph 2, subparagraph (D) of this Section.

4. Procedure for destruction by smashing:

(A) a heavy steel wrecking ball, or the equivalent, shall be dropped repeatedly onto the hull and the turret, if any, until the hull is cracked in at least three separate places and the turret, if any, in one place;

(B) in addition, for heavy armament combat vehicles:

(1) the hits of the ball on the turret shall render either of the gun trunnions and its trunnion mount inoperative, and shall deform visibly the breech ring; and

(2) the gun tube shall be visibly cracked or bent.

Section V. Procedures for the reduction of artillery by destruction

1. Each State Party shall have the right to choose any one of the following sets of procedures each time it carries out the destruction of guns, howitzers, artillery pieces combining the characteristics of guns and howitzers, multiple launch rocket systems or mortars at reduction sites.

2. Procedure for destruction by severing of guns, howitzers, artillery pieces combining the characteristics of guns and howitzers, or mortars, that are not self-propelled:

(A) removal of special equipment, including detachable equipment, that ensures the operation of the gun, howitzer, artillery piece combining the characteristics of guns and howitzers or mortar;

(B) for the breech system, if any, of the gun, howitzer, artillery piece combining the characteristics of guns and howitzers or mortar, either:

(1) welding the breech block to the breech ring in at least two places; or

(2) cutting of at least one side of the breech ring along the long axis of the cavity that receives the breech block;

(C) severing of the tube into two parts at a distance of no more than 100 millimetres from the breech ring;

(D) severing of the left trunnion of the

cradle and the mounting area of that trunnion in the upper carriage; and

(E) severing of the trails, or the base plate of the mortar, into two approximately equal parts.

3. Procedure for destruction by explosive demolition of guns, howitzers, or artillery pieces combining the characteristics of guns and howitzers that are not self-propelled:

(A) explosive charges shall be placed in the tube, on one cradle mount in the upper carriage and on the trails, and detonated so that:

(1) the tube is split or longitudinally torn within 1.5 metres of the breech;

(2) the breech block is torn off, deformed or partially melted;

(3) the attachments between the tube and the breech ring and between one of the trunnions of the cradle and the upper carriage are destroyed or sufficiently damaged to make them further inoperative; and

(4) the trails are separated into two approximately equal parts or sufficiently damaged to make them further inoperative.

4. Procedure for destruction by explosive demolition of mortars that are not self-propelled:

explosive charges shall be placed in the mortar tube and on the base plate so that, when the charges are detonated, the mortar tube is ruptured in its lower half and the base plate is severed into two approximately equal parts.

5. Procedure for destruction by deformation of mortars that are not self-propelled:

(A) the mortar tube shall be visibly bent approximately at its mid-point; and

(B) the base plate shall be bent approximately on the centreline at an angle of at least 45 degrees.

6. Procedure for destruction by severing of self-propelled guns, howitzers, artillery pieces combining the characteristics of guns and howitzers or mortars:

(A) removal of special equipment, including detachable equipment, that ensures the operation of the gun, howitzer, artillery piece combining the characteristics of guns and howitzers or mortar;

(B) for the breech system, if any, of the gun, howitzer, artillery piece combining the characteristics of guns and howitzers or mortar, either:

(1) welding the breech block to the breech ring in at least two places; or

(2) cutting of at least one side of the breech ring along the long axis of the cavity that receives the breech block;

(C) severing of the tube into two parts at a distance of no more than 100 millimetres from the breech ring;

(D) severing of the left trunnion and trunnion mount; and

(E) severing of sections of both sides from the hull which include the final drive apertures, by vertical and horizontal cuts in the side plates and diagonal cuts in the deck or belly plates and front or rear plates, so that the final drive apertures are contained in the severed portions.

7. Procedure for destruction by explosive demolition of self-propelled guns, howitzers, artillery pieces combining the characteristics of guns and howitzers or mortars:

(A) for self-propelled guns, howitzers, artillery pieces combining the characteristics of guns and howitzers or mortars with a turret: the method specified for battle tanks in Section III, paragraph 3 of this Protocol shall be applied in order to achieve results equivalent to those specified in that provision; and

(B) for self-propelled guns, howitzers, artillery pieces combining the characteristics of guns and howitzers or mortars without a turret: an explosive charge shall be placed in the hull under the forward edge of the traversing deck that supports the tube, and detonated so as to separate the deck plate from the hull. For the destruction of the weapon system, the method specified for guns, howitzers, or artillery pieces combining the characteristics of guns and howitzers in paragraph 3 of this Section shall be applied in order to achieve results equivalent to those specified in that provision.

8. Procedure for destruction by smashing of self-propelled guns, howitzers, artillery pieces combining the characteristics of guns and howitzers or mortars:

(A) a heavy steel wrecking ball, or the equivalent, shall be dropped repeatedly onto the hull and turret, if any, until the hull is cracked in at least three separate places and the turret in at least one place;

(B) the hits of the ball on the turret shall render either of the trunnions and its trunnion mount inoperative, and deform visibly the breech ring; and

(C) the tube shall be visibly cracked or bent at approximately its mid-point.

9. Procedure for destruction by severing of multiple launch rocket systems:

(A) removal of special equipment from the multiple launch rocket system, including detachable equipment, that ensures the operation of its combat systems; and

(B) removal of tubes or launch rails, screws (gears) of elevation mechanism sectors, tube bases or launch rail bases and their rotatable parts and severing them into two approximately equal parts in areas that are not assembly joints.

10. Procedure for destruction by explosive demolition of multiple launch rocket systems:

a linear shaped charge shall be placed across the tubes or launcher rails, and tube or launcher rail bases. When detonated, the charge shall sever the tubes or launcher rails, and tube or launcher rail bases and their rotatable parts, into two approximately equal parts in areas that are not assembly joints.

11. Procedure for destruction by deformation of multiple launch rocket systems:

all tubes or launch rails, tube or launcher rail bases and the sighting system shall be visibly bent at approximately the mid-point.

Section VI. Procedures for the reduction of combat aircraft by destruction

1. Each State Party shall have the right to choose any one of the following sets of procedures each time it carries out the destruction of combat aircraft at reduction sites.

2. Procedure for destruction by severing:

the fuselage of the aircraft shall be divided into three parts not on assembly joints by severing its nose immediately forward of the cockpit and its tail in the central wing section area so that assembly joints, if there are any in the areas to be severed, shall be contained in the severed portions.

3. Procedure for destruction by deformation:

the fuselage shall be deformed throughout by compression, so that its height, width or length is reduced by at least 30 percent.

4. Procedure for destruction by use as target drones:

(A) each State Party shall have the right to reduce by use as target drones no more than 200 combat aircraft during the 40-month reduction period;

(B) the target drone shall be destroyed in flight by munitions fired by the armed forces of the State Party owning the target drone;

(C) if the attempt to shoot down the target drone fails and it is subsequently destroyed by a self-destruct mechanism, the procedures of this paragraph shall continue to apply. Otherwise the target drone may be recovered or may be claimed destroyed by accident in accordance with Section IX of this Protocol, depending on the circumstances; and

(D) notification of destruction shall be made to all other States Parties. Such notification shall include the type of the destroyed target drone and the location where it was destroyed. Within 90 days of the notification, the State Party claiming such reduction shall send documentary evidence, such as a report of the investigation, to all other States Parties. In the event of ambiguities relating to the destruction of a particular target drone, reduction shall not be considered complete until final resolution of the matter.

Section VII. Procedure for the reduction of attack helicopters by destruction

1. Each State Party shall have the right to choose any one of the following sets of procedures each time it carries out the destruction of attack helicopters at reduction sites.

2. Procedure for destruction by severing:

(A) the tail boom or tail part shall be severed from the fuselage so that the assembly joint is contained in the severed portion; and

(B) at least two transmission mounts on the fuselage shall be severed, fused or deformed.

3. Procedure for destruction by explosive demolition:

any type and number of explosives may be used so that, at a minimum, after detonation the fuselage is cut into two pieces through that section of the fuselage that contains the transmission mounting area.

4. Procedure for destruction by deformation:

the fuselage shall be deformed throughout by compression so that its height, width or length is reduced by at least 30 percent.

Section VIII. Rules and procedures for reduction of conventional armaments and equipment limited by the Treaty by conversion for non-military purposes

1. Each State Party shall have the right to reduce a certain number of battle tanks and armoured combat vehicles by conversion. The

types of vehicles that may be converted are listed in paragraph 3 of this Section and the specific non-military purposes for which they may be converted are listed in paragraph 4 of this Section. Converted vehicles shall not be placed in service with the conventional armed forces of a State Party.

2. Each State Party shall determine the number of battle tanks and armoured combat vehicles it will convert. This number shall not exceed:

(A) for battle tanks, 5.7 percent (not to exceed 750 battle tanks) of the maximum level for holdings of battle tanks it notified at the signature of the Treaty pursuant to Article VII of the Treaty, or 150 items whichever is the greater; and

(B) for armoured combat vehicles, 15 percent (not to exceed 3 000 armoured combat vehicles) of the maximum level for holdings of armoured combat vehicles it notified at the signature of the Treaty pursuant to Article VII of the Treaty, or 150 items whichever is the greater.

3. The following vehicles may be converted for non-military purposes: T-54, T-55, T-62, T-64, T-72, Leopard 1, BMP-l, BTR-60, OT-64. The States Parties, within the framework of the Joint Consultative Group, may make changes to the list of vehicles which may be converted to non-military purposes. Such changes, pursuant to Article XVI, paragraph 5 of the Treaty shall be deemed improvements to the viability and effectiveness of the Treaty relating only to minor matters of a technical nature.

4. Such vehicles shall be converted for the following specific non-military purposes:

(A) general purpose prime movers;

(B) bulldozers;

(C) fire fighting vehicles;

(D) cranes;

(E) power unit vehicles;

(F) mineral fine crushing vehicles;

(G) quarry vehicles;

(H) rescue vehicles;

(I) casualty evacuation vehicles;

(J) transportation vehicles;

(K) oil rig vehicles;

(L) oil and chemical product spill cleaning vehicles;

(M) tracked ice breaking prime movers;

(N) environmental vehicles.

The States Parties, within the framework of the Joint Consultative Group, may make changes to the list of specific non-military pur-

poses. Such changes, pursuant to Article XVl, paragraph 5 of the Treaty shall be deemed improvements to the viability and effectiveness of the Treaty relating only to minor matters of a technical nature.

5. On entry into force of the Treaty, each State Party shall notify to all other States Parties the number of battle tanks and armoured combat vehicles that it plans to convert in accordance with the provisions of the Treaty. Notification of a State Party's intention to carry out conversion in accordance with this Section shall be given to all other Parties at least 15 days in advance in accordance with Section X, paragraph 5 of the Protocol on Inspection. It shall specify the number and types of vehicles to be converted, the starting date and completion date of conversion, as well as the specific non-military purpose vehicles to emerge after conversion.

6. The following procedures shall be carried out before conversion of battle tanks and armoured combat vehicles at reduction sites:

(A) for battle tanks:

(1) removal of special equipment from the chassis, including detachable equipment, that ensures the operation of on-board armament systems;

(2) removal of the turret, if any;

(3) for the gun breech system, either:

(*a*) welding the breech block to the breech ring in at least two places; or

(*b*) cutting of at least one side of the breech ring along the long axis of the cavity that receives the breech block;

(4) severing of the gun tube into two parts at a distance of no more than 100 millimetres from the breech ring;

(5) severing of either of the gun trunnions and its trunnion mount in the turret; and

(6) cutting out and removal of a portion of the hull top armour beginning from the front glacis to the middle of the hull turret aperture, together with the associated portions of the side armour at a height of no less than 200 millimetres (for the T-64 and T-72, no less than 100 millimetres) below the level of the hull top armour, as well as the associated portion of the front glacis plate severed at the same height. The severed portion of this front glacis plate shall consist of no less than the upper third; and

(B) for armoured combat vehicles:

(1) for all armoured combat vehicles, removal of special equipment from the chassis,

including detachable equipment, that ensures the operation of on-board armament systems;

(2) for rear-engined vehicles, cutting out and removal of a portion of the hull top armour from the front glacis to the bulkhead of the engine-transmission compartment, together with the associated portions of the side and front armour at a height of no less than 300 millimetres below the level of the top of the assault crew compartment;

(3) for front-engined vehicles, cutting out and removal of a portion of the hull top armour plate from the bulkhead of the engine-transmission compartment to the rear of the vehicle, together with the associated portions of the side armour at a height of no less than 300 millimetres below the level of the top of the assault crew compartment; and

(4) in addition, for armoured infantry fighting vehicles and heavy armament combat vehicles:

(*a*) removal of the turret;

(*b*) severing of either of the gun trunnions and its trunnion mount in the turret;

(*c*) for the gun breech system:

(i) welding the breech block to the breech ring in at least two places;

(ii) cutting of at least one side of the breech ring along the long axis of the cavity that receives the breech block; or

(iii) severing of the breech casing into two approximately equal parts; and

(*d*) severing of the gun tube into two parts at a distance of no more than 100 millimetres from the breech ring.

7. Battle tanks and armoured combat vehicles being reduced pursuant to paragraph 6 of this Section shall be subject to inspection, without right of refusal, in accordance with Section X of the Protocol on Inspection. Battle tanks and armoured combat vehicles shall be deemed reduced upon completion of the procedures specified in paragraph 6 of this Section and notification in accordance with Section X of the Protocol on Inspection.

8. Vehicles reduced pursuant to paragraph 7 of this Section shall remain subject to notification pursuant to Section IV of the Protocol on Information Exchange until final conversion for non-military purposes has been completed and notification has been made in accordance with Section X, paragraph 12 of the Protocol on Inspection.

9. Vehicles undergoing final conversion for non-military purposes shall also be subject to inspection in accordance with Section X of the Protocol on Inspection, with the following changes:

(A) the process of final conversion at a reduction site shall not be subject to inspection; and

(B) all other States Parties shall have the right to inspect fully converted vehicles, without right of refusal, upon receipt of a notification from the State Party conducting final conversion specifying when final conversion procedures will be completed.

10. If, having completed the procedures specified in paragraph 6 of this Section on a given vehicle, it is decided not to proceed with final conversion, then the vehicle shall be destroyed within the time limits for conversion set forth in Article VIII of the Treaty in accordance with the appropriate procedures set forth elsewhere in this Protocol.

Section IX. Procedure in the event of destruction by accident

1. Each State Party shall have the right to reduce its reduction liability for each category of conventional armaments and equipment limited by the Treaty in the event of destruction by accident by an amount no greater than 1.5 percent of the maximum levels for holdings it notified at the signature of the Treaty for that category.

2. An item of conventional armaments and equipment limited by the Treaty shall be deemed reduced, according to Article VIII of the Treaty, if the accident in which it was destroyed is notified to all other States Parties within seven days of its occurrence. Notification shall include the type of the destroyed item, the date of the accident, the approximate location of the accident and the circumstances related to the accident.

3. Within 90 days of the notification, the State Party claiming such reduction shall provide documentary evidence, such as a report of the investigation, to all other States Parties in accordance with Article XVII of the Treaty. In the event of ambiguities relating to the accident, such reduction shall not be considered complete until final resolution of the matter.

Section X. Procedure for reduction by means of static display

1. Each State Party shall have the right to reduce by means of static display a certain number of conventional armaments and equipment limited by the Treaty.

2. No State Party shall use static display to reduce more than one percent or eight items, whichever is the greater number, of its maximum levels for holdings it declared at the signature of the Treaty for each category of conventional armaments and equipment limited by the Treaty.

3. Notwithstanding paragraphs 1 and 2 of this Section, each State Party also shall have the right to retain in working order two items of each existing type of conventional armaments and equipment limited by the Treaty for the purpose of static display. Such conventional armaments and equipment shall be displayed at museums or other similar sites.

4. Conventional armaments and equipment placed on static display or in museums prior to the signature of the Treaty shall not be subject to any numerical limitations set forth in the Treaty, including the numerical limitations set forth in paragraphs 2 and 3 of this Section.

5. Such items to be reduced by means of static display shall undergo the following procedures at reduction sites:

(A) all items to be displayed that are powered by self-contained engines shall have their fuel tanks rendered incapable of holding fuel and:

(1) have their engine(s) and transmission removed and their mounts damaged so that these pieces cannot be refitted; or

(2) have their engine compartment filled with concrete or a polymer resin;

(B) all items to be displayed equipped with 75 millimetre or larger guns with permanently fixed elevation and traversing mechanisms shall have their elevation and traversing mechanisms welded so that the tube can be neither traversed nor elevated. In addition, those items to be displayed which use pinion and rack or pinion and ring mechanisms for traversing or elevating shall have three consecutive gear teeth cut off from the rack or ring on each side of the pinion of the gun tube;

(C) all items to be displayed which are equipped with weapon systems that do not meet the criteria set forth in subparagraph (B) of this paragraph shall have their barrel and receiver group filled with either concrete or a polymer resin, beginning at the face of the bolt/breech and ending within 100 millimetres of the muzzle.

Section XI. Procedure for reduction by use as ground targets

1. Each State Party shall have the right to reduce by use as ground targets a certain number of battle tanks, armoured combat vehicles and self-propelled pieces of artillery.

2. No State Party shall reduce by use as ground targets numbers of battle tanks or armoured combat vehicles greater than 2.5 percent of its maximum level for holdings in each of those two categories as notified at the signature of the Treaty pursuant to Article VII of the Treaty. In addition, no State Party shall have the right to reduce by use as ground targets more than 50 self-propelled pieces of artillery.

3. Conventional armaments and equipment in use as ground targets prior to the signature of the Treaty shall not be subject to any numerical limitations set forth in Articles IV, V or VI of the Treaty, or to the numerical limitations set forth in paragraph 2 of this Section.

4. Such items to be reduced by use as ground targets shall undergo the following procedures at reduction sites:

(A) for battle tanks and self-propelled pieces of artillery:

(1) for the breech system, either:

(a) welding the breech block to the breech ring in at least two places; or

(b) cutting of at least one side of the breech ring along the long axis of the cavity that receives the breech block;

(2) severing of either of the trunnions and its trunnion mount in the turret; and

(3) severing of sections from both sides of the hull which include the final drive apertures, by vertical and horizontal cuts in the side plates and diagonal cuts in the deck or belly plates and front or rear plates, such that the final drive apertures are contained in the severed portions; and

(B) for armoured combat vehicles:

(1) for the gun breech system:

(a) welding the breech block to the breech ring in at least two places;

(b) cutting of at least one side of the breech ring along the axis of the cavity that receives the breech block; or

(c) severing of the breech casing into two approximately equal parts;

(2) severing of either of the gun trunnions and its trunnion mount in the turret;

(3) for tracked armoured combat vehicles, severing of sections from both sides of the hull which include the final drive apertures, by vertical and horizontal cuts in the side plates and diagonal cuts in the deck or belly plates

and front or rear plates, so that the final drive apertures are contained in the severed portions; and

(4) for wheeled armoured combat vehicles, severing of sections from both sides of the hull which include the front wheel final gearbox mounting areas by vertical, horizontal and irregular cuts in the side, front, deck and belly plates so that the front wheel final gearbox mounting areas are included in the severed portions at a distance of no less than 100 millimetres from the cuts.

Section XII. Procedure for reduction by use for ground instructional purposes

1. Each State Party shall have the right to reduce by use for ground instructional purposes a certain number of combat aircraft and attack helicopters.

2. No State Party shall reduce by use for ground instructional purposes numbers of combat aircraft or attack helicopters greater than five percent of its maximum level for holdings in each of those two categories as notified at the signature of the Treaty pursuant to Article VII of the Treaty.

3. Conventional armaments and equipment limited by the Treaty in use for ground instructional purposes prior to the signature of the Treaty shall not be subject to any numerical limitations set forth in Articles IV, V or VI of the Treaty, or the numerical limitations set forth in paragraph 2 of this Section.

4. Such items to be reduced by use for ground instructional purposes shall undergo the following procedures at reduction sites:

(A) for combat aircraft:

(1) severing of the fuselage into two parts in the central wing area;

(2) removal of engines, mutilation of engine mounting points and either filling of all fuel tanks with concrete, polymer or resin setting compounds or removal of the fuel tanks and mutilation of the fuel tank mounting points; or

(3) removal of all internal, external and removable armament and armament systems equipment, removal of the tail fin and mutilation of the tail fin mounting points, and filling of all but one fuel tank with concrete, polymer or resin setting compounds; and

(B) for attack helicopters:

severing of the tail boom or tail part from the fuselage so that the assembly joint is contained in the severed portion.

PROTOCOL ON PROCEDURES GOVERNING THE CATEGORISATION OF COMBAT HELICOPTERS AND THE RECATEGORISATION OF MULTI-PURPOSE ATTACK HELICOPTERS

The States Parties hereby agree upon procedures and provisions governing the categorisation of combat helicopters and recategorisation of multi-purpose attack helicopters as provided for in Article VIII of the Treaty on Conventional Armed Forces in Europe of November 19, 1990, hereinafter referred to as the Treaty.

Section I. General requirements for the categorisation of combat helicopters

1. Combat helicopters shall be categorised as specialised attack, multi-purpose attack or combat support helicopters and shall be listed as such in the Protocol on Existing Types.

2. All models or versions of a specialised attack helicopter type shall be categorised as specialised attack helicopters.

3. Notwithstanding the provisions in paragraph 2 of this Section and as a unique exception to that paragraph, the Union of Soviet Socialist Republics may hold an aggregate total not to exceed 100 Mi-24R and Mi-24K helicopters equipped for reconnaissance, spotting, or chemical/biological/radiological sampling which shall not be subject to the limitations on attack helicopters in Articles IV and VI of the Treaty. Such helicopters shall be subject to exchange of information in accordance with the Protocol on Information Exchange and to internal inspection in accordance with Section VI, paragraph 30 of the Protocol on Inspection. Mi-24R and Mi-24K helicopters in excess of this limit shall be categorised as specialised attack helicopters regardless of how they are equipped and shall count against the limitations on attack helicopters in Articles IV and VI of the Treaty.

4. Each State Party that holds both combat support and multi-purpose attack models or versions of a helicopter type shall categorise as attack helicopters all helicopters which have any of the features listed in Section III, paragraph 1 of this Protocol and shall have the right to categorise as combat support helicopters any helicopters that have none of the features listed in Section III, paragraph 1 of this Protocol.

5. Each State Party that holds only combat support models or versions of a helicopter type included on both the Multi-Purpose

Attack Helicopter and the Combat Support Helicopter lists in the Protocol on Existing Types shall have the right to categorise such helicopters as combat support helicopters.

Section II. General requirements for recategorisation

1. Only combat helicopters that are categorised as multi-purpose attack helicopters in accordance with the categorisation requirements set forth in this Protocol shall be eligible for recategorisation as combat support helicopters.

2. Each State Party shall have the right to recategorise individual multi-purpose attack helicopters that have any of the features set forth in Section III, paragraph I of this Protocol only by conversion and certification. Each State Party shall have the right to recategorise individual multi-purpose attack helicopters that do not have any of the features set forth in Section III, paragraph 1 of this Protocol by certification alone.

3. Each State Party shall use whatever technological means it deems necessary to implement the conversion procedures set forth in Section III of this Protocol.

4. Each combat helicopter subject to the recategorisation procedure shall bear the original manufacturer's serial number permanently stamped in a main airframe structural member.

Section III. Procedures for conversion

1. Multi-purpose attack helicopters being converted shall be rendered incapable of further employment of guided weapons by the removal of the following components:

(A) provisions specifically for the attachment of guided weapons, such as special hardpoints or launching devices. Any such special hardpoints which are integral to the helicopter, as well as any special elements of general purpose hardpoints which are designed for use only by guided weapons, shall be rendered incapable of further employment with guided weapons; and

(B) all integrated fire control and aiming systems for guided weapons, including wiring.

2. A State Party shall provide to all other States Parties the following information, either at least 42 days in advance of the conversion of the first helicopter of a type or at entry into force of the Treaty in the event that a State Party declares both multi-purpose attack helicopters and combat support helicopters of the same type:

(A) a basic block diagram portraying all major components of guided weapon integrated fire control and aiming systems as well as components of equipment designed for the attachment of guided weapons, the basic function of the components described in paragraph 1 of this Section, and the functional connections of such components to each other;

(B) a general description of the conversion process including a list of components to be removed; and

(C) a photograph of each component to be removed, illustrating its position in the helicopter prior to its removal, and a photograph of the same position after the corresponding component has been removed.

Section IV. Procedures for certification

1. Each State Party that is recategorising multi-purpose attack helicopters shall comply with the following certification procedures, in order to ensure that such helicopters do not possess any of the features listed in Section III, paragraph 1 of this Protocol.

2. Each State Party shall notify all other States Parties of each certification in accordance with Section IX, paragraph 3 of the Protocol on Inspection.

3. Each State Party shall have the right to inspect the certification of helicopters in accordance with Section IX of the Protocol on Inspection.

4. The process of recategorisation shall be deemed completed when the certification procedures set forth in this Section have been completed regardless of whether any State Party exercises the certification inspection rights described in paragraph 3 of this Section and Section IX of the Protocol on Inspection, provided that within 30 days of receipt of the notification of completion of the certification and recategorisation provided pursuant to paragraph 5 of this Section no State Party has notified all other States Parties that it considers that there is an ambiguity relating to the certification and recategorisation process. In the event of such an ambiguity being raised, such recategorisation shall not be deemed complete until the matter relating to the ambiguity is resolved.

5. The State Party conducting the certification shall notify all other States Parties in accordance with Section IX of the Protocol on Inspection of completion of the certification and recategorisation.

6. Certification shall be conducted within the area of application. States Parties belong-

ing to the same group of States Parties shall have the right to share locations for certification.

Section V. Procedures for information exchange and verification

All combat helicopters within the area of application shall be subject to information exchange in accordance with the provisions of the Protocol on Information Exchange and Verification, including inspection, in accordance with the Protocol on Inspection.

PROTOCOL ON NOTIFICATION AND EXCHANGE OF INFORMATION

The States Parties hereby agree on procedures and provisions regarding notification and exchange of information pursuant to Article XIII of the Treaty on Conventional Armed Forces in Europe of November 19, 1990, hereinafter referred to as the Treaty.

Section I. Information on the structure of each State Party's land forces and air and air defence aviation forces within the area of application

1. Each State Party shall provide to all other States Parties the following information about the structure of its land forces and air and air defence aviation forces within the area of application:

(A) the command organisation of its land forces, specifying the designation and subordination of all combat, combat support and combat service support formations and units at each level of command down to the level of brigade/regiment or equivalent level, including air defence formations and units subordinated at or below the military district or equivalent level. Independent units at the next level of command below the brigade/regiment level directly subordinate to formations above the brigade/regiment level (i.e., independent battalions) shall be identified, with the information indicating the formation or unit to which such units are subordinated; and

(B) the command organisation of its air and air defence aviation forces, specifying the designation and subordination of formations and units at each level of command down to wing/air regiment or equivalent level. Independent units at the next level of command below the wing/air regiment level directly subordinate to formations above the wing/air regiment level (i.e., independent squadrons) shall be identified, with the information indi-

cating the formation or unit to which such units are subordinated.

Section II. Information on the overall holdings in each category of conventional armaments and equipment limited by the Treaty

1. Each State Party shall provide to all other States Parties information on:

(A) overall numbers and numbers by type of its holdings in each category of conventional armaments and equipment limited by the Treaty; and

(B) overall numbers and numbers by type of its holdings of battle tanks, armoured combat vehicles and artillery limited by the Treaty in each of the areas described in Articles IV and V of the Treaty.

Section III. Information on the location, numbers and types of conventional armaments and equipment in service with the conventional armed forces of the States Parties

1. For each of its formations and units notified pursuant to Section I, paragraph 1, subparagraphs (A) and (B) of this Protocol, as well as separately located battalions/squadrons or equivalents subordinate to those formations and units, each State Party shall provide to all other States Parties the following information:

(A) the designation and peacetime location of its formations and units at which conventional armaments and equipment limited by the Treaty in the following categories are held, including headquarters, specifying the geographic name and coordinates:

(1) battle tanks;
(2) armoured combat vehicles;
(3) artillery;
(4) combat aircraft; and
(5) attack helicopters;

(B) the holdings of its formations and units notified pursuant to subparagraph (A) of this paragraph, giving numbers (by type in the case of formations and units at the level of division or equivalent and below) of the conventional armaments and equipment listed in subparagraph (A) of this paragraph, and of:

(1) combat support helicopters;
(2) unarmed transport helicopters;
(3) armoured vehicle launched bridges, specifying those in active units;
(4) armoured infantry fighting vehicle look-alikes;

(5) armoured personnel carrier look-alikes;

(6) primary trainer aircraft;

(7) reclassified combat-capable trainer aircraft; and

(8) Mi-24R and Mi-24K helicopters not subject to the numerical limitations set forth in Article IV, paragraph 1 and Article VI of the Treaty;[*]

(C) the designation and peacetime location of its formations and units, other than those notified pursuant to subparagraph (A) of this paragraph, at which the following categories of conventional armaments and equipment, as defined in Article II of the Treaty, specified in the Protocol on Existing Types, or enumerated in the Protocol on Aircraft Reclassification, are held, including headquarters, specifying the geographic name and coordinates:

(1) combat support helicopters;

(2) unarmed transport helicopters;

(3) armoured vehicle launched bridges;

(4) armoured infantry fighting vehicle look-alikes;

(5) armoured personnel carrier look-alikes;

(6) primary trainer aircraft;

(7) reclassified combat-capable trainer aircraft; and

(8) Mi-24R and Mi-24K helicopters not subject to the numerical limitations set forth in Article IV, paragraph 1 and Article VI of the Treaty;[**] and

(D) the holdings of its formations and units notified pursuant to subparagraph (C) of this paragraph giving numbers (by type in the case of formations and units at the level of division or equivalent and below) in each category specified above; and, in the case of armoured vehicle launched bridges, those which are in active units.

2. Each State Party shall provide to all other States Parties information on conventional armaments and equipment in service with its conventional armed forces but not held by its land forces or air or air defence aviation forces, specifying:

(A) the designation and peacetime location of its formations and units down to the level of brigade/regiment, wing/air regiment or equi-valent as well as units at the next level of command below the brigade/regiment, wing/air regiment level which are separately located or are independent (i.e., battalions/squadrons or equivalent) at which conventional armaments and equipment limited by the Treaty in the following categories are held, including headquarters, specifying the geographic name and coordinates:

(1) battle tanks;

(2) armoured combat vehicles;

(3) artillery;

(4) combat aircraft; and

(5) attack helicopters; and

(B) the holdings of its formations and units notified pursuant to subparagraph (A) of this paragraph, giving numbers (by type in the case of formations and units at the level of division or equivalent and below) of conventional armaments and equipment listed in subparagraph (A) of this paragraph, and of:

(1) combat support helicopters;

(2) unarmed transport helicopters;

(3) armoured vehicle launched bridges, specifying those in active units;

(4) armoured infantry fighting vehicle look-alikes;

(5) armoured personnel carrier look-alikes;

(6) primary trainer aircraft;

(7) reclassified combat-capable trainer aircraft; and

(8) Mi-24R and Mi-24K helicopters not subject to the numerical limitations set forth in Article IV, paragraph 1 and Article VI of the Treaty;[*]

3. Each State Party shall provide to all other States Parties the following information:

(A) the location of its designated permanent storage sites, specifying geographic name and coordinates, and the numbers and types of conventional armaments and equipment in the categories listed in paragraph 1, subparagraphs (A) and (B) of this Section held at such sites;

(B) the location of its military storage sites not organic to formations and units identified as objects of verification, independent repair and maintenance units, military training establishments and military airfields, specifying geographic name and coordinates, at which conventional armaments and equipment in the

---

[*] Pursuant to Section I, paragraph 3 of the Protocol on Helicopter Recategorisation.

[**] Pursuant to Section I, paragraph 3 of the Protocol on Helicopter Recategorisation.

---

[*] Pursuant to Section I, paragraph 3 of the Protocol on Helicopter Recategorisation.

categories listed in paragraph 1, subparagraphs (A) and (B) of this Section are held or routinely present, giving the holdings by type in each category at such locations; and

(C) the location of its sites at which the reduction of conventional armaments and equipment limited by the Treaty will be undertaken pursuant to the Protocol on Reduction, specifying the location by geographic name and coordinates, the holdings by type in each category of conventional armaments and equipment limited by the Treaty awaiting reduction at such locations, and indicating that it is a reduction site.

Section IV. Information on the location and numbers of battle tanks, armoured combat vehicles, artillery, combat aircraft and attack helicopters within the area of application but not in service with conventional armed forces

1. Each State Party shall provide information to all other States Parties on the location and numbers of its battle tanks, armoured combat vehicles, artillery, combat aircraft and attack helicopters within the area of application not in service with its conventional armed forces but of potential military significance.

(A) Accordingly, each State Party shall provide the following information:

(1) in respect of its battle tanks, artillery, combat aircraft and specialised attack helicopters, as well as armoured infantry fighting vehicles as specified in Article XII of the Treaty, held by organisations down to the independent or separately located battalion or equivalent level designed and structured to perform in peacetime internal security functions, the location, including geographic name and coordinates, of sites at which such armaments and equipment are held and the numbers and types of conventional armaments and equipment in these categories held by each such organisation;

(2) in respect of its armoured personnel carriers, heavy armament combat vehicles and multi-purpose attack helicopters held by organisations designed and structured to perform in peacetime internal security functions, the aggregate numbers in each category of such armaments and equipment in each administrative region or division;

(3) in respect of its battle tanks, armoured combat vehicles, artillery, combat aircraft and attack helicopters awaiting disposal having been decommissioned in accordance with the provisions of Article IX of the Treaty, the location, including geographic name and coordinates, of sites at which such armaments and equipment are held and the numbers and types at each site;

(4) in respect of its battle tanks, armoured combat vehicles, artillery, combat aircraft and attack helicopters, each State Party shall provide to all other States Parties, following entry into force of the Treaty and coincident with each annual exchange of information pursuant to Section VII, paragraph 1, subparagraph (C) of this Protocol, an identifiable location of sites at which there are normally more than a total of 15 battle tanks, armoured combat vehicles and pieces of artillery or more than five combat aircraft or more than 10 attack helicopters which are, pursuant to Article III, paragraph 1, subparagraph (E) of the Treaty, awaiting or are being refurbished for export or re-export and are temporarily retained within the area of application. Each State Party shall provide to all other States Parties, following entry into force of the Treaty and coincident with each annual exchange of information pursuant to Section VII, paragraph 1, subparagraph (C) of this Protocol, the numbers of such battle tanks, armoured combat vehicles, artillery, combat aircraft and attack helicopters. The States Parties shall, within the framework of the Joint Consultative Group, agree as to the form in which the information on the numbers shall be provided pursuant to this provision;

(5) in respect of its battle tanks and armoured combat vehicles which have been reduced and are awaiting conversion pursuant to Section VIII of the Protocol on Reduction, the location, including geographic name and coordinates, of each site at which such armaments and equipment are held and the numbers and types at each site; and

(6) in respect of its battle tanks, armoured combat vehicles, artillery, combat aircraft and attack helicopters used exclusively for the purpose of research and development pursuant to Article III, paragraph 1, subparagraph (B) of the Treaty, each State Party shall provide to all other States Parties following entry into force of the Treaty and coincident with each annual exchange of information pursuant to Section VII, paragraph 1, subparagraph (C) of this Protocol the aggregate numbers in each category of such conventional armaments and equipment.

Section V. Information on objects of verification and declared sites

1. Each State Party shall provide to all other States Parties information specifying its objects of verification, including the total number and the designation of each object of verification, and enumerating its declared sites, as defined in Section I of the Protocol on Inspection, providing the following information on each site:

(A) the site's designation and location, including geographic names and coordinates;

(B) the designation of all objects of verification, as specified in Section I, paragraph 1, subparagraph (J) of the Protocol on Inspection, at that site, it being understood that subordinate elements at the next level of command below the brigade/regiment or wing/air regiment level located in the vicinity of each other or of the headquarters immediately superior to such elements may be deemed as not separately located, if the distance between such separately located battalions/squadrons or equivalent or to their headquarters does not exceed 15 kilometres;

(C) the overall numbers by type of conventional armaments and equipment in each category specified in Section III of this Protocol held at that site and by each object of verification, as well as those belonging to any object of verification located at another declared site, specifying the designation of each such object of verification;

(D) in addition, for each such declared site, the number of conventional armaments and equipment not in service with its conventional armed forces, indicating those that are:

(1) battle tanks, armoured combat vehicles, artillery, combat aircraft and attack helicopters awaiting disposal having been decommissioned in accordance with the provisions of Article IX of the Treaty or reduced and awaiting conversion pursuant to the Protocol on Reduction; and

(2) battle tanks, armoured combat vehicles, artillery, combat aircraft and attack helicopters held by organisations designed and structured to perform in peacetime internal security functions;

(E) declared sites that hold battle tanks, armoured combat vehicles, artillery, combat aircraft or attack helicopters awaiting or being refurbished for export or re-export and temporarily retained within the area of application or used exclusively for research and development shall be identified as such, and the aggregate numbers in each category at that site shall be provided; and

(F) point(s) of entry/exit associated with each declared site, including geographic name and coordinates.

Section VI. Information on the location of sites from which conventional armaments and equipment have been withdrawn

1. Each State Party shall provide annually to all other States Parties, coincident with the annual exchange of information provided pursuant to Section VII, paragraph 1, subparagraph (C) of this Protocol, information about the locations of sites which have been notified previously as declared sites from which all conventional armaments and equipment in the categories listed in Section III, paragraph 1 of this Protocol have been withdrawn since the signature of the Treaty if such sites continue to be used by the conventional armed forces of that State Party. The locations of such sites shall be notified for three years following such withdrawal.

Section VII. Timetable for the provision of information in Sections I to V of this Protocol

1. Each State Party shall provide to all other States Parties the information pursuant to Sections I to V of this Protocol as follows:

(A) upon signature of the Treaty, with information effective as of that date; and, no later than 90 days after signature of the Treaty, each State Party shall provide to all other States Parties within the framework of the Joint Consultative Group any necessary corrections to its information reported pursuant to Sections III, IV and V of this Protocol. Such corrected information shall be deemed information provided at Treaty signature and valid as of that date;

(B) 30 days following entry into force of the Treaty, with information effective as of the date of entry into force;

(C) on the 15th day of December of the year in which the Treaty comes into force (unless entry into force occurs within 60 days of the 15th day of December), and on the 15th day of December of every year thereafter, with the information effective as of the first day of January of the following year; and

(D) following completion of the 40-month reduction period specified in Article VIII of the Treaty, with information effective as of that date.

Section VIII. Information on changes in organisational structures or force levels

1. Each State Party shall notify all other States Parties of:

(A) any permanent change in the organisational structure of its conventional armed forces within the area of application as notified pursuant to Section I of this Protocol at least 42 days in advance of that change; and

(B) any change of 10 percent or more in any one of the categories of conventional armaments and equipment limited by the Treaty assigned to any of its combat, combat support or combat service support formations and units down to the brigade/regiment, wing/air regiment, independent or separately located battalion/squadron or equivalent level as notified in Section III, paragraph 1, subparagraphs (A) and (B) and paragraph 2, subparagraphs (A) and (B) of this Protocol since the last annual exchange of information. Such notification shall be given no later than five days after such change occurs, indicating actual holdings after the notified change.

Section IX. Information on the entry into and removal from service with the conventional armed forces of a State Party of conventional armaments and equipment limited by the Treaty

1. Each State Party shall provide to all other States Parties following entry into force of the Treaty coincident with each annual exchange of information provided pursuant to Section VII, paragraph 1, subparagraph (C) of this Protocol:

(A) aggregate information on the numbers and types of conventional armaments and equipment limited by the Treaty which entered into service with its conventional armed forces within the area of application during the previous 12 months; and

(B) aggregate information on the numbers and types of conventional armaments and equipment limited by the Treaty which have been removed from service with its conventional armed forces within the area of application during the previous 12 months.

Section X. Information on entry into and exit from the area of application of conventional armaments and equipment limited by the Treaty in service with the conventional armed forces of the States Parties

1. Each State Party shall provide annually to all other States Parties following entry into force of the Treaty and coincident with each annual exchange of information provided pursuant to Section VII, paragraph 1, subparagraph (C) of this Protocol:

(A) aggregate information on the numbers and types of each category of conventional armaments and equipment limited by the Treaty in service with its conventional armed forces that have entered the area of application within the last 12 months and whether any of these armaments and equipment were organised in a formation or unit;

(B) aggregate information on the numbers and types of each category of conventional armaments and equipment limited by the Treaty in service with its conventional armed forces that have been removed from, and remain outside of, the area of application within the last 12 months and the last reported locations within the area of application of such conventional armaments and equipment; and

(C) conventional armaments and equipment limited by the Treaty in service with its conventional armed forces within the area of application which exit and re-enter the area of application, including for purposes such as training or military activities, within a seven-day period shall not be subject to the reporting provisions in this Section.

Section XI. Conventional armaments and equipment in transit through the area of application

1. The provisions of this Protocol shall not apply to conventional armaments and equipment that are in transit through the area of application from a location outside the area of application to a final destination outside the area of application. Conventional armaments and equipment in the categories specified in Section III of this Protocol which entered the area of application in transit shall be reported pursuant to this Protocol if they remain within the area of application for a period longer than seven days.

Section XII. Format for the provision of information

1. Each State Party shall provide to all other States Parties the information specified in this Protocol in accordance with the procedures set forth in Article XVII of the Treaty and the Annex on Format. In accordance with Article XVI, paragraph 5 of the Treaty, changes to the Annex on Format shall be deemed improvements to the viability and effectiveness of the

Treaty relating only to minor matters of a technical nature.

Section XIII. Other notifications pursuant to the Treaty

1. After signature of the Treaty and prior to its entry into force, the Joint Consultative Group shall develop a document relating to notifications required by the Treaty. Such document shall list all such notifications, specifying those that shall be made in accordance with Article XVII of the Treaty, and shall include appropriate formats, as necessary, for such notifications. In accordance with Article XVI, paragraph 5 of the Treaty, changes to this document, including any formats, shall be deemed to be improvements to the viability and effectiveness of the Treaty relating only to minor matters of a technical nature.

Annex on the Format for the Exchange of Information

1. Each State Party shall provide to all other States Parties information pursuant to the Protocol on Information Exchange, hereinafter referred to as the Protocol, in accordance with the formats specified in this Annex. The information in each data listing shall be provided in mechanically or electronically printed form and in one of the six official languages of the Conference on Security and Cooperation in Europe. In each table (column a), each data entry shall be assigned a sequential line number.

2. Each set of listings shall begin with a cover page showing the name of the State Party providing the listings, the language in which the listings are being provided, the date on which the listings are to be exchanged and the effective date of the information set forth in the listings.

(A) Each organisation shall be identified (column b) by a unique designator (i.e., formation or unit record number) which shall be used on subsequent listings with that organisation and for all subsequent information exchanges; its national designation (i.e., name) (column c); and, in the case of divisions, brigades/regiments, independent battalions, and wings/air regiments, independent squadrons or equivalent organisations, where appropriate, the formation or unit type (e.g., infantry, tank, artillery, fighter, bomber, supply); and

(B) for each organisation, the two levels of command within the area of application immediately superior to that organisation shall be designated (columns d and e).

Section I. Information on the structure of land forces and air and air defence aviation forces within the area of application

1. Pursuant to Section I of the Protocol, each State Party shall provide information on the command organisation of its land forces, including air defence formations and units subordinated at or below the military district or equivalent level, and air and air defence aviation forces in the form of two separate hierarchical data listings as set forth in Chart I.

2. The data listings shall be provided beginning at the highest level and proceeding through each level of command down to the level of brigade/regiment, independent battalion, and wing/air regiment, independent squadron or their equivalent. For example, a military district/army/corps would be followed by any subordinate independent regiments, independent battalions, depots, training establishments, then each subordinate division with its regiments/independent battalions. After all the subordinate organisations are listed, entries shall begin for the next military district/army/corps. An identical procedure shall be followed for air and air defence aviation forces.

(A) Each organisation shall be identified (column b) by a unique designator (i.e., formation or unit record number) which shall be used on subsequent listings with that organisation and for all subsequent information exchanges; its national designation (i.e., name) (column c); and, in the case of divisions, brigades/regiments, independent battalions, and wings/air regiments, independent squadrons or equivalent organisations, where appropriate, the formation or unit type (e.g., infantry, tank, artillery, fighter, bomber, supply); and

(B) for each organisation, the two levels of command within the area of application immediately superior to that organisation shall be designated (columns d and e).

CHART I. Command organisation of the land forces and air and air defence aviation forces of (State Party) valid as of (date)

Section II. Information on overall holdings of conventional armaments and equipment subject to numerical limitations pursuant to Articles IV and V of the Treaty

1. Pursuant to Section II of the Protocol, each State Party shall provide data on its overall holdings by type of battle tanks, armoured combat vehicles and artillery (Chart IIA) subject to the numerical limitations set forth in Articles IV and V of the Treaty (column b), and on its overall holdings by type of combat aircraft and attack helicopters (Chart IIB) subject to the numerical limitations set forth in Article IV of the Treaty (column b).

2. Data on armoured combat vehicles shall include the total numbers of heavy armament combat vehicles, armoured infantry fighting vehicles and armoured personnel carriers, and their number (column f/e) and type (column e/d) in each of these subcategories (column d/c).

3. In the case of battle tanks, armoured combat vehicles, artillery and armoured vehicle launched bridges, stored in accordance with Article X of the Treaty, the total of such equipment in designated permanent storage sites shall be specified (column g).

CHART IIA. Overall holdings of battle tanks, armoured combat vehicles and artillery subject to numerical limitation of (State Party) valid as of (date)

CHART IIB. Overall holdings of combat aircraft and attack helicopters subject to numerical limitation of (State Party) valid as of (date)

Section III. Information on the location, numbers and types of conventional armaments and equipment in service with the conventional armed forces

1. Each State Party shall provide a hierarchical data listing of all its land forces' and air and air defence aviation forces' organisations reported pursuant to Section III, paragraph 1 of the Protocol, formations and units reported pursuant to Section III, paragraph 2 of the Protocol and installations at which conventional armaments and equipment are held as specified in Section III, paragraph 3 of the Protocol.

2. For each organisation and installation, the information shall reflect:

(A) the formation or unit record number (column b) and designation of the organisation (column c) reported in Chart I. Separately located battalions/squadrons specified pursuant to paragraph 1 of this Section, formations and units reported pursuant to Section III, paragraph 2 of the Protocol and installations listed in accordance with Section III, paragraph 3 of the Protocol shall also be given a unique formation or unit record number (column b), and their national designation (i.e., name) (column c) shall be provided. Their position on the listing shall reflect their subordination with the exception of formations and units reported pursuant to Section III, paragraph 2 of the Protocol which shall be specified together at the conclusion of the listing:

(1) designated permanent storage sites shall be identified with the notation 'DPSS' following the national designation; and

(2) reduction sites shall be identified with the notation 'reduction' following the national designation;

(B) location (column d), including the geographic name and coordinates accurate to the nearest 10 seconds. For locations containing stationed forces, the host State Party shall also be included;

(C) for each level of command from the highest down to the division/air division level, the overall total of conventional armaments and equipment in each category (columns f to m/l). For example, the overall total held by a division would be the sum of the holdings of all its subordinate organisations; and

(D) for each level of command at the division level and below as specified in paragraph 1 of this Section, the number of conventional armaments and equipment by type under the headings specified in Charts IIIA and IIIB (columns f to m/l). In the armoured combat vehicle column in Chart IIIA (column g), the subcategories (i.e., armoured personnel carriers, armoured infantry fighting vehicles, heavy armament combat vehicles shall be presented separately. In the attack helicopter column (column k/i), the subcategories (i.e., specialised attack, multi-purpose attack) shall be presented separately. The column (l) labelled 'other' in Chart IIIB shall include battle tanks, armoured combat vehicles, artillery, armoured personnel carrier look-alikes, armoured infantry fighting vehicle look-alikes, and armoured vehicle launched bridges, if any, in service with the air and air defence aviation forces.

CHART IIIA. Information on the location, numbers and types of conventional armaments and equipment provided pursuant to section III pf the Protocal on information exchange of (state party) valid as of (date)

CHART IIIB. Information on the location, numbers and types of conventional armaments and equipment provided pursuant to section III pf the Protocal on information exchange of (state party) valid as of (date)

Section IV. Information on conventional armaments and equipment not in service with the conventional armed forces provided pursuant to Section IV of the Protocol on Information Exchange

1. Pursuant to Section IV of the Protocol, each State Party shall provide information on the location, number and type of its battle tanks, armoured combat vehicles, artillery, combat aircraft and attack helicopters within the area of application but not in service with its conventional armed forces.

2. For each location, the information shall reflect:

(A) the provision of Section IV of the Protocol pursuant to which the information is being provided (column b);

(B) the location (column c):

(1) in respect of conventional armaments and equipment reported pursuant to Section IV, paragraph 1, subparagraph (A), sub-sub-paragraphs (1), (3) and (5) of the Protocol, the geographic name and coordinates accurate to the nearest 10 seconds of sites containing such equipment; and

(2) in respect of conventional armaments and equipment reported pursuant to Section IV, paragraph 1, subparagraph (A), sub-sub-paragraph (2) of the Protocol, the national designation of the administrative region or division containing such equipment;

(C) in respect of conventional armaments and equipment reported pursuant to Section IV, paragraph 1, subparagraph (A), sub-subparagraphs (1) and (2) of the Protocol, the national-level designation of organisations holding the equipment specified (column c); and

(D) for each location, the number by type

under the headings specified in Chart IV (columns d to h), except as follows:

in respect of conventional armaments and equipment reported pursuant to Section IV, paragraph 1, subparagraph (A), sub-subparagraph (2) of the Protocol, only the numbers in each category shall be provided solely for the administrative region or division specified (column c).

CHART IV. Information on the location of conventional armaments and equipment provided pursuant to Section IV of the Protocol on Information Exchange of (State Party) valid as of (date)

Section V. Information on objects of verification and declared sites

1. Pursuant to Section V of the Protocol, each State Party shall provide a listing of its objects of verification and declared sites, as defined in Section I of the Protocol on Inspection. Declared sites (Chart V) shall be listed in alphabetical order.

2. Information about each declared site shall include:

(A) a unique designator (i.e., declared site record number) (column b) which shall be used with that site for all subsequent information exchanges;

(B) the site's name and location using geographic name and coordinates accurate to the nearest 10 seconds (column c). For locations containing objects of verification of stationed forces, the host State Party shall also be included;

(C) the point(s) of entry/exit associated with the declared site (column d);

(D) a unique sequential number and the designation and formation or unit record number of all objects of verification stationed at the declared site as specified in Section III of this Annex (column e). Unique sequential numbers shall be assigned such that the number assigned to the last object of verification appearing in the listing shall equal the State Party's total number of objects of verification; and

(E) the overall number of conventional armaments and equipment in each category specified in Section III of the Protocol held at the declared site and by each object of verification (columns f to p) and specifying, in addition:

(1) conventional armaments and equipment held in each category on the declared site belonging to an object of verification located at another declared site, specifying the designation and formation or unit record number of each such object of verification (column e); and

(2) conventional armaments and equipment not belonging to an object of verification shall be identified with the following notations immediately following/below each such entry in columns f to p:

(*a*) equipment held by organisations designed and structured to perform in peacetime internal security functions, with the notation 'security';

(*b*) decommissioned equipment, with the notation 'decommissioned';

(*c*) equipment awaiting or being refurbished for export or re-export, with the notation 'export';

(*d*) reduced equipment awaiting conversion, with the notation 'reduced'; and

(*e*) equipment used exclusively for research and development, with the notation 'research'.

CHART V: Information on objects of verification and declared sites of (State Party) valid as of (date)

3. Each State Party shall provide a listing of points of entry/exit (Chart VI). The listing shall assign a unique sequential numerical designator (column b) which shall be used to indicate the point(s) of entry/exit for each site provided pursuant to paragraph 2, subparagraph (C) of this Section. The location shall include the geographic name (column c) and coordinates accurate to the nearest 10 seconds (column d). The type(s) of transportation acceptable—'air', 'sea', 'ground'—for each point of entry/exit also shall be specified (column e).

CHART VI: Points of entry/exit (POE) of (State Party) valid as of (date)

Chart I. Command organisation of the land forces and air and air defence aviation forces of (State Party) valid as of (date)

Line Number	Formation or Unit Record	Designation of Formation or Unit	Subordination	
			1st Higher Echelon	2nd Higher Echelon
(a)	(b)	(c)	(d)	(e)

Chart IIA. Overall holdings of battle tanks, armoured combat vehicles and artillery subject to numerical limitation of (State Party) valid as of (date)

Line Number	Area	Category	Sub-Category	Type	Overall Number (including in DPSSs)	Number in DPSSs
(a)	(b)	(c)	(d)	(e)	(f)	(g)

Chart IIB. Overall holdings of combat aircraft and attack helicopters subject to numerical limitation of (State Party) valid as of (date)

Line Number	Category	Sub-Category	Type	Overall Number
(a)	(b)	(c)	(d)	(e)

Chart IIIA. Information on the location, numbers and types of conventional armaments and equipment provided pursuant to Section III of the Protocol on Information Exchange of (State Party) valid as of (Date)

Line Number	Formation or Unit Record Number	Designation of Formation or Unit	Peacetime Location	NOT USED	Battle Tanks	Armoured Combat Vehicles	APC & AIFV Look-Alikes	Artillery	AVLBs	Attack Helicopters	Combat Support Helicopters	Unarmed Transport Helicopters
(a)	(b)	(c)	(d)	(e)	(f)	(g)	(h)	(i)	(j)	(k)	(l)	(m)

Chart IIIB. Information on the location, numbers and types of conventional armaments and equipment provided pursuant to Section III of the Protocol on Information Exchange of (State Party) valid as of (date)

Line Number	Formation or Unit Record Number	Designation of Formation or Unit	Peacetime Location	NOT USED	Combat Aircraft	Reclassified CCT Aircraft	Primary Trainer Aircraft	Attack Helicopters	Combat Support Helicopters	Unarmed Transport Helicopters	Other
(a)	(b)	(c)	(d)	(e)	(f)	(g)	(h)	(i)	(j)	(k)	(l)

Chart IV. Information on the location of conventional armaments and equipment provided pursuant to Section IV of the Protocol on Information Exchange of (State Party) valid as of (date)

Line number	Protocol Reference	Location	Battle Tanks	Armoured Combat Vehicles	Artillery	Attack Heli-copters	Combat Aircraft
(a)	(b)	(c)	(d)	(e)	(f)	(g)	(h)

Chart V. Information on objects of verification and declared sites (State Party) valid as of (date)

Line Number	Declared Site Record Number	Location	Point of Entry/Exit	Object of Verifica-tion	Battle Tanks	Armoured Combat Vehicles	APC & AIFV Look-Alikes	Artillery	AVLBs	Attack Heli-copters	Combat Support Heli-copters	Unarmed Transport Heli-copters	Combat Aircraft	Reclass-ified CCT Aircraft	Primary Trainer Aircraft
(a)	(b)	(c)	(d)	(e)	(f)	(g)	(h)	(i)	(j)	(k)	(l)	(m)	(n)	(o)	(p)

Chart VI. Points of entry/exit (POE) of (State Party) valid as of (date)

Line number	POE Record Number	Name of POE	Location	Type(s)
(a)	(b)	(c)	(d)	(e)

PROTOCOL ON INSPECTION

The States Parties hereby agree on procedures and other provisions governing the conduct of inspections as provided for in Article XIV of the Treaty on Conventional Armed Forces in Europe of November 19, 1990, hereinafter referred to as the Treaty.

Section I. Definitions

1. For the purposes of the Treaty:

(A) The term 'inspected State Party' means a State Party on whose territory an inspection is carried out in compliance with Article XIV of the Treaty:

(1) in the case of inspection sites where only a stationing State Party's conventional armaments and equipment limited by the Treaty are present, such a stationing State Party shall exercise, in compliance with the provisions of this Protocol, the rights and obligations of the inspected State Party as set forth in this Protocol for the duration of the inspection within that inspection site where its conventional armaments and equipment limited by the Treaty are located; and

(2) in the case of inspection sites containing conventional armaments and equipment limited by the Treaty of more than one State Party, each such State Party shall exercise, in compliance with the provisions of this Protocol, each in respect of its own conventional armaments and equipment limited by the Treaty, the rights and obligations of the inspected State Party as set forth in this Protocol for the duration of the inspection within that inspection site where its conventional armaments and equipment limited by the Treaty are located.

(B) The term 'stationing State Party' means a State Party stationing conventional armaments and equipment in service with its conventional armed forces outside its own territory and within the area of application.

(C) The term 'host State Party' means a State Party receiving on its territory within the area of application conventional armaments and equipment in service with the conventional armed forces of another State Party stationed by that State Party.

(D) The term 'inspecting State Party' means a State Party which requests and is therefore responsible for carrying out an inspection.

(E) The term 'inspector' means an individual designated by one of the States Parties to carry out an inspection and who is included on that State Party's accepted list of inspectors in accordance with the provisions of Section III of this Protocol.

(F) The term 'transport crew member' means an individual who performs duties related to the operation of a transportation means and who is included on a State Party's accepted list of transport crew members in accordance with the provisions of Section III of this Protocol.

(G) The term 'inspection team' means a group of inspectors designated by an inspecting State Party to conduct a particular inspection.

(H) The term 'escort team' means a group of individuals assigned by an inspected State Party to accompany and to assist inspectors conducting a particular inspection, as well as to assume other responsibilities as set forth in this Protocol. In the case of inspection of a stationing State Party's conventional armaments and equipment limited by the Treaty, an escort team shall include individuals assigned by both the host and stationing States Parties, unless otherwise agreed between them.

(I) The term 'inspection site' means an area, location or facility where an inspection is carried out.

(J) The term 'object of verification' means:

(1) any formation or unit at the organisational level of brigade/regiment, wing/air regiment, independent battalion/artillery battalion, independent squadron or equivalent as well as any separately located battalion/squadron or equivalent unit at the next level of command below the brigade/regiment, wing/air regiment level holding conventional armaments and equipment limited by the Treaty at a location notified pursuant to Section III, paragraph 1, sub–paragraph (A) of the Protocol on Information Exchange;

(2) any designated permanent storage site, military storage site not organic to formations and units referred to in sub-subparagraph (l) of this subparagraph, independent repair or maintenance unit, military training establishment or military airfield at which conventional armaments and equipment limited by the Treaty are notified pursuant to Section III, paragraph 3, subparagraphs (A) and (B) of the Protocol on Information Exchange as being permanently or routinely present;

(3) a reduction site for conventional armaments and equipment limited by the Treaty as notified pursuant to Section III,

paragraph 3, subparagraph (C) of the Protocol on Information Exchange;

(4) in the case of units below the level of battalion holding conventional armaments and equipment limited by the Treaty that are directly subordinate to a unit or formation above the level of brigade/regiment or equivalent, that unit or formation to which the units below the level of battalion are subordinated shall be considered an object of verification, if it has no subordinate unit or formation at the level of brigade/regiment or equivalent; and

(5) a formation or unit holding conventional armaments and equipment subject to the Treaty, but not in service with the conventional armed forces of a State Party shall not be considered an object of verification.

(K) The term 'military airfield' means a permanent military complex, not otherwise containing an object of verification, at which the frequent operation, i.e., launch and recovery, of at least six combat aircraft or combat helicopters limited by the Treaty or subject to internal inspection is routinely performed.

(L) The term 'military training establishment' means a facility, not otherwise containing an object of verification, at which a military unit or subunit using at least 30 conventional armaments and equipment limited by the Treaty or more than 12 of any single category of conventional armaments and equipment limited by the Treaty is organised to train military personnel.

(M) The term 'military storage site' not organic to formations and units identified as objects of verification means any storage site, other than designated permanent storage sites or sites subordinate to organisations designed and structured for internal security purposes, holding conventional armaments and equipment limited by the Treaty without respect to organisational or operational status. Conventional armaments and equipment limited by the Treaty contained in such sites shall constitute a portion of the permitted holdings counted in active units pursuant to Article IV of the Treaty.

(N) The term 'declared site' means a facility or precisely delineated geographic location which contains one or more objects of verification. A declared site shall consist of all territory within its man-made or natural outer boundary or boundaries as well as associated territory comprising firing ranges, training areas, maintenance and storage areas, helicopter airfields and railroad loading facilities at which battle tanks, armoured combat vehicles, artillery, combat helicopters, combat aircraft, reclassified combat-capable trainer aircraft, armoured personnel carrier look-alikes, armoured infantry fighting vehicle look-alikes or armoured vehicle launched bridges are permanently or routinely present.

(O) The term 'specified area' means an area anywhere on the territory of a State Party within the area of application other than a site inspected pursuant to Section VII, IX or X of this Protocol within which a challenge inspection is conducted pursuant to Section VIII of this Protocol. A specified area shall not exceed 65 square kilometres. No straight line between any two points in that area shall exceed 16 kilometres.

(P) The term 'sensitive point' means any equipment, structure or location which has been designated to be sensitive by the inspected State Party or the State Party exercising the rights and obligations of the inspected State Party through the escort team and to which access or overflight may be delayed, limited or refused.

(Q) The term 'point of entry/exit' means a point designated by a State Party on whose territory an inspection is to be carried out, through which inspection teams and transport crews arrive on the territory of that State Party and through which they depart from the territory of that State Party.

(R) The term 'in-country period' means the total time spent continuously on the territory of the State Party where an inspection is carried out by an inspection team for inspections pursuant to Sections VII and VIII of this Protocol from arrival of the inspection team at the point of entry/exit until the return of the inspection team to a point of entry/exit after completion of that inspection team's last inspection.

(S) The term 'baseline validation period' means, for the purpose of calculating inspection quotas, the specified time period consisting of the first 120 days following entry into force of the Treaty.

(T) The term 'reduction period' means, for the purpose of calculating inspection quotas, the specified time period consisting of the three years following the 120-day baseline validation period.

(U) The term 'residual level validation period' means, for the purpose of calculating inspection quotas, the specified time period consisting of the 120 days following the three-year reduction period.

(V) The term 'residual period' means, for the purpose of calculating inspection quotas, the specified time period following the 120-day residual level validation period for the duration of the Treaty.

(W) The term 'passive declared site inspection quota' means the total number of inspections of objects of verification pursuant to Section VII of this Protocol that each State Party shall be obliged to receive within a specified time period at inspection sites where its objects of verification are located.

(X) The term 'passive challenge inspection quota' means the maximum number of challenge inspections within specified areas pursuant to Section VIII of this Protocol that each State Party with territory within the area of application shall be obliged to receive within a specified time period.

(Y) The term 'active inspection quota' means the total number of inspections pursuant to Sections VII and VIII of this Protocol that each State Party shall be entitled to conduct within a specified time period.

(Z) The term 'certification site' means a clearly designated location where the certification of recategorised multi-purpose attack helicopters and reclassified combat-capable trainer aircraft in accordance with the Protocol on Helicopter Recategorisation and the Protocol on Aircraft Reclassification takes place.

(AA) The term 'calendar reporting period' means a period of time defined in days during which the intended reduction of the planned number of items of conventional armaments and equipment limited by the Treaty in accordance with Article VIII of the Treaty is to be carried out.

Section II. General obligations

1. For the purpose of ensuring verification of compliance with the provisions of the Treaty, each State Party shall facilitate inspections pursuant to this Protocol.

2. In the case of conventional armaments and equipment in service with the conventional armed forces of a State Party stationed in the area of application outside national territory, the host State Party and the stationing State Party shall, in fulfilment of their respective responsibilities, cooperatively ensure compliance with the relevant provisions of this Protocol. The stationing State Party shall be fully responsible for compliance with the Treaty obligations in respect of its conventional armaments and equipment in service with its conventional armed forces stationed in the territory of the host State Party.

3. The escort team shall be placed under the responsibility of the inspected State Party:

(A) in the case of inspection sites at which only a stationing State Party's conventional armaments and equipment limited by the Treaty are present and are under this State Party's command, the escort team shall be placed under the responsibility of a representative of the stationing State Party for the duration of the inspection within that inspection site where the stationing State Party's conventional armaments and equipment limited by the Treaty are located; and

(B) in the case of inspection sites containing conventional armaments and equipment limited by the Treaty of both the host State Party and the stationing State Party, the escort team shall be composed of representatives from both States Parties when conventional armaments and equipment limited by the Treaty of the stationing State Party are actually inspected. During the inspection within that inspection site, the host State Party shall exercise the rights and obligations of the inspected State Party with the exception of those rights and obligations related to the inspection of the conventional armaments and equipment limited by the Treaty of the stationing State Party, which will be exercised by this stationing State Party.

4. If an inspection team requests access to a structure or premises utilised by another State Party by agreement with the inspected State Party, such other State Party shall, in cooperation with the inspected State Party and to the extent consistent with the agreement on utilisation, exercise the rights and obligations set forth in this Protocol with respect to inspections involving equipment or materiel of the State Party utilising the structure or premises.

5. Structures or premises utilised by another State Party by agreement with the inspected State Party shall be subject to inspection only when that other State Party's representative is on the escort team.

6. Inspection teams and sub-teams shall be under the control and responsibility of the inspecting State Party.

7. No more than one inspection team conducting an inspection pursuant to Section VII or VIII of this Protocol may be present at the same time at any one inspection site.

8. Subject to the other provisions of this Protocol, the inspecting State Party shall decide for how long each inspection team will

stay on the territory of the State Party where an inspection is to be carried out and at how many and at which inspection sites it will conduct inspections during the in-country period.

9. Travel expenses of an inspection team to the point of entry/exit prior to conducting an inspection and from the point of entry/exit after completion of the last inspection shall be borne by the inspecting State Party.

10. Each State Party shall be obliged to receive a number of inspections pursuant to Section VII or VIII of this Protocol not to exceed its passive declared site inspection quota for each specified time period: a 120-day baseline validation period, a three-year reduction period, a 120-day residual level validation period and a residual period for the duration of the Treaty. The passive declared site inspection quota shall be determined for each specified period as a percentage of that State Party's objects of verification, excluding reduction sites and certification sites, located within the area of application of the Treaty:

(A) during the first 120 days after entry into force of the Treaty, the passive declared site inspection quota shall be equal to 20 percent of a State Party's objects of verification notified pursuant to Section V of the Protocol on Information Exchange;

(B) during each year of the reduction period, after completion of the initial 120-day period, the passive declared site inspection quota shall be equal to 10 percent of a State Party's objects of verification notified pursuant to Section V of the Protocol on Information Exchange;

(C) during the first 120 days after completion of the three-year reduction period, the passive declared site inspection quota shall be equal to 20 percent of a State Party's objects of verification notified pursuant to Section V of the Protocol on Information Exchange; and

(D) each year, commencing after completion of the 120-day residual level validation period, for the duration of the Treaty, the passive declared site inspection quota shall be equal to 15 percent of a State Party's objects of verification notified pursuant to Section V of the Protocol on Information Exchange.

11. Each State Party with territory within the area of application shall be obliged to accept challenge inspections as follows:

(A) during the baseline validation period, during each year of the reduction period and during the residual level validation period, up to 15 percent of the number of inspections of declared sites which that State Party is obliged to receive on its territory of its own objects of verification as well as of objects of verification belonging to stationing States Parties; and

(B) during each year of the residual period, up to 23 percent of the number of inspections of declared sites which that State Party is obliged to receive on its territory of its own objects of verification and of objects of verification belonging to stationing States Parties.

12. Notwithstanding any other limitations in this Section, each State Party shall be obliged to accept a minimum of one inspection each year of its objects of verification pursuant to Section VII of this Protocol, and each State Party with territory within the area of application shall be obliged to accept a minimum of one inspection each year within a specified area pursuant to Section VIII of this Protocol.

13. Inspection pursuant to Section VII of this Protocol of one object of verification at an inspection site shall count as one inspection against the passive declared site inspection quota of that State Party whose object of verification is inspected.

14. The proportion of inspections pursuant to Section VII of this Protocol on the territory of a host State Party within a specified time period used to inspect objects of verification belonging to a stationing State Party shall be no greater than the proportion which that stationing State Party's objects of verification constitute of the total number of objects of verification located on the territory of that host State Party.

15. The number of inspections pursuant to Section VII of this Protocol of objects of verification within a specified time period on any State Party's territory shall be calculated as a percentage of the total number of objects of verification present on that State Party's territory.

16. Inspection pursuant to Section VIII of this Protocol within one specified area shall count as one inspection against the passive challenge inspection quota and one inspection against the passive declared site inspection quota of the State Party on whose territory the inspection is conducted.

17. Unless otherwise agreed between the escort team and the inspection team, an inspection team's in-country period shall, up to a total of 10 days, not exceed the total number of hours calculated according to the following formula:

(A) 48 hours for the first inspection of an object of verification or within a specified area; plus

(B) 36 hours for each sequential inspection of an object of verification or within a specified area.

18. Subject to the limitations in paragraph 17 of this Section, an inspection team conducting an inspection pursuant to Section VII or VIII of this Protocol shall spend no more than 48 hours at a declared site and no more than 24 hours in inspection within a specified area.

19. The inspected State Party shall ensure that the inspection team travels to a sequential inspection site by the most expeditious means available. If the time between completion of one inspection and arrival of the inspection team at a sequential inspection site exceeds nine hours, or if the time between completion of the last inspection conducted by an inspection team on the territory of the State Party where an inspection is carried out and the arrival of that inspection team at the point of entry/exit exceeds nine hours, such excess time shall not count against that inspection team's in-country period.

20. Each State Party shall be obliged to accept on its territory within the area of application simultaneously no more than either two inspection teams conducting inspections pursuant to Section VII or VIII of this Protocol or a number of inspection teams conducting inspections pursuant to Section VII or Section VIII of this Protocol equal to two percent of the total number of objects of verification that are to be inspected during a specified time period on the territory of that State Party, whichever number is greater.

21. Each State Party shall be obliged to accept simultaneously no more than either two inspection teams conducting inspections of its conventional armed forces pursuant to Section VII or Section VIII of this Protocol or a number of inspection teams conducting inspections of its conventional armed forces pursuant to Section VII or Section VIII of this Protocol equal to two percent of the total number of its objects of verification that are to be inspected during a specified time period, whichever number is greater.

22. Notwithstanding the provisions of paragraphs 20 and 21 of this Section, each State Party with military districts specified in Articles IV and V of the Treaty shall be obliged to accept on its territory within the area of application simultaneously no more than two inspection teams conducting inspections pursuant to Sections VII and VIII of this Protocol within any one of those military districts.

23. No State Party shall be obliged to accept inspections pursuant to Section VII or VIII of this Protocol representing more than 50 percent of its passive declared site inspection quota in a calendar year from the same State Party.

24. Each State Party shall have the right to conduct inspections within the area of application on the territory of other States Parties. However, no State Party shall conduct more than five inspections annually pursuant to Sections VII and VIII of this Protocol of another State Party belonging to the same group of States Parties. Any such inspections shall count against the passive declared site inspection quota of the State Party being inspected. It shall otherwise be the responsibility solely of each group of States Parties to determine the allocation of inspections for each State Party within its group of States Parties. Each State Party shall notify to all other States Parties its active inspection quota:

(A) for the baseline validation period, no later than 120 days after signature of the Treaty;

(B) for the first year of the reduction period, no later than 60 days after entry into force of the Treaty; and

(C) for each subsequent year of the reduction period, for the residual level validation period and for each year of the residual period, no later than the 15th day of January preceding each such specified time period.

Section III. Pre-inspection requirements

1. Inspections conducted pursuant to the Treaty shall be carried out by inspectors designated in accordance with paragraphs 3 to 7 of this Section.

2. Inspectors shall be nationals of the inspecting State Party or other States Parties.

3. Within 90 days after signature of the Treaty, each State Party shall provide to all other States Parties a list of its proposed inspectors and a list of its proposed transport crew members, containing the full names of inspectors and transport crew members, their gender, date of birth, place of birth and passport number. No list of proposed inspectors provided by a State Party shall contain at any time more than 400 individuals, and no list of proposed transport crew members provided by

a State Party shall contain at any time more than 600 individuals.

4. Each State Party shall review the lists of inspectors and transport crew members provided to it by other States Parties and, within 30 days after receipt of each list, shall provide notification to the State Party providing that list of any individual whose name it wishes to be deleted from that list.

5. Subject to paragraph 7 of this Section, inspectors and transport crew members for whom deletion has not been requested within the time interval specified in paragraph 4 of this Section shall be considered as accepted for the purposes of issuing visas and any other documents in accordance with paragraph 8 of this Section.

6. Each State Party shall have the right to amend its lists within one month after entry into force of the Treaty. Thereafter, each State Party may once every six months propose additions to or deletions from its lists of inspectors and transport crew members, provided that such amended lists do not exceed the numbers specified in paragraph 3 of this Section. Proposed additions shall be reviewed in accordance with paragraphs 4 and 5 of this Section.

7. A State Party may request, without right of refusal, deletion of any individual it wishes from lists of inspectors and transport crew members provided by any other State Party.

8. The State Party on whose territory an inspection is conducted shall provide to the inspectors and transport crew members accepted in accordance with paragraph 5 of this Section visas and any other documents as required to ensure that these inspectors and transport crew members may enter and remain in the territory of that State Party for the purpose of carrying out inspection activities in accordance with the provisions of this Protocol. Such visas and any other necessary documents shall be provided either:

(A) within 30 days after the acceptance of the lists or subsequent changes in such lists, in which case the visa shall be valid for a period of no less than 24 months; or

(B) within one hour after the arrival of the inspection team and transport crew members at the point of entry/exit, in which case the visa shall be valid for the duration of their inspection activities.

9. Within 90 days after signature of the Treaty, each State Party shall provide notification to all other States Parties of the standing diplomatic clearance number for the transportation means of that State Party transporting inspectors and equipment necessary for an inspection into and out of the territory of the State Party in which such an inspection is conducted. Routings to and from the designated point(s) of entry/exit shall be along established international airways or other routes that are agreed upon by the States Parties concerned as the basis for such diplomatic clearance. Inspectors may use commercial flights for travel to those points of entry/exit that are served by airlines. The provisions of this paragraph relating to diplomatic clearance numbers shall not apply to such flights.

10. Each State Party shall indicate in the notification provided pursuant to Section V of the Protocol on Information Exchange a point or points of entry/exit in respect of each declared site with its objects of verification. Such points of entry/exit may be ground border crossing points, airports or seaports which must have the capacity to receive the transportation means of the inspecting State Party. At least one airport shall be notified as a point of entry/exit in respect of each declared site. The location of any point of entry/exit notified as associated with a declared site shall be such as to allow access to that declared site within the time specified in Section VII, paragraph 8 of this Protocol.

11. Each State Party shall have the right to change the point or points of entry/exit to its territory by notifying all other States Parties no less than 90 days before such a change becomes effective.

12. Within 90 days after signature of the Treaty, each State Party shall provide notification to all other States Parties of the official language or languages of the Conference on Security and Cooperation in Europe to be used by inspection teams conducting inspections of its conventional armed forces.

Section IV. Notification of intent to inspect

1. The inspecting State Party shall notify the inspected State Party of its intention to carry out an inspection provided for in Article XIV of the Treaty. In the case of inspection of stationed conventional armed forces, the inspecting State Party shall simultaneously notify the host and stationing States Parties. In the case of inspection of certification or reduction procedures carried out by a stationing State Party, the inspecting State Party shall simultaneously notify the host and stationing States Parties.

2. For inspections conducted pursuant to Sections VII and VIII of this Protocol, such notifications shall be made in accordance with Article XVII of the Treaty no less than 36 hours in advance of the estimated time of arrival of the inspection team at the point of entry/exit on the territory of the State Party where an inspection is to be carried out and shall include:

(A) the point of entry/exit to be used;

(B) the estimated time of arrival at the point of entry/exit;

(C) the means of arrival at the point of entry/exit;

(D) a statement of whether the first inspection shall be conducted pursuant to Section VII or VIII of this Protocol and whether the inspection will be conducted on foot, by cross-country vehicle, by helicopter or by any combination of these;

(E) the time interval between the arrival at the point of entry/exit and the designation of the first inspection site;

(F) the language to be used by the inspection team, which shall be a language designated in accordance with Section III, paragraph 12 of this Protocol;

(G) the language to be used for the inspection report prepared in accordance with Section XII of this Protocol;

(H) the full names of inspectors and transport crew members, their gender, date of birth, place of birth and passport number; and

(I) the likely number of sequential inspections.

3. For inspections conducted pursuant to Section IX and X of this Protocol, such notifications shall be made in accordance with Article XVII of the Treaty no less than 96 hours in advance of the estimated time of arrival of the inspection team at the designated point of entry/exit on the territory of the State Party where an inspection is to be carried out and shall include:

(A) the point of entry/exit to be used;

(B) the estimated time of arrival at the point of entry/exit;

(C) the means of arrival at the point of entry/exit;

(D) for each inspection at a reduction or certification site, reference to the notification provided pursuant to Section IX, paragraph 3 or Section X, paragraph 5 of this Protocol;

(E) the language to be used by the inspection team, which shall be a language designated in accordance with Section III, para-

graph 12 of this Protocol;

(F) the language to be used for the inspection report prepared in accordance with Section XII of this Protocol; and

(G) the full names of inspectors and transport crew members, their gender, date of birth, place of birth and passport number.

4. The States Parties notified pursuant to paragraph 1 of this Section shall acknowledge in accordance with Article XVII of the Treaty receipt of notification within three hours. Subject to the provisions set forth in this Section, the inspection team shall be permitted to arrive at the point of entry/exit at the estimated time of arrival notified pursuant to paragraph 2, subparagraph (B) or paragraph 3, subparagraph (B) of this Section.

5. An inspected State Party receiving a notification of intent to inspect shall immediately upon its receipt send copies of such notification to all other States Parties in accordance with Article XVII of the Treaty.

6. If the State Party on whose territory an inspection is to be carried out is unable to allow the entry of the inspection team at the estimated time of arrival, the inspection team shall be permitted to enter the territory of that State Party within two hours before or after the notified estimated time of arrival. In such a case, the State Party on whose territory an inspection is to be carried out shall notify the inspecting State Party of the new time of arrival no later than 24 hours following the issuance of the original notification.

7. If the inspection team finds itself delayed more than two hours beyond the notified estimated time of arrival or beyond the new time of arrival communicated pursuant to paragraph 6 of this Section, the inspecting State Party shall inform the States Parties notified pursuant to paragraph 1 of this Section of:

(A) a new estimated time of arrival, which in no case shall be more than six hours beyond the initial estimated time of arrival or beyond the new time of arrival communicated pursuant to paragraph 6 of this Section; and

(B) if the inspecting State Party desires, a new time interval between arrival at the point of entry/exit and the designation of the first inspection site.

8. In the event non-commercial flights are used to transport the inspection team to the point of entry/exit, no less than 10 hours before the planned time of entry into the air space of the State Party on whose territory the inspection is to be carried out, the inspecting

State Party shall provide that State Party with a flight plan in accordance with Article XVII of the Treaty. The flight plan shall be filed in accordance with the procedures of the International Civil Aviation Organisation applicable to civil aircraft. The inspecting State Party shall include in the remarks section of each flight plan the standing diplomatic clearance number and the notation: 'CFE inspection aircraft. Priority clearance processing required'.

9. No more than three hours following the receipt of a flight plan that has been filed in accordance with paragraph 8 of this Section, the State Party on whose territory an inspection is to be carried out shall ensure that the flight plan is approved so that the inspection team may arrive at the point of entry/exit at the estimated time of arrival.

Section V. Procedures upon arrival at point of entry/exit

1. The escort team shall meet the inspection team and transport crew members at the point of entry/exit upon their arrival.

2. A State Party which utilises structures or premises by agreement with the inspected State Party will designate a liaison officer to the escort team who will be available as needed at the point of entry/exit to accompany the inspection team at any time as agreed with the escort team.

3. Times of arrival at and return to a point of entry/exit shall be agreed and recorded by both the inspection team and the escort team.

4. The State Party on whose territory an inspection is to be carried out shall ensure that luggage, equipment and supplies of the inspection team are exempt from all customs duties and are expeditiously processed at the point of entry/exit.

5. Equipment and supplies that the inspecting State Party brings into the territory of the State Party where an inspection is to be carried out shall be subject to examination each time they are brought into that territory. This examination shall be completed prior to the departure of the inspection team from the point of entry/exit to the inspection site. Such equipment and supplies shall be examined by the escort team in the presence of the inspection team members.

6. If the escort team determines upon examination that an item of equipment or supplies brought by inspectors is capable of performing functions inconsistent with the inspection requirements of this Protocol or does not meet the requirements set forth in Section VI, para-

graph 15 of this Protocol, then the escort team shall have the right to deny permission to use that item and to impound it at the point of entry/exit. The inspecting State Party shall remove such impounded equipment or supplies from the territory of the State Party where an inspection is to be carried out at the earliest opportunity at its own discretion, but no later than the time when the inspection team which brought that impounded equipment or supplies leaves the country.

7. If a State Party has not participated during examination of equipment of an inspection team at the point of entry/exit, that State Party shall be entitled to exercise the rights of the escort team pursuant to paragraphs 5 and 6 of this Section prior to inspection at a declared site at which its conventional armed forces are present or of a structure or premises it utilises by agreement with the inspected State Party.

8. Throughout the period in which the inspection team and transport crew remain on the territory of the State Party where the inspection site is located, the inspected State Party shall provide or arrange for the provision of meals, lodging, work space, transportation and, as necessary, medical care or any other emergency assistance.

9. The State Party on whose territory an inspection is carried out shall provide accommodation, security protection, servicing and fuel for the transportation means of the inspecting State Party at the point of entry/exit.

Section VI. General rules for conducting inspections

1. An inspection team may include inspectors from States Parties other than the inspecting State Party.

2. For inspections conducted in accordance with Sections VII, VIII, IX and X of this Protocol, an inspection team shall consist of up to nine inspectors and may divide itself into up to three sub-teams. In the case of simultaneous inspections on the territory of States Parties that do not have military districts specified in Articles IV and V of the Treaty or within a single military district of a State Party with such military districts, only one inspection team may divide itself at the inspection site into three sub-teams, the others into two sub-teams.

3. Inspectors and escort team members shall wear some clear identification of their respective roles.

4. An inspector shall be deemed to have assumed his or her duties upon arrival at the

point of entry/exit on the territory of the State Party where an inspection is to be carried out and shall be deemed to have ceased performing those duties after leaving the territory of that State Party through the point of entry/exit.

5. The number of transport crew members shall not exceed 10.

6. Without prejudice to their privileges and immunities, inspectors and transport crew members shall respect the laws and regulations of the State Party on whose territory an inspection is carried out and shall not interfere in the internal affairs of that State Party. Inspectors and transport crew members shall also respect regulations at an inspection site, including safety and administrative procedures. In the event that the inspected State Party determines that an inspector or transport crew member has violated such laws and regulations or other conditions governing the inspection activities set forth in this Protocol, it shall so notify the inspecting State Party, which upon the request of the inspected State Party shall immediately delete the name of the individual from the list of inspectors or transport crew members. If the individual is on the territory of the State Party where an inspection is carried out, the inspecting State Party shall promptly remove that individual from that territory.

7. The inspected State Party shall be responsible for ensuring the safety of the inspection team and transport crew members from the time they arrive at the point of entry/exit until the time they leave the point of entry/exit to depart the territory of that State Party.

8. The escort team shall assist the inspection team in carrying out its functions. At its discretion, the escort team may exercise its right to accompany the inspection team from the time it enters the territory of the State Party where an inspection is to be carried out until the time it departs that territory.

9. The inspecting State Party shall ensure that the inspection team and each sub-team have the necessary linguistic ability to communicate freely with the escort team in the language notified in accordance with Section IV, paragraph 2, subparagraph (F) and paragraph 3, subparagraph (E) of this Protocol. The inspected State Party shall ensure that the escort team has the necessary linguistic ability to communicate freely in this language with the inspection team and each sub-team. Inspectors and members of the escort team may also communicate in other languages.

10. No information obtained during inspections shall be publicly disclosed without the express consent of the inspecting State Party.

11. Throughout their presence on the territory of the State Party where an inspection is to be carried out, inspectors shall have the right to communicate with the embassy or consulate of the inspecting State Party located on that territory, using appropriate telecommunications means provided by the inspected State Party. The inspected State Party shall also provide means of communication between the sub-teams of an inspection team.

12. The inspected State Party shall transport the inspection team to, from and between inspection sites by a means and route selected by the inspected State Party. The inspecting State Party may request a variation in the selected route. The inspected State Party shall if possible grant such a request. Whenever mutually agreed, the inspecting State Party will be permitted to use its own land vehicles.

13. If an emergency arises that necessitates travel of inspectors from an inspection site to a point of entry/exit or to the embassy or consulate of the inspecting State Party on the territory of the State Party where an inspection is carried out, the inspection team shall so notify the escort team, which shall promptly arrange such travel, and if necessary, shall provide appropriate means of transportation.

14. The inspected State Party shall provide for use by the inspection team at the inspection site an administrative area for storage of equipment and supplies, report writing, rest breaks and meals.

15. The inspection team shall be permitted to bring such documents as needed to conduct the inspection, in particular its own maps and charts. Inspectors shall be permitted to bring and use portable passive night vision devices, binoculars, video and still cameras, dictaphones, tape measures, flashlights, magnetic compasses and lap-top computers. The inspectors shall be permitted to use other equipment, subject to the approval of the inspected State Party. Throughout the in-country period, the escort team shall have the right to observe the equipment brought by inspectors, but shall not interfere with the use of equipment that has been approved by the escort team in accordance with Section V, paragraphs 5 to 7 of this Protocol.

16. In the case of an inspection conducted pursuant to Sections VII or VIII of this Protocol, the inspection team shall specify on each occasion it designates the inspection site to be

inspected whether the inspection will be conducted on foot, by cross-country vehicle, by helicopter or by any combination of these. Unless otherwise agreed, the inspected State Party shall provide and operate the appropriate cross-country vehicles at the inspection site.

17. Whenever possible, subject to the safety requirements and flight regulations of the inspected State Party and subject to the provisions of paragraphs 18 to 21 of this Section, the inspection team shall have the right to conduct helicopter overflights of the inspection site, using a helicopter provided and operated by the inspected State Party, during inspections conducted pursuant to Sections VII and VIII of this Protocol.

18. The inspected State Party shall not be obliged to provide a helicopter at any inspection site that is less than 20 square kilometres in area.

19. The inspected State Party shall have the right to delay, limit or refuse helicopter overflights above sensitive points, but the presence of sensitive points shall not prevent helicopter overflight of the remaining areas of the inspection site. Photography of or above sensitive points during helicopter overflights shall be permitted only with the approval of the escort team.

20. The duration of such helicopter overflights at an inspection site shall not exceed a cumulative total of one hour, unless otherwise agreed between the inspection team and the escort team.

21. Any helicopter provided by the inspected State Party shall be large enough to carry at least two members of the inspection team and at least one member of the escort team. Inspectors shall be allowed to take and use on overflights of the inspection site any of the equipment specified in paragraph 15 of this Section. The inspection team shall advise the escort team during inspection flights whenever it intends to take photographs. A helicopter shall afford the inspectors a constant and unobstructed view of the ground.

22. In discharging their functions, inspectors shall not interfere directly with ongoing activities at the inspection site and shall avoid unnecessarily hampering or delaying operations at the inspection site or taking actions affecting safe operation.

23. Except as provided for in paragraphs 24 to 29 of this Section, during an inspection of an object of verification or within a specified area, inspectors shall be permitted access, entry and unobstructed inspection:

(A) in the case of a specified area, within the entire specified area; or

(B) in the case of an object of verification, within the entire territory of the declared site except within those areas delineated on the site diagram as belonging exclusively to another object of verification which the inspection team has not designated for inspection.

24. During an inspection of an object of verification or within a specified area pursuant to Section VII or VIII of this Protocol and subject to the provisions of paragraph 25 of this Section, inspectors shall have the right, within the areas cited in paragraph 23 of this Section, to enter any location, structure or area within a structure in which battle tanks, armoured combat vehicles, artillery, combat helicopters, combat aircraft, reclassified combat-capable trainer aircraft, armoured personnel carrier look-alikes, armoured infantry fighting vehicle look-alikes or armoured vehicle launched bridges are permanently or routinely present. Inspectors shall not have the right to enter other structures or areas within structures the entry points to which are physically accessible only by personnel doors not exceeding two metres in width and to which access is denied by the escort team.

25. During an inspection of an object of verification or within a specified area pursuant to Section VII or VIII of this Protocol, inspectors shall have the right to look into a hardened aircraft shelter to confirm visually whether any battle tanks, armoured combat vehicles, artillery, combat helicopters, combat aircraft, reclassified combat-capable trainer aircraft, armoured personnel carrier look-alikes, armoured infantry fighting vehicle look-alikes or armoured vehicle launched bridges are present and, if so, their number and type, model or version. Notwithstanding the provisions of paragraph 24 of this Section, inspectors shall enter the interior of such hardened aircraft shelters only with the approval of the escort team. If such approval is denied and if the inspectors so request, any battle tanks, armoured combat vehicles, artillery, combat helicopters, combat aircraft, reclassified combat-capable trainer aircraft, armoured personnel carrier look-alikes, armoured infantry fighting vehicle look-alikes or armoured vehicle launched bridges in such hardened aircraft shelters shall be displayed outside.

26. During an inspection of an object of verification or within a specified area pursuant to Section VII or VIII of this Protocol, except

as provided in paragraphs 27 to 33 of this Section, inspectors shall have the right to have access to conventional armaments and equipment only in so far as is necessary to confirm visually their number and type, model or version.

27. The inspected State Party shall have the right to shroud individual sensitive items of equipment.

28. The escort team shall have the right to deny access to sensitive points, the number and extent of which should be as limited as possible, to shrouded objects and to containers any dimension (width, height, length or diameter) of which is less than two metres. Whenever a sensitive point is designated, or shrouded objects or containers are present, the escort team shall declare whether the sensitive point, shrouded object or container holds any battle tanks, armoured combat vehicles, artillery, combat helicopters, combat aircraft, reclassified combat-capable trainer aircraft, armoured personnel carrier look-alikes, armoured infantry fighting vehicle look-alikes or armoured vehicle launched bridges and, if so, their number and type, model or version.

29. If the escort team declares that a sensitive point, shrouded object or container does contain any of the conventional armaments and equipment specified in paragraph 28 of this section, then the escort team shall display or declare such conventional armaments and equipment to the inspection team and shall take steps to satisfy the inspection team that no more than the declared number of such conventional armaments and equipment are present.

30. If, during an inspection of an object of verification or within a specified area pursuant to Section VII or VIII of this Protocol, a helicopter of a type that is or has been on the multi-purpose attack helicopter list in the Protocol on Existing Types is present at an inspection site and is declared by the escort team to be a combat support helicopter, or if an Mi-24R or Mi-24K helicopter is present at an inspection site and is declared by the escort team to be limited pursuant to Section I, paragraph 3 of the Protocol on Helicopter Recategorisation, such a helicopter shall be subject to internal inspection in accordance with Section IX, paragraphs 4 to 6 of this Protocol.

31. If, during an inspection of an object of verification or within a specified area pursuant to Section VII or VIII of this Protocol, an aircraft of a specific model or version of combat-capable trainer aircraft listed in Section II of the Protocol on Aircraft Reclassification is present at an inspection site and is declared by the escort team to have been certified as unarmed in accordance with the Protocol on Aircraft Reclassification, such an aircraft shall be subject to internal inspection in accordance with Section IX, paragraphs 4 and 5 of this Protocol.

32. If, during an inspection of an object of verification or within a specified area pursuant to Section VII or Section VIII of this Protocol, an armoured vehicle declared by the escort team to be an armoured personnel carrier look-alike or an armoured infantry fighting vehicle look-alike is present at an inspection site, the inspection team shall have the right to determine that such vehicle cannot permit the transport of a combat infantry squad. Inspectors shall have the right to require the doors and/or hatches of the vehicle to be opened so that the interior can be visually inspected from outside the vehicle. Sensitive equipment in or on the vehicle may be shrouded.

33. If, during an inspection of an object of verification or within a specified area pursuant to Section VII or Section VIII of this Protocol, items of equipment declared by the escort team to have been reduced in accordance with the provisions in the Protocol on Reduction are present at an inspection site, the inspection team shall have the right to inspect such items of equipment to confirm that they have been reduced in accordance with the procedures specified in Sections III to XII of the Protocol on Reduction.

34. Inspectors shall have the right to take photographs, including video, for the purpose of recording the presence of conventional armaments and equipment subject to the Treaty, including within designated permanent storage sites, or other storage sites containing more than 50 such conventional armaments and equipment. Still cameras will be limited to 35-mm cameras and to cameras capable of producing instantly developed photographic prints. The inspection team shall advise the escort team in advance whether it plans to take photographs. The escort team shall cooperate with the inspection team's taking of photographs.

35. Photography of sensitive points shall be permitted only with the approval of the escort team.

36. Except as provided for in paragraph 38 of this Section, photography of interiors of structures other than storage sites specified in

paragraph 34 of this Section shall be permitted only with the approval of the escort team.

37. Inspectors shall have the right to take measurements to resolve ambiguities that might arise during inspections. Such measurements recorded during inspections shall be confirmed by a member of the inspection team and a member of the escort team immediately after they are taken. Such confirmed data shall be included in the inspection report.

38. States Parties shall, whenever possible, resolve during an inspection any ambiguities that arise regarding factual information. Whenever inspectors request the escort team to clarify such an ambiguity, the escort team shall promptly provide the inspection team with clarifications. If inspectors decide to document an unresolved ambiguity with photographs, the escort team shall, subject to the provision in paragraph 35 of this Section, cooperate with the inspection team's taking of appropriate photographs using a camera capable of producing instantly developed photographic prints. If an ambiguity cannot be resolved during the inspection, then the question, relevant clarifications and any pertinent photographs shall be included in the inspection report in accordance with Section XII of this Protocol.

39. For inspections conducted pursuant to Sections VII and VIII of this Protocol, the inspection shall be deemed to have been completed once the inspection report has been signed and countersigned.

40. No later than completion of an inspection at a declared site or within a specified area, the inspection team shall inform the escort team whether the inspection team intends to conduct a sequential inspection. If the inspection team intends to conduct a sequential inspection, the inspection team shall designate at that time the next inspection site. In such cases, subject to the provisions in Section VII, paragraphs 6 and 17 and Section VIII, paragraph 6, subparagraph (A) of this Protocol, the inspected State Party shall ensure that the inspection team arrives at the sequential inspection site as soon as possible after completion of the previous inspection. If the inspection team does not intend to conduct a sequential inspection, then the provisions in paragraphs 42 and 43 of this Section shall apply.

41. An inspection team shall have the right to conduct a sequential inspection, subject to the provisions of Sections VII and VIII of this Protocol, on the territory of the State Party on which that inspection team has conducted the preceding inspection:

(A) at any declared site associated with the same point of entry/exit as the preceding inspection site or the same point of entry/exit at which the inspection team arrived; or

(B) within any specified area for which the point of entry/exit at which the inspection team arrived is the nearest point of entry/exit notified pursuant to Section V of the Protocol on Information Exchange; or

(C) at any location within 200 kilometres of the preceding inspection site within the same military district; or

(D) at the location which the inspected State Party claims, pursuant to Section VII, paragraph 11, subparagraph (A) of this Protocol, is the temporary location of battle tanks, armoured combat vehicles, artillery, combat helicopters, combat aircraft or armoured vehicle launched bridges which were absent during inspection of an object of verification at the preceding inspection site, if such conventional armaments and equipment constitute more than 15 percent of the number of such conventional armaments and equipment notified in the most recent notification pursuant to the Protocol on Information Exchange; or

(E) at the declared site which the inspected State Party claims, pursuant to Section VII, paragraph 11, subparagraph (B) of this Protocol, is the site of origin for battle tanks, armoured combat vehicles, artillery, combat helicopters, combat aircraft or armoured vehicle launched bridges at the preceding inspection site which are in excess of the number provided in the most recent notification pursuant to the Protocol on Information Exchange as being present at that preceding inspection site, if such conventional armaments and equipment exceed by 15 percent the number of such conventional armaments and equipment so notified.

42. After completion of an inspection at a declared site or within a specified area, if no sequential inspection has been declared, then the inspection team shall be transported to the appropriate point of entry/exit as soon as possible and shall depart the territory of the State Party where the inspection was carried out within 24 hours.

43. The inspection team shall leave the territory of the State Party where it has been conducting inspections from the same point of entry/exit at which it entered, unless otherwise agreed. If an inspection team chooses to proceed to a point of entry/exit on the territory of

another State Party for the purpose of conducting inspections, it shall have the right to do so provided that the inspecting State Party has provided the necessary notification in accordance with Section IV, paragraph 1 of this Protocol.

Section VII. Declared site inspection

1. Inspection of a declared site pursuant to this Protocol shall not be refused. Such inspections may be delayed only in cases of force majeure or in accordance with Section II, paragraphs 7 and 20 to 22 of this Protocol.

2. Except as provided for in paragraph 3 of this Section, an inspection team shall arrive on the territory of the State Party where an inspection is to be carried out through a point of entry/exit associated under Section V of the Protocol on Information Exchange with the declared site it plans to designate as the first inspection site pursuant to paragraph 7 of this Section.

3. If an inspecting State Party desires to use a ground border crossing point or seaport as a point of entry/exit and the inspected State Party has not previously notified a ground border crossing point or seaport as a point of entry/exit pursuant to Section V of the Protocol on Information Exchange as associated with the declared site the inspecting State Party desires to designate as the first inspection site pursuant to paragraph 7 of this Section, the inspecting State Party shall indicate in the notification provided pursuant to Section IV, paragraph 2 of this Protocol the desired ground border crossing point or seaport as point of entry/exit. The inspected State Party shall indicate in its acknowledgement of receipt of notification, as provided for in Section IV, paragraph 4 of this Protocol, whether this point of entry/exit is acceptable or not. In the latter case, the inspected State Party shall notify the inspecting State Party of another point of entry/exit which shall be as near as possible to the desired point of entry/exit and which may be an airport notified pursuant to Section V of the Protocol on Information Exchange, a seaport or a ground border crossing point through which the inspection team and transport crew members may arrive on its territory.

4. If an inspecting State Party notifies its desire to use a ground border crossing point or seaport as a point of entry/exit pursuant to paragraph 3 of this Section, it shall determine prior to such notification that there is reasonable certainty that its inspection team can reach the first declared site where the State Party desires to carry out an inspection within the time specified in paragraph 8 of this Section using ground transportation means.

5. If an inspection team and transport crew arrive pursuant to paragraph 3 of this Section on the territory of the State Party on which an inspection is to be carried out through a point of entry/exit other than a point of entry/exit that was notified pursuant to Section V of the Protocol on Information Exchange as being associated with the declared site it desires to designate as the first inspection site, the inspected State Party shall facilitate access to this declared site as expeditiously as possible, but shall be permitted to exceed, if necessary, the time limit specified in paragraph 8 of this Section.

6. The inspected State Party shall have the right to utilise up to six hours after designation of a declared site to prepare for the arrival of the inspection team at that site.

7. At the number of hours after arrival at the point of entry/exit notified pursuant to Section IV, paragraph 2, subparagraph (E) of this Protocol, which shall be no less than one hour and no more than 16 hours after arrival at the point of entry/exit, the inspection team shall designate the first declared site to be inspected.

8. The inspected State Party shall ensure that the inspection team travels to the first declared site by the most expeditious means available and arrives as soon as possible but no later than nine hours after the designation of the site to be inspected, unless otherwise agreed between the inspection team and the escort team, or unless the inspection site is located in mountainous terrain or terrain to which access is difficult. In such case, the inspection team shall be transported to the inspection site no later than 15 hours after designation of that inspection site. Travel time in excess of nine hours shall not count against that inspection team's in-country period.

9. Immediately upon arrival at the declared site, the inspection team shall be escorted to a briefing facility where it shall be provided with a diagram of the declared site, unless such a diagram has been provided in a previous exchange of site diagrams. The declared site diagram, provided upon arrival at the declared site, shall contain an accurate depiction of the:

(A) geographic coordinates of a point within the inspection site, to the nearest 10 seconds, with indication of that point and of true north;

(B) scale used in the site diagram;

(C) perimeter of the declared site;

(D) precisely delineated boundaries of those areas belonging exclusively to each object of verification, indicating the formation or unit record number of each object of verification to which each such area belongs and including those separately located areas where battle tanks, armoured combat vehicles, artillery, combat aircraft, combat helicopters, reclassified combat-capable trainer aircraft, armoured personnel carrier look-alikes, armoured infantry fighting vehicle look-alikes or armoured vehicle launched bridges belonging to each object of verification are permanently assigned;

(E) major buildings and roads on the declared site;

(F) entrances to the declared site; and

(G) location of an administrative area for the inspection team provided in accordance with Section VI, paragraph 14 of this Protocol.

10. Within one-half hour after receiving the diagram of the declared site, the inspection team shall designate the object of verification to be inspected. The inspection team shall then be given a pre-inspection briefing which shall last no more than one hour and shall include the following elements:

(A) safety and administrative procedures at the inspection site;

(B) modalities of transportation and communication for inspectors at the inspection site; and

(C) holdings and locations at the inspection site, including within the common areas of the declared site, of battle tanks, armoured combat vehicles, artillery, combat aircraft, combat helicopters, reclassified combat-capable trainer aircraft, armoured personnel carrier look-alikes, armoured infantry fighting vehicle look-alikes and armoured vehicle launched bridges, including those belonging to separately located subordinate elements belonging to the same object of verification to be inspected.

11. The pre-inspection briefing shall include an explanation of any differences between the numbers of battle tanks, armoured combat vehicles, artillery, combat aircraft, combat helicopters or armoured vehicle launched bridges present at the inspection site and the corresponding numbers provided in the most recent notification pursuant to the Protocol on Information Exchange, in accordance with the following provisions:

(A) if the numbers of such conventional armaments and equipment present at the inspection site are less than the numbers provided in that most recent notification, such explanation shall include the temporary location of such conventional armaments and equipment; and

(B) if the numbers of such armaments and equipment present at the inspection site exceed the numbers provided in that most recent notification, such explanation shall include specific information on the origin, departure times from origin, time of arrival and projected stay at the inspection site of such additional conventional armaments and equipment.

12. When an inspection team designates an object of verification to be inspected, the inspection team shall have the right, as part of the same inspection of that object of verification, to inspect all territory delineated on the site diagram as belonging to that object of verification, including those separately located areas on the territory of the same State Party where conventional armaments and equipment belonging to that object of verification are permanently assigned.

13. The inspection of one object of verification at a declared site shall permit the inspection team access, entry and unobstructed inspection within the entire territory of the declared site except within those areas delineated on the site diagram as belonging exclusively to another object of verification which the inspection team has not designated for inspection. During such inspections, the provisions of Section VI of this Protocol shall apply.

14. If the escort team informs the inspection team that battle tanks, armoured combat vehicles, artillery, combat helicopters, combat aircraft, reclassified combat-capable trainer aircraft, armoured personnel carrier look-alikes, armoured infantry fighting vehicle look-alikes or armoured vehicle launched bridges that have been notified as being held by one object of verification at a declared site are present within an area delineated on the site diagram as belonging exclusively to another object of verification, then the escort team shall ensure that the inspection team, as part of the same inspection, has access to such conventional armaments and equipment.

15. If conventional armaments and equipment limited by the Treaty or armoured vehi-

cle launched bridges are present within areas of a declared site not delineated on the site diagram as belonging exclusively to one object of verification, the escort team shall inform the inspection team to which object of verification such conventional armaments and equipment belong.

16. Each State Party shall be obliged to account for the aggregate total of any category of conventional armaments and equipment limited by the Treaty notified pursuant to Section III of the Protocol on Information Exchange, at the organisational level above brigade/regiment or equivalent, if such an accounting is requested by another State Party.

17. If, during an inspection at a declared site, the inspection team decides to conduct at the same declared site an inspection of an object of verification that had not been previously designated, the inspection team shall have the right to commence such inspection within three hours of that designation. In such case, the inspection team shall be given a briefing on the object of verification designated for the next inspection in accordance with paragraphs 10 and 11 of this Section.

Section VIII. Challenge inspection within specified areas

1. Each State Party shall have the right to conduct challenge inspections within specified areas in accordance with this Protocol.

2. If the inspecting State Party intends to conduct a challenge inspection within a specified area as the first inspection after arrival at a point of entry/exit:

(A) it shall include in its notification pursuant to Section IV of this Protocol the designated point of entry/exit nearest to or within that specified area capable of receiving the inspecting State Party's chosen means of transportation; and

(B) at the number of hours after arrival at the point of entry/exit notified pursuant to Section IV, paragraph 2, subparagraph (E) of this Protocol, which shall be no less than one hour and no more than 16 hours after arrival at the point of entry/exit, the inspection team shall designate the first specified area it wishes to inspect. Whenever a specified area is designated, the inspection team shall, as part of its inspection request, provide to the escort team a geographic description delineating the outer boundaries of that area. The inspection team shall have the right, as part of that request, to identify any structure or facility it

wishes to inspect.

3. The State Party on whose territory a challenge inspection is requested shall, immediately upon receiving a designation of a specified area, inform other States Parties which utilise structures or premises by agreement with the inspected State Party of that specified area, including its geographical description delineating the outer boundaries.

4. The inspected State Party shall have the right to refuse challenge inspections within specified areas.

5. The inspected State Party shall inform the inspection team within two hours after the designation of a specified area whether the inspection request will be granted.

6. If access to a specified area is granted:

(A) the inspected State Party shall have the right to use up to six hours after it accepts the inspection to prepare for the arrival of the inspection team at the specified area;

(B) the inspected State Party shall ensure that the inspection team travels to the first specified area by the most expeditious means available and arrives as soon as possible after the designation of the site to be inspected, but no later than nine hours from the time such an inspection is accepted, unless otherwise agreed between the inspection team and the escort team, or unless the inspection site is located in mountainous terrain or terrain to which access is difficult. In such case, the inspection team shall be transported to the inspection site no later than 15 hours after such an inspection is accepted. Travel time in excess of nine hours shall not count against that inspection team's in-country period; and

(C) the provisions of Section VI of this Protocol shall apply. Within such specified area the escort team may delay access to or overflight of particular parts of that specified area. If the delay exceeds more than four hours the inspection team shall have the right to cancel the inspection. The period of delay shall not count against the in-country period or the maximum time allowed within a specified area.

7. If an inspection team requests access to a structure or premises which another State Party utilises by agreement with the inspected State Party, the inspected State Party shall immediately inform that State Party of such a request. The escort team shall inform the inspection team that the other State Party, by agreement with the inspected State Party,

shall, in cooperation with the inspected State Party and to the extent consistent with the agreement on utilisation, exercise the rights and obligations set forth in this Protocol with respect to inspections involving equipment or materiel of the State Party utilising the structure or premises.

8. If the inspected State Party so wishes, the inspection team may be briefed on arrival at the specified area. This briefing is to last no more than one hour. Safety procedures and administrative arrangements may also be covered in this briefing.

9. If access to a specified area is denied:

(A) the inspected State Party or the State Party exercising the rights and obligations of the inspected State Party shall provide all reasonable assurance that the specified area does not contain conventional armaments and equipment limited by the Treaty. If such armaments and equipment are present and assigned to organisations designed and structured to perform in peacetime internal security functions in the area defined in Article V of the Treaty, the inspected State Party or the State Party exercising the rights and obligations of the inspected State Party shall allow visual confirmation of their presence, unless precluded from so doing by force majeure, in which case visual confirmation shall be allowed as soon as practicable; and

(B) no inspection quota shall be counted, and the time between the designation of the specified area and its subsequent refusal shall not count against the in-country period. The inspection team shall have the right to designate another specified area or declared site for inspection or to declare the inspection concluded.

Section IX. Inspection of certification

1. Each State Party shall have the right to inspect, without right of refusal, the certification of recategorised multi-purpose attack helicopters and reclassified combat-capable trainer aircraft in accordance with the provisions of this Section, the Protocol on Helicopter Recategorisation and the Protocol on Aircraft Reclassification. Such inspections shall not count against the quotas established in Section II of this Protocol. Inspection teams conducting such inspections may be composed of representatives of different States Parties. The inspected State Party shall not be obliged to accept more than one inspection team at a time at each certification site.

2. In conducting an inspection of certification in accordance with this Section, an inspection team shall have the right to spend up to two days at a certification site, unless otherwise agreed.

3. No less than 15 days before the certification of recategorised multi-purpose attack helicopters or reclassified combat-capable trainer aircraft, the State Party conducting the certification shall provide to all other States Parties notification of:

(A) the site at which the certification is to take place, including geographic coordinates;

(B) the scheduled dates of the certification process;

(C) the estimated number and type, model or version of helicopters or aircraft to be certified;

(D) the manufacturer's serial number for each helicopter or aircraft;

(E) the unit or location to which the helicopters or aircraft were previously assigned;

(F) the unit or location to which the certified helicopters or aircraft will be assigned in the future;

(G) the point of entry/exit to be used by an inspection team; and

(H) the date and time by which an inspection team shall arrive at the point of entry/exit in order to inspect the certification.

4. Inspectors shall have the right to enter and inspect visually the helicopter or aircraft cockpit and interior to include checking the manufacturer's serial number, without right of refusal on the part of the State Party conducting the certification.

5. If requested by the inspection team, the escort team shall remove, without right of refusal, any access panels covering the position from which components and wiring were removed in accordance with the provisions of the Protocol on Helicopter Recategorisation or the Protocol on Aircraft Reclassification.

6. Inspectors shall have the right to request and observe, with the right of refusal on the part of the State Party conducting the certification, the activation of any weapon system component in multi-purpose attack helicopters being certified or declared to have been recategorised.

7. At the conclusion of each inspection of certification, the inspection team shall complete an inspection report in accordance with the provisions of Section XII of this Protocol.

8. Upon completion of an inspection at a certification site, the inspection team shall

have the right to depart the territory of the inspected State Party or to conduct a sequential inspection at another certification site or at a reduction site if the appropriate notification has been provided by the inspection team in accordance with Section IV, paragraph 3 of this Protocol. The inspection team shall notify the escort team of its intended departure from the certification site and, if appropriate, of its intention to proceed to another certification site or to a reduction site at least 24 hours before the intended departure time.

9. Within seven days after completion of the certification, the State Party responsible for the certification shall notify all other States Parties of the completion of the certification. Such notification shall specify the number, types, models or versions and manufacturer's serial numbers of certified helicopters or aircraft, the certification site involved, the actual dates of the certification, and the units or locations to which the recategorised helicopters or reclassified aircraft will be assigned.

Section X. Inspection of reduction

1. Each State Party shall have the right to conduct inspections, without the right of refusal by the inspected State Party, of the process of reduction carried out pursuant to Sections I to VIII and X to XII of the Protocol on Reduction in accordance with the provisions of this Section. Such inspections shall not count against the quotas established in Section II of this Protocol. Inspection teams conducting such inspections may be composed of representatives of different States Parties. The inspected State Party shall not be obliged to accept more than one inspection team at a time at each reduction site.

2. The inspected State Party shall have the right to organise and implement the process of reduction subject only to the provisions set forth in Article VIII of the Treaty and in the Protocol on Reduction. Inspections of the process of reduction shall be conducted in a manner that does not interfere with the ongoing activities at the reduction site or unnecessarily hamper, delay or complicate the implementation of the process of reduction.

3. If a reduction site notified pursuant to Section III of the Protocol on Information Exchange is used by more than one State Party, inspections of the reduction process shall be conducted in accordance with schedules of such use provided by each State Party using the reduction site.

4. Each State Party that intends to reduce conventional armaments and equipment limited by the Treaty shall notify all other States Parties which conventional armaments and equipment are to be reduced at each reduction site during a calendar reporting period. Each such calendar reporting period shall have a duration of no more than 90 days and no less than 30 days. This provision shall apply whenever reduction is carried out at a reduction site, without regard to whether the reduction process is to be carried out on a continuous or intermittent basis.

5. No less than 15 days before the initiation of reduction for a calendar reporting period, the State Party intending to implement reduction procedures shall provide to all other States Parties the calendar reporting period notification. Such notification shall include the designation of the reduction site with geographic coordinates, the scheduled date for initiation of reduction and the scheduled date for completion of the reduction of conventional armaments and equipment identified for reduction during the calendar reporting period. In addition, the notification shall identify:

(A) the estimated number and type of conventional armaments and equipment to be reduced;

(B) the object or objects of verification from which the items to be reduced have been withdrawn;

(C) the reduction procedures to be used, pursuant to Sections III to VIII and Sections X to XII of the Protocol on Reduction, for each type of conventional armaments and equipment to be reduced;

(D) the point of entry/exit to be used by an inspection team conducting an inspection of reduction notified for that calendar reporting period; and

(E) the date and time by which an inspection team must arrive at the point of entry/exit in order to inspect the conventional armaments and equipment before the initiation of their reduction.

6. Except as specified in paragraph 11 of this Section, an inspection team shall have the right to arrive at or depart from a reduction site at any time during the calendar reporting period, including three days beyond the end of a notified calendar reporting period. In addition, the inspection team shall have the right to remain at the reduction site throughout one or more calendar reporting periods provided that these periods are not separated by more than three days. Throughout the period that

the inspection team remains at the reduction site, it shall have the right to observe all the reduction procedures carried out in accordance with the Protocol on Reduction.

7. In accordance with the provisions established in this Section, the inspection team shall have the right to freely record factory serial numbers from the conventional armaments and equipment to be reduced or to place special marks on such equipment before reduction and to record subsequently such numbers or marks at the completion of the reduction process. Parts and elements of reduced conventional armaments and equipment as specified in Section II, paragraphs 1 and 2 of the Protocol on Reduction or, in the case of conversion, the vehicles converted for non-military purposes shall be available for inspection for at least three days after the end of the notified calendar reporting period, unless inspection of those reduced elements has been completed earlier.

8. The State Party engaged in the process of reducing conventional armaments and equipment limited by the Treaty shall establish at each reduction site a working register in which it shall record the factory serial numbers of each item undergoing reduction as well as the dates on which the reduction procedures were initiated and completed. This register shall also include aggregate data for each calendar reporting period. The register shall be made available to the inspection team for the period of inspection.

9. At the conclusion of each inspection of the reduction process, the inspection team shall complete a standardised report which shall be signed by the inspection team leader and a representative of the inspected State Party. The provisions of Section XII of this Protocol shall apply.

10. Upon completion of an inspection at a reduction site, the inspection team shall have the right to depart the territory of the inspected State Party or to conduct a sequential inspection at another reduction site or at a certification site if the appropriate notification has been provided in accordance with Section IV, paragraph 3 of this Protocol. The inspection team shall notify the escort team of its intended departure from the reduction site and, if appropriate, of its intention to proceed to another reduction site or to a certification site at least 24 hours before the intended departure time.

11. Each State Party shall be obliged to accept up to 10 inspections each year to vali-date the completion of conversion of conventional armaments and equipment into vehicles for non-military purposes pursuant to Section VIII of the Protocol on Reduction. Such inspections shall be conducted in accordance with the provisions of this Section with the following exceptions:

(A) the notification pursuant to paragraph 5, subparagraph (E) of this Section shall identify only the date and time by which an inspection team must arrive at the point of entry/exit in order to inspect the items of equipment at the completion of their conversion into vehicles for non-military purposes; and

(B) the inspection team shall have the right to arrive at or depart from the reduction site only during the three days beyond the end of the notified completion date of conversion.

12. Within seven days after the completion of the process of reduction for a calendar reporting period, the State Party responsible for reductions shall notify all other States Parties of the completion of reduction for that period. Such notification shall specify the number and types of conventional armaments and equipment reduced, the reduction site involved, the reduction procedures employed and the actual dates of the initiation and completion of the reduction process for that calendar reporting period. For conventional armaments and equipment reduced pursuant to Sections X, XI and XII of the Protocol on Reduction, the notification shall also specify the location at which such conventional armaments and equipment will be permanently located. For conventional armaments and equipment reduced pursuant to Section VIII of the Protocol on Reduction, the notification shall specify the reduction site at which final conversion will be carried out or the storage site to which each item designated for conversion will be transferred.

Section XI. Cancellation of inspections

1. If an inspection team finds itself unable to arrive at the point of entry/exit within six hours after the initial estimated time of arrival or after the new time of arrival communicated pursuant to Section IV, paragraph 6 of this Protocol, the inspecting State Party shall so inform the States Parties notified pursuant to Section IV, paragraph 1 of this Protocol. In such a case the notification of intent to inspect shall lapse and the inspection shall be cancelled.

2. In the case of delay, due to circumstances

beyond the control of the inspecting State Party, occurring after the inspection team has arrived at the point of entry/exit and which has prevented the inspection team from arriving at the first designated inspection site within the time specified in Section VII, paragraph 8 or Section VIII, paragraph 6, subparagraph (B) of this Protocol, the inspecting State Party shall have the right to cancel the inspection. If an inspection is cancelled under such circumstances, it shall not be counted against any quotas provided for in the Treaty.

Section XII. Inspection reports

1. In order to complete the inspection carried out in accordance with Section VII, VIII, IX or X of this Protocol, and before leaving the inspection site:

(A) the inspection team shall provide the escort team with a written report; and

(B) the escort team shall have the right to include its written comments in the inspection report and shall countersign the report within one hour after having received the report from the inspection team, unless an extension has been agreed between the inspection team and the escort team.

2. The report shall be signed by the inspection team leader and receipt acknowledged in writing by the leader of the escort team.

3. The report shall be factual and standardised. Formats for each type of inspection shall be agreed by the Joint Consultative Group prior to entry into force of the Treaty, taking into account paragraphs 4 and 5 of this Section.

4. Reports of inspections conducted pursuant to Sections VII and VIII of this Protocol shall include:

(A) the inspection site;

(B) the date and time of arrival of the inspection team at the inspection site;

(C) the date and time of departure of the inspection team from the inspection site; and

(D) the number and type, model or version of any battle tanks, armoured combat vehicles, artillery, combat aircraft, combat helicopters, reclassified combat-capable trainer aircraft, armoured personnel carrier look-alikes, armoured infantry fighting vehicle look-alikes or armoured vehicle launched bridges that were observed during the inspection, including, if appropriate, an indication of the object of verification to which they belonged.

5. Reports of inspections conducted pursuant to Sections IX and X of this Protocol shall include:

(A) the reduction or certification site at which the reduction or certification procedures were carried out;

(B) the dates the inspection team was present at the site;

(C) the number and type, model or version of conventional armaments and equipment for which the reduction or certification procedures were observed;

(D) a list of any serial numbers recorded during the inspections;

(E) in the case of reductions, the particular reduction procedures applied or observed; and

(F) in the case of reductions, if an inspection team was present at the reduction site throughout the calendar reporting period, the actual dates on which the reduction procedures were initiated and completed.

6. The inspection report shall be written in the official language of the Conference on Security and Cooperation in Europe designated by the inspecting State Party in accordance with Section IV, paragraph 2, subparagraph (G) and paragraph 3, subparagraph (F) of this Protocol.

7. The inspecting State Party and the inspected State Party shall each retain one copy of the report. At the discretion of either State Party, the inspection report may be forwarded to other States Parties and, as a rule, made available to the Joint Consultative Group.

8. The stationing State Party shall in particular:

(A) have the right to include written comments related to the inspection of its stationed conventional armed forces; and

(B) retain one copy of the inspection report in the case of inspection of its stationed conventional armed forces.

Section XIII. Privileges and immunities of inspectors and transport crew members

1. To exercise their functions effectively, for the purpose of implementing the Treaty and not for their personal benefit, inspectors and transport crew members shall be accorded the privileges and immunities enjoyed by diplomatic agents pursuant to Article 29; Article 30, paragraph 2; Article 31, paragraphs 1, 2 and 3; and Articles 34 and 35 of the Vienna Convention on Diplomatic Relations of April 18, 1961.

2. In addition, inspectors and transport crew members shall be accorded the privileges enjoyed by diplomatic agents pursuant to Article 36, paragraph 1, subparagraph (b) of the Vienna Convention on Diplomatic Relations of April 18, 1961. They shall not be permitted to bring into the territory of the State Party where the inspection is to be carried out articles the import or export of which is prohibited by law or controlled by quarantine regulations of that State Party.

3. The transportation means of the inspection team shall be inviolable, except as otherwise provided for in the Treaty.

4. The inspecting State Party may waive the immunity from jurisdiction of any of its inspectors or transport crew members in those cases when it is of the opinion that immunity would impede the course of justice and that it can be waived without prejudice to the implementation of the provisions of the Treaty. The immunity of inspectors and transport crew members who are not nationals of the inspecting State Party may be waived only by the States Parties of which those inspectors are nationals. Waiver must always be express.

5. The privileges and immunities provided for in this Section shall be accorded to inspectors and transport crew members:

(A) while transiting through the territory of any State Party for the purpose of conducting an inspection on the territory of another State Party;

(B) throughout their presence on the territory of the State Party where the inspection is carried out; and

(C) thereafter with respect to acts previously performed in the exercise of official functions as an inspector or transport crew member.

6. If the inspected State Party considers that an inspector or transport crew member has abused his or her privileges and immunities, then the provisions set forth in Section VI, paragraph 6 of this Protocol shall apply. At the request of any of the States Parties concerned, consultations shall be held between them in order to prevent a repetition of such an abuse.

PROTOCOL ON THE JOINT CONSULTATIVE GROUP

The States Parties hereby agree upon procedures and other provisions relating to the Joint Consultative Group established by Article XVI of the Treaty on Conventional Armed Forces in Europe of November 19, 1990, hereinafter referred to as the Treaty.

1. The Joint Consultative Group shall be composed of representatives designated by each State Party. Alternates, advisers and experts of a State Party may take part in the proceedings of the Joint Consultative Group as deemed necessary by that State Party.

2. The first session of the Joint Consultative Group shall open no later than 60 days after the signing of the Treaty. The Chairman of the opening meeting shall be the representative of the Kingdom of Norway.

3. The Joint Consultative Group shall meet for regular sessions to be held two times per year.

4. Additional sessions shall be convened at the request of one or more States Parties by the Chairman of the Joint Consultative Group, who shall promptly inform all other States Parties of the request. Such sessions shall open no later than 15 days after receipt of such a request by the Chairman.

5. Sessions of the Joint Consultative Group shall last no longer than four weeks, unless it decides otherwise.

6. States Parties shall assume in rotation, determined by alphabetical order in the French language, the Chairmanship of the Joint Consultative Group.

7. The Joint Consultative Group shall meet in Vienna, unless it decides otherwise.

8. Representatives at meetings shall be seated in alphabetical order of the States Parties in the French language.

9. The official languages of the Joint Consultative Group shall be English, French, German, Italian, Russian and Spanish.

10. The proceedings of the Joint Consultative Group shall be confidential, unless it decides otherwise.

11. The scale of distribution for the common expenses associated with the operation of the Joint Consultative Group shall be applied, unless otherwise decided by the Joint Consultative Group, as follows:

10.35%	for the French Republic, the Federal Republic of Germany, the Italian Republic, the Union of Soviet Socialist Republics, the United Kingdom of Great Britain and Northern Ireland and the United States of America;
6.50%	for Canada;
5.20%	for the Kingdom of Spain;
4.00%	for the Kingdom of Belgium,

the Kingdom of the Netherlands and the Republic of Poland;

2.34% for the Czech and Slovak Federal Republic, the Kingdom of Denmark, the Republic of Hungary and the Kingdom of Norway;

0.88% for the Hellenic Republic, Romania and the Republic of Turkey;

0.68% for the Republic of Bulgaria, the Grand Duchy of Luxembourg and the Portuguese Republic; and

0.16% for the Republic of Iceland.

12. During the period that this Protocol is applied provisionally in accordance with the Protocol on Provisional Application, the Joint Consultative Group shall:

(A) work out or revise, as necessary, rules of procedure, working methods, the scale of distribution of expenses of the Joint Consultative Group and of conferences, and the distribution of the costs of inspections between or among States Parties, in accordance with Article XVI, paragraph 2, subparagraph (F) of the Treaty; and

(B) consider, upon the request of any State Party, issues relating to the provisions of the Treaty that are applied provisionally.

PROTOCOL ON THE PROVISIONAL APPLICATION OF CERTAIN PROVISIONS OF THE TREATY ON CONVENTIONAL ARMED FORCES IN EUROPE

To promote the implementation of the Treaty on Conventional Armed Forces in Europe of November 19, 1990, hereinafter referred to as the Treaty, the States Parties hereby agree to the provisional application of certain provisions of the Treaty.

1. Without detriment to the provisions of Article XXII of the Treaty, the States Parties shall apply provisionally the following provisions of the Treaty:

(A) Article VII, paragraphs 2, 3 and 4;

(B) Article VIII, paragraphs 5, 6 and 8;

(C) Article IX;

(D) Article XIII;

(E) Article XVI, paragraphs 1, 2(F), 2(G), 4, 6, and 7;

(F) Article XVII;

(G) Article XVIII;

(H) Article XXI, paragraph 2;

(I) Protocol on Existing Types, Sections III and IV;

(J) Protocol on Information Exchange, Sections VII, XII and XIII;

(K) Protocol on Inspection, Section II, paragraph 24, subparagraph (A) and Section III, paragraphs 3, 4, 5, 7, 8, 9, 10, 11 and 12;

(L) Protocol on the Joint Consultative Group; and

(M) Protocol on Reduction, Section IX.

2. The States Parties shall apply provisionally the provisions listed in paragraph 1 of this Protocol in the light of and in conformity with the other provisions of the Treaty.

3. This Protocol shall enter into force at the signature of the Treaty. It shall remain in force for 12 months, but shall terminate earlier if:

(A) the Treaty enters into force before the period of 12 months expires; or

(B) a State Party notifies all States Parties that it does not intend to become a party to the Treaty.

The period of application of this Protocol may be extended if all the States Parties so decide.

————

Source: Treaty on Conventional Armed Forces in Europe (United States Information Agency: Paris, 1990).

Appendix B. The Vienna Document 1992

Vienna, 4 March 1992

(1) Representatives of the participating States of the Conference on Security and Co-operation in Europe (CSCE), Albania, Armenia, Austria, Azerbaijan, Belarus, Belgium, Bulgaria, Canada, Cyprus, the Czech and Slovak Federal Republic, Denmark, Estonia, Finland, France, Germany, Greece, the Holy See, Hungary, Iceland, Ireland, Italy, Kazakhstan, Kyrgyzstan, Latvia, Liechtenstein, Lithuania, Luxembourg, Malta, Moldova, Monaco, the Netherlands, Norway, Poland, Portugal, Romania, the Russian Federation, San Marino, Spain, Sweden, Switzerland, Tajikistan, Turkey, Turkmenistan, Ukraine, the United Kingdom, the United States of America, Uzbekistan and Yugoslavia, met in Vienna in accordance with the provisions relating to the Conference on Confidence- and Security-Building Measures and Disarmament in Europe contained in the Concluding Documents of the Madrid and Vienna Follow-up Meetings of the CSCE.

(2) The Negotiations were conducted from 9 March 1989 to 4 March 1992.

(3) The participating States recalled that the aim of the Conference on Confidence- and Security- Building Measures and Disarmament in Europe is, as a substantial and integral part of the multilateral process initiated by the Conference on Security and Co-operation in Europe, to undertake, in stages, new, effective and concrete actions designed to make progress in strengthening confidence and security and in achieving disarmament, so as to give effect and expression to the duty of States to refrain from the threat or use of force in their mutual relations as well as in their international relations in general.

(4) The participating States recognized that the mutually complementary confidence- and security-building measures which are adopted in the present document and which are in accordance with the mandates of the Madrid and Vienna Follow-up Meetings of the CSCE serve by their scope and nature and by their implementation to strengthen confidence and security among the participating States.

(5) The participating States recalled the declaration on Refraining from the Threat or Use of Force contained in paragraphs (9) to (27) of the Document of the Stockholm Conference and stressed its continuing validity as seen in the light of the Charter of Paris for a New Europe.

(6) From 8 to 18 October 1991, the participating States held discussions in a seminar setting on military doctrine in relation to the posture, structure and activities of conventional forces in the zone of application for confidence- and security-building measures*. The discussions built on the results of the first such seminar, which had been held in Vienna from 16 January to 5 February 1990.

(7) On 17 November 1990, the participating States adopted the Vienna Document 1990, which built upon and added to the confidence- and security-building measures contained in the Document of the Stockholm Conference 1986.

(8) In fulfilment of the Charter of Paris for a New Europe of November 1990, they continued the CSBM negotiations under the same mandate, and have adopted the present document which integrates a set of new confidence- and security-building measures with measures previously adopted.

(9) The participating States have adopted the following:

1. ANNUAL EXCHANGE OF MILITARY INFORMATION

Information on Military Forces

(10) The participating States will exchange annually information on their military forces concerning the military organization, manpower and major weapon and equipment systems, as specified below, in the zone of application for confidence- and security-building measures (CSBMs).

(11) The information will be provided in an agreed format to all other participating States not later than 15 December of each year. It will be valid as of 1 January of the following year and will include:

---

*Annex 1

(11.1) 1. Information on the command organization of those military forces referred to under points 2 and 3 specifying the designation and subordination of all formations* and units** at each level of command down to and including brigade/regiment or equivalent level.

(11.1.1) Each participating State providing information on military forces will include a statement indicating the total number of units contained therein and the resultant annual evaluation quota as provided for in paragraph (114).

(11.2) 2. For each formation and combat unit*** of land forces down to and including brigade/regiment or equivalent level the information will indicate:

(11.2.1) – the designation and subordination;

(11.2.2) – whether it is active or non-active****;

(11.2.3) – the normal peacetime location of its headquarters indicated by exact geographic terms and/or co-ordinates;

(11.2.4) – the peacetime authorized personnel strength;

(11.2.5) – the major organic weapon and equipment systems, specifying the numbers of each type of:

(11.2.5.1) – battle tanks;

(11.2.5.2) – helicopters;

(11.2.5.3) – armoured combat vehicles (armoured personnel carriers, armoured infantry fighting vehicles, heavy armament combat vehicles);

(11.2.5.4) – armoured personnel carrier look-alikes and armoured infantry fighting vehicle look-alikes;

(11.2.5.5) – anti-tank guided missile launchers permanently/integrally mounted on armoured vehicles;

---

* In this context, formations are armies, corps and divisions and their equivalents.
** In this context, units are brigades, regiments and their equivalents.
*** In this context, combat units are infantry, armoured, mechanized, motorized rifle, artillery, combat engineer and army aviation units. Those combat units which are airmobile or airborne will also be included.
**** In this context, non-active formations or combat units are those manned from zero to fifteen per cent of their authorized combat strength. This term includes low strength formations and units.

(11.2.5.6) – self-propelled and towed artillery pieces, mortars and multiple rocket launchers (100 mm calibre and above);

(11.2.5.7) – armoured vehicle launched bridges.

(11.3.1) For planned increases in personnel strength above that reported under paragraph (11.2.4) for more than 21 days by more than 1,500 troops for each active combat unit and by more than 5,000 troops for each active formation, excluding personnel increases in the formation's subordinate formations and/or combat units subject to separate reporting under paragraph (11.2); as well as

(11.3.2) for each non-active formation and non-active combat unit which is planned to be temporarily activated for routine military activities or for any other purpose with more than 2,000 troops for more than 21 days

(11.3.3) the following additional information will be provided in the annual exchange of military information:

(11.3.3.1) – designation and subordination of the formation or combat unit;

(11.3.3.2) – purpose of the increase or activation;

(11.3.3.3) – for active formations and combat units the planned number of troops exceeding the personnel strength indicated under paragraph (11.2.4) or for non-active formations and combat units the number of troops involved during the period of activation;

(11.3.3.4) – start and end dates of the envisaged increase in personnel strength or activation;

(11.3.3.5) – planned location/area of activation;

(11.3.3.6) – the numbers of each type of the major weapon and equipment systems as listed in paragraphs (11.2.5.1) to (11.2.5.7) which are planned to be used during the period of the personnel increase or activation.

(11.3.4) In cases where the information required under paragraphs (11.3.1) to (11.3.3.6) cannot be provided in the annual exchange of military information, or in cases of changes in the information already provided, the required information will be communicated at least 42 days prior to such a personnel increase or temporary activation taking effect or, in cases when the personnel increase or temporary activation is carried out without advance notice to the troops involved, at the latest at the time the increase or the activation has taken effect.

(11.4) For each amphibious formation and amphibious combat unit* permanently located in the zone of application down to and including brigade/regiment or equivalent level, the information will include the items as set out above.

(11.5) 3. For each air formation and air combat unit** of the air forces, air defence aviation and of naval aviation permanently based on land down to and including wing/air regiment or equivalent level the information will include:

(11.5.1) – the designation and subordination;

(11.5.2) – the normal peacetime location of the headquarters indicated by exact geographic terms and/or co-ordinates;

(11.5.3) – the normal peacetime location of the unit indicated by the air base or military airfield on which the unit is based, specifying:

(11.5.3.1) – the designation or, if applicable, name of the air base or military airfield and

(11.5.3.2) – its location indicated by exact geographic terms and/or co-ordinates;

(11.5.4) – the peacetime authorized personnel strength***;

(11.5.5) – the numbers of each type of:

(11.5.5.1) – combat aircraft;

(11.5.5.2) – helicopters

organic to the formation or unit.

Data Relating to Major Weapon and Equipment Systems

(12) The participating States will exchange data relating to their major weapon and equipment systems as specified in the provisions on Information on Military Forces within the zone of application for CSBMs.

(12.1) Data on existing weapon and equipment systems will be provided once to all other participating States not later than 15 December 1992.

(12.2) Data on new types or versions of major weapon and equipment systems will be provided by each State when its deployment plans for the systems concerned are provided for the first time in accordance with para-

---

* Combat units as defined above.
** In this context, air combat units are units, the majority of whose organic aircraft are combat aircraft.
***As an exception, this information need not be provided on air defence aviation units.

graphs (14) and (15) below or, at the latest, when it deploys the systems concerned for the first time in the zone of application for CSBMs. If a participating State has already provided data on the same new type or version, other participating States may, if appropriate, certify the validity of those data as far as their system is concerned.

(13) The following data will be provided for each type or version of major weapon and equipment systems:

(13.1) BATTLE TANKS

(13.1.1) Type

(13.1.2) National Nomenclature/Name

(13.1.3) Main Gun Calibre

(13.1.4) Unladen Weight

(13.1.5) Data on new types or versions will, in addition, include:

(13.1.5.1) Night Vision Capability   yes/no

(13.1.5.2) Additional Armour   yes/no

(13.1.5.3) Track Width   cm

(13.1.5.4) Floating Capability   yes/no

(13.1.5.5) Snorkelling Equipment   yes/no

(13.2) ARMOURED COMBAT VEHICLES

(13.2.1) Armoured Personnel Carriers

(13.2.1.1) Type

(13.2.1.2) National Nomenclature/Name

(13.2.1.3) Type and Calibre of Armaments, if any

(13.2.1.4) Data on new types or versions will, in addition, include:

(13.2.1.4.1) Night Vision Capability
yes/no

(13.2.1.4.2) Seating Capacity

(13.2.1.4.3) Floating Capability   yes/no

(13.2.1.4.4) Snorkelling equipment yes/no

(13.2.2) Armoured Infantry Fighting Vehicles

(13.2.2.1) Type

(13.2.2.2) National Nomenclature/Name

(13.2.2.3) Type and Calibre of Armaments

(13.2.2.4) Data on new types or versions will, in addition, include:

(13.2.2.4.1) Night Vision Capability
yes/no

(13.2.2.4.2) Additional Armour   yes/no

(13.2.2.4.3) Floating Capability   yes/no

(13.2.2.4.4) Snorkelling Equipment yes/no

(13.2.3) Heavy Armament Combat Vehicles

(13.2.3.1) Type

(13.2.3.2) National Nomenclature/Name

(13.2.3.3) Main Gun Calibre

(13.2.3.4) Unladen Weight

(13.2.3.5) Data on new types or versions will, in addition, include:

(13.2.3.5.1) Night Vision Capability
yes/no
(13.2.3.5.2) Additional Armour   yes/no
(13.2.3.5.3) Floating Capability   yes/no
(13.2.3.5.4) Snorkelling Equipment yes/no
(13.3) ARMOURED PERSONNEL CARRIER LOOK-ALIKES AND ARMOURED INFANTRY FIGHTING VEHICLE LOOK-ALIKES
(13.3.1) Armoured Personnel Carrier Look-Alikes
(13.3.1.1) Type
(13.3.1.2) National Nomenclature/Name
(13.3.1.3) Type and Calibre of Armaments, if any
(13.3.2) Armoured Infantry Fighting Vehicle Look-Alikes
(13.3.2.1) Type
(13.3.2.2) National Nomenclature/Name
(13.3.2.3) Type and Calibre of Armaments, if any
(13.4) ANTI-TANK GUIDED MISSILE LAUNCHERS PERMANENTLY/INTEGRALLY MOUNTED ON ARMOURED VEHICLES
(13.4.1) Type
(13.4.2) National Nomenclature/Name
(13.5) SELF-PROPELLED AND TOWED ARTILLERY PIECES, MORTARS AND MULTIPLE ROCKET LAUNCHERS (100 mm CALIBRE AND ABOVE)
(13.5.1) Artillery pieces
(13.5.1.1) Type
(13.5.1.2) National Nomenclature/Name
(13.5.1.3) Calibre
(13.5.2) Mortars
(13.5.2.1) Type
(13.5.2.2) National Nomenclature/Name
(13.5.2.3) Calibre
(13.5.3) Multiple Launch Rocket Systems
(13.5.3.1) Type
(13.5.3.2) National Nomenclature/Name
(13.5.3.3) Calibre
(13.5.3.4) Data on new types or versions will, in addition, include:
(13.5.3.4.1) Number of Tubes
(13.6) ARMOURED VEHICLE LAUNCHED BRIDGES
(13.6.1) Type
(13.6.2) National Nomenclature/Name
(13.6.3) Data on new types or versions will, in addition, include:
(13.6.3.1) Span of the Bridge   — m
(13.6.3.2) Carrying Capacity/Load Classification   — metric tons
(13.7) COMBAT AIRCRAFT
(13.7.1) Type

(13.7.2) National Nomenclature/Name
(13.7.3) Data on new types or versions will, addition, include:
(13.7.3.1) Type of Integrally Mounted Armaments, if any
(13.8) HELICOPTERS
(13.8.1) Type
(13.8.2) National Nomenclature/Name
(13.8.3) Data on new types or versions will, in addition, include:
(13.8.3.1) Primary Role (e.g. specialized attack, multi-purpose attack, combat support, transport)
(13.8.3.2) Type of Integrally Mounted Armaments, if any
(13.9) Each participating State will, at the time the data are presented, ensure that other participating States are provided with photographs presenting the right or left side, top and front views for each of the types of major weapon and equipment systems concerned.
(13.10) Photographs of armoured personnel carrier look-alikes and armoured infantry fighting vehicle look-alikes will include a view of such vehicles so as to show clearly their internal configuration illustrating the specific characteristic which distinguishes each particular vehicle as a look-alike.
(13.11) The photographs of each type will be accompanied by a note giving the type designation and national nomenclature for all models and versions of the type which the photographs represent. The photographs of a type will contain an annotation of the data for that type.

Information on Plans for the Deployment of Major Weapon and Equipment Systems

(14) The participating States will exchange annually information on their plans for the deployment of major weapon and equipment systems as specified in the provisions on Information on Military Forces within the zone of application for CSBMs.
(15) The information will be provided in an agreed format to all other participating States not later than 15 December of each year. It will cover plans for the following year and will include:
(15.1) – the type and name of the weapon/equipment systems to be deployed;
(15.2) – the total number of each weapon/equipment system;
(15.3) – whenever possible, the number of each weapon/equipment system planned to be allocated to each formation or unit;

(15.4) – the extent to which the deployment will add to or replace existing weapon/equipment systems.

Information on Military Budgets

(16) The participating State will exchange annually information on their military budgets for the forthcoming fiscal year, itemising defence expenditures on the basis of the categories set out in the United Nations 'Instrument for Standardised International Reporting of Military Expenditures' adopted on 12 December 1980.

(16.1) The information will be provided to all other participating States not later than two months after the military budget has been approved by the competent national authorities.

(16.2) Each participating State may ask for clarification from any other participating State of the budgetary information provided. Questions should be submitted within a period of two months following the receipt of a participating State's budgetary information. Participating States will make every effort to answer such questions fully and promptly. The questions and replies may be transmitted to all other participating States.

II. RISK REDUCTION

Mechanism for Consultation and Co-operation as Regards Unusual Military Activities

(17) Participating States will, in accordance with the following provisions, consult and co-operate with each other about any unusual and unscheduled activities of their military forces outside their normal peacetime locations which are militarily significant, within the zone of application for CSBMs and about which a participating State expresses its security concern.

(17.1) The participating State which has concerns about such an activity may transmit a request for an explanation to other participating State where the activity is taking place.

(17.1.1) The request will state the cause, or causes, of the concern and, to the extent possible, the type and location, or area, of the activity.

(17.1.2) The reply will be transmitted within not more than 48 hours.

(17.1.3) The reply will give answers to questions raised, as well as any other relevant information which might help to clarify the activity giving rise to concern.

(17.1.4) The request and the reply will be transmitted to all other participating States without delay.

(17.2) The requesting State, after considering the reply provided, may then request a meeting to discuss the matter.

(17.2.1) The requesting State may ask for a meeting with the responding State.

(17.2.1.1) Such a meeting will be convened within not more than 48 hours.

(17.2.1.2) The request for such a meeting will be transmitted to all participating States without delay.

(17.2.1.3) The responding State is entitled to ask other interested participating States, in particular those which might be involved in the activity, to participate in the meeting.

(17.2.1.4) Such a meeting will be held at a venue to be mutually agreed upon by the requesting and the responding States. If there is no agreement, the meeting will be held at the Conflict Prevention Centre.

(17.2.1.5) The requesting and responding States will, jointly or separately, transmit a report of the meeting to all other participating States without delay.

(17.2.2) The requesting State may ask for a meeting of all participating States.

(17.2.2.1) Such a meeting will be convened within not more than 48 hours.

(17.2.2.2) The Conflict Prevention Centre will serve as the forum for such a meeting.

(17.2.2.3) Participating States involved in the matter to be discussed undertake to be represented at such a meeting.

(17.3) The communications between participating States provided for above will be transmitted preferably through the CSBM communications network.

Co-operation as Regards Hazardous Incidents of a Military Nature

(18) Participating States will co-operate by reporting and clarifying hazardous incidents of a military nature within the zone of application for CSBMs in order to prevent possible misunderstandings and mitigate the effects on another participating State.

(18.1) Each participating State will designate a point to contact in case of such hazardous incidents and will so inform all other participating States. A list of such points will be kept available at the Conflict Prevention Centre.

(18.2) In the event of such a hazardous incident the participating State whose military forces are involved in the incident should provide the information available to other participating States in an expeditious manner. Any participating State affected by such an incident may also request clarification as appropriate. Such requests will receive a prompt response.

(18.3) Communications between participating States will be transmitted preferably through the CSBM communications network.

(18.4) Matters relating to information about such hazardous incidents may be discussed by participating States at the Conflict Prevention Centre, either at the annual implementation assessment meeting at the Centre, or at additional meetings convened there.

(18.5) These provisions will not affect the rights and obligations of participating States under any international agreement concerning hazardous incidents, nor will they preclude additional methods of reporting and clarifying hazardous incidents.

Voluntary Hosting of Visits to Dispel Concerns about Military Activities

(19) In order to help to dispel concerns about military activities in the zone of application for CSBMs, participating States are encouraged to invite, at their discretion, other participating States to designate personnel accredited to the host State or other representatives to take part in visits to areas on the territory of the host State in which there may be cause for such concerns. Such invitations will be without prejudice to any action taken under paragraphs (17) to (17.3).

(19.1) States invited to participate in such visits will include those which are understood to have concerns. At the time invitations are issued, the host State will communicate to all other participating States its intention to conduct the visit, indicating the reasons for the visit, the area to be visited, the States invited and the general arrangements to be adopted.

(19.2) Arrangements for such visits, including the number of the representatives from other participating States to be invited, will be at the discretion of the host State, which will bear the in-country costs. However, the host State should take appropriate account of the need to ensure the effectiveness of the visit, the maximum amount of openness and transparency and the safety and security of the invited representatives. It should also take account, as far as practicable, of the wishes of visiting representatives as regards the itinerary of the visit. The host State and the States which provide visiting personnel may circulate joint or individual comments on the visit to all other participating States.

III. CONTACTS

Visits to Air Bases

(20) Each participating State with air combat units reported under paragraph (11) will arrange visits for representatives of all other participating States to one of its normal peacetime air bases* on which such units are located in order to provide the visitors with the opportunity to view activity at the air base, including preparations to carry out the functions of the air base and to gain an impression of the appropriate number of air sorties and type of missions being flown.

(21) No participating State will be obliged to arrange more than one such visit in any five-year period. Prior indications given by participating States of forthcoming schedules for such visits for the subsequent year(s) may be discussed at the annual implementation assessment meetings.

(22) As a rule, up to two visits from each participating State will be invited.

(23) Invitations will be extended to all participating States 42 days or more in advance of the visit. The invitation will indicate a preliminary programme, including: place, date and time of assembly; planned duration; languages to be used; arrangements for board, lodging and transportation; equipment permitted to be used during the visit; and any other information that may be considered useful.

(24) When the air base to be visited is located on the territory of another participating State, the invitations will be issued by the participating State on whose territory the air base is located. In such cases, the responsibilities as host delegated by this State to the participating States arranging the visit will be specified in the invitation.

(25) The invited State may decide whether to send military and/or civilian visitors, including personnel accredited to the host State. Military visitors will normally wear their uniforms and insignia during the visit..

(26) Replies, indicating whether or not the invitation is accepted, will be given not later than 21 days after the issue of the invitation. Participating States accepting an invitation

---

* In this context, the term normal peacetime air base is understood to mean the normal peacetime location of the air combat unit indicated by the air base or military airfield on which the unit is based.

will provide the names and ranks of the visitors in their replies. If the invitation is not accepted in time, it will be assumed that no visitors will be sent

(27) The visit to the air base will last for a minimum of 24 hours. In the course of the visit, the visitors will be given a briefing on the purpose and functions of the air base and on current activity at the air base. They will have the opporunity to communicate with commanders and troops, including those of support/logistic units located at the air base.

(28) The visitors will be provided with the opportunity to view all types of aircraft located at the air base.

(29) At the close of the visit, the host State will provide an opporunity for the visitors to meet together and also with host State officials and senior air base personnel to discuss the course of the visit.

(30) The host State will determine the programme for the visit and access granted to visitors at the air base. The visitors will follow the instructions issued by the host State in accordance with the provisions set out in this document.

(31) The visitors will be provided with appropriate accommodation in a location suitable for carrying out the visit.

(32) The invited State will cover the travel expenses of its representatives to and from the place of assembly specified in the invitation.

(33) Participating States should, in due cooperation with the visitors, ensure that no action is taken which could be harmful to the safety of visitors.

Military Contacts

(34) To improve further their mutual relations in the interest of strengthening the process of confidence- and security-building, the participating States will, as appropriate, promote and facilitate:

(34.1) – exchanges and visits between senior military/defence representatives;

(34.2) – contacts between relevant military institutions;

(34.3) – attendance by military representatives of other participating States at courses of instruction;

(34.4) – exchanges between military commanders and officers of commands down to brigade/regiment or equivalent level;

(34.5) – exchanges and contacts between academics and experts in military studies and related areas;

(34.6) – sporting and cultural events between members of their armed forces.

Demonstration of New Types of Major Weapon and Equipment Systems

(35) The first participating State which deploys with its military forces in the zone of application a new type of major weapon and equipment system as specified in the provisions on Information on Military Forces will arrange at the earliest opportunity (e.g. during an observation) a demonstration for representatives of all other participating States.*

(35.1) The host State will determine the duration, the programme and other modalities of the demonstration.

(35.2) Invitations will be extended to all participating States 42 days or more in advance of visits. The invitation will indicate a preliminary programme, including: the number of visitors invited from each participating State; the type(s) of major weapon and equipment system(s) to be viewed; place, date and time of assembly; planned duration; languages to be used; arrangements for board, lodging and transportation, where necessary; equipment permitted to be used during the visit; and any other information that may be considered useful.

(35.3) Replies, indicating whether or not the invitation is accepted, will be given not later than 21 days after the issue of the invitation. Participating States accepting an invitation will provide the names and ranks of the visitors in their replies. If the invitation is not accepted in time, it will be assumed that no visitors will be sent.

(35.4) The invited State will cover the travel expenses of its representatives to and from the place of assembly and, if applicable, costs for accommodation during the visit.

IV. PRIOR NOTIFICATION OF CERTAIN MILITARY ACTIVITIES

(36) The participating States will give notification in writing through diplomatic channels in an agreed form of content, to all other participating States 42 days or more in

---

*This provision will not apply if another participating State has already arranged a demonstration of the same type of major weapon and equipment system.

advance of the start of notifiable* military activities in the zone of application for CSBMs.

(37) Notification will be given by the participating State on whose territory the activity in question is planned to take place even if the forces of that State are not engaged in the activity or their strength is below the notifiable level. This will not relieve other participating States of their obligation to give notification, if their involvement in the planned military activity reaches the notifiable level.

(38) Each of the following military activities in the field conducted as a single activity in the zone of application for CSBMs at or above the levels defined below, will be notified:

(38.1) The engagement of formations of land forces** of the participating States in the same exercise activity conducted under a single operational command independently or in combination with any possible air or naval components.

(38.1.1) This military activity will be subject to notification whenever it involves at any time during the activity:
− at least 9,000 troops, including support troops, or
− at least 250 battle tanks if organized into a divisional structure or at least two brigades/regiments, not necessarily subordinate to the same division.

(38.1.2) The participation of air forces of the participating States will be included in the notification if it is foreseen that in the course of the activity 200 or more sorties by aircraft, excluding helicopters, will be flown.

(38.2) The engagement of military forces either in an amphibious landing or in a parachute assault by airborne forces in the zone of application for CSBMs.

(38.2.1) These military activities will be subject to notification whenever the amphibious landing involves at least 3,000 troops or whenever the parachute drop involves at least 3,000 troops.

(38.3) The engagement of formations of land forces of the participating States in a transfer from outside the zone of application

for CSBMs to arrival points in the zone, or from inside the zone of application for CSBMs to points of concentration in the zone, to participate in a notifiable exercise activity or to be concentrated.

(38.3.1) The arrival or concentration of these forces will be subject to notification whenever it involves, at any time during the activity:
− at least 9,000 troops, including support troops, or
− at least 250 battle tanks
if organized into a divisional structure or at least two brigades/regiments, not necessarily subordinate to the same division.

(38.3.2) Forces which have been transferred into the zone will be subject to all provisions of agreed CSBMs when they depart their arrival points to participate in a notifiable exercise activity or to be concentrated within the zone of application for CSBMs.

(39) Notifiable military activities carried out without advance notice to the troops involved, are exceptions to the requirement for prior notification to be made 42 days in advance.

(39.1) Notification of such activities, above the agreed thresholds, will be given at the time the troops involved commence such activities.

(40) Notification will be given in writing of each notifiable military activity in the following agreed form:

(41) A—General Information

(41.1) The designation of the military activity;

(41.2) The general purpose of the military activity;

(41.3) The names of the States involved in the military activity,

(41.4) The level of command, organizing and commanding the military activity;

(41.5) The start and end dates of the military activity.

(42) B—Information on different types of notifiable military activities

(42.1) The engagement of formations of land forces of the participating States in the same exercise activity conducted under a single operational command independently or in combination with any possible air or naval components:

(42.1.1) The total number of troops taking part in the military activity (i.e. ground troops, amphibious troops, airmobile and airborne troops) and the number of troops participating for each State involved, if applicable;

(42.1.2) The designation, subordination,

---

* In this document, the term notifiable means subject to notification.
** In this context, the term land forces includes amphibious, airmobile and airborne forces.

number and type of formations and units participating for each State down to and including brigade/regiment or equivalent level;

(42.1.3) The total number of battle tanks for each State and the total number of anti-tank guided missile launchers mounted on armoured vehicles;

(42.1.4) The total number of artillery pieces and multiple rocket launchers (100 mm calibre or above);

(42.1.5) The total number of helicopters, by category;

(42.1.6) Envisaged number of sorties by aircraft, excluding helicopters;

(42.1.7) Purpose of air missions;

(42.1.8) Categories of aircraft involved;

(42.1.9) The level of command, organizing and commanding the air force participation;

(42.1.10) Naval ship-to-shore gunfire;

(42.1.11) Indication of other naval ship-to-shore support;

(42.1.12) The level of command, organizing and commanding the naval force participation.

(42.2) The engagement of military forces either in an amphibious landing or in a parachute assault by airborne forces in the zone of application for CSBMs:

(42.2.1) The total number of amphibious troops involved in notifiable amphibious landings, and/or the total number of airborne troops involved in notifiable parachute assaults;

(42.2.2) In the case of a notifiable amphibious landing, the point or points of embarkation, if in the zone of application for CSBMs.

(42.3) The engagement of formations of land forces of the participating States in a transfer from outside the zone of application for CSBMs to arrival points in the zone, or from inside the zone of application for CSBMs to points of concentration in the zone, to participate in a notifiable exercise activity or to be concentrated:

(42.3.1) The total number of troops transferred;

(42.3.2) Number and type of divisions participating in the transfer;

(42.3.3) The total number of battle tanks participating in a notifiable arrival or concentration;

(42.3.4) Geographical co-ordinates for the points of arrival and for the points of concentration.

(43) C—The envisaged area and time-frame of the activity

(43.1) The area of the military activity delimited by geographic features together with geographic co-ordinates, as appropriate;

(43.2) The start and end dates of each phase (transfers, deployment, concentration of forces, active exercise phase, recovery phase) of activities in the zone of application for CSBMs of participating formations, the tactical purpose and corresponding geographical areas (delimited by geographical co-ordinates) for each phase;

(43.3) Brief description of each phase.

(44) D—Other information

(44.1) Changes, if any, in relation to information provided in the annual calendar regarding the activity;

(44.2) Relationship of the activity to other notifiable activities.

V. OBSERVATION OF CERTAIN MILITARY ACTIVITIES

(45) The participating States will invite observers from all other participating States to the following notifiable military activities:

(45.1) – The engagement of formations of land forces* of the participating States in the same exercise activity conducted under a single operational command independently or in combination with any possible air or naval components.

(45.2) – The engagement of military forces either in an amphibious landing or in a parachute assault by airborne forces in the zone of application for CSBMs.

(45.3) – In the case of the engagement of formations of land forces of the participating States in a transfer from outside the zone of application for CSBMs to arrival points in the zone, or from inside the zone of application for CSBMs to points of concentration in the zone, to participate in a notifiable exercise activity or to be concentrated, the concentration of these forces. Forces which have been transferred into the zone will be subject to all provisions of agreed confidence- and security-building measures when they depart their arrival points to participate in a notifiable exercise activity or to be concentrated within the zone of application for CSBMs.

---

*In this context, the term land forces includes amphibious, airmobile and airborne forces.

(45.4) The above-mentioned activities will be subject to observation whenever the number of troops engaged meets or exceeds 13,000 or where the number of battle tanks engaged meets or exceeds 300, except in the case of either an amphibious landing or a parachute assault by airborne forces, which will be subject to observation whenever the number of troops engaged meets or exceeds 3,500.

(46) The host State will extend the invitations in writing through diplomatic channels to all other participating States at the time of notification. The host State will be the participating State on whose territory the notified activity will take place.

(47) The host State may delegate some of its responsibilities as host to another participating State engaged in the military activity on the territory of the host State. In such cases, the host State will specify the allocation of responsibilities in its invitation to observe the activity.

(48) Each participating State may send up to two observers to the military activity to be observed.

(49) The invited State may decide whether to send military and/or civilian observers, including personnel accredited to the host State. Military observers will normally wear their uniforms and insignia while performing their tasks.

(50) Replies, indicating whether or not the invitation is accepted, will be given in writing not later than 21 days after the issue of the invitation.

(51) The participating States accepting an invitation will provide the names and ranks of their observers in their reply to the invitation. If the invitation is not accepted in time, it will be assumed that no observers will be sent.

(52) Together with the invitation the host State will provide a general observation programme, including the following information:

(52.1) – the date, time and place of assembly of observers;

(52.2) – planned duration of the observation programme;

(52.3) – languages to be used in interpretation and/or translation;

(52.4) – arrangements for board, lodging and transportation of the observers;

(52.5) – arrangements for observation equipment which will be issued to the observers by the host State;

(52.6) – possible authorization by the host State of the use of special equipment that the observers may bring with them;

(52.7) – arrangements for special clothing to be issued to the observers because of weather or environmental factors.

(53) The observers may make requests with regard to the observation programme. The host State will, if possible, accede to them.

(54) The host State will determine a duration of observation which permits the observers to observe a notifiable military activity from the time that agreed thresholds for observation are met or exceeded until, for the last time during the activity, the thresholds for observation are no longer met.

(55) The host State will provide the observers with transportation to the area of the notified activity and back. This transportation will be provided from either the capital or another suitable location to be announced in the invitation, so that the observers are in position before the start of the observation programme.

(56) The invited State will cover the travel expenses for its observers to the capital, or another suitable location specified in the invitation, of the host State, and back.

(57) The observers will be provided equal treatment and offered equal opportunities to carry out their functions.

(58) The observers will be granted, during their mission, the privileges and immunities accorded to diplomatic agents in the Vienna Convention on Diplomatic Relations.

(59) The participating States will ensure that official personnel and troops taking part in an observed military activity, as well as other armed personnel located in the area of the military activity, are adequately informed regarding the presence, status and functions of observers. Participating States should, in due co-operation with the observers, ensure that no action is taken which could be harmful to the safety of observers.

(60) The host State will not be required to permit observation of restricted locations, installations or defence sites.

(61) In order to allow the observers to confirm that the notified activity is non-threatening in character and that it is carried out in conformity with the appropriate provisions of the notification, the host State will:

(61.1) – at the commencement of the observation programme give a briefing on the purpose, the basic situation, the phases of the activity and possible changes as compared with the notification and provide the observers with an observation programme with a daily schedule;

(61.2) – provide the observers with a map with a scale of 1 to not more than 250,000 depicting the area of the notified military activity and the initial tactical situation in this area. To depict the entire area of the notified military activity, smaller-scale maps may be additionally provided;

(61.3) – provide the observers with appropriate observation equipment; in addition, the observers will be permitted to use their own binoculars, maps, photo and video cameras, dictaphones and hand-held passive night-vision devices. The above-mentioned equipment will be subject to examination and approval by the host State. It is understood that the host State may limit the use of certain equipment in restricted locations, installations or defence sites;

(61.4) – be encouraged, whenever feasible and with due consideration for the security of the observers, to provide an aerial survey, preferably by helicopter, of the area of the military activity. If carried out, such a survey should provide the observers with the opportunity to observe from the air the disposition of forces engaged in the activity in order to help them gain a general impression of its scope and scale. At least one observer from each participating State represented at the observation should be given the opportunity to participate in the survey. Helicopters and/or aircraft may be provided by the host State or by another participating State at the request of and in agreement with the host State;

(61.5) – in the course of the observation programme give the observers daily briefings with the help of maps on the various phases of the military activity and their development and inform the observers about their positions geographically; in the case of a land force activity conducted in combination with air or naval components, briefings will be given by representatives of these forces;

(61.6) – provide opportunities to observe directly forces of the State(s) engaged in the military activity so that the observers get an impression of the flow of the entire activity; to this end, the observers will be given the opportunity to observe combat and support units of all participating formations of a divisional or equivalent level and, whenever possible, to visit units below divisional or equivalent level and communicate with commanders and troops. Commanders and other senior personnel of the participating formations as well as of the visited units will inform the

observers of the mission and disposition of their respective units;

(61.7) – guide the observers in the area of the military activity; the observers will follow the instructions issued by the host State in accordance with the provisions set out in this document;

(61.8) – provide the observers with appropriate means of transportation in the area of the military activity;

(61.9) – provide the observers with opportunities for timely communication with their embassies or other official missions and consular posts; the host State is not obligated to cover the communication expense of the observers;

(61.10) – provide the observers with appropriate board and lodging in a location suitable for carrying out the observation programme and, when necessary, medical care;

(61.11) – at the close of each observation, provide an opportunity for the observers to meet together and also with host State officials to discuss the course of the observed activity. Where States other than the host State have been engaged in the activity, military representatives of those States will also be invited to take part in this discussion.

(62) The participating States need not invite observers to notifiable military activities which are carried out without advance notice to the troops involved unless these notifiable activities have a duration of more than 72 hours. The continuation of these activities beyond this time will be subject to observation while the agreed thresholds for observation are met or exceeded. The observation programme will follow as closely as practically possible all the provisions for observation set out in this document.

(63) The participating States are encouraged to permit media representatives from all participating States to attend observed military activities in accordance with accreditation procedures set down by the host State. In such instances, media representatives from all participating States will be treated without discrimination and given equal access to those facets of the activity open to media representatives.

(64) The presence of media representatives will not interfere with the observers carrying out their functions nor with the flow of the military activity.

VI. ANNUAL CALENDARS

(65) Each participating State will exchange,

with all other participating States, an annual calendar of its military activities subject to prior notification,* within the zone of application for CSBMs, forecast for the subsequent calendar year. A participating State which is to host military activities subject to prior notification conducted by any other participating State(s) will include these activities in its annual calendar. It will be transmitted every year, in writing, through diplomatic channels, not later than 15 November for the following year.

(66) If a participating State does not forecast any military activity subject to prior notification it will so inform all other participating States in the same manner as prescribed for the exchange of annual calendars.

(67) Each participating State will list the above-mentioned activities chronologically and will provide information on each activity in accordance with the following model:

(67.1) – type of military activity and its designation;

(67.2) – general characteristics and purpose of the military activity;

(67.3) – States involved in the military activity;

(67.4) – area of the military activity, indicated by geographic features where appropriate and defined by geographic co-ordinates;

(67.5) – planned duration of the military activity, indicated by envisaged start and end dates;

(67.6) – the envisaged total number of troops* engaged in the military activity. For activities involving more than one State, the host State will provide such information for each State involved;

(67.7) – the types of armed forces involved in the military activity;

(67.8) – the envisaged level of the military activity and designation of direct operational command, under which this military activity will take place;

(67.9) – the number and type of divisions whose participation in the military activity is envisaged;

(67.10) – any additional information concerning, *inter alia,* components of armed forces, which the participating State planning the military activity considers relevant.

(68) – Should changes regarding the military activities in the annual calendar prove necessary, they will be communicated to all other participating States no later than in the appropriate notification.

(69) – Should a participating State cancel a military activity included in its annual calendar or reduce it to a level below notification thresholds, that State will inform the other participating States immediately.

(70) – Information on military activities subject to prior notification not included in an annual calendar will be communicated to all participating States as soon as possible, in accordance with the model provided in the annual calendar.

VII. CONSTRAINING PROVISIONS

(71.1) No participating State will carry out within two calendar years more than one military activity subject to prior notification* involving more than 40,000 troops or 900 battle tanks.

(71.2) No participating State will carry out within a calendar year more than six military activities subject to prior notification* each one involving more than 13,000 troops or 300 battle tanks but not more than 40,000 troops or 900 battle tanks.

(71.2.1) Of these six military activities no participating State will carry out within a calendar year more than three military activities subject to prior notification* each one involving more than 25,000 troops or 400 battle tanks.

(71.3) No participating State will carry out simultaneously more than three military activities subject to prior notification* each one involving more than 13,000 troops or 300 battle tanks.

(72) Each participating State will communicate, in writing, to all other participating States, by 15 November each year, information concerning military activities subject to prior notification* involving more than 40,000 troops or 900 battle tanks, which it plans to carry out or host in the second subsequent calendar year. Such a communication will include preliminary information on the activity, as to its general purpose, timeframe and duration, area, size and States involved.

(73) No participating State will carry out a military activity subject to prior notification* involving more than 40,000 troops or 900 battle tanks, unless it has been the object of a communication as defined above and unless it has been included in the annual calendar, not later than 15 November each year.

---

*as defined in the provisions on Prior Notification of Certain Military Activities.

(74) If military activities subject to prior notification* are carried out in addition to those contained in the annual calendar, they should be as few as possible.

VIII. COMPLIANCE AND VERIFICATION

(75) According to the Madrid Mandate, the confidence- and security-building measures to be agreed upon 'will be provided with adequate forms of verification which correspond to their content'.

(76) The participating States recognize that national technical means can play a role in monitoring compliance with agreed confidence- and security-building measures.

Inspection

(77) In accordance with the provisions contained in this document each participating State has the right to conduct inspections on the territory of any other participating State within the zone of application for CSBMs. The inspecting State may invite other participating States to participate in an inspection.

(78) Any participating State will be allowed to address a request for inspection to another participating State on whose territory, within the zone of application for CSBMs, compliance with the agreed confidence- and security-building measures is in doubt.

(79) No participating State will be obliged to accept on its territory within the zone of application for CSBMs, more than three inspections per calendar year.

(80) No participating State will be obliged to accept more than one inspection per calendar year from the same participating State.

(81) An inspection will not be counted if, due to force majeure, it cannot be carried out.

(82) The participating State which requests an inspection will state the reasons for such a request.

(83) The participating State which has received such a request will reply in the affirmative to the request within the agreed period of time, subject to the provisions contained in paragraphs (79) and (80).

(84) Any possible dispute as to the validity of the reasons for a request will not prevent or delay the conduct of an inspection.

*as defined in the provisions on Prior Notification of Certain Military Activities.

(85) The participating State which requests an inspection will be permitted to designate for inspection on the territory of another State within the zone of application for CSBMs, a specific area. Such an area will be referred to as the 'specified area'. The specified area will comprise terrain where notifiable military activities are conducted or where another participating State believes a notifiable military activity is taking place. The specified area will be defined and limited by the scope and scale of notifiable military activities but will not exceed that required for an army level military activity.

(86) In the specified area the inspection team accompanied by the representatives of the receiving State will be permitted access, entry and unobstructed survey, except for areas or sensitive points to which access is normally denied or restricted, military and other defence installations, as well as naval vessels, military vehicles and aircraft. The number and extent of the restricted areas should be as limited as possible. Areas where notifiable military activities can take place will not be declared restricted areas, except for certain permanent or temporary military installations which, in territorial terms, should be as small as possible, and consequently those areas will not be used to prevent inspection of notifiable military activities. Restricted areas will not be employed in a way inconsistent with the agreed provisions on inspection.

(87) Within the specified area, the forces of participating States other than the receiving State will also be subject to the inspection.

(88) Inspection will be permitted on the ground, from the air, or both.

(89) The representatives of the receiving State will accompany the inspection team, including when it is in land vehicles and an aircraft from the time of their first employment until the time they are no longer in use for the purposes of inspection.

(90) In its request, the inspecting State will notify the receiving State of:

(90.1) – the reasons for the request;

(90.2) – the location of the specified area defined by geographical co-ordinates;

(90.3) – the preferred point(s) of entry for the inspection team;

(90.4) – mode of transport to and from the point(s) of entry and, if applicable, to and from the specified area;

(90.5) – where in the specified area the inspection will begin;

(90.6) – whether the inspection will be conducted from the ground, from the air, or both simultaneously;

(90.7) – whether aerial inspection will be conducted using an airplane, a helicopter, or both;

(90.8) – whether the inspection team will use land vehicles provided by the receiving State or, if mutually agreed, its own vehicles;

(90.9) – other participating States participating in the inspection, if applicable;

(90.10) – information for the issuance of diplomatic visas to inspectors entering the receiving State.

(91) The reply to the request will be given in the shortest possible period of time, but within not more than twenty-four hours. Within thirty-six hours after the issuance of the request, the inspection team will be permitted to enter the territory of the receiving State.

(92) Any request for inspection as well as the reply thereto will be communicated to all participating States without delay.

(93) The receiving State should designate the point(s) of entry as close as possible to the specified area. The receiving State will ensure that the inspection team will be able to reach the specified area without delay from the point(s) of entry.

(94) All participating States will facilitate the passage of the inspection teams through their territory.

(95) Within 48 hours after the arrival of the inspection team at the specified area, the inspection will be terminated.

(96) There will be no more than four inspectors in an inspection team. The inspecting State may invite other participating States to participate in an inspection. The inspection team will be headed by a national of the inspecting State, which will have at least as many inspectors in the team as any invited State. The inspection team will be under the responsibility of the inspecting State, against whose quota the inspection is counted. While conducting the inspection, the inspection team may divide into two sub-teams.

(97) The inspectors and, if applicable, auxiliary personnel, will be granted during their mission the privileges and immunities in accordance with the Vienna Convention on Diplomatic Relations.

(98) The participating States will ensure that troops, other armed personnel and officials in the specified area are adequately informed regarding the presence, status and functions of inspectors and, if applicable, auxiliary personnel. The receiving State will ensure that no action is taken by its representatives which could endanger inspectors and, if applicable, auxiliary personnel. In carrying out their duties, inspectors and, if applicable, auxiliary personnel will take into account safety concerns expressed by representatives of the receiving State.

(99) The receiving State will provide the inspection team with appropriate board and lodging in a location suitable for carrying out the inspection, and, when necessary, medical care; however this does not exclude the use by the inspection team of its own tents and rations.

(100) The inspection team will have use of its own maps and charts, photo and video cameras, binoculars, hand-held passive night vision devices and dictaphones. Upon arrival in the specified area the inspection team will show the equipment to the representatives of the receiving State. In addition, the receiving State may provide the inspection team with a map depicting the area specified for the inspection.

(101) The inspection team will have access to appropriate telecommunications equipment of the receiving State for the purpose of communicating with the embassy or other official missions and consular posts of the inspecting State accredited to the receiving State.

(102) The receiving State will provide the inspection team with access to appropriate telecommunications equipment for the purpose of continuous communication between the sub-teams.

(103) Inspectors will be entitled to request and to receive briefings at agreed times by military representatives of the receiving State. At the inspectors' request, such briefings will be given by commanders of formations or units in the specified area. Suggestions of the receiving State as to the briefings will be taken into consideration.

(104) The inspecting State will specify whether aerial inspection will be conducted using an airplane, a helicopter or both. Aircraft for inspection will be chosen by mutual agreement between the inspecting and receiving States. Aircraft will be chosen which provide the inspection team with a continuous view of the ground during the inspection.

(105) After the flight plan, specifying, *inter alia,* the inspection team's choice of flight path, speed and altitude in the specified area, has been filed with the competent air traffic

control authority the inspection aircraft will be permitted to enter the specified area without delay. Within the specified area, the inspection team will, at its request, be permitted to deviate from the approved flight plan to make specific observations provided such deviation is consistent with paragraph (86) as well as flight safety and air traffic requirements. Directions to the crew will be given through a representative of the receiving State on board the aircraft involved in the inspection.

(106) One member of the inspection team will be permitted, if such a request is made, at any time to observe data on navigational equipment of the aircraft and to have access to maps and charts used by the flight crew for the purpose of determining the exact location of the aircraft during the inspection flight.

(107) Aerial and ground inspectors may return to the specified area as often as desired within the 48-hour inspection period.

(108) The receiving State will provide for inspection purposes land vehicles with cross country capability. Whenever mutually agreed taking into account the specific geography relating to the area to be inspected, the inspecting State will be permitted to use its own vehicles.

(109) If land vehicles or aircraft are provided by the inspecting State, there will be one accompanying driver for each land vehicle, or accompanying aircraft crew.

(110) The inspecting State will prepare a report of its inspection and will provide a copy of that report to all participating States without delay.

(111) The inspection expenses will be incurred by the receiving State except when the inspecting State uses its own aircraft and/or land vehicles. The inspecting State will be responsible for travel expenses to and from the point(s) of entry.

Evaluation

(112) Information provided under the provisions on Information on Military Forces and on Information on Plans for the Deployment of Major Weapon and Equipment Systems will be subject to evaluation.

(113) Subject to the provisions below each participating State will provide the opportunity to visit active formations and units in their normal peacetime locations as specified in point 2 and 3 of the provisions on Information on Military Forces to allow the other participating States to evaluate the information provided.

(113.1) Non-active formations and combat units temporarily activated will be made available for evaluation during the period of temporary activation and in the area/location of activation indicated under paragraph (11.3.3). In such cases the provisions for the evaluation of active formations and units will be applicable, *mutatis mutandis.* Evaluation visits conducted under this provision will count against the quotas established under paragraph (114).

(114) Each participating State will be obliged to accept a quota of one evaluation visit per calendar year for every sixty units, or portion thereof, reported under paragraph (11). However, no participating State will be obliged to accept more than fifteen visits per calendar year. No participating State will be obliged to accept more than one fifth of its quota of visits from the same participating State; a participating State with a quota of less than five visits will not be obliged to accept more than one visit from the same participating State during a calendar year. No formation or unit may be visited more than twice during a calendar year and more than once by the same participating State during a calendar year.

(115) No participating State will be obliged to accept more than one visit at any given time on its territory.

(116) If a participating State has formations or units stationed on the territory of other participating States (host States) in the zone of application for CSBMs, the maximum number of evaluation visits permitted to its forces in each of the States concerned will be proportional to the number of its units in each State. The application of this provision will not alter the number of visits this participating State (stationing State) will have to accept under paragraph (114).

(117) Requests for such visits will be submitted giving 5 days notice.

(118) The request will specify:

(118.1) – the formation or unit to be visited;

(118.2) – the proposed date of the visit;

(118.3) – the preferred point(s) of entry as well as the date and estimated time of arrival for the evaluation team;

(118.4) – the mode of transport to and from the point(s) of entry and, if applicable, to and from the formation or unit to be visited;

(118.5) – the names and ranks of the members of the team and, if applicable, information for the issue of diplomatic visas;

(119) If a formation or unit of a participat-

ing State is stationed on the territory of another participating State, the request will be addressed to the host State and sent simultaneously to the stationing State.

(120) The reply to the request will be given within 48 hours after the receipt of the request.

(121) In the case of formations or units of a participating State stationed on the territory of another participating State, the reply will be given by the host State in consultation with the stationing State. After consultation between the host State and the stationing State the host State will specify in its reply any of its responsibilities which it agrees to delegate to the stationing State.

(122) The reply will indicate whether the formation or unit will be available for evaluation at the proposed date at its normal peacetime location.

(123) Formations or units may be in their normal peacetime location but be unavailable for evaluation. Each participating State will be entitled in such cases not to accept a visit; the reasons for the non-acceptance and the number of days that the formation or unit will be unavailable for evaluation will be stated in the reply. Each participating State will be entitled to invoke this provision up to a total of five times for an aggregate of no more than 30 days per calendar year.

(124) If the formation or unit is absent from its normal peacetime location, the reply will indicate the reasons for and the duration of its absence. The requested State may offer the possibility of a visit to the formation or unit outside its normal peacetime location. If the requested State does not offer this possibility, the requesting State will be able to visit the normal peacetime location of the formation or unit. The requesting State may however refrain in either case from the visit.

(125) Visits will not be counted against the quotas of receiving States, if they are not carried out. Likewise, if visits are not carried out, due to force majeure, they will not be counted.

(126) The reply will designate the point(s) of entry and indicate, if applicable, the time and place of assembly of the team. The point(s) of entry and, if applicable, the place of assembly will be designated as close as possible to the formation or unit to be visited. The receiving State will ensure that the team will be able to reach the formation or unit without delay.

(127) The request and the reply will be communicated to all participating States without delay.

(128) Participating States will facilitate the passage of teams through their territory.

(129) The team will have no more than two members. It may be accompanied by an interpreter as auxiliary personnel.

(130) The members of the team and, if applicable, auxiliary personnel, will be granted during their mission the privileges and immunities in accordance with the Vienna Convention on Diplomatic Relations.

(131) The visit will take place in the course of a single working day and last up to 12 hours.

(132) The visit will begin with a briefing by the officer commanding the formation or unit, or his deputy, in the headquarters of the formation or unit, concerning the personnel as well as the major weapon and equipment systems reported under paragraph (11).

(132.1) In the case of a visit to a formation, the receiving State may provide the possibility to see personnel and major weapon and equipment systems reported under paragraph (11) for that formation, but not for any of its formations or units, in their normal locations.

(132.2) In the case of a visit to a unit, the receiving State will provide the possibility to see the personnel and the major weapon and equipment systems of the unit reported under paragraph (11) in their normal locations.

(133) Access will not have to be granted to sensitive points, facilities and equipment.

(134) The team will be accompanied at all times by representatives of the receiving State.

(135) The receiving State will provide the team with appropriate transportation during the visit to the formation or unit.

(136) Personal binoculars and dictaphones may be used by the team.

(137) The visit will not interfere with activities of the formation or unit.

(138) The participating States will ensure that troops, other armed personnel and officials in the formation or unit are adequately informed regarding the presence, status and functions of members of teams and, if applicable, auxiliary personnel. Participating States will also ensure that no action is taken by their representatives which could endanger the members of teams and, if applicable, auxiliary personnel. In carrying out their duties, members of teams and, if applicable, auxiliary personnel will take into account safety concerns expressed by representatives of the receiving State.

(139) Travel expenses to and from the point(s) of entry, including expenses for re-

fuelling, maintenance and parking of aircraft and/or land vehicles of the visiting State, will be borne by the visiting State according to existing practices established under the CSBM inspection provisions.

(139.1) Expenses for evaluation visits incurred beyond the point(s) of entry will be borne by the receiving State, except when the visiting State uses its own aircraft and/or land vehicles in accordance with paragraph (118.4).

(139.2) The receiving State will provide appropriate board and, when necessary, lodging in a location suitable for carrying out the evaluation as well as any urgent medical care which may be required.

(139.3) In the case of visits to formations or units of a participating State stationed on the territory of another participating State, the stationing State will bear the costs for the discharge of those responsibilities which have been delegated to it by the host State under the terms of paragraph (121).

(140) The visiting State will prepare a report of its visit which will be communicated to all participating States expeditiously.

(141) Each participating State will be entitled to obtain timely clarification from any other participating State concerning the application of agreed confidence- and security-building measures. Communications in this context will, if appropriate, be transmitted to all other participating States.

(142) The communications concerning compliance and verification will be transmitted preferably through the CSBM communications network.

IX. COMMUNICATIONS

(143) The participating States have established a network of direct communications between their capitals for the transmission of messages relating to agreed measures. The network will complement the existing use of diplomatic channels. Participating States undertake to use the network flexibly, efficiently and in a cost-effective way.

(144) Each participating State will designate a point of contact capable of transmitting and receiving such messages from other participating States on a 24-hour-a-day basis and will notify in advance any change in this designation.

(145) Cost-sharing arrangements are set out in documents CSCE/WV/Dec. 2 and CSCE/WV/Dec. 4.

(146) Communications may be in any one of the six working languages of the CSCE.

(147) Details on the use of these six languages are set out in Annex II. The provisions of this annex have been elaborated for the practical purposes of the communication system only. They are not intended to change the existing use of all six working languages of the CSCE according to established rules and practice as set out in the Final Recommendations of the Helsinki Consultations.

(148) Messages will be considered official communications of the sending State. If the content of a message is not related to an agreed measure, the receiving State has the right to reject it by so informing the other participating States.

(149) Participating States may agree among themselves to use the network for other purposes.

(150) All aspects of the implementation of the network may be discussed at the annual implementation assessment meeting.

X. ANNUAL IMPLEMENTATION ASSESSMENT MEETING

(151) The participating States will hold each year a meeting to discuss the present and future implementation of agreed CSBMs. Discussion may extend to:

(151.1) – clarification of questions arising from such implementation;

(151.2) – operation of agreed measures;

(151.3) – implications of all information originating from the implementation of any agreed measures for the processs of confidence- and security-building in the framework of the CSCE.

(152) Before the conclusion of each year's meeting the participating States will normally agree upon the agenda and dates for the subsequent year's meeting. Lack of agreement will not constitute sufficient reason to extend a meeting, unless otherwise agreed. Agenda and dates may, if necessary, be agreed between meetings.

(153) The Conflict Prevention Centre will serve as the forum for such meetings.

* * *

(154) The participating States will implement this new set of mutually complementary confidence- and security-building measures in order to promote security co-operation and to reduce the risk of military conflict.

(155) Reaffirming the relevant objectives of the Final Act and the Charter of Paris, the participating States are determined to continue building confidence and to enhance security

for all.

(156) The measures adopted in this document are politically binding and will come into force on 1 May 1992.

(157) The Government of Austria is requested to transmit the present document to the Helsinki Follow-up Meeting of the CSCE. The Government of Austria is also requested to transmit the present document to the Secretary-General of the United Nations and to the Governments of the non-participating Mediterranean States.

(158) The text of this document will be published in each participating State, which will disseminate it and make it known as widely as possible.

(159) The representatives of the participating States express their profound gratitude to the Government and people of Austria for the excellent arrangements they have made for the Vienna CSBM Negotiations and the warm hospitality they have extended to the delegations which participated in the Negotiations.

Vienna, 4 March 1992

ANNEX I

Under the terms of the Madrid mandate, the zone of application for CSBMs is defined as follows:

'On the basis of equality of rights, balance and reciprocity, equal respect for the security interests of all CSCE participating States, and of their respective obligations concerning confidence- and security-building measures and disarmament in Europe, these confidence- and security-building measures will cover the whole of Europe as well as the adjoining sea area* and air space. They will be of military significance and politically binding and will be provided with adequate forms of verification which correspond to their content.

As far as the adjoining sea area* and air space is concerned, the measures will be applicable to the military activities of all the participating States taking place there whenever these activities affect security in Europe as well as constitute a part of activities taking place within the whole of Europe as referred to above, which they will agree to notify.

_____

*In this context, the notion of adjoining sea area is understood to refer also to ocean areas adjoining Europe.

Necessary specifications will be made through the negotiations on the confidence- and security-building measures at the Conference. Nothing in the definition of the zone given above will diminish obligations already undertaken under the Final Act. The confidence- and security-building measures to be agreed upon at the Conference will also be applicable in all areas covered by any of the provisions in the Final Act relating to confidence-building measures and certain aspects of security and disarmament.

Wherever the term 'the zone of application for CSBMs' is used in this document, the above definition will apply. The following understanding will apply as well:

The commitments undertaken in letters to the Chairman-in-Office of the CSCE Council by Armenia, Azerbaijan, Belarus, Kazakhstan, Kyrgyzstan, Moldova, Tajikistan, Turkmenistan, Ukraine and Uzbekistan on 29 January 1992 have the effect of extending the application of CSBMs in the Vienna Document 1992 to the territories of the above-mentioned States insofar as their territories were not covered already by the above.

ANNEX II

Use of the six CSCE working languages

Messages will, wherever possible, be transmitted in formats with headings in all six CSCE working languages.

Such formats, agreed among the participating States with a view to making transmitted messages immediately understandable by reducing the language element to a minimum, are annexed to document CSCE/WV/ Dec. 4. The formats may be subject to agreed modifications as required. Partcipating States will co-operate in this respect.

Any narrative text, to the extent it is required in such formats, and messages that do not lend themselves to formatting will be transmitted in the CSCE working language chosen by the transmitting State.

Each participating State has the right to ask for clarification of messages in cases of doubt.

ANNEX III

Chairman's Statement

The participating States, in order to facilitate an efficient use of the communications network, will give due consideration to practical needs of rapid transmission of their messages and of immediate understandability. A translation into another CSCE working language will be added where needed to meet that principle. The participating States have indicated at least two CSCE working languages in which they would prefer to receive the translation.

These provisions do not prejudice in any way the future continued use of all six working languages of the CSCE according to established rules and practice as set out in the Final Recommendations of the Helsinki Consultations.

This statement will be an annex to the Vienna Document 1992 and will be published with it.

Vienna, 4 March 1992

ANNEX IV

Chairman's Statement

It is understood that the implementation aspects of CSBMs in the case of contiguous areas of participating States specified in the understanding of Annex I which share frontiers with non-European non-participating States may be discussed at future Annual Implementation Assessment Meetings.

This statement will be an annex to the Vienna Document 1992 and will be published with it.

Vienna, 4 March 1992

ANNEX V

Chairman's Statement

It is understood that the participating States will take into consideration practical problems which may arise at an initial stage in implementing CSBMs on the territories of new participating States.

This statement will not constitute a precedent.

This statement will be an annex to the Vienna Document 1992 and will be published with it.

Source: The Vienna Document 1992 of the Negotiations on Confidence- and Security-Building Measures Convened in Accordance with the Relevant Provisions of the Concluding Document of the Vienna Meeting of the Conference on Security and Co-operation in Europe, Vienna, 4 Mar. 1992

Appendix C. The Treaty on Open Skies

Helsinki, 24 March 1992

The States concluding this Treaty, hereinafter referred to collectively as the States Parties or individually as a State Party,

Recalling the commitments they have made in the Conference on Security and Co-operation in Europe to promoting greater openness and transparency in their military activities and to enhancing security by means of confidence- and security-building measures,

Welcoming the historic events in Europe which have transformed the security situation from Vancouver to Vladivostok,

Wishing to contribute to the further development and strengthening of peace, stability and co-operative security in that area by the creation of an Open Skies regime for aerial observation,

Recognizing the potential contribution which an aerial observation regime of this type could make to security and stability in other regions as well,

Noting the possibility of employing such a regime to improve openness and transparency, to facilitate the monitoring of compliance with existing or future arms control agreements and to strengthen the capacity for conflict prevention and crisis management in the framework of the Conference on Security and Co-operation in Europe and in other relevant international institutions,

Envisaging the possible extension of the Open Skies regime into additional fields, such as the protection of the environment,

Seeking to establish agreed procedures to provide for aerial observation of all the territories of States Parties, with the intent of observing a single State Party or groups of States Parties, on the basis of equity and effectiveness while maintaining flight safety,

Noting that the operation of such an Open Skies regime will be without prejudice to States not participating in it,

Have agreed as follows:

Article I. General provisions

1. This Treaty establishes the regime, to be known as the Open Skies regime, for the conduct of observation flights by States Parties over the territories of other States Parties, and sets forth the rights and obligations of the States Parties relating thereto.

2. Each of the Annexes and their related Appendices constitutes an integral part of this Treaty.

Article II. Definitions

For the purposes of this Treaty:

1. The term 'observed Party' means the State Party or group of States Parties over whose territory an observation flight is conducted or is intended to be conducted, from the time it has received notification thereof from an observing Party until completion of the procedures relating to that flight, or personnel acting on behalf of that State Party or group of States Parties.

2. The term 'observing Party' means the State Party or group of States Parties that intends to conduct or conducts an observation flight over the territory of another State Party or group of States Parties, from the time that it has provided notification of its intention to conduct an observation flight until completion of the procedures relating to that flight, or personnel acting on behalf of that State Party or group of States Parties.

3. The term 'group of States Parties' means two or more States Parties that have agreed to form a group for the purposes of this Treaty.

4. The term 'observation aircraft' means an unarmed, fixed wing aircraft designated to make observation flights, registered by the relevant authorities of a State Party and equipped with agreed sensors. The term 'unarmed' means that the observation aircraft used for the purposes of this Treaty is not equipped to carry and employ weapons.

5. The term 'observation flight' means the flight of the observation aircraft conducted by an observing Party over the territory of an observed Party, as provided in the flight plan, from the point of entry or Open Skies airfield to the point of exit or Open Skies airfield.

6. The term 'transit flight' means a flight of an observation aircraft or transport aircraft conducted by or on behalf of an observing

Party over the territory of a third State Party en route to or from the territory of the observed Party.

7. The term 'transport aircraft' means an aircraft other than an observation aircraft that, on behalf of the observing Party, conducts flights to or from the territory of the observed Party exclusively for the purposes of this Treaty.

8. The term 'territory' means the land, including islands, and internal and territorial waters, over which a State Party exercises sovereignty.

9. The term 'passive quota' means the number of observation flights that each State Party is obliged to accept as an observed Party.

10. The term 'active quota' means the number of observation flights that each State Party has the right to conduct as an observing Party.

11. The term 'maximum flight distance' means the maximum distance over the territory of the observed Party from the point at which the observation flight may commence to the point at which that flight may terminate, as specified in Annex A to this Treaty.

12. The term 'sensor' means equipment of a category specified in Article IV, paragraph 1 that is installed on an observation aircraft for use during the conduct of observation flights.

13. The term 'ground resolution' means the minimum distance on the ground between two closely located objects distinguishable as separate objects.

14. The term 'infra-red line-scanning device' means a sensor capable of receiving and visualizing thermal electro-magnetic radiation emitted in the invisible infra-red part of the optical spectrum by objects due to their temperature and in the absence of artificial illumination.

15. The term 'observation period' means a specified period of time during an observation flight when a particular sensor installed on the observation aircraft is operating.

16. The term 'flight crew' means individuals from any State Party who may include, if the State Party so decides, interpreters and who perform duties associated with the operation or servicing of an observation aircraft or transport aircraft.

17. The term 'pilot-in-command' means the pilot on board the observation aircraft who is responsible for the operation of the observation aircraft, the execution of the flight plan, and the safety of the observation aircraft.

18. The term 'flight monitor' means an individual who, on behalf of the observed Party, is on board an observation aircraft provided by the observing Party during the observation flight and who performs duties in accordance with Annex G to this Treaty.

19. The term 'flight representative' means an individual who, on behalf of the observing Party, is on board an observation aircraft provided by the observed Party during an observation flight and who performs duties in accordance with Annex G to this Treaty.

20. The term 'representative' means an individual who has been designated by the observing Party and who performs activities on behalf of the observing Party in accordance with Annex G during an observation flight on an observation aircraft designated by a State Party other than the observing Party or the observed Party.

21. The term 'sensor operator' means an individual from any State Party who performs duties associated with the functioning, operation and maintenance of the sensors of an observation aircraft.

22. The term 'inspector' means an individual from any State Party who conducts an inspection of sensors or observation aircraft of another State Party.

23. The term 'escort' means an individual from any State Party who accompanies the inspectors of another State Party.

24. The term 'mission plan' means a document, which is in a format established by the Open Skies Consultative Commission, presented by the observing Party that contains the route, profile, order of execution and support required to conduct the observation flight, which is to be agreed upon with the observed Party and which will form the basis for the elaboration of the flight plan.

25. The term 'flight plan' means a document elaborated on the basis of the agreed mission plan in the format and with the content specified by the International Civil Aviation Organization, hereinafter referred to as the ICAO, which is presented to the air traffic control authorities and on the basis of which the observation flight will be conducted.

26. The term 'mission report' means a document describing an observation flight completed after its termination by the observing Party and signed by both the observing and observed Parties, which is in a format established by the Open Skies Consultative Commission.

27. The term 'Open Skies airfield' means an airfield designated by the observed Party as a point where an observation flight may com-

mence or terminate.

28. The term 'point of entry' means a point designated by the observed Party for the arrival of personnel of the observing Party on the territory of the observed Party.

29. The term 'point of exit' means a point designated by the observed Party for the departure of personnel of the observing Party from the territory of the observed Party.

30. The term 'refuelling airfield' means an airfield designated by the observed Party used for fuelling and servicing of observation aircraft and transport aircraft.

31. The term 'alternate airfield' means an airfield specified in the flight plan to which an observation aircraft or transport aircraft may proceed when it becomes inadvisable to land at the airfield of intended landing.

32. The term 'hazardous airspace' means the prohibited areas, restricted areas and danger areas, defined on the basis of Annex 2 to the Convention on International Civil Aviation, that are established in accordance with Annex 15 to the Convention on International Civil Aviation in the interests of flight safety, public safety and environmental protection and about which information is provided in accordance with ICAO provisions.

33. The term 'prohibited area' means an airspace of defined dimensions, above the territory of a State Party, within which the flight of aircraft is prohibited.

34. The term 'restricted area' means an airspace of defined dimensions, above the territory of a State Party, within which the flight of aircraft is restricted in accordance with specified conditions.

35. The term 'danger area' means an airspace of defined dimensions within which activities dangerous to the flight of aircraft may exist at specified times.

Article III. Quotas

SECTION I. GENERAL PROVISIONS

1. Each State Party shall have the right to conduct observation flights in accordance with the provisions of this Treaty.

2. Each State Party shall be obliged to accept observation flights over its territory in accordance with the provisions of this Treaty.

3. Each State Party shall have the right to conduct a number of observation flights over the territory of any other State Party equal to the number of observation flights which that other State Party has the right to conduct over it.

4. The total number of observation flights that each State Party is obliged to accept over its territory is the total passive quota for that State Party. The allocation of the total passive quota to the States Parties is set forth in Annex A, Section I to this Treaty.

5. The number of observation flights that a State Party shall have the right to conduct each year over the territory of each of the other States Parties is the individual active quota of that State Party with respect to that other State Party. The sum of the individual active quotas is the total active quota of that State Party. The total active quota of a State Party shall not exceed its total passive quota.

6. The first distribution of active quotas is set forth in Annex A, Section II to this Treaty.

7. After entry into force of this Treaty, the distribution of active quotas shall be subject to an annual review for the following calendar year within the framework of the Open Skies Consultative Commission. In the event that it is not possible during the annual review to arrive within three weeks at agreement on the distribution of active quotas with respect to a particular State Party, the previous year's distribution of active quotas with respect to that State Party shall remain unchanged.

8. Except as provided for by the provisions of Article VIII, each observation flight conducted by a State Party shall be counted against the individual and total active quotas of that State Party.

9. Notwithstanding the provisions of paragraphs 3 and 5 of this Section, a State Party to which an active quota has been distributed may, by agreement with the State Party to be overflown, transfer a part or all of its total active quota to other States Parties and shall promptly notify all other States Parties and the Open Skies Consultative Commission thereof. Paragraph 10 of this Section shall apply.

10. No State Party shall conduct more observation flights over the territory of another State Party than a number equal to 50 per cent, rounded up to the nearest whole number, of its own total active quota, or of the total passive quota of that other State Party, whichever is less.

11. The maximum flight distances of observation flights over the territories of the States Parties are set forth in Annex A, Section III to this Treaty.

SECTION II. PROVISIONS FOR A GROUP OF STATES PARTIES

1. (A) Without prejudice to their rights and

obligations under this Treaty, two or more States Parties which hold quotas may form a group of States Parties at signature of this Treaty and thereafter. For a group of States Parties formed after signature of this Treaty, the provisions of this Section shall apply no earlier than six months after giving notice to all other States Parties, and subject to the provisions of paragraph 6 of this Section.

(B) A group of States Parties shall co-operate with regard to active and passive quotas in accordance with the provisions of either paragraph 2 or 3 of this Section.

2. (A) The members of a group of States Parties shall have the right to redistribute amongst themselves their active quotas for the current year, while retaining their individual passive quotas. Notification of the redistribution shall be made immediately to all third States Parties concerned.

(B) An observation flight shall count as many observation flights against the individual and total active quotas of the observing Party as observed Parties belonging to the group are overflown. It shall count one observation flight against the total passive quota of each observed Party.

(C) Each State Party in respect of which one or more members of a group of States Parties hold active quotas shall have the right to conduct over the territory of any member of the group 50 per cent more observation flights, rounded up to the nearest whole number, than its individual active quota in respect of that member of the group or to conduct two such overflights if it holds no active quota in respect of that member of the group.

(D) In the event that it exercises this right the State Party concerned shall reduce its active quotas in respect of other members of the group in such a way that the total sum of observation flights it conducts over their territories shall not exceed the sum of the individual active quotas that the State Party holds in respect of all the members of the group in the current year.

(E) The maximum flight distances of observation flights over the territories of each member of the group shall apply. In case of an observation flight conducted over several members, after completion of the maximum flight distance for one member all sensors shall be switched off until the observation aircraft reaches the point over the territory of the next member of the group of States Parties where the observation flight is planned to begin. For such follow-on observation flight the maxi-

mum flight distance related to the Open Skies airfield nearest to this point shall apply.

3. (A) A group of States Parties shall, at its request, be entitled to a common total passive quota which shall be allocated to it and common individual and total active quotas shall be distributed in respect of it.

(B) In this case, the total passive quota is the total number of observation flights that the group of States Parties is obliged to accept each year. The total active quota is the sum of the number of observation flights that the group of States Parties has the right to conduct each year. Its total active quota shall not exceed the total passive quota.

(C) An observation flight resulting from the total active quota of the group of States Parties shall be carried out on behalf of the group.

(D) Observation flights that a group of States Parties is obliged to accept may be conducted over the territory of one or more of its members.

(E) The maximum flight distances of each group of States Parties shall be specified pursuant to Annex A, Section III and Open Skies airfields shall be designated pursuant to Annex E to this Treaty.

4. In accordance with the general principles set out in Article X, paragraph 3, any third State Party that considers its rights under the provisions of Section 1, paragraph 3 of this Article to be unduly restricted by the operation of a group of States Parties may raise this problem before the Open Skies Consultative Commission.

5. The group of States Parties shall ensure that procedures are established allowing for the conduct of observation flights over the territories of its members during one single mission, including refuelling if necessary. In the case of a group of States Parties established pursuant to paragraph 3 of this Section, such observation flights shall not exceed the maximum flight distance applicable to the Open Skies airfields at which the observation flights commence.

6. No earlier than six months after notification of the decision has been provided to all other States Parties:

(A) a group of States Parties established pursuant to the provisions of paragraph 2 of this Section may be transformed into a group of States Parties pursuant to the provisions of paragraph 3 of this Section;

(B) a group of States Parties established pursuant to the provisions of paragraph 3 of this Section may be transformed into a group of States Parties pursuant to the provisions of paragraph 2 of this Section;

(C) a State Party may withdraw from a group of States Parties; or

(D) a group of States Parties may admit further States Parties which hold quotas.

7. Following entry into force of this Treaty, changes in the allocation or distribution of quotas resulting from the establishment of or an admission to or a withdrawal from a group of States Parties according to paragraph 3 of this Section shall become effective on 1 January following the first annual review within the Open Skies Consultative Commission occurring after the six-month notification period. When necessary, new Open Skies airfields shall be designated and maximum flight distances established accordingly.

Article IV. Sensors

1. Except as otherwise provided for in paragraph 3 of this Article, observation aircraft shall be equipped with sensors only from amongst the following categories:

(A) optical panoramic and framing cameras;

(B) video cameras with real-time display;

(C) infra-red line-scanning devices; and

(D) sideways-looking synthetic aperture radar.

2. A State Party may use, for the purposes of conducting observation flights, any of the sensors specified in paragraph 1 above, provided that such sensors are commercially available to all States Parties, subject to the following performance limits:

(A) in the case of optical panoramic and framing cameras a ground resolution of no better than 30 centimetres at the minimum height above ground level determined in accordance with the provisions of Annex D, Appendix 1, obtained from no more than one panoramic camera, one vertically-mounted framing camera and two obliquely-mounted framing cameras, one on each side of the aircraft, providing coverage, which need not be continuous, of the ground up to 50 kilometres of each side of the flight path of the aircraft;

(B) in the case of video cameras, a ground resolution of no better than 30 centimetres determined in accordance with the provisions of Annex D, Appendix 1;

(C) in the case of infra-red line-scanning devices, a ground resolution of no better than 50 centimetres at the minimum height above ground level determined in accordance with the provisions of Annex D, Appendix 1, obtained from a single device; and

(D) in the case of sideways-looking synthetic aperture radar, a ground resolution of no better than three metres calculated by the impulse response method, which, using the object separation method, corresponds to the ability to distinguish on a radar image two corner reflectors, the distance between the centres of which is no less than five metres, over a swath width of no more than 25 kilometres, obtained from a single radar unit capable of looking from either side of the aircraft, but not both simultaneously.

3. The introduction of additional categories and improvements to the capabilities of existing categories of sensors provided for in this Article shall be addressed by the Open Skies Consultative Commission pursuant to Article X of this Treaty.

4. All sensors shall be provided with aperture covers or other devices which inhibit the operation of sensors so as to prevent collection of data during transit flights or flights to points of entry or from points of exit over the territory of the observed Party. Such covers or other devices shall be removable or operable only from outside the observation aircraft.

5. Equipment that is capable of annotating data collected by sensors in accordance with Annex B, Section II shall be allowed on observation aircraft. The State Party providing the observation aircraft for an observation flight shall annotate the data collected by sensors with the information provided for in Annex B, Section II to this Treaty.

6. Equipment that is capable of displaying data collected by sensors in real-time shall be allowed on observation aircraft for the purposes of monitoring the functioning and operation of the sensors during the conduct of an observation flight.

7. Except as required for the operation of the agreed sensors, or as required for the operation of the observation aircraft, or as provided for in paragraphs 5 and 6 of this Article, the collection, processing, retransmission or recording of electronic signals from electromagnetic waves are prohibited on board the observation aircraft and equipment for such operations shall not be on that observation aircraft.

8. In the event that the observation aircraft is provided by the observing Party, the observing Party shall have the right to use an obser-

vation aircraft equipped with sensors in each sensor category that do not exceed the capability specified in paragraph 2 of this Article.

9. In the event that the observation aircraft used for an observation flight is provided by the observed Party, the observed Party shall be obliged to provide an observation aircraft equipped with sensors from each sensor category specified in paragraph 1 of this Article, at the maximum capability and in the numbers specified in paragraph 2 of this Article, subject to the provisions of Article XVIII, Section II, unless otherwise agreed by the observing and observed Parties. The package and configuration of such sensors shall be installed in such a way so as to provide coverage of the ground provided for in paragraph 2 of this Article. In the event that the observation aircraft is provided by the observed Party, the latter shall provide a sideways-looking synthetic aperture radar with a ground resolution of no worse than six metres, determined by the object separation method.

10. When designating an aircraft as an observation aircraft pursuant to Article V of this Treaty, each State Party shall inform all other States Parties of the technical information on each sensor installed on such aircraft as provided for in Annex B to this Treaty.

11. Each State Party shall have the right to take part in the certification of sensors installed on observation aircraft in accordance with the provisions of Annex D. No observation aircraft of a given type shall be used for observation flights until such type of observation aircraft and its sensors has been certified in accordance with the provisions of Annex D to this Treaty.

12. A State Party designating an aircraft as an observation aircraft shall, upon 90-day prior notice to all other States Parties and subject to the provisions of Annex D to this Treaty, have the right to remove, replace or add sensors, or amend the technical information it has provided in accordance with the provisions of paragraph 10 of this Article and Annex B to this Treaty. Replacement and additional sensors shall be subject to certification in accordance with the provisions of Annex D to this Treaty prior to their use during an observation flight.

13. In the event that a State Party or group of States Parties, based on experience with using a particular observation aircraft, considers that any sensor or its associated equipment installed on an aircraft does not correspond to those certified in accordance with the provisions of Annex D, the interested States Parties shall notify all other States Parties of their concern. The State Party that designated the aircraft shall:

(A) take the steps necessary to ensure that the sensor and its associated equipment installed on the observation aircraft correspond to those certified in accordance with the provisions of Annex D, including, as necessary, repair, adjustment or replacement of the particular sensor or its associated equipment; and

(B) at the request of an interested State Party, by means of a demonstration flight set up in connection with the next time that the aforementioned observation aircraft is used, in accordance with the provisions of Annex F, demonstrate that the sensor and its associated equipment installed on the observation aircraft correspond to those certified in accordance with the provisions of Annex D. Other States Parties that express concern regarding a sensor and its associated equipment installed on an observation aircraft shall have the right to send personnel to participate in such a demonstration flight.

14. In the event that, after the steps referred to in paragraph 13 of this Article have been taken, the States Parties remain concerned as to whether a sensor or its associated equipment installed on an observation aircraft correspond to those certified in accordance with the provisions of Annex D, the issue may be referred to the Open Skies Consultative Commission.

Article V. Aircraft designation

1. Each State Party shall have the right to designate as observation aircraft one or more types or models of aircraft registered by the relevant authorities of a State Party.

2. Each State Party shall have the right to designate types or models of aircraft as observation aircraft or add new types or models of aircraft to those designated earlier by it, provided that it notifies all other States Parties 30 days in advance thereof. The notification of the designation of aircraft of a type or model shall contain the information specified in Annex C to this Treaty.

3. Each State Party shall have the right to delete types or models of aircraft designated earlier by it, provided that it notifies all other States Parties 90 days in advance thereof.

4. Only one exemplar of a particular type and model of aircraft with an identical set of associated sensors shall be required to be

offered for certification in accordance with the provisions of Annex D to this Treaty.

5. Each observation aircraft shall be capable of carrying the flight crew and the personnel specified in Article VI, Section III.

Article VI. Choice of observation aircraft, general provisions for the conduct of observation flights, and requirements for mission planning

SECTION I. CHOICE OF OBSERVATION AIRCRAFT AND GENERAL PROVISIONS FOR THE CONDUCT OF OBSERVATION FLIGHTS

1. Observation flights shall be conducted using observation aircraft that have been designated by a State Party pursuant to Article V. Unless the observed Party exercises its right to provide an observation aircraft that it has itself designated, the observing Party shall have the right to provide the observation aircraft. In the event that the observing Party provides the observation aircraft, it shall have the right to provide an aircraft that it has itself designated or an aircraft designated by another State Party. In the event that the observed Party provides the observation aircraft, the observing Party shall have the right to be provided with an aircraft capable of achieving a minimum unrefuelled range, including the necessary fuel reserves, equivalent to one-half of the flight distance, as notified in accordance with paragraph 5, subparagraph (G) of this Section.

2. Each State Party shall have the right, pursuant to paragraph 1 of Section, to use an observation aircraft designated by another State Party for observation flights. Arrangements for the use of such aircraft shall be worked out by the States Parties involved to allow for active participation in the Open Skies regime.

3. States Parties having the right to conduct observation flights may co-ordinate their plans for conducting observation flights in accordance with Annex H to this Treaty. No State Party shall be obliged to accept more than one observation flight at any one time during the 96-hour period specified in paragraph 9 of this Section, unless that State Party has requested a demonstration flight pursuant to Annex F to this Treaty. In that case, the observed Party shall be obliged to accept an overlap for the observation flights of up to 24 hours. After having been notified of the results of the co-ordination of plans to conduct observation flights, each State Party over whose territory observation flights are to be conducted shall inform other States Parties, in accordance with the provisions of Annex H, whether it will exercise, with regard to each specific observation flight, its right to provide its own observation aircraft.

4. No later than 90 days after signature of this Treaty, each State Party shall provide notification to all other States Parties:

(A) of the standing diplomatic clearance number for Open Skies observation flights, flights of transport aircraft and transit flights; and

(B) of which languages of the Open Skies Consultative Commission specified in Annex L, Section I, paragraph 7 to this Treaty shall be used by personnel for all activities associated with the conduct of observation flights over its territory, and for completing the mission plan and mission report, unless the language to be used is the one recommended in Annex 10 to the Convention on International Civil Aviation, Volume II, paragraph 5.2.1.1.2.

5. The observing Party shall notify the observed Party of its intention to conduct an observation flight, no less than 72 hours prior to the estimated time of arrival of the observing Party at the point of entry of the observed Party. States Parties providing such notifications shall make every effort to avoid using the minimum pre-notification period over weekends. Such notification shall include:

(A) the desired point of entry and, if applicable, Open Skies airfield where the observation flight shall commence;

(B) the date and estimated time of arrival of the observing Party at the point of entry and the date and estimated time of departure for the flight from the point of entry to the Open Skies airfield, if applicable, indicating specific accommodation needs;

(C) the location, specified in Annex E, Appendix 1, where the conduct of the pre-flight inspection is desired and the date and start time of such pre-flight inspection in accordance with the provisions of Annex F;

(D) the mode of transport and, if applicable, type and model of the transport aircraft used to travel to the point of entry in the event that the observation aircraft used for the observation flight is provided by the observed Party;

(E) The diplomatic clearance number for the observation flight or for the flight of the transport aircraft used to bring the personnel in and out of the territory of the observed Party to conduct an observation flight;

(F) the identification of the observation aircraft, as specified in Annex C;

(G) the approximate observation flight distance; and

(H) the names of the personnel, their gender, date and place of birth, passport number and issuing State Party, and their function.

6. The observed Party that is notified in accordance with paragraph 5 of this Section shall acknowledge receipt of the notification within 24 hours. In the event that the observed Party exercises its right to provide the observation aircraft, the acknowledgement shall include the information about observation aircraft specified in paragraph 5, subparagraph (F) of this Section. The observing Party shall be permitted to arrive at the point of entry at the estimated time of arrival as notified in accordance with paragraph 5 of this Section. The estimated time of departure for the flight from the point of entry to the Open Skies airfield where the observation flight shall commence and the location, the date and the start time of the pre-flight inspection shall be subject to confirmation by the observed Party.

7. Personnel of the observing Party may include personnel designated pursuant to Article XIII by other States Parties.

8. The observing Party, when notifying the observed Party in accordance with paragraph 5 of this Section, shall simultaneously notify all other States Parties of its intention to conduct the observation flight.

9. The period from the estimated time of arrival at the point of entry until completion of the observation flight shall not exceed 96 hours, unless otherwise agreed. In the event that the observed Party requests a demonstration flight pursuant to Annex F to the Treaty, it shall extend the 96-hour period pursuant to Annex F, Section III, paragraph 4, if additional time is required by the observing Party for the unrestricted execution of the mission plan.

10. Upon arrival of the observation aircraft at the point of entry, the observed Party shall inspect the covers for sensor apertures or other devices that inhibit the operation of sensors to confirm that they are in their proper position pursuant to Annex E, unless otherwise agreed by all States Parties involved.

11. In the event that the observation aircraft is provided by the observing Party, upon the arrival of the observation aircraft at the point of entry or at the Open Skies airfield where the observation flight commences, the observed Party shall have the right to carry out the pre-flight inspection pursuant to Annex F, Section I. In the event that, in accordance with paragraph 1 of this Section, an observation aircraft is provided by the observed Party, the observing Party shall have the right to carry out the pre-flight inspection of sensors pursuant to Annex F, Section II. Unless otherwise agreed, such inspections shall terminate no less than four hours prior to the scheduled commencement of the observation flight set forth in the flight plan.

12. The observing Party shall ensure that its flight crew includes at least one individual who has the necessary linguistic ability to communicate freely with the personnel of the observed Party and its air traffic control authorities in the language or languages notified by the observed Party in accordance with paragraph 4 of this Section.

13. The observed Party shall provide the flight crew, upon its arrival at the point of entry or at the Open Skies airfield where the observation flight commences, with the most recent weather forecast and air navigation information and information on flight safety, including Notices to Airmen. Updates of such information shall be provided as requested. Instrument procedures, and information about alternate airfields along the flight route shall be provided upon approval of the mission plan in accordance with the requirements of Section II of this Article.

14. While conducting observation flights pursuant to this Treaty, all observation aircraft shall be operated in accordance with the provisions of this Treaty and in accordance with the approved flight plan. Without prejudice to the provisions of Section II, paragraph 2 of this Article, observation flights shall also be conducted in compliance with:

(A) published ICAO standards and recommended procedures; and

(B) published national air traffic control rules, procedures and guidelines on flight safety of the State Party whose territory is being overflown.

15. Observation flights shall take priority over any regular air traffic. The observed Party shall ensure that its air traffic control authorities facilitate the conduct of observation flights in accordance with this Treaty.

16. On board the aircraft the pilot-in-command shall be the sole authority for the safe conduct of the flight and shall be responsible for the execution of the flight plan.

17. The observed Party shall provide:

(A) a calibration target suitable for confirming the capability of sensors in accordance with the procedures set forth in Annex D, Section III to this Treaty, to be overflown during the demonstration flight or the observation flight upon the request of either Party, for each sensor that is to be used during the observation flight. The calibration target shall be located in the vicinity of the airfield at which the pre-flight inspection is conducted pursuant to Annex F to this Treaty;

(B) customary commercial aircraft fuelling and servicing for the observation aircraft or transport aircraft at the point of entry, at the Open Skies airfield, at any refuelling airfield, and at the point of exit specified in the flight plan, according to the specifications that are published about the designated airfield;

(C) meals and the use of accommodation for the personnel of the observing Party; and

(D) upon the request of the observing Party, further services, as may be agreed upon between the observing and observed Parties, to facilitate the conduct of the observation flight.

18. All costs involved in the conduct of the observation flight, including the costs of the recording media and the processing of the data collected by sensors, shall be reimbursed in accordance with Annex L, Section I, paragraph 9 to this Treaty.

19. Prior to the departure of the observation aircraft from the point of exit, the observed Party shall confirm that the covers for sensor apertures or other devices that inhibit the operation of sensors are in their proper position pursuant to Annex E to this Treaty.

20. Unless otherwise agreed, the observing Party shall depart from the point of exit no later than 24 hours following completion of the observation flight, unless weather conditions or the airworthiness of the observation aircraft or transport aircraft do not permit, in which case the flight shall commence as soon as practicable.

21. The observing Party shall compile a mission report of the observation flight using the appropriate format developed by the Open Skies Consultative Commission. The mission report shall contain pertinent data on the date and time of the observation flight, its route and profile, weather conditions, time and location of each observation period for each sensor, the approximate amount of data collected by sensors, and the result of inspection of covers for sensor apertures or other devices that inhibit the operation of sensors in accordance with Article VII and Annex E. The mission report shall be signed by the observing and observed Parties at the point of exit and shall be provided by the observing Party to all other States Parties within seven days after departure of the observing Party from the point of exit.

SECTION II. REQUIREMENTS FOR MISSION PLANNING

1. Unless otherwise agreed, the observing Party shall, after arrival at the Open Skies airfield, submit to the observed Party a mission plan for the proposed observation flight that meets the requirements of paragraphs 2 and 4 of this Section.

2. The mission plan may provide for an observation flight that allows for the observation of any point on the entire territory of the observed Party, including areas designated by the observed Party as hazardous airspace in the source specified in Annex I. The flight path of an observation aircraft shall not be closer than, but shall be allowed up to, ten kilometres from the border with an adjacent State that is not a State Party.

3. The mission plan may provide that the Open Skies airfield where the observation flight terminates, as well as the point of exit, may be different from the Open Skies airfield where the observation flight commences or the point of entry. The mission plan shall specify, if applicable, the commencement time of the observation flight, the desired time and place of planned refuelling stops or rest periods, and the time of continuation of the observation flight after a refuelling stop or rest period within the 96-hour period specified in Section I, paragraph 9 of this Article.

4. The mission plan shall include all information necessary to file the flight plan and shall provide that:

(A) the observation flight does not exceed the relevant maximum flight distance as set forth in Annex A, Section I;

(B) the route and profile of the observation flight satisfies observation flight safety conditions in conformity with ICAO standards and recommended practices, taking into account existing differences in national flight rules, without prejudice to the provisions of paragraph 2 of this Section;

(C) the mission plan takes into account information on hazardous airspace, as provided in accordance with Annex I;

(D) the height above ground level of the observation aircraft does not permit the observing Party to exceed the limitation on ground resolution for each sensor, as set forth in Article IV, paragraph 2;

(E) the estimated time of commencement of the observation flight shall be no less than 24 hours after the submission of the mission plan, unless otherwise agreed;

(F) the observation aircraft flies a direct route between the co-ordinates or navigation fixes designated in the mission plan in the declared sequence; and

(G) the flight path does not intersect at the same point more than once, unless otherwise agreed, and the observation aircraft does not circle around a single point, unless otherwise agreed. The provisions of this subparagraph do not apply for the purposes of taking off, flying over calibration targets, or landing by the observation aircraft.

5. In the event that the mission plan filed by the observing Party provides for flights through hazardous airspace, the observed Party shall:

(A) specify the hazard to the observation aircraft;

(B) facilitate the conduct of the observation flight by co-ordination or suppression of the activity specified pursuant to subparagraph (A) of this paragraph; or

(C) propose an alternative flight altitude, route, or time.

6. No later than four hours after submission of the mission plan, the observed Party shall accept the mission plan or propose changes to it in accordance with Article VIII, Section I, paragraph 4 and paragraph 5 of this Section. Such changes shall not preclude observation of any point on the entire territory of the observed Party, including areas designated by the observed Party as hazardous airspace in the source specified in Annex I to this Treaty. Upon agreement, the mission plan shall be signed by the observing and observed Parties. In the event that the Parties do not reach agreement on the mission plan within eight hours of the submission of the original mission plan, the observing Party shall have the right to decline to conduct the observation flight in accordance with the provisions of Article VIII of this Treaty.

7. If the planned route of the observation flight approaches the border of other States Parties or other States, the observed Party may notify that State or those States of the esti-mated route, date and time of the observation flight.

8. On the basis of the agreed mission plan the State Party providing the observation aircraft shall, in co-ordination with the other State Party, file the flight plan immediately, which shall have the content specified in Annex 2 to the Convention on International Civil Aviation and shall be in the format specified by ICAO Document No. 4444-RAC/501/12, 'Rules of the Air and Air Traffic Services', as revised or amended.

SECTION III. SPECIAL PROVISIONS

1. In the event that observation aircraft is provided by the observing Party, the observed Party shall have the right to have on board the observation aircraft two flight monitors and one interpreter, in addition to one flight monitor for each sensor control station on board the observation aircraft, unless otherwise agreed. Flight monitors and interpreters shall have the rights and obligations specified in Annex G to this Treaty.

2. Notwithstanding paragraph 1 of this Section, in the event that an observing Party uses an observation aircraft which has a maximum take-off gross weight of no more than 35 000 kilograms for an observation flight distance of no more than 1500 kilometres as notified in accordance with Section I, paragraph 5, sub-paragraph (G) of this Article, it shall be obliged to accept only two flight monitors and one interpreter on board the observation aircraft, unless otherwise agreed.

3. In the event that the observation aircraft is provided by the observed Party, the observed Party shall permit the personnel of the observing Party to travel to the point of entry of the observed Party in the most expeditious manner. The personnel of the observing Party may elect to travel to the point of entry using ground, sea, or air transportation, including transportation by an aircraft owned by any State Party. Procedures regarding such travel are set forth in Annex E to this Treaty.

4. In the event that the observation aircraft is provided by the observed Party, the observing Party shall have the right to have on board the observation aircraft two flight representatives and one interpreter, in addition to one flight representative for each sensor control station on the aircraft, unless otherwise agreed. Flight representatives and interpreters shall have the rights and obligations set forth in Annex G to this Treaty.

5. In the event that the observing State Party

provides an observation aircraft designated by a State Party other than the observing or observed Party, the observing Party shall have the right to have on board the observation aircraft two representatives and one interpreter, in addition to one representative for each sensor control station on the aircraft, unless otherwise agreed. In this case, the provisions on flight monitors set forth in paragraph 1 of this Section shall also apply. Representatives and interpreters shall have the rights and obligations set forth in Annex G to this Treaty.

Article VII. Transit flights

1. Transit flights conducted by an observing Party to and from the territory of an observed Party for the purposes of this Treaty shall originate on the territory of the observing Party or of another State Party.

2. Each State Party shall accept transit flights. Such transit flights shall be conducted along internationally recognized Air Traffic Services routes, unless otherwise agreed by the States Parties involved, and in accordance with the instructions of the national air traffic control authorities of each State Party whose airspace is transited. The observing Party shall notify each State Party whose airspace is to be transited at the same time that it notifies the observed Party in accordance with Article VI.

3. The operation of sensors on an observation aircraft during transit flights is prohibited. In the event that, during the transit flight, the observation aircraft lands on the territory of a State Party, that State Party shall, upon landing and prior to departure, inspect the covers of sensor apertures or other devices that inhibit the operation of sensors to confirm that they are in their proper position.

Article VIII. Prohibitions, deviations from flight plans and emergency situations

SECTION I. PROHIBITION OF OBSERVATION FLIGHTS AND CHANGES TO MISSION PLANS

1. The observed Party shall have the right to prohibit an observation flight that is not in compliance with the provisions of this Treaty.

2. The observed Party shall have the right to prohibit an observation flight prior to its commencement in the event that the observing Party fails to arrive at the point of entry within 24 hours after the estimated time of arrival specified in the notification provided in accordance with Article VI, Section I, paragraph 5, unless otherwise agreed between the States Parties involved.

3. In the event that an observed State Party prohibits an observation flight pursuant to this Article or Annex F, it shall immediately state the facts for the prohibition in the mission plan. Within seven days the observed Party shall provide to all States Parties, through diplomatic channels, a written explanation for this prohibition in the mission report provided pursuant to Article VI, Section 1, paragraph 21. An observation flight that has been prohibited shall not be counted against the quota of either State Party.

4. The observed Party shall have the right to propose changes to the mission plan as a result of any of the following circumstances:

(A) the weather conditions affect flight safety;

(B) the status of the Open Skies airfield to be used, alternate airfields, or refuelling airfields prevents their use; or

(C) the mission plan is inconsistent with Article VI, Section II, paragraphs 2 and 4.

5. In the event that the observing Party disagrees with the proposed changes to the mission plan, it shall have the right to submit alternatives to the proposed changes. In the event that agreement on a mission plan is not reached within eight hours of the submission of the original mission plan, and if the observing Party considers the changes to the mission plan to be prejudicial to its rights under this Treaty with respect to the conduct of the observation flight, the observing Party shall have the right to decline to conduct the observation flight, which shall not be recorded against the quota of either State Party.

6. In the event that an observing Party declines to conduct an observation flight pursuant to this Article or Annex F, it shall immediately provide an explanation of its decision in the mission plan prior to the departure of the observing Party. Within seven days after departure of the observing Party, the observing Party shall provide to all other States Parties, through diplomatic channels, a written explanation for this decision in the mission report provided pursuant to Article VI, Section I, paragraph 21.

SECTION II. DEVIATIONS FROM THE FLIGHT PLAN

1. Deviations from the flight plan shall be permitted during the observation flight if necessitated by:

(A) weather conditions affecting flight safety;

(B) technical difficulties relating to the observation aircraft;

(C) a medical emergency of any person on board; or

(D) air traffic control instructions related to circumstances brought about by *force majeure*.

2. In addition, if weather conditions prevent effective use of optical sensors and infra-red line-scanning devices, deviations shall be permitted, provided that:

(A) flight safety requirements are met;

(B) in cases where national rules so require, permission is granted by air traffic control authorities; and

(C) the performance of the sensors does not exceed the capabilities specified in Article IV, paragraph 2, unless otherwise agreed.

3. The observed Party shall have the right to prohibit the use of a particular sensor during a deviation that brings the observation aircraft below the minimum height above ground level for operating that particular sensor, in accordance with the limitation on ground resolution specified in Article IV, paragraph 2. In the event that a deviation requires the observation aircraft to alter its flight path by more than 50 kilometres from the flight path specified in the flight plan, the observed Party shall have the right to prohibit the use of all the sensors installed on the observation aircraft beyond that 50-kilometre limit.

4. The observing Party shall have the right to curtail an observation flight during its execution in the event of sensor malfunction. The pilot-in-command shall have the right to curtail an observation flight in the event of technical difficulties affecting the safety of the observation aircraft.

5. In the event that a deviation from the flight plan permitted by paragraph 1 of this Section results in curtailment of the observation flight, or a curtailment occurs in accordance with paragraph 4 of this Section, an observation flight shall be counted against the quotas of both States Parties, unless the curtailment is due to:

(A) sensor malfunction on an observation aircraft provided by the observed Party;

(B) technical difficulties relating to the observation aircraft provided by the observed Party;

(C) a medical emergency of a member of the flight crew of the observed Party or of flight monitors; or

(D) air traffic control instructions related to circumstances brought about by *force majeure*.

In such cases the observing Party shall have the right to decide whether to count it against the quotas of both States Parties.

6. The data collected by the sensors shall be retained by the observing Party only if the observation flight is counted against the quotas of both States Parties.

7. In the event that a deviation is made from the flight plan, the pilot-in-command shall take action in accordance with the published national flight regulations of the observed Party. Once the factors leading to the deviation have ceased to exist, the observation aircraft may, with the permission of the air traffic control authorities, continue the observation flight in accordance with the flight plan. The additional flight distance of the observation aircraft due to the deviation shall not count against the maximum flight distance.

8. Personnel of both States Parties on board the observation aircraft shall be immediately informed of all deviations from the flight plan.

9. Additional expenses resulting from provisions of this Article shall be reimbursed in accordance with Annex L, Section I, paragraph 9 to this Treaty.

SECTION III. EMERGENCY SITUATIONS

1. In the event that an emergency situation arises, the pilot-in-command shall be guided by 'Procedures for Air Navigation Services—Rules of the Air and Air Traffic Services', ICAO Document No. 4444-RAC/501/12, as revised or amended, the national flight regulations of the observed Party, and the flight operation manual of the observation aircraft.

2. Each observation aircraft declaring an emergency shall be accorded the full range of distress and navigational facilities of the observed Party in order to ensure the most expeditious recovery of the aircraft to the nearest suitable airfield.

3. In the event of an aviation accident involving the observation aircraft on the territory of the observed Party, search and rescue operations shall be conducted by the observed Party in accordance with its own regulations and procedures for such operations.

4. Investigation of an aviation accident or incident involving an observation aircraft shall be conducted by the observed Party, with the participation of the observing party, in accordance with the ICAO recommendations set forth in Annex 13 to the Convention on Inter-

national Civil Aviation ('Investigation of Aviation Accidents') as revised or amended and in accordance with the national regulations of the observed Party.

5. In the event that the observation aircraft is not registered with the observed Party, at the conclusion of the investigation all wreckage and debris of the observation aircraft and sensors, if found and recovered, shall be returned to the observing Party or to the Party to which the aircraft belongs, if so requested.

Article IX. Sensor output from observation flights

SECTION I. GENERAL PROVISIONS

1. For the purposes of recording data collected by sensors during observation flights, the following recording media shall be used:

(A) in the case of optical panoramic and framing cameras, black and white photographic film;

(B) in the case of video cameras, magnetic tape;

(C) in the case of infra-red line-scanning devices, black and white photographic film or magnetic tape; and

(D) in the case of sideways-looking synthetic aperture radar, magnetic tape.

The agreed format in which such data is to be recorded and exchanged on other recording media shall be decided within the Open Skies Consultative Commission during the period of provisional application of this Treaty.

2. Data collected by sensors during observation flights shall remain on board the observation aircraft until completion of the observation flight. The transmission of data collected by sensors from the observation aircraft during the observation flight is prohibited.

3. Each roll of photographic film and cassette or reel of magnetic tape used to collect data by a sensor during an observation flight shall be placed in a container and sealed in the presence of the States Parties as soon as is practicable after it has been removed from the sensor.

4. Data collected by sensors during observation flights shall be made available to States Parties in accordance with the provisions of this Article and shall be used exclusively for the attainment of the purposes of this Treaty.

5. In the event that, on the basis of data provided pursuant to Annex B, Section I to this Treaty, a data recording medium to be used by a State Party during an observation flight is incompatible with the equipment of another State Party for handling that data recording medium, the States Parties involved shall establish procedures to ensure that all data collected during observation flights can be handled, in terms of processing, duplication and storage, by them.

SECTION II. OUTPUT FROM SENSORS THAT USE PHOTOGRAPHIC FILM

1. In the event that output from duplicate optical cameras is to be exchanged, the cameras, film and film processing shall be of an identical type.

2. Provided that the data collected by a single optical camera is subject to exchange, the States Parties shall consider, within the Open Skies Consultative Commission during the period of provisional application of this Treaty, the issue of whether the responsibility for the development of the original film negative shall be borne by the observing Party or by the State Party providing the observation aircraft. The State Party developing the original film negative shall be responsible for the quality of processing the original negative film and producing the duplicate positive or negative. In the event that States Parties agree that the film used during the observation flight conducted on an observation aircraft provided by the observed Party shall be processed by the observing Party, the observed Party shall bear no responsibility for the quality of the processing of the original negative film.

3. All the film used during the observation flight shall be developed:

(A) in the event that the original film negative is developed at a film processing facility arranged for by the observed Party, no later than three days, unless otherwise agreed, after the arrival of the observation aircraft at the point of exit; or

(B) in the event that the original film negative is developed at a film processing facility arranged for by the observing Party, no later than ten days after the departure of the observation aircraft from the territory of the observed Party.

4. The State Party that is developing the original film negative shall be obliged to accept at the film processing facility up to two officials from the other State Party to monitor the unsealing of the film cassette or container and each step in the storage, processing, duplication and handling of the original film negative, in accordance with the provisions of

Annex K, Section II to this Treaty. The State Party monitoring the film processing and duplication shall have the right to designate such officials from among its nationals present on the territory on which the film processing facility arranged for by the other State Party is located, provided that such individuals are on the list of designated personnel in accordance with Article XIII, Section I of this Treaty. The State Party developing the film shall assist the officials of the other State Party in their functions provided for in this paragraph to the maximum extent possible.

5. Upon completion of an observation flight, the State Party that is to develop the original film negative shall attach a 21-step sensitometric test strip of the same film type used during the observation flight or shall expose a 21-step optical wedge onto the leader or trailer of each roll of original film negative used during the observation flight. After the original film negative has been processed and duplicate film negative or positive has been produced, the States Parties shall assess the image quality of the 21-step sensitometric test strips or images of the 21-step optical wedge against the characteristics provided for that type of original film negative or duplicate film negative or positive in accordance with the provisions of Annex K, Section I to this Treaty.

6. In the event that only one original film negative is developed:

(A) the observing Party shall have the right to retain or receive the original film negative; and

(B) the observed Party shall have the right to select and receive a complete first generation duplicate or part thereof, either positive or negative, of the original film negative. Unless otherwise agreed, such duplicate shall be:

(1) of the same format and film size as the original film negative;

(2) produced immediately after development of the original film negative; and

(3) provided to the officials of the observed Party immediately after the duplicate has been produced.

7. In the event that two original film negatives are developed:

(A) if the observation aircraft is provided by the observing Party, the observed Party shall have the right, at the completion of the observation flight, to select either of the two original film negatives, and the original film negative not selected shall be retained by the observing Party; or

(B) if the observation aircraft is provided by the observed Party, the observing Party shall have the right to select either of the original film negatives, and the original film negative not selected shall be retained by the observed Party.

SECTION III. OUTPUT FROM SENSORS THAT USE OTHER RECORDING MEDIA

1. The State Party that provides the observation aircraft shall record at least one original set of data collected by sensors using other media.

2. In the event that only one original set is made:

(A) if the observation aircraft is provided by the observing Party, the observing Party shall have the right to retain the original set and the observed Party shall have the right to receive a first generation duplicate copy; or

(B) if the observation aircraft is provided by the observed Party, the observing Party shall have the right to receive the original set and the observed Party shall have the right to receive a first generation duplicate copy.

3. In the event that two original sets are made:

(A) if the observation aircraft is provided by the observing Party, the observed Party shall have the right, at the completion of the observation flight, to select either of the two sets of recording media, and the set not selected shall be retained by the observing Party; or

(B) if the observation aircraft is provided by the observed Party, the observing Party shall have the right to select either of the two sets of recording media, and the set not selected shall be retained by the observed Party.

4. In the event that the observation aircraft is provided by the observing Party, the observed Party shall have the right to receive the data collected by a sideways-looking synthetic aperture radar in the form of either initial phase information or a radar image, at its choice.

5. In the event that the observation aircraft is provided by the observed Party, the observing Party shall have the right to receive the data collected by a sideways-looking synthetic aperture radar in the form of either initial phase information or a radar image, at its choice.

SECTION IV. ACCESS TO SENSOR OUTPUT

Each State Party shall have the right to request and receive from the observing Party copies of data collected by sensors during an observation flight. Such copies shall be in the form of first generation duplicates produced from the original data collected by sensors during an observation flight. The State Party requesting copies shall also notify the observed Party. A request for duplicates of data shall include the following information:

(A) the observing Party ;

(B) the observed Party ;

(C) the date of the observation flight;

(D) the sensor by which the data was collected;

(E) the portion or portions of the observation period during which the data was collected; and

(F) the type and format of duplicate recording medium, either negative or positive film, or magnetic tape.

Article X. Open Skies Consultative Commission

1. In order to promote the objectives and facilitate the implementation of the provisions of this Treaty, the States Parties hereby establish an Open Skies Consultative Commission.

2. The Open Skies Consultative Commission shall take decisions or make recommendations by consensus. Consensus shall be understood to mean the absence of any objection by any State Party to the taking of a decision or the making of a recommendation.

3. Each State Party shall have the right to raise before the Open Skies Consultative Commission, and have placed on its agenda, any issue relating to this Treaty, including any issue related to the case when the observed Party provides an observation aircraft.

4. Within the framework of the Open Skies Consultative Commission the States Parties to this Treaty shall:

(A) consider questions relating to compliance with the provisions of this Treaty;

(B) seek to resolve ambiguities and differences of interpretation that may become apparent in the way this Treaty is implemented;

(C) consider and take decisions on applications for accession to this Treaty; and

(D) agree as to those technical and adminis trative measures, pursuant to the provisions of this Treaty, deemed necessary following the accession to this Treaty by other States.

5. The Open Skies Consultative Commission may propose amendments to this Treaty for consideration and approval in accordance with Article XVI. The Open Skies Consultative Commission may also agree on improvements to the viability and effectiveness of this Treaty, consistent with its provisions. Improvements relating only to modification of the annual distribrution of active quotas pursuant to Article III and Annex A, to updates and additions to the categories or capabilities of sensors pursuant to Article IV, to revision of the share of costs pursuant to Annex L, Section I, paragraph 9, to arrangements for the sharing and availability of data pursuant to Article IX, Sections III and IV and to the handling of mission reports pursuant to Article VI, Section I, paragraph 21, as well as to minor matters of an administrative or technical nature, shall be agreed upon within the Open Skies Consultative Commission and shall not be deemed to be amendments to this Treaty.

6. The Open Skies Consultative Commission shall request the use of the facilities and administrative support of the Conflict Prevention Centre of the Conference on Security and Co-operation in Europe, or other existing facilities in Vienna, unless it decides otherwise.

7. Provisions for the operation of the Open Skies Consultative Commission are set forth in Annex L to this Treaty.

Article XI. Notifications and reports

The States Parties shall transmit notifications and reports required by this Treaty in written form. The States Parties shall transmit such notifications and reports through diplomatic channels or, at their choice, through other official channels, such as the communications network of the Conference on Security and Co-operation in Europe.

Article XII. Liability

A State Party shall, in accordance with international law and practice, be liable to pay compensation for damage to other States Parties, or to their natural or juridical persons or their property, caused by it in the course of the implementation of this Treaty.

Article XIII. Designation of personnel and privileges and immunities

SECTION I. DESIGNATION OF PERSONNEL

1. Each State Party shall, at the same time that it deposits its instrument of ratification to either of the Depositaries, provide to all other States Parties, for their review, a list of designated personnel who will carry out all duties relating to the conduct of observation flights for that State Party, including monitoring the processing of the sensor output. No such list of designated personnel shall include more than 400 individuals at any time. It shall contain the name, gender, date of birth, place of birth, passport number, and function for each individual included. Each State Party shall have the right to amend its list of designated personnel until 30 days after entry into force of this Treaty and once every six months thereafter.

2. In the event that any individual included on the original or any amended list is unacceptable to a State Party reviewing the list, that State Party shall, no later than 30 days after receipt of each list, notify the State Party providing that list that such individual shall not be accepted with respect to the objecting State Party. Individuals not declared unacceptable within that 30-day period shall be deemed accepted. In the event that a State Party subsequently determines that an individual is unacceptable, that State Party shall so notify the State Party that designated such individual. Individuals who are declared unacceptable shall be removed from the list previously submitted to the objecting State Party.

3. The observed Party shall provide visas and any other documents as required to ensure that each accepted individual may enter and remain on the territory of that State Party for the purpose of carrying out duties relating to the conduct of observation flights, including monitoring the processing of the sensor output. Such visas and any other necessary documents shall be provided either:

(A) no later than 30 days after the individual is deemed to be accepted, in which case the visa shall be valid for a period of no less than 24 months; or

(B) no later than one hour after the arrival of the individual at the point of entry, in which case the visa shall be valid for the duration of that individual's duties; or

(C) at any other time, by mutual agreement of the States Parties involved.

SECTION II. PRIVILEGES AND IMMUNITIES

1. In order to exercise their functions effectively, for the purpose of implementing this Treaty and not for their personal benefit, personnel designated in accordance with the provisions of Section I, paragraph 1 of this Article shall be accorded the privileges and immunities enjoyed by diplomatic agents pursuant to Article 29; Article 30, paragraph 2; Article 31, paragraphs 1, 2 and 3; and Articles 34 and 35 of the Vienna Convention on Diplomatic Relations of 18 April 1961, hereinafter referred to as the Vienna Convention. In addition, designated personnel shall be accorded the privileges enjoyed by diplomatic agents pursuant to Article 36, paragraph 1, subparagraph (b) of the Vienna Convention, except in relation to articles, the import or export of which is prohibited by law or controlled by quarantine regulations.

2. Such privileges and immunities shall be accorded to designated personnel for the entire period between arrival on and departure from the territory of the observed Party, and thereafter with respect to acts previously performed in the exercise of their official functions. Such personnel shall also, when transiting the territory of other States Parties, be accorded the privileges and immunities enjoyed by diplomatic agents pursuant to Article 40, paragraph 1 of the Vienna Convention.

3. The immunity from jurisdiction may be waived by the observing Party in those cases when it would impede the course of justice and can be waived without prejudice to this Treaty. The immunity of personnel who are not nationals of the observing Party may be waived only by the States Parties of which such personnel are nationals. Waiver must always be express.

4. Without prejudice to their privileges and immunities or the rights of the observing Party set forth in this Treaty, it is the duty of designated personnel to respect the laws and regulations of the observed Party.

5. The transportation means of the personnel shall be accorded the same immunities from search, requisition, attachment or execution as those of a diplomatic mission pursuant to Article 22, paragraph 3 of the Vienna Convention, except as otherwise provided for in this Treaty.

Article XIV. Benelux

1. Solely for the purposes of Articles II to IX and Article XI, and of Annexes A to I and

Annex K to this Treaty, the Kingdom of Belgium, the Grand Duchy of Luxembourg, and the Kingdom of the Netherlands shall be deemed a single State Party, hereinafter referred to as the Benelux.

2. Without prejudice to the provisions of Article XV, the above-mentioned States Parties may terminate this arrangement by notifying all other States Parties thereof. This arrangement shall be deemed to be terminated on the next 31 December following the 60-day period after such notification.

Article XV. Duration and withdrawal

1. This Treaty shall be of unlimited duration.

2. A State Party shall have the right to withdraw from this Treaty. A State Party intending to withdraw shall provide notice of its decision to withdraw to either Depositary at least six months in advance of the date of its intended withdrawal and to all other States Parties. The Depositaries shall promptly inform all other States Parties of such notice.

3. In the event that a State Party provides notice of its decision to withdraw from this Treaty in accordance with paragraph 2 of this Article, the Depositaries shall convene a conference of the States Parties no less than 30 days and no more than 60 days after they have received such notice, in order to consider the effect of the withdrawal on this Treaty.

Article XVI. Amendments and periodic review

1. Each State Party shall have the right to propose amendments to this Treaty. The text of each proposed amendment shall be submitted to either Depositary, which shall circulate it to all States Parties for consideration. If so requested by no less than three States Parties within a period of 90 days after circulation of the proposed amendment, the Depositaries shall convene a conference of the States Parties to consider the proposed amendment. Such a conference shall open no earlier than 30 days and no later than 60 days after receipt of the third of such requests.

2. An amendment to this Treaty shall be subject to the approval of all States Parties, either by providing notification, in writing, of their approval to a Depositary within a period of 90 days after circulation of the proposed amendment, or by expressing their approval at a conference convened in accordance with paragraph 1 of this Article. An amendment so approved shall be subject to ratification in accordance with the provisions of Article XVII, paragraph 1, and shall enter into force 60 days after the deposit of instruments of ratification by the States Parties.

3. Unless requested to do so earlier by no less than three States Parties, the Depositaries shall convene a conference of the States Parties to review the implementation of this Treaty three years after entry into force of this Treaty and at five-year intervals thereafter.

Article XVII. Depositaries, entry into force and accession

1. This Treaty shall be subject to ratification by each State Party in accordance with its constitutional procedures. Instruments of ratification and instruments of accession shall be deposited with the Government of Canada or the Government of the Republic of Hungary or both, hereby designated the Depositaries. This Treaty shall be registered by the Depositaries pursuant to Article 102 of the Charter of the United Nations.

2. This Treaty shall enter into force 60 days after the deposit of 20 instruments of ratification, including those of the Depositaries, and of States Parties whose individual allocation of passive quotas as set forth in Annex A is eight or more.

3. This Treaty shall be open for signature by Armenia, Azerbaijan, Georgia, Kazakhstan, Kirgistan, Moldova, Tajikistan, Turkmenistan and Uzbekistan and shall be subject to ratification by them. Any of these States which do not sign this Treaty before it enters into force in accordance with the provisions of paragraph 2 of this Article may accede to it at any time by depositing an instrument of accession with one of the Depositaries.

4. For six months after entry into force of this Treaty, any other State participating in the Conference on Security and Co-operation in Europe may apply for accession by submitting a written request to one of the Depositaries. The Depositary receiving such a request shall circulate it promptly to all States Parties. The States applying for accession to this Treaty may also, if they so wish, request an allocation of a passive quota and the level of this quota.

The matter shall be considered at the next regular meeting of the Open-Skies Consultative Commission and decided in due course.

5. Following six months after entry into force of this Treaty, the Open Skies Consultative Commission may consider the accession to this Treaty of any State which, in the judgement of the Commission, is able and willing to

contribute to the objectives of this Treaty.

6. For any State which has not deposited an instrument of ratification by the time of entry into force, but which subsequently ratifies or accedes to this Treaty, this Treaty shall enter into force 60 days after the date of deposit of its instrument of ratification or accession.

7. The Depositaries shall promptly inform all States Parties of:

(A) the date of deposit of each instrument of ratification and the date of entry into force of this Treaty;

(B) the date of an application for accession, the name of the requesting State and the result of the procedure;

(C) the date of deposit of each instrument of accession and the date of entry into force of this Treaty for each State that subsequently accedes to it;

(D) the convening of a conference pursuant to Articles XV and XVI;

(E) any withdrawal in accordance with Article XV and its effective date;

(F) the date of entry into force of any amendments to this Treaty; and

(G) any other matters of which the Depositaries are required by this Treaty to inform the States Parties.

Article XVIII. Provisional application and phasing of implementation of the Treaty

In order to facilitate the implementation of this Treaty, certain of its provisions shall be provisionally applied and others shall be implemented in phases.

SECTION I. PROVISIONAL APPLICATION

1. Without detriment to Article XVII, the signatory States shall provisionally apply the following provisions of this Treaty:

(A) Article VI, Section I, paragraph 4;

(B) Article X, paragraphs 1, 2, 3, 6 and 7;

(C) Article XI;

(D) Article XIII, Section I, paragraphs 1 and 2;

(E) Article XIV; and

(F) Annex L, Section I.

2. This provisional application shall be effective for a period of 12 months from the date when this Treaty is opened for signature. In the event that this Treaty does not enter into force before the period of provisional application expires, that period may be extended if all the signatory States so decide. The period of provisional application shall in any event ter-

minate when this Treaty enters into force. However, the States Parties may then decide to extend the period of provisional application in respect of signatory States that have not ratified this Treaty.

SECTION II. PHASING OF IMPLEMENTATION

1. After entry into force, this Treaty shall be implemented in phases in accordance with the provisions set forth in this Section. The provisions of paragraphs 2 to 6 of this Section shall apply during the period from entry into force of this Treaty until 31 December of the third year following the year during which entry into force takes place.

2. Notwithstanding the provisions of Article IV, paragraph 1, no State Party shall during the period specified in paragraph 1 above use an infra-red line-scanning device if one is installed on an observation aircraft, unless otherwise agreed between the observing and observed Parties. Such sensors shall not be subject to certification in accordance with Annex D. If it is difficult to remove such sensor from the observation aircraft, then it shall have covers or other devices that inhibit its operation in accordance with the provisions of Article IV, paragraph 4 during the conduct of observation flights.

3. Notwithstanding the provisions of Article IV, paragraph 9, no State Party shall, during the period specified in paragraph 1 of this Section, be obliged to provide an observation aircraft equipped with sensors from each sensor category, at the maximum capability and in the numbers specified in Article IV, paragraph 2, provided that the observation aircraft is equipped with:

(A) a single optical panoramic camera; or

(B) not less than a pair of optical framing cameras.

4. Notwithstanding the provisions of Annex B, Section II, paragraph 2, subparagraph (A) to this Treaty, data recording media shall be annotated with data in accordance with existing practice of States Parties during the period specified in paragraph 1 of this Section.

5. Notwithstanding the provisions of Article VI, Section I, paragraph 1, no State Party during the period specified in paragraph 1 of this Section shall have the right to be provided with an aircraft capable of achieving any specified unrefuelled range.

6. During the period specified in para-

graph 1 of this Section, the distribution of active quotas shall be established in accordance with the provisions of Annex A, Section II, paragraph 2 to this Treaty.

7. Further phasing in respect of the introduction of additional categories of sensors or improvements to the capabilities of existing categories of sensors shall be addressed by the Open Skies Consultative Commission in accordance with the provisions of Article IV, paragraph 3 concerning such introduction or improvement.

Article XIX. Authentic texts

The originals of this Treaty, of which the English, French, German, Italian, Russian and Spanish texts are equally authentic, shall be deposited in the archives of the Depositaries. Duly certified copies of this Treaty shall be transmitted by the Depositaries to all the States Parties.

[Annexes:

A. Quotas and Maximum Flight Distances;

B. Information on Sensors (including Appendix on Annotation of Data collected during an Observation Flight);

C. Information on Observation Aircraft;

D. Certification of Observation Aircraft and Sensors (including Appendix on Methodologies for the Verification of the Performance of Sensors installed on an Observation Aircraft);

E. Procedures for Arrivals and Departures (Including Appendix on Designation of Sites);

F. Pre-flight Inspections and Demonstration Flights;

G. Flight Monitors, Flight Representatives and Representatives;

H. Co-ordination of Planned Observation Flights;

I. Information on Airspace and Flights in Hazardous Airspace;

J. Montreux Convention;

K. Information on Film Processors, Duplicators and Photographic Films, and Procedures for Monitoring the Processing of Photographic Film; and

L. Open Skies Consultative Commission not reproduced here.]

Source: Treaty on Open Skies. Copy supplied by the Canadian Embassy, Stockholm, Oct. 1993..

Index

air bases 146
aircraft:
  CBMs and 152
  CFE and 3–4, 24, 25, 26, 27, 29, 30, 33,
    34, 35, 36, 37, 38, 72–73, 101
  CFE Negotiation and 92, 95, 96, 97–98
  counting 72
  CSBMs and 142, 146
  inspections by 127–28, 131, 140–41
  Iraq, monitoring by 197
  Open Skies, types used 167
  Persian Gulf War and 204
  stand-down 72
  trainers 73, 96
air forces: CFE and 3, 73, 94
Alexander, Michael 86
ambulances 64
America see United States of America
Arens, Moshe 199
Armenia:
  CFE and 27, 29, 36, 37, 38, 39, 44, 50
  USSR's military legacy 112
armoured combat vehicles (ACV):
  CFE and 3, 23, 24, 25, 27, 28, 30, 31, 34,
    35, 36, 38, 39, 63
  CSBMs and 151
armoured combat vehicle look-alikes 71
armoured infantry fighting vehicles (AIFV):
  CFE and 23, 25, 26, 35, 39
  CSBMs and 151
armoured infantry fighting vehicle look-alikes
  47–48
armoured personnel carriers (APC):
  CFE and 23, 34, 35, 39, 63–64, 91, 93, 94,
    96
  CSBMs and 151
armoured personnel carrier look-alikes 47,
  63–64
armoured vehicle launched bridges (AVLB)
  24, 37, 48, 69–70, 98:
  CBMs and 152
  CFE and 94
arms control:
  change and 207
  'cheating' 12, 14
  political changes and 4

politics and 207
predictability and 6
see also verification and under names of
  treaties
artillery:
  CFE and 3, 23, 24, 25, 26, 27, 29, 30, 34,
    35, 36, 38, 39, 71–72
  CFE Negotiation and 91, 93, 96
  CSBMs and 152
atomic weapons: prohibition of 157
ATTU zone 21–23, 24, 67
AWACS aircraft 58, 59, 202
Azerbaijan:
  arms imports 114–15, 116
  CFE and 27, 29, 31, 36, 37, 38, 39, 44, 50
  USSR's military legacy 112, 113

Baker, James 57, 65fn., 67, 106, 107, 144,
  163
Balkans: cascading and 36, 39
Baltic MD 21, 22, 37
Bauch, Johannes 61
Belarus:
  CFE and 27, 29, 31, 36, 37, 38, 40, 44, 50,
    119
  CFE-1A and 109
  Open Skies Treaty and 183, 188
  USSR's military legacy 112
  weapons destruction 118
Belgium:
  CFE and 27, 29, 30, 31, 44, 50
  CFE-1A and 109
  Open Skies and 187, 188
  satellites and 198
Bessmertnykh, Alexander 67
Black Sea Fleet 112, 119
bombs, guided 204
Borawski, John 133–34
Boren, David 192
Brussels Declaration 88, 163
Bulganin, Prime Minister Nicolai 160–61
Bulgaria 27, 29, 30, 31, 44, 50:
  CFE-1A and 109
Bush, President George;
  CFE and 18, 97, 100
  Open Skies 156, 163